ASPEN PUBLISHERS

Casenote™ Legal Briefs

AGENCY AND PARTNERSHIP

Keyed to Courses Using

Hynes and Loewenstein's
Agency, Partnership, and the LLC
Seventh Edition

Wolters Kluwer
Law & Business

AUSTIN BOSTON CHICAGO NEW YORK THE NETHERLANDS

a Wolters Kluwer business
http://lawschool.aspenpublishers.com

To contact Customer Care, e-mail customer.care@aspenpublishers.com, call 1-800-234-1660, fax 1-800-901-9075, or mail correspondence to:

Aspen Publishers
Attn: Order Department
P.O. Box 990
Frederick, MD 21705

Printed in the United States of America.

1 2 3 4 5 6 7 8 9 0

ISBN 978-0-7355-6984-3

About Wolters Kluwer Law & Business

Wolters Kluwer Law & Business is a leading provider of research information and workflow solutions in key specialty areas. The strengths of the individual brands of Aspen Publishers, CCH, Kluwer Law International and Loislaw are aligned within Wolters Kluwer Law & Business to provide comprehensive, in-depth solutions and expert-authored content for the legal, professional and education markets.

CCH was founded in 1913 and has served more than four generations of business professionals and their clients. The CCH products in the Wolters Kluwer Law & Business group are highly regarded electronic and print resources for legal, securities, antitrust and trade regulation, government contracting, banking, pension, payroll, employment and labor, and health-care reimbursement and compliance professionals.

Aspen Publishers is a leading information provider for attorneys, business professionals and law students. Written by preeminent authorities, Aspen products offer analytical and practical information in a range of specialty practice areas from securities law and intellectual property to mergers and acquisitions and pension/benefits. Aspen's trusted legal education resources provide professors and students with high-quality, up-to-date and effective resources for successful instruction and study in all areas of the law.

Kluwer Law International supplies the global business community with comprehensive English-language international legal information. Legal practitioners, corporate counsel and business executives around the world rely on the Kluwer Law International journals, loose-leafs, books and electronic products for authoritative information in many areas of international legal practice.

Loislaw is a premier provider of digitized legal content to small law firm practitioners of various specializations. Loislaw provides attorneys with the ability to quickly and efficiently find the necessary legal information they need, when and where they need it, by facilitating access to primary law as well as state-specific law, records, forms and treatises.

Wolters Kluwer Law & Business, a unit of Wolters Kluwer, is headquartered in New York and Riverwoods, Illinois. Wolters Kluwer is a leading multinational publisher and information services company.

Format for the Casenote Legal Brief

Nature of Case: This section identifies the form of action (e.g., breach of contract, negligence, battery), the type of proceeding (e.g., demurrer, appeal from trial court's jury instructions) or the relief sought (e.g., damages, injunction, criminal sanctions).

Party ID: Quick identification of the relationship between the parties.

Fact Summary: This is included to refresh your memory and can be used as a quick reminder of the facts.

Rule of Law: Summarizes the general principle of law that the case illustrates. It may be used for instant recall of the court's holding and for classroom discussion or home review.

Facts: This section contains all relevant facts of the case, including the contentions of the parties and the lower court holdings. It is written in a logical order to give the student a clear understanding of the case. The plaintiff and defendant are identified by their proper names throughout and are always labeled with a (P) or (D).

Palsgraf v. Long Island R.R. Co.

Injured bystander (P) v. Railroad company (D)

N.Y. Ct. App., 248 N.Y. 339, 162 N.E. 99 (1928).

NATURE OF CASE: Appeal from judgment affirming verdict for plaintiff seeking damages for personal injury.

FACT SUMMARY: Helen Palsgraf (P) was injured on R.R.'s (D) train platform when R.R.'s (D) guard helped a passenger aboard a moving train, causing his package to fall on the tracks. The package contained fireworks which exploded, creating a shock that tipped a scale onto Palsgraf (P).

RULE OF LAW

The risk reasonably to be perceived defines the duty to be obeyed.

FACTS: Helen Palsgraf (P) purchased a ticket to Rockaway Beach from R.R. (D) and was waiting on the train platform. As she waited, two men ran to catch a train that was pulling out from the platform. The first man jumped aboard, but the second man, who appeared as if he might fall, was helped aboard by the guard on the train who had kept the door open so they could jump aboard. A guard on the platform also helped by pushing him onto the train. The man was carrying a package wrapped in newspaper. In the process, the man dropped his package, which fell on the tracks. The package contained fireworks and exploded. The shock of the explosion was apparently of great enough strength to tip over some scales at the other end of the platform, which fell on Palsgraf (P) and injured her. A jury awarded her damages, and R.R. (D) appealed.

ISSUE: Does the risk reasonably to be perceived define the duty to be obeyed?

HOLDING AND DECISION: (Cardozo, C.J.) Yes. The risk reasonably to be perceived defines the duty to be obeyed. If there is no foreseeable hazard to the injured party as the result of a seemingly innocent act, the act does not become a tort because it happened to be a wrong as to another. If the wrong was not willful, the plaintiff must show that the act as to her had such great and apparent possibilities of danger as to entitle her to protection. Negligence in the abstract is not enough upon which to base liability. Negligence is a relative concept, evolving out of the common law doctrine of trespass on the case. To establish liability, the defendant must owe a legal duty of reasonable care to the injured party. A cause of action in tort will lie where harm, though unintended, could have been averted or avoided by observance of such a duty. The scope of the duty is limited by the range of danger that a reasonable person could foresee. In this case, there was nothing to suggest from the appearance of the parcel or otherwise that the parcel contained fireworks. The guard could not reasonably have had any warning of a threat to Palsgraf (P), and R.R. (D) therefore cannot be held liable. Judgment is reversed in favor of R.R. (D).

DISSENT: (Andrews, J.) The concept that there is no negligence unless R.R. (D) owes a legal duty to take care as to Palsgraf (P) herself is too narrow. Everyone owes to the world at large the duty of refraining from those acts that may unreasonably threaten the safety of others. If the guard's action was negligent as to those nearby, it was also negligent as to those outside what might be termed the "danger zone." For Palsgraf (P) to recover, R.R.'s (D) negligence must have been the proximate cause of her injury, a question of fact for the jury.

ANALYSIS

The majority defined the limit of the defendant's liability in terms of the danger that a reasonable person in defendant's situation would have perceived. The dissent argued that the limitation should not be placed on liability, but rather on damages. Judge Andrews suggested that only injuries that would not have happened but for R.R.'s (D) negligence should be compensable. Both the majority and dissent recognized the policy-driven need to limit liability for negligent acts, seeking, in the words of Judge Andrews, to define a framework "that will be practical and in keeping with the general understanding of mankind." The Restatement (Second) of Torts has accepted Judge Cardozo's view.

Quicknotes

FORESEEABILITY A reasonable expectation that change is the probable result of certain acts or omissions.

NEGLIGENCE Conduct falling below the standard of care that a reasonable person would demonstrate under similar conditions.

PROXIMATE CAUSE The natural sequence of events without which an injury would not have been sustained.

Concurrence/Dissent: All concurrences and dissents are briefed whenever they are included by the casebook editor.

Analysis: This last paragraph gives you a broad understanding of where the case "fits in" with other cases in the section of the book and with the entire course. It is a hornbook-style discussion indicating whether the case is a majority or minority opinion and comparing the principal case with other cases in the casebook. It may also provide analysis from restatements, uniform codes, and law review articles. The analysis will prove to be invaluable to classroom discussion.

Issue: The issue is a concise question that brings out the essence of the opinion as it relates to the section of the casebook in which the case appears. Both substantive and procedural issues are included if relevant to the decision.

Holding and Decision: This section offers a clear and in-depth discussion of the rule of the case and the court's rationale. It is written in easy-to-understand language and answers the issue presented by applying the law to the facts of the case. When relevant, it includes a thorough discussion of the exceptions to the case as listed by the court, any major cites to the other cases on point, and the names of the judges who wrote the decisions.

Quicknotes: Conveniently defines legal terms found in the case and summarizes the nature of any statutes, codes, or rules referred to in the text.

Note to Students

Aspen Publishers is proud to offer *Casenote Legal Briefs*—continuing thirty years of publishing America's best-selling legal briefs.

Casenote Legal Briefs are designed to help you save time when briefing assigned cases. Organized under convenient headings, they show you how to abstract the basic facts and holdings from the text of the actual opinions handed down by the courts. Used as part of a rigorous study regimen, they can help you spend more time analyzing and critiquing points of law than on copying bits and pieces of judicial opinions into your notebook or outline.

Casenote Legal Briefs should never be used as a substitute for assigned casebook readings. They work best when read as a follow-up to reviewing the underlying opinions themselves. Students who try to avoid reading and digesting the judicial opinions in their casebooks or on-line sources will end up shortchanging themselves in the long run. The ability to absorb, critique, and restate the dynamic and complex elements of case law decisions is crucial to your success in law school and beyond. It cannot be developed vicariously.

Casenote Legal Briefs represents but one of the many offerings in Aspen's Study Aid Timeline, which includes:

- *Casenote Legal Briefs*
- *Emanuel Law Outlines*
- *Examples & Explanations* Series
- *Introduction to Law* Series
- Emanuel *Law in a Flash* Flashcards
- Emanuel *CrunchTime* Series

Each of these series is designed to provide you with easy-to-understand explanations of complex points of law. Each volume offers guidance on the principles of legal analysis and, consulted regularly, will hone your ability to spot relevant issues. We have titles that will help you prepare for class, prepare for your exams, and enhance your general comprehension of the law along the way.

To find out more about Aspen Study Aid publications, visit us on-line at *http://lawschool.aspenpublishers.com* or e-mail us at *legaledu@aspenpubl.com.* We'll be happy to assist you.

Free access to Briefs online!

Download cases from this Casenote Legal Brief. Simply fill out this form for full access to this useful feature provided by Loislaw. Learn more about Loislaw services on the inside front cover of this book or visit *www.loislawschool.com.*

Name		**Phone** ( )
Address		**Apt. No.**
City	**State**	**ZIP Code**
Law School		**Year** (check one) ☐ **1st** ☐ **2nd** ☐ **3rd**

Cut out the UPC found on the lower left-hand corner of the back cover of this book. Staple the UPC inside this box. Only the original UPC from the book cover will be accepted. No photocopies or store stickers are allowed.

Attach UPC inside this box.

Email (Print legibly or you may not get access!)
Title of this book (course subject)
Used with which casebook (provide author's name)

Mail the completed form to:

Aspen Publishers, Inc.
Legal Education Division
Casenote Online Access
130 Turner Street, Building 3, 4th Floor
Waltham, MA 02453-8901

I understand that online access is granted solely to the purchaser of this book for the academic year in which it was purchased. Any other usage is not authorized and will result in immediate termination of access. Sharing of codes is strictly prohibited.

Signature ____________________

Upon receipt of this completed form, you will be emailed codes with which to access the briefs for this Casenote Legal Brief. Online briefs are not available for all titles. For a full list of Casenote Legal Brief titles, please visit *http://lawschool.aspenpublishers.com.*

How to Brief a Case

A. Decide on a Format and Stick to It

Structure is essential to a good brief. It enables you to arrange systematically the related parts that are scattered throughout most cases, thus making manageable and understandable what might otherwise seem to be an endless and unfathomable sea of information. There are, of course, an unlimited number of formats that can be utilized. However, it is best to find one that suits your needs and stick to it. Consistency breeds both efficiency and the security that when called upon you will know where to look in your brief for the information you are asked to give.

Any format, as long as it presents the essential elements of a case in an organized fashion, can be used. Experience, however, has led *Casenotes* to develop and utilize the following format because of its logical flow and universal applicability.

NATURE OF CASE: This is a brief statement of the legal character and procedural status of the case (e.g., "Appeal of a burglary conviction").

There are many different alternatives open to a litigant dissatisfied with a court ruling. The key to determining which one has been used is to discover *who is asking this court for what.*

This first entry in the brief should be kept as *short as possible.* Use the court's terminology if you understand it. But since jurisdictions vary as to the titles of pleadings, the best entry is the one that addresses who wants what in this proceeding, not the one that sounds most like the court's language.

RULE OF LAW: A statement of the general principle of law that the case illustrates (e.g., "An acceptance that varies any term of the offer is considered a rejection and counteroffer").

Determining the rule of law of a case is a procedure similar to determining the issue of the case. Avoid being fooled by red herrings; there may be a few rules of law mentioned in the case excerpt, but usually only one is *the* rule with which the casebook editor is concerned. The techniques used to locate the issue, described below, may also be utilized to find the rule of law. Generally, your best guide is simply the chapter heading. It is a clue to the point the casebook editor seeks to make and should be kept in mind when reading every case in the respective section.

FACTS: A synopsis of only the essential facts of the case, i.e., those bearing upon or leading up to the issue.

The facts entry should be a short statement of the events and transactions that led one party to initiate legal proceedings against another in the first place. While some cases conveniently state the salient facts at the beginning of the decision, in other instances they will have to be culled from hiding places throughout the text, even from concurring and dissenting opinions. Some of the "facts" will often be in dispute and should be so noted. Conflicting evidence may be briefly pointed up. "Hard" facts must be included. Both must be *relevant* in order to be listed in the facts entry. It is impossible to tell what is relevant until the entire case is read, as the ultimate determination of the rights and liabilities of the parties may turn on something buried deep in the opinion.

Generally, the facts entry should not be longer than three to five *short* sentences.

It is often helpful to identify the role played by a party in a given context. For example, in a construction contract case the identification of a party as the "contractor" or "builder" alleviates the need to tell that that party was the one who was supposed to have built the house.

It is always helpful, and a good general practice, to identify the "plaintiff" and the "defendant." This may seem elementary and uncomplicated, but, especially in view of the creative editing practiced by some casebook editors, it is sometimes a difficult or even impossible task. Bear in mind that the *party presently* seeking something from this court may not be the plaintiff, and that sometimes only the cross-claim of a defendant is treated in the excerpt. Confusing or misaligning the parties can ruin your analysis and understanding of the case.

ISSUE: A statement of the general legal question answered by or illustrated in the case. For clarity, the issue is best put in the form of a question capable of a "yes" or "no" answer. In reality, the issue is simply the Rule of Law put in the form of a question (e.g., "May an offer be accepted by performance?").

The major problem presented in discerning what is *the* issue in the case is that an opinion usually purports to raise and answer several questions. However, except for rare cases, only one such question is really the issue in the case. Collateral issues not necessary to the resolution of the matter in controversy are handled by the court by language known as *"obiter dictum"* or merely *"dictum."* While dicta may be included later in the brief, they have no place under the issue heading.

To find the issue, ask *who wants what* and then go on to ask *why did that party succeed or fail in getting it.* Once this is determined, the "why" should be turned into a question.

The complexity of the issues in the cases will vary, but in all cases a single-sentence question should sum up the issue. *In a few cases,* there will be two, or even more rarely, three issues of equal importance to the resolution of the case. Each should be expressed in a single-sentence question.

Since many issues are resolved by a court in coming to a final disposition of a case, the casebook editor will reproduce the portion of the opinion containing the issue or issues most relevant to the area of law under scrutiny. A noted law professor gave this advice: "Close the book; look at the title on the cover." Chances are, if it is Property, you need not concern yourself with whether, for example, the federal government's treatment of the plaintiff's land really raises a federal question sufficient to support jurisdiction on this ground in federal court.

The same rule applies to chapter headings designating sub-areas within the subjects. They tip you off as to what the text is designed to teach. The cases are arranged in a casebook to show a progression or development of the law, so that the preceding cases may also help.

It is also most important to remember to *read the notes and questions* at the end of a case to determine what the editors wanted you to have gleaned from it.

HOLDING AND DECISION: This section should succinctly explain the rationale of the court in arriving at its decision. In capsulizing the "reasoning" of the court, it should always include an application of the general rule or rules of law to the specific facts of the case. Hidden justifications come to light in this entry; the reasons for the state of the law, the public policies, the biases and prejudices, those considerations that influence the justices' thinking and, ultimately, the outcome of the case. At the end, there should be a short indication of the disposition or procedural resolution of the case (e.g., "Decision of the trial court for Mr. Smith (P) reversed").

The foregoing format is designed to help you "digest" the reams of case material with which you will be faced in your law school career. Once mastered by practice, it will place at your fingertips the information the authors of your casebooks have sought to impart to you in case-by-case illustration and analysis.

B. Be as Economical as Possible in Briefing Cases

Once armed with a format that encourages succinctness, it is as important to be economical with regard to the time spent on the actual reading of the case as it is to be economical in the writing of the brief itself. This does not mean "skimming" a case. Rather, it means reading the case with an "eye" trained to recognize into which "section" of your brief a particular passage or line fits and having a system for quickly and precisely marking the case so that the passages fitting any one particular part of the brief can be easily identified and brought together in a concise and accurate manner when the brief is actually written.

It is of no use to simply repeat everything in the opinion of the court; record only enough information to trigger your recollection of what the court said. Nevertheless, an accurate statement of the "law of the case," i.e., the legal principle applied to the facts, is absolutely essential to class preparation and to learning the law under the case method.

To that end, it is important to develop a "shorthand" that you can use to make margin notations. These notations will tell you at a glance in which section of the brief you will be placing that particular passage or portion of the opinion.

Some students prefer to underline all the salient portions of the opinion (with a pencil or colored underliner marker), making marginal notations as they go along. Others prefer the color-coded method of underlining, utilizing different colors of markers to underline the salient portions of the case, each separate color being used to represent a different section of the brief. For example, blue underlining could be used for passages relating to the rule of law, yellow for those relating to the issue, and green for those relating to the holding and decision, etc. While it has its advocates, the color-coded method can be confusing and time-consuming (all that time spent on changing colored markers). Furthermore, it can interfere with the continuity and concentration many students deem essential to the reading of a case for maximum comprehension. In the end, however, it is a matter of personal preference and style. Just remember, whatever method you use, underlining must be used sparingly or its value is lost.

If you take the marginal notation route, an efficient and easy method is to go along underlining the key portions of the case and placing in the margin alongside them the following "markers" to indicate where a particular passage or line "belongs" in the brief you will write:

- N (NATURE OF CASE)
- RL (RULE OF LAW)
- I (ISSUE)
- HL (HOLDING AND DECISION, relates to the RULE OF LAW behind the decision)
- HR (HOLDING AND DECISION, gives the RATIONALE or reasoning behind the decision)
- HA (HOLDING AND DECISION, APPLIES the general principle(s) of law to the facts of the case to arrive at the decision)

Remember that a particular passage may well contain information necessary to more than one part of your brief, in which case you simply note that in the margin. If you are using the color-coded underlining method instead of margin notation, simply make asterisks or checks in the margin next to the passage in question in the colors that indicate the additional sections of the brief where it might be utilized.

The economy of utilizing "shorthand" in marking cases for briefing can be maintained in the actual brief writing process itself by utilizing "law student shorthand" within the brief. There are many commonly used words and phrases for which abbreviations can be substituted in your briefs (and in your class notes also). You can develop abbreviations that are personal to you and which will save you a lot of time. A reference list of briefing abbreviations can be found on page xii of this book.

C. Use Both the Briefing Process and the Brief as a Learning Tool

Now that you have a format and the tools for briefing cases efficiently, the most important thing is to make the time spent in briefing profitable to you and to make the most advantageous use of the briefs you create. Of course, the briefs are invaluable for classroom reference when you are called upon to explain or analyze a particular case. However, they are also useful in reviewing for exams. A quick glance at the fact summary should bring the case to mind, and a rereading of the rule of law should enable you to go over the underlying legal concept in your mind, how it was applied in that particular case, and how it might apply in other factual settings.

As to the value to be derived from engaging in the briefing process itself, there is an immediate benefit that arises from being forced to sift through the essential facts and reasoning from the court's opinion and to succinctly express them in your own words in your brief. The process ensures that you understand the case and the point that it illustrates, and that means you will be ready to absorb further analysis and information brought forth in class. It also ensures you will have something to say when called upon in class. The briefing process helps develop a mental agility for getting to the *gist* of a case and for identifying, expounding on, and applying the legal concepts and issues found there. The briefing process is the mental process on which you must rely in taking law school examinations; it is also the mental process upon which a lawyer relies in serving his clients and in making his living.

Abbreviations for Briefs

acceptance	acp
affirmed	aff
answer	ans
assumption of risk	a/r
attorney	atty
beyond a reasonable doubt	b/r/d
bona fide purchaser	BFP
breach of contract	br/k
cause of action	c/a
common law	c/l
Constitution	Con
constitutional	con
contract	K
contributory negligence	c/n
cross	x
cross-complaint	x/c
cross-examination	x/ex
cruel and unusual punishment	c/u/p
defendant	D
dismissed	dis
double jeopardy	d/j
due process	d/p
equal protection	e/p
equity	eq
evidence	ev
exclude	exc
exclusionary rule	exc/r
felony	f/n
freedom of speech	f/s
good faith	g/f
habeas corpus	h/c
hearsay	hr
husband	H
in loco parentis	ILP
injunction	inj
inter vivos	I/v
joint tenancy	j/t
judgment	judgt
jurisdiction	jur
last clear chance	LCC
long-arm statute	LAS
majority view	maj
meeting of minds	MOM
minority view	min
Miranda warnings	Mir/w
Miranda rule	Mir/r
negligence	neg
notice	ntc
nuisance	nus
obligation	ob
obscene	obs
offer	O
offeree	OE
offeror	OR
ordinance	ord
pain and suffering	p/s
parol evidence	p/e
plaintiff	P
prima facie	p/f
probable cause	p/c
proximate cause	px/c
real property	r/p
reasonable doubt	r/d
reasonable man	r/m
rebuttable presumption	rb/p
remanded	rem
res ipsa loquitur	RIL
respondeat superior	r/s
Restatement	RS
reversed	rev
Rule Against Perpetuities	RAP
search and seizure	s/s
search warrant	s/w
self-defense	s/d
specific performance	s/p
statute of limitations	S/L
statute of frauds	S/F
statute	S
summary judgment	s/j
tenancy in common	t/c
tenancy at will	t/w
tenant	t
third party	TP
third party beneficiary	TPB
transferred intent	TI
unconscionable	uncon
unconstitutional	unconst
undue influence	u/e
Uniform Commercial Code	UCC
unilateral	uni
vendee	VE
vendor	VR
versus	v
void for vagueness	VFV
weight of the evidence	w/e
weight of authority	w/a
wife	W
with	w/
within	w/i
without prejudice	w/o/p
without	w/o
wrongful death	wr/d

Table of Cases

CHAPTER 1

The Agency Relationship; The Ambiguous Principal Problem; Subagency

Quick Reference Rules of Law

Carrier v. McLlarky

Principal/Home owner (P) v. Agent/Plumber (D)

N.H. Sup. Ct., 693 A.2d. 76 (1997).

NATURE OF CASE: Appeal from a judgment awarding replacement value for breach of duty.

FACT SUMMARY: When McLlarky (D), a plumber, failed to obtain payment from the manufacturer for a defective unit he had to replace, Carrier (P), the customer, sued McLlarky (D) under an agency theory, claiming he had breached his duty to her.

RULE OF LAW

The promise to act as an agent is interpreted as a promise only to make reasonable efforts to accomplish the directed result.

FACTS: When McLlarky (D) installed a replacement hot water heater in the home of Carrier (P), he said he would try to obtain a credit for her against its cost since he thought the old unit was still under warranty. When McLlarky (D) failed to credit Carrier (P) because he had not received payment from the manufacturer, Carrier (P) successfully sued McLlarky (D) in small claims court for the replacement value of the water heater plus costs. McLlarky (D) appealed.

ISSUE: Does the promise to act as an agent guarantee that the desired result will be obtained?

HOLDING AND DECISION: (Johnson, J.) No. The promise to act as an agent is interpreted as a promise only to make reasonable efforts to accomplish the directed result. In this case, McLlarky (D) did make a reasonable attempt, as promised, to obtain a refund for Carrier (P). He did not guarantee that a credit would be obtained. Therefore, the trial court's findings that McLlarky (D) was not sufficiently diligent were unreasonable and unsupported by the record. Reversed.

ANALYSIS

The court noted that whether an agency agreement has been created is a question of fact. In this case, although an agency relationship was found to have been created, no breach was found. In other cases, courts have not found an agency relationship to be created when a person merely offered help or made a suggestion.

M.D. & Associates and Paul D. Hogg v. Sears, Roebuck & Co.

Landlord (P) v. Tenant (D)

Mo. Ct. App., 749 S.W.2d 454 (1988).

NATURE OF CASE: Appeal from judgment for tenant in action claiming unlawful possession of leasehold premises.

FACT SUMMARY: A co-worker was considered to be M.D. & Associates' (P) agent when she signed the return receipt for a registered letter from Sears, Roebuck & Co. (D).

RULE OF LAW

Implied agency may be inferred from a prior course of conduct between the alleged principal and agent if there was knowing acquiescence of the principal in the past acts.

FACTS: M.D. & Associates (P) sued Sears, Roebuck & Co. (D) for unlawful possession of its leasehold premises following termination of the lease. For several months prior to the suit, Fraley, who worked with the president of M.D. & Associates' (P), had been picking up the mail at a P.O. box and taking it back to the office. When Sears (D) produced a return receipt for a registered letter informing M.D. & Associates (P) that Sears (D) was exercising its option to extend the lease in a timely manner, the signature of Fraley was considered by the court to be sufficient evidence to show timely notice had been received by the principal, M.D. & Associates (P). M.D. & Associates (P) appealed.

ISSUE: May implied agency be inferred from a prior course of conduct between the alleged principal and agent if there was knowing acquiescence of the principal in the past acts?

HOLDING AND DECISION: (Prewitt, J.) Yes. Implied agency may be inferred from a prior course of conduct between the alleged principal and agent if there was knowing acquiescence of the principal in the past acts. Fraley's had M.D. & Associates' (P) authorization to pick up the mail. Since she had been doing so for several months, agency may be inferred based on past course of conduct. The president's implied consent to Fraley's conduct created the agency relationship. Affirmed.

ANALYSIS

The Restatement (Second) of Agency lists three elements necessary to establish an agency relationship. They are as follows: the acting party must be acting "on behalf of" the principal, must be subject to his control, and must act with the consent of both parties. This case stands for the rule that consent can be implied as well as express.

Hunter Mining Laboratories, Inc. v. Management Assistance, Inc.

Buyer (P) v. Manufacturer (D)

Nev. Sup. Ct., 763 P.2d 350 (1988).

NATURE OF CASE: Appeal from a judgment n.o.v. in action for breach of contract.

FACT SUMMARY: Management Assistance, Inc. (MAI) (D), a software manufacturer, was sued by Hunter Mining Laboratories, Inc. (P) on contracts entered into by two dealers who were alleged to be agents of MAI (D).

RULE OF LAW

In an agency relationship, the principal possesses the right to control the agent's conduct and the agent has a fiduciary obligation to act primarily for the benefit of the principal.

FACTS: When Management Assistance, Inc. (MAI) (D), a software manufacturer, and its subsidiary (D) were sued for breach of the contracts Hunter Mining Laboratories, Inc. (P) had entered into with two distributors of MAI's (D) software, the jury found the MAI companies (D) liable for breach of contract. However, the trial court determined that no evidence supported the jury's implicit finding of an agency relationship between the MAI companies (D) and the two distributors. Consequently, the court granted MAI's (D) motion for judgment notwithstanding the verdict. Hunter Mining (P) appealed.

ISSUE: In an agency relationship, does the principal possess the right to control the agent's conduct and does the agent have a fiduciary obligation to act primarily for the benefit of the principal?

HOLDING AND DECISION: (Per curiam) Yes. In an agency relationship, the principal possesses the right to control the agent's conduct and the agent has a fiduciary obligation to act primarily for the benefit of the principal. In this case, the software dealers set their own prices and had no duty to account to MAI (D) for prices charged or profits received. They acted at all times independently and in their own names. The district court was correct in finding that the relationship between MAI (D) and the software dealers was not that of principal and agent, but rather that of seller and buyer. Affirmed.

ANALYSIS

For an agency relationship to be found, the seller must be selling the goods not as his own property, but as the property of the principal, who remains the owner of the goods and therefore has the right to fix the price and the terms of the sale. The principal must receive the proceeds from the sale, less the agent's commission. One who is acting primarily for his own benefit in a sale is generally not considered an agent of another.

United States v. General Electric Co.

Federal government (P) v. Corporation (D)

272 U.S. 476 (1926).

NATURE OF CASE: Bill in equity to enjoin antitrust violation.

FACT SUMMARY: General Electric Co. (GE) (D) used 21,000 distributors under consignment to sell lamps to the public.

RULE OF LAW

If title in goods sold to the public by a middleman under consignment passes directly from the manufacturer to the ultimate purchaser, a true agency exists between the middleman and the manufacturer.

FACTS: General Electric Co. (GE) (D) produced lamps which were sold to the general public through 21,000 distributors acting on consignment. Under the distributorship appointments, GE (D) set the sale prices and determined the quantity and types of lamps held in stock. The distributors had to pay expenses minus commissions. Title of lamps went from GE (D) to the ultimate purchaser. The Government (P) sued under the antitrust laws to enjoin this plan of distribution as resale price maintenance, an illegal restraint of trade, arguing that a true agency relationship between GE (D) and its distributors did not exist.

ISSUE: If title in goods sold to the public by a middleman under consignment passes directly from the manufacturer to the ultimate purchaser, does a true agency exist between the middleman and manufacturer?

HOLDING AND DECISION: (Taft, C.J.) Yes. If title in goods sold to the public by a middleman under consignment passes directly from the manufacturer to the ultimate purchaser, a true agency exists between the middleman and the manufacturer. Here GE (D) wanted to avoid selling to jobbers or dealers who would sell its lamps to consumers at different prices and hired distributors to sell goods on consignment. Title of goods did not pass from GE (D) to the distributors but to the ultimate purchasers. The fact that the distributors were not obliged to pay for stock held until it was sold and were required to return unsold stock was consistent with GE's (D) retention of title. The distributors' duty to account for lost, missing, or damaged lamps was only a reasonable provision to ensure careful handling of the entrusted goods; their expenses in storing and selling the goods were a cost of doing business recoverable in their commissions. The decree of the trial court dismissing the bill is affirmed.

ANALYSIS

Despite the Court's holding, there have been later cases which find consignments not to give rise to agency relationships such as to avoid the antitrust laws. See, e.g., *Simpson v. Union Oil*, 377 U.S. 13 (1964) (Union Oil's consignment agreements with lessee dealers are illegal restraints of trade). The Court's focus on passage of title seems unduly limited, and the better test remains whether the alleged consignee or agent is principally acting for his own benefit or the benefit of the alleged consignor or principal.

A. Gay Jenson Farms Co. v. Cargill, Inc.

Creditor (P) v. Debtor's alleged principal (D)

Minn. Sup. Ct., 309 N.W.2d 285 (1981).

NATURE OF CASE: Appeal from damages award for breach of a supply contract.

FACT SUMMARY: When Warren defaulted on contracts it had made with A. Gay Jenson Farms (P), the latter sued Cargill (D) as Warren's principal on the grounds that Cargill (D) had assumed de facto control of Warren's business.

RULE OF LAW

A creditor who assumes control of his debtor's business may become liable as principal for the debtor's acts in connection with the business.

FACTS: Warren Grain & Seed Co. operated a grain elevator and purchased grain from local farmers for resale through an exchange. In 1964, Warren received working capital financing from Cargill (D) on "open account." Warren also agreed to provide Cargill (D) with annual financial statements and access to its financial records and to seek Cargill's (D) consent for capital improvements and repairs, stock transactions, issuance of dividends and guaranty of third party loans. Cargill's (D) memos stated that Warren needed "very strong parental guidance." Over the course of the next 13 years, Cargill (D) intervened in Warren's internal management extensively, including directing Warren to negotiate contracts with farmers in a variety of activities. By 1977, many farmers, including A. Gay Jenson Farms (P), were owed $2 million by Warren. An audit of Warren revealed that Warren had falsified financial statements and was $4 million in debt. The farmers sued Cargill (D) as well as Warren, alleging that Cargill (D) was jointly liable as principal for operation of the grain elevator. The trial court agreed, and Cargill (D) appealed.

ISSUE: May a creditor who assumes control of its debtor's business become liable as principal for the debtor's acts in connection with the business?

HOLDING AND DECISION: (Peterson, J.) Yes. A creditor who assumes control of its debtor's business may become liable as principal for the debtor's acts in connection with the business. An agreement may result in the creation of an agency relationship although the parties did not call it an agency and did not intend the legal consequences of the relation to follow. Existence of the agency may be proved by circumstantial evidence which shows a course of dealing between the two parties. Here Cargill (D) controlled Warren and continually infused it with capital to avoid establishing another line elevator of its own. This control is shown by Cargill's (D) recommendations and criticisms concerning Warren's management and financial decisions; the right of entry to carry on periodic checks and audits; provision of printed business forms; financing all of Warren's grain purchases and operating expenses; power to discontinue financing; right of first refusal on grain; and determination that Warren needed "parental guidance." These factors must be viewed in light of all the circumstances surrounding Cargill's (D) aggressive financing of Warrren. Furthermore, the lower court did not err in refusing to submit a jury instruction that agency to perform a particular act cannot be inferred by the existence of agency relationship at another time and in a different capacity since a court is not required to instruct against every improper inference that a jury could draw. Nor did the lower court err in the denial of Cargill's (D) motion for a change of venue since the mere fact that the jury had knowledge of the financial collapse of Warren and its connection with Cargill (D) does not indicate that it could not render a fair decision. Affirmed.

ANALYSIS

As the *A. Gay Jenson* case notes, under the Restatement approach, it must be shown that a supplier has an independent business before it can be concluded that he or she is not an agent. Furthermore, the Restatement (Second) of Agency § 14 O (1958) expressly states that a creditor who assumes control of the debtor's business may become liable as principal for the debtor's acts in connection with the business.

Jones v. Taylor

Automobile owner (P) v. Driver (D)

Mo. Ct. App., 401 S.W.2d 183 (1966).

NATURE OF CASE: Appeal from denial of recovery for property damage.

FACT SUMMARY: Jones (P), who appealed from a judgment rendered in favor of Taylor (D), who collided with Jones' (P) automobile driven by one Lester Jones, who in turn, rented the car as a taxi, contended that because he and Lester Jones were in a bailor-bailee relationship and Taylor (D) admitted negligence, the court should have found in his favor.

RULE OF LAW

The negligence of a bailee in handling the subject of the bailment will not be imputed to the bailor so as to bar the bailor's recovery against a third party whose negligence also contributed to the bailor's loss, unless there is some element of agency in the contract of bailment.

FACTS: Jones (P) owned a vehicle which he rented to Lester Jones for $12.00 a day for use as a taxicab. Lester Jones' fares were arranged and dispatched through the Marcella Cab Company. Jones (P) paid $110.00 a month to Marcella Cab Company for the use of its franchise name. It was Jones (P) who had the right to, and in fact did, select Lester Jones to operate his vehicle, and who had the right to terminate the rental relationship with him at any time. Jones (P) did not control the vehicle when it was being used by Lester Jones as a taxicab, and Lester Jones retained no control over the vehicle when he was not using it as a taxicab. Jones (P) brought an action against Taylor (D), who was driving another vehicle, to recover for damage to his vehicle and loss of rental as a result of an automobile collision, at which time Lester Jones was driving. It was stipulated at the time of trial that both Taylor (D) and Lester Jones were negligently driving. From a judgment in favor of Taylor (D), Jones (P) appealed, contending that the negligence of Lester Jones should not bar his recovery against Taylor (D) because they were in a bailor-bailee relationship.

ISSUE: Will the negligence of a bailee in handling the subject of the bailment be imputed to the bailor so as to bar the bailor's recovery against a third party whose negligence also contributed to the bailor's loss?

HOLDING AND DECISION: (Anderson, J.) No. The negligence of a bailee in handling the subject of the bailment will not be imputed to the bailor so as to bar the bailor's recovery against a third party whose negligence also contributed to the bailor's loss, unless there is one element of agency in the contract of bailment. A bailment for hire created in the present case, since the vehicle was hired out to Lester Jones for his use, and Jones (P) retained no control over the car while it was used as a taxicab. It was stipulated that all fares were dispatched and arranged through Marcella. None of the facts stipulated to demonstrate any element of agency, partnership, or master-servant relationship in the bailment for hire was created. Absent such an element, and given the fact that Taylor (D) admitted negligence, judgment should have been for Jones (P). Reversed and remanded.

ANALYSIS

In the present case, the court noted that an agent could also fit within the definition of a bailee. Some jurisdictions hold, however, that a servant has only custody, and not possession, of goods placed in his charge, precluding him from maintaining any possessory action against one who perhaps converts those goods.

Dierksen v. Albert

Parents (P) v. Daughter (D)

N.J. Super. Ct., 254 A.2d 809 (1969).

NATURE OF CASE: Appeal from denial of declaratory relief to revest title to stock.

FACT SUMMARY: The Dierksens (P) appealed from a denial of their declaratory relief action seeking a declaration revesting title of stock previously placed in the name of their daughter, Albert (D), claiming that under the facts of this case, an effective trust was not created.

RULE OF LAW

Where one delivers property in trust in the name of another but retains substantial, detailed directional control over the disposition of the trust property, an effective trust is not created.

FACTS: In November 1962, the Dierksens (P) were contemplating the transfer of certain securities to their daughter, Albert (D), memorializing their intention in written form. The memorandum provided that the Dierksens (P) would retain substantial, detailed control over the disposition of the stock during their lifetime, including the right to a majority of the dividends and interest generated thereon, and the right to add stock or dispose of stock at their discretion. Stock was subsequently delivered to Albert (D) and registered in her name. Accounts were opened and Albert (D) executed a will in accordance with the memorandum. In March 1965, Mr. Dierksen (P) visited Albert (D) to help salvage her marriage. At that time, at the suggestion of his son-in-law, the shares of stock were redelivered to him. Dividends were last sent to the Dierksens (P) in accordance with the memorandum in August 1965. Albert (D) disappeared a month later and has not since been heard from. The Dierksens (P) moved for a judicial declaration revesting full title in the stock originally transferred back in their name. The trial court denied their request, finding that the agreement created an express trust which could not be revoked by the Dierksens (P) absent a reservation of power to do so. From this decision, the Dierksens (P) appealed, contending that an effective trust was not created under the terms of the memorandum.

ISSUE: When one delivers property in trust in the name of another but retains substantial, detailed directional control over the disposition of the trust property, is an effective trust created?

HOLDING AND DECISION: (Conford, J.) No. Where one delivers property in trust in the name of another but retains substantial, detailed directional control over the trust property, an effective trust is not created. A relationship characterized by such control is more akin to a principal-agent relationship, and as such the principles of agency are applicable. In the present case, the Dierksens (P) clearly retained this control, reserving the right to control and dispose of the property effectively throughout their lifetimes. Thus, applying the principles of agency to this situation, the relationship between the Dierksens (D) and Albert (D) was revocable at any time, and the Dierksens (P) were entitled to the declaration revesting title of the stock in their name. Reversed.

ANALYSIS

Among the other distinctions between a trust relationship and an agency relationship are that the trustee cannot subject the beneficiary of the trust to personal liabilities, and that the trust can be created without the consent or knowledge of the beneficiary. In addition, not discussed in the present case, the trust is not ordinarily terminable at the will of either the beneficiary or the trustee. Thus in the present case, had an effective trust been created, Albert (D) as well would have been unable to terminate the relationship.

King v. First National Bank

Purchaser of land (P) v. Bank (D)

Alaska Sup. Ct., 647 P.2d 596 (1982).

NATURE OF CASE: Appeal from grant of defense motion for partial summary judgment in action for breach of escrow agreement.

FACT SUMMARY: The Kings (P) appealed from a decision granting First National Bank's (Bank) (D) motion for partial summary judgment in their action for the Bank's (D) alleged breach of an "escrow agreement."

RULE OF LAW

An agent who acts on behalf of one person may be held liable to a third person for failure to perform a contract intended to benefit that third person.

FACTS: The Kings (P) agreed to purchase some real property from the Olsons. The real property had been purchased by the Olsons from the state and was subject to a long-term purchase agreement, with the state retaining legal title to the property, pending full payment of the purchase price. The Kings (P) hired an attorney to prepare the necessary documents. Also drafted were "collection instructions," signed only by the Olsons, which provided that the First National Bank's (Bank) (D) was to credit a portion of each payment to the Olsons' savings account and to the state in satisfaction of the Olsons' purchase contract. Upon full payment of the note, the Bank (D) was to forward the note, the executed request for reconveyance, and the deed trust to the Kings (P). Subsequently, and without knowledge of the Kings (P), Mr. Olson altered the collection instructions such that the entire amount of each payment was credited to his savings account. After having paid the note in full, the Kings (P) were informed that the state had terminated the purchase agreement with the Olsons because of the failure to make an annual installment payment. The Kings (P) sued the Bank (D) for its alleged breach of this so-called escrow agreement. The Bank (D) successfully moved for a partial summary judgment on the grounds that there was no escrow agreement because there was no contract between it and the Kings (P). From this decision, the Kings (P) appealed.

ISSUE: May an agent who acts on behalf on one person be held liable to a third person for failure to perform a contract intended to benefit that third person?

HOLDING AND DECISION: (Connor, J.) Yes. An agent who acts on behalf on one person may be held liable to a third person for failure to perform a contract intended to benefit that third person. The Bank (D) was correct in asserting that there was no escrow agreement because there was no contract between it and the Kings (P). In the present case, however, the Kings (P) occupied a third party beneficiary position to the Bank (D) as to the collection instructions. The original instructions were drafted by the Kings' (P) attorney and were intended in part to benefit the Kings (P). Since it may have been possible for the Kings (P) to recover under the third party beneficiary theory, the grant of the motion for summary judgment was improper. Reversed in part.

ANALYSIS

In the present case, it may have been critical that the collection instructions were drafted by the Kings' (P) attorney for their benefit. In *Bescor, Inc. v. Chicago Title & Trust Co.* (1983) 446 N.E.2d 1209, a plaintiff subcontractor was denied recovery for negligently disbursed proceeds under an escrow agreement, since the court found that the subcontractor was merely an incidental beneficiary under the agreement, which was primarily intended to protect the security interests of the lender.

Thayer v. Pacific Electric Railway

Purchaser (P) v. Railroad (D)

Cal. Sup. Ct., 55 Cal.2d 430, 360 P.2d 56 (1961).

NATURE OF CASE: Appeal from award of recovery for damages to freight.

FACT SUMMARY: The Pacific Electric Railway (Pacific) (D) appealed from a judgment in favor of Thayer (P) in his action for damages to freight shipped by Pacific (D), contending in part that the notation on the freight bill referencing damage could not be construed as a written claim as required because it was made by an agent for Pacific (D).

RULE OF LAW

The existence of an agency relationship is a question of fact which can be inferred from the conduct of the parties.

FACTS: Thayer (P) purchased a precision grinding machine and arranged for its shipment. The machine was in good condition when delivered to the originating carrier but arrived damaged. The Pacific Electric Railway's (Pacific) (D) agent, Hileman, notified Thayer (P) of the damage, who inspected the machine and had photographs taken of the damage before it was moved. The bill of lading required that a written claim for damage must be made within nine months of the machine's delivery. A dispute arose over the payment of the freight charges, with Thayer (P) contending that he not pay them the money owed because of the damage to the machine. Within a month of delivery, Hileman went to Thayer's (P) office and obtained payment of the freight charges, but only after Hileman annotated the freight bill "Damage on this shipment, 4/20/55, C.D. Hileman." The annotated freight bill was kept as part of the permanent file. Thayer (P) had been provided standard claim forms and was told by Hileman that they could be submitted when the extent of the damage was ascertained. Over nine moths later, the extent of the damage was ascertained, and Thayer's (P) attorney made a written claim for the damages, which was denied because of the provision on the bill of lading. Thayer (P) successfully brought suit against Pacific (D) for the damages to the machine and Pacific (D) appealed, contending in part that the annotated freight bill would not satisfy the written claim requirement.

ISSUE: Can the existence of an agency relationship be inferred from the conduct of the parties?

HOLDING AND DECISION: (White, J.) Yes. The existence of an agency relationship is a question of fact which can be inferred from the conduct of the parties. The notice requirement does not require documents in any particular form, and therefore the annotated freight bill could qualify as notice. The fact that the freight bill was annotated by Hileman, Pacific's (D) agent, is not fatal to Thayer's (P) claim. He signed the freight bill at Thayer's (P) insistence, and thus even though Pacific's (D) agent, he was Thayer's (P) agent for the purpose of annotating the freight bill. Affirmed.

ANALYSIS

The dual agency rule provides that an agent cannot act on behalf of an adverse party in a transaction without the permission of this principal. In reality, however, there are many situations where one is not the exclusive agent of one party to a transaction. One of the most common situations is when a home is purchased, where the real estate agent often acts on behalf of both buyer and seller.

Kilbourn v. Henderson

Employee (P) v. Insurance Agency (D)

Ohio Ct. App., 577 N.E.2d 1132 (1989).

NATURE OF CASE: Appeal from grant of defendant's motion for summary judgment in an action to recover health care costs.

FACT SUMMARY: When the group insurance plan used by OTC (D), Kilbourn's (P) employer, refused to cover the cost of Kilbourn's (P) inpatient treatment for alcoholism, he sued OTC (D) as the insurance company's agent to recover the cost of that treatment.

RULE OF LAW

An employer's administration of a group insurance plan does not create an agency relationship between the employer and the insurance carrier.

FACTS: Kilbourn (P), an employee of the Ohio Turnpike Commission (OTC) (D), was covered by OTC's (D) group health insurance plan, which was administered for OTC (D) by Laura Fitzgerald. Coverage was provided by CNA (D) through the Henderson (D) insurance agency. After Fitzgerald assured Kilbourn (P) that inpatient treatment for his alcoholism would be covered by the insurance plan, he checked into a treatment center. When coverage for that treatment was denied, Kilbourn (P) filed this suit against Henderson (D), CNA (D), and OTC (D), contending that Fitzgerald had acted as agent to bind Henderson (D) and CNA (D) by her statements. The trial court granted the joint motion for summary judgment filed by Henderson (D) and CNA (D) and denied OTC's (D) motion of summary judgment. This appeal followed.

ISSUE: Does an employer's administration of a group insurance plan create an agency relationship between the employer and the insurance carrier?

HOLDING AND DECISION: (Krupansky, J.) No. An employer's administration of a group insurance plan does not create an agency relationship between the employer and the insurance carrier. OTC's (D) employee, Fitzgerald, was not acting for the benefit of Henderson (D) and CNA (D). Rather, in administrating the plan, she was acting for the benefit of OTC (D) and its employees. Therefore, Henderson (D) and CNA (D) are not bound by her statements. Moreover, the insurance policy plainly states that it covers treatment for alcoholism on an outpatient basis, but not on an inpatient basis. Accordingly, there are no genuine issues of material facts upon which reasonable minds can differ, and Henderson (D) and CNA (D) were entitled to judgment as a matter of law. Affirmed.

ANALYSIS

An agency relationship is generally based upon consent by one person that another shall act in his behalf and be subject to his control. To the extent that an employer, with the insurer's consent, performs the functions of the insurer, it may be considered the insurer's agent. However, courts have generally decided not to find an agency relationship between an employer and an insurance company providing group insurance where the employer actively participates in the administration of that group plan. In *Elfstrom v. New York Life Insurance Co.*, 432 P.2d 731, 737 (Cal. 1967), the court stated that the employer and the employees are allied in their interests and that these interests are adverse to the insurer.

Norby v. Bankers Life Co.

Employee (P) v. Insurance company (D)

Minn. Sup. Ct., 304 Minn. 464, 231 N.W.2d 665 (1975).

NATURE OF CASE: Appeal from award of recovery on medical insurance policy.

FACT SUMMARY: The Bankers Life Co. (Bankers) (D) appealed from a judgment in favor of Norby (P) on his action regarding a group accident and sickness insurance policy issued by Bankers (D), contending that Hoffman, Norby's (P) employer, did not act as Bankers' (D) agent in accepting Norby's (P) initial application, and as such it was not binding on Bankers (D).

RULE OF LAW

To the extent that an employer, with the consent of the insurer, performs the functions of an insurer in the administration of a group policy, it may be considered the insurer's agent.

FACTS: Hoffman, Norby's (P) employer, was a member of the Association, which was the policyholder in a group accident and sickness policy issued by Bankers Life Co. (Bankers) (D). Norby (P) became employed in August 1970, and submitted his initial application for coverage in September 1970. The policy provided for partial reimbursement for medical expenses incurred by covered employees for illness or accidents, including dependent coverage. His initial application was never transmitted to Bankers (D). When Norby (P) learned of this, he submitted a second application, with coverage beginning January 20, 1971, if the first application was not binding on Bankers (D). Norby's (P) child was injured on January 19, 1971, and he made a claim under the policy, which was rejected. Norby (P) successfully brought an action to recover benefits under the policy, the court finding that the initial application was binding upon Bankers (D) because Hoffman was acting as the agent of Bankers (D) in accepting the initial application. From this decision, Bankers (D) appealed.

ISSUE: Will an employer be considered the insurer's agent to the extent that the employer, with the insurer's consent, performs the functions of the insurer in the administration of a group policy?

HOLDING AND DECISION: (Peterson, J.) Yes. To the extent that an employer, with the consent of the insurer, performs the functions of an insurer in the administration of a group policy, it may be considered the insurer's agent. Group insurance is a widespread and very significant form of insurance protection. Administration of such a policy includes the collecting and remitting of insurance premiums, terminating and reinstating insurance, assistance in the processing of claims, and to a certain extent, determining eligibility. When an employer performs a substantial or significant portion of these duties, the group policy can be considered "employer-administered." Both the insurer and the employer exercise some choice and control over the administration of said policies, whereas the employee is limited to the knowledge of benefits under the policy. In such a situation, it would be unfair to frustrate the expectations of the employee because of the employer's negligence in administering the plan. There are no hard and fast rules established here, as an employer may be determined to be the insurer's agent for some purposes and not for others. In this case, Norby (P) was plainly eligible except for Hoffman's mishandling of his initial application, a function clearly delegated to Hoffman by Bankers (D). Thus, with respect to this function, Hoffman acted as the agent of Bankers (D), and as such the initial application was binding on Bankers (D), entitling Norby (P) to benefits under the policy. Affirmed.

ANALYSIS

Often, a group insurance policy will attempt to fix the agency relationship among the parties by express provision in the policy. Courts have held, however, that where the agency relationship as described in the policy is untrue in fact, the nature of the relationship will be determined from the evidence as to how the parties actually stand and perform in relation to one another. See *Bell v. Riggs* (1912) 34 Okla. 834, 841–43.

Stortroen v. Beneficial Finance Co.

Home owner/buyer (P) v. Broker (D)

Colo. Sup. Ct., 736 P.2d 391 (1987).

NATURE OF CASE: Appeal from summary judgment in action for specific performance.

FACT SUMMARY: Stortroen (P) appealed from a decision granting Beneficial Finance Co.'s (Beneficial) (D) motion for summary judgment in their action for specific performance of a real estate purchase, contending Panio, the selling broker, was a subagent of Beneficial (D) when they accepted a counterproposal to buy the home.

RULE OF LAW

In a multiple listing real estate transaction involving residential property, the selling broker or salesperson, absent a written agreement establishing a different agency relationship, is an agent of the listing broker and a subagent of the seller.

FACTS: The Stortroens (P) wanted to sell their home and buy another. For these purposes, they contacted Panio, a broker associate with Foremost, who listed their home. Panio contacted Metrolist, Inc., a multiple listing service, to find them a new home. As to that new home, Beneficial Finance Co.'s (Beneficial) (D) had entered into an exclusive listing arrangement with Olthoff, which in addition to granting the exclusive right to sell the property, granted Olthoff the right to list the property with any multiple listing service. Olthoff listed the property with Metrolist, where Panio found the property. Stortroen (P) made an offer on the property which was rejected. Reh, an officer of Beneficial (P), made a counterproposal, which had to be accepted before 9:00 p.m. on February 3, 1984. On February 3, 1984, the Carellis (D) made an offer to purchase the property for an amount in excess of the amount set forth in Reh's counterproposal. Wanting to accept the Carelli (D) offer, Reh instructed Olthoff to withdraw the counterproposal. At 4:30 p.m., a phone message was left with Panio, withdrawing the counterproposal, not knowing that at 4:10 p.m., Stortroen (P), with Panio present, had accepted the counterproposal. Satisfied that notice had been given, Reh accepted the Carelli (D) offer, which Panio learned of the following Monday. Unable to work things out, Stortroen (P) sued Beneficial (D) and Carelli (D) for specific performance of the sale in accordance with the terms of the counterproposal. Beneficial (D) successfully moved for summary judgment, and Stortroen (P) appealed, contending in part that Panio was Beneficial's (D) subagent when the counterproposal was accepted.

ISSUE: In a multiple listing real estate transaction involving residential property, is the selling broker or salesperson a subagent of the seller?

HOLDING AND DECISION: (Quinn, C.J.) Yes. In a multiple listing real estate transaction involving residential real estate, the selling broker or salesperson, absent a written agreement establishing a different agency relationship, is an agent of the listing broker and subagent of the seller. No such agreement exists in this case, and it would be detrimental to imply such an agency relationship, since the purchaser could lose his right to sue for rescission. The listing broker's act of listing property with a multiple listing service constitutes an offer of subagency by the listing broker to other multiple service members to get a buyer for the home for a split of the commission. Although not a classic example of an agency relationship, good reasons exist to support the traditional rule that a principal-agent relationship flows from the seller to the selling broker in a multiple listing transaction. The relationship is structured by the listing agreement with the seller, and the agreement between the listing broker and the other members of the multiple listing service. Finding a broker, like Panio, to be the agent of Stortroen (P), will lead to serious conflict of interest situations in typical real estate transactions. In this case, Olthoff, by listing the property with Metrolist, offered the "subagency" to Panio, who accepted it by making her efforts to secure Stortroen (P) as a purchaser. Since the counterproposal was accepted before Panio's agency was revoked, summary judgment in favor of Beneficial (D) was improper. Reversed and remanded.

ANALYSIS

The consequences of a subagency relationship are far-reaching. A subagent is often an employee of the agent, and the principal will be held liable for the mistake or misconduct of the subagent. Further, although there is no evidence that Olthoff was sued in the present case, the agent is usually liable as well for the acts of the subagent. See *Colony Assocs. v. Fred L. Clapp & Co.*, 300 S.E. 2d 37 (1983).

CHAPTER 2

Rights and Duties Between Principal and Agent

Quick Reference Rules of Law

Admiral Oriental Line v. United States

Ship's agent (P) v. Federal government (D)

86 F.2d 201 (2d Cir. 1936).

NATURE OF CASE: Appeal from dismissal of cross-claims for damages incurred from legal fees.

FACT SUMMARY: In Atlantic Gulf and Oriental Company's (company) (D) cross-claim for damages against the United States (Board) (D), the trial court ruled, as a matter of law, that the Board (D), and the company's (D) principal, were not responsible for the legal expenses the Admiral Oriental Line (Line) (P), the company's (D) agent, incurred as a result of defending a baseless suit brought against it in connection with its duties for the company (D) and for which the Line (P) sought indemnity from the company (D).

RULE OF LAW

An agent, compelled to defend a baseless suit, grounded upon the acts performed in his principal's business, may recover from the principal the expenses of his defense.

FACTS: Atlantic Gulf and Oriental Company (company) (D) employed the Admiral Oriental Line (Line) (P) to fit out the steamship "Elkton" on a voyage out of Pulupandan. This steamship was owned by the United States (Board) (D), and had been entrusted to the company (D) as ship's agent under an operating contract. While the Line (P) was performing its contractual duties, a typhoon arose and caused the entire ship, along with its crew and cargo, to be lost at sea. As a result, the Elkton's cargo owners brought suit for damages against the Line (P) for the losses they suffered in the storm. Moreover, although the suit was unsuccessful, the Line (P) suffered legal expenses in defending the suit and, as a result, cross-claimed against the company (D), contending that the latter, as principal, was responsible for the legal expenses it had incurred. Subsequently, the company (D) in turn, cross-claimed against the Board (D), contending that the latter was the principal in the whole venture and as such was responsible to its immediate agent, the company (D), for any legal expenses the company (D) might be compelled to pay the Line (P). Notwithstanding these cross-claims' contentions, the district court dismissed them both for failure to state a cause of action. The company (D) and the Line (P) appealed.

ISSUE: May an agent, compelled to defend a baseless suit, grounded upon acts performed in his principal's business, recover from the principal the expenses of his defense?

HOLDING AND DECISION: (Hand, J.) Yes. An agent, compelled to defend a baseless suit, grounded upon acts performed in his principal's business, may recover from the principal the expenses of his defense. The right of recovery grounded in this rule is founded on the general doctrine that an agent may recover any expenses necessarily incurred in the transaction of his principal's affairs. This doctrine stands upon the fact that the venture is the principal's, and that, as the profits will be his, so should be the expenses. Moreover, since, by hypothesis, the agent's outlay is not due to his management, it should be regarded only as a loss, unexpected it is true, but inextricably interwoven with the enterprise. In the instant case, the company (D) contractually agreed with the Board (D) to maintain the latter's ships and keep them in seaworthy condition, and coordinate administrative and general expenses. Moreover, the company (D) employed the Line (P) to perform all the principal's duties under its contract with the Board (D) in areas where it has no offices of its own. Hence, in reasonably construing both contracts, the company (D) was an agent of the Board (D) and the Line (P) was an agent of the company (D). Consequently, although the Board (D)—Company (D) contract contained language which prohibited agents of the company (D) from presumably being considered agents of the Board (D), the Board (D) is responsible for any expenses the Line (P) incidently incurred as a result of forming its contractual duties for the company (D) since there is no difference between payment by an agent of his sub-agent's expenses and payment of his own expenses. Reversed and remanded.

ANALYSIS

An agent's right to indemnity, unless expressly agreed to, depends on reasonable inferences drawn from the circumstances. Thus, a real estate broker, who is paid by commission, ordinarily is expected to bear certain expenses, like the cost of gasoline used in transporting potential purchases to the property his principal is trying to sell. The general standard is expressed by Seavey to be that "the principal bears the burdens to the extent that courts believe to be just, considering the customs of the business and the nature of the particular relation." W. Seavey, Law of Agency § 266 (1964).

Roberts Associates v. Blazer International Corp.

Manufacturer's representative (P) v. Manufacturer (D)

741 F. Supp. 650 (E.D. Mich. 1990).

NATURE OF CASE: Defense motion for summary judgment in suit for the recovery of a sales commission.

FACT SUMMARY: When Roberts Associates, Inc. (P), a sales agent of Blazer International Corp. (D), sued Blazer (D) for commission on a sale which Roberts (P) allegedly procured for Blazer (D) but which was not completed until after Blazer's (D) dismissal of Roberts (P), Roberts (P) sued Blazer (D) for its commission.

RULE OF LAW

A sales agent may recover commissions only on sales which were the subject or result of discussions, negotiations, quotations, or pre-sale customer services in which the sales agent actually participated.

FACTS: Blazer International Corp. (D) terminated Roberts Associates, Inc. (P) as its exclusive manufacturers' representative for certain parts sold to the automobile industry. On December 15, 1982, Blazer (D) sent Roberts (P) a letter confirming its understanding of the scope of Roberts' agency relationship and the rate of compensation. The letter stated that Roberts (P) was Blazer's (D) exclusive representative for certain accounts, listed the products sold to those accounts, and provided that Roberts (P) would be paid a 5% commission on these items and any other items sold to those accounts. In 1982, Blazer (D) was awarded a large contract for the Fisher Guide Division of General Motors. Subsequently, Blazer (D) then reduced its commission to Roberts (P). Several years later, Blazer (D) terminated its relationship with Roberts (P). Roberts (P) brought suit against Blazer (D) for its commission, contending that it was Roberts (P) that was responsible for securing the large Fisher Guide account for Blazer (D), notwithstanding that Blazer (D) closed the deal after Roberts (P) was terminated. Blazer (D) moved for summary judgment on the grounds that Roberts (P) was not the procuring cause of the Fisher Guide account.

ISSUE: May a sales agent recover commissions only on sales which were the subject or result of discussions, negotiations, quotations, or pre-sale customer services in which the sales agent actually participated?

HOLDING AND DECISION: (Cohn, J.) Yes. A sales agent may recover commissions only on sales which were the subject or result of discussions, negotiations, quotations, or pre-sale customer services in which the sales agent actually participated. Obligations of the parties to a sales agency agreement are primarily governed by the terms of the contract. Where the contract is silent, the agent is entitled to recover a commission on a sale, whether or not the agent personally concluded it only where it can be shown that his or her efforts were the "procuring cause." Under the Restatement (Second) Agency § 449, where a principal enters into a non-exclusive representation agreement with an agent, the principal is not therefore precluded from competing with the agent personally or through another agent. Both the Restatement and Michigan cases interpret the concept of "procuring cause" quite narrowly. Here, it is clear that Roberts (P) has no valid claim to commissions on the Fisher Guide account after the date of Roberts' (P) termination. There is no allegation that Roberts (P) had an exclusive agency agreement as to the parts sold to the Fisher Guide account which would preclude Blazer (D) from approaching the accounts during the life of the agreement. Nor did the 1982 agency agreement guarantee commissions for all sales to customers procured by Roberts (P). It is undisputed that Roberts (P) had nothing to do with sales to Fisher Guide following its termination. As a matter of law, Roberts (P) could not have been the procuring cause of those sales. Accordingly, this claim is dismissed. On reconsideration, the court, while adhering to its previous decision to grant the dismissal, notes, however, for purposes of clarification, that if subsequent purchase orders are submitted by a customer that involve no additional servicing or negotiation, then the salesperson securing the original account may well be entitled to commissions on those sales.

ANALYSIS

Most jurisdictions distinguish between two types of exclusive representation agreements. The first type, known as an "exclusive right to sell" confers on the agent the sole right to sell certain goods or property for a stipulated period or in a given geographic area. Under this agreement, the agent is entitled to all commissions on all sales regardless of whether they are made by another agent or the principal himself. The exclusive agent need not be the procuring cause. The second, and more common type, of exclusive representation contract is known as an "exclusive agency." Under this arrangement, the principal is only precluded from employing other agents to sell the goods or property.

McCollum v. Clothier

Trustee's agent (P) v. Mortgagee (D)

Utah Sup. Ct., 121 Utah 311, 241 P.2d 468 (1952).

NATURE OF CASE: Appeal from award of damages for services rendered.

FACT SUMMARY: In McCollum's (P) suit for damages against Clothier (D), the trial court found that the services McCollum (P) rendered to Clothier (D) contractually bound the latter, as implied from the circumstances, to make compensation for them.

RULE OF LAW

Except where circumstances indicate that the parties have agreed otherwise, it is inferred that one who requests or permits another to perform services for him as his agent promises to pay for them.

FACTS: Clothier (D) instituted foreclosure proceedings and procured judgment on certain property, machinery, and equipment upon which he held a mortgage. However, before the sheriff's sale could be held, Clothier's (D) attorney, Iverson, enlisted McCollum's (P) services in checking and inventorying the property as well as in lining up prospective buyers, pursuant to what McCollum (P) was already doing for the trustee in bankruptcy in regards to the upcoming sheriff's sale. Moreover, as McCollum (P) carried out these requested duties, he talked and made reports to both Iverson and Clothier (D) concerning his activities. Subsequently, as a result of McCollum's (P) efforts, certain buyers he had contracted were at the sale, and Clothier (D) realized more money than he had anticipated. However, McCollum (P) was never compensated for his services rendered. As a result, he brought this suit for damages against Clothier (D), contending that he had rendered services for Clothier (D) under such circumstances that Clothier (D) is obligated under implied contract to pay for them. On the other hand, Clothier (D) maintained that McCollum's (P) activities were officious and without any express or implied promise that Clothier (D) would pay therefore. Despite Clothier's (D) contention, however, McCollum (P) recovered a judgment in quantum meruit for the services he rendered. Clothier (D) appealed.

ISSUE: Except where circumstances indicate that the parties have agreed otherwise, will it be inferred that one who requests or permits another to perform services for him as his agent promises to pay for them?

HOLDING AND DECISION: (Crockett, J.) Yes. Except where circumstances indicate that the parties have agreed otherwise, it is inferred that one who requests or permits another to perform services for him as his agent promises to pay for them. This rule merely restates Restatement of Agency, vol. 2, § 441, which, in effect, specifies when an agency relationship is created between two parties. However, this Restatement section was not intended to be applied to bind one under an implied contract who merely permits services to be rendered to him, or accept benefits from another, under such circumstances that he may reasonably assume they are given gratuitously. Hence, the test is whether the circumstances were such that a person rendering services for, or transferring benefits to, another reasonably assumes to be paid and the latter reasonably expects to pay for such services. In the instant case, the fact that McCollum (P) had been working previously for the trustee in a similar capacity, for which he had been paid, coupled with the request made by Clothier's (D) attorney and agent to continue the work, and the knowledge of Clothier (D) himself that the work was being done, are all factors the trial court could take into consideration in applying the above rule. Hence, the evidence was sufficient to support these findings of the court that there was an implied contract to pay for the reasonable value of McCollum's (P) services. Affirmed.

ANALYSIS

With regard to one common circumstance where the recipient of services can reasonably assume they are rendered gratuitously, it has been frequently stated that the law will presume that services rendered by members of a family living in one household "were gratuitous favors merely, prompted by friendship, kindness, and the relationship between them." *Hartley v. Bohrer*, 52 Idaho 72, II F.2d 616 (1932).

McKnight v. Peoples-Pittsburgh Trust Co.

Theatre manager (P) v. Bank (D)

Pa. Sup. Ct., 360 Pa. 290, 61 A.2d 820 (1948).

NATURE OF CASE: Appeal from directed verdict denying damages for services rendered.

FACT SUMMARY: In McKnight's (P) suit for damages against Peoples-Pittsburgh Trust Co. (Bank) (D), the trial court entered a directed verdict in favor of the Bank (D), thereby denying McKnight (P) damages allegedly resulting from the Bank's (D) refusal to pay McKnight (P) for services rendered in connection with an alleged agency relationship.

RULE OF LAW

Except where there is an express or implied promise otherwise, a principal has no obligation to compensate his sub-agent for services the latter rendered to him pursuant to a contractual agreement between the sub-agent and the principal's immediate agent.

FACTS: George Brothers, a Pittsburg real estate firm, put McKnight (P), its employee, in charge of two theatres which the theatre owners conveyed to him as a strawman for Peoples-Pittsburgh Trust Co. (Bank) (D) after the Bank (D), in lieu of the foreclosure of a mortgage that it held against the theatres, took possession of them as mortgagee in possession. Moreover, McKnight (P) received compensation from George Brothers on a commission basis to run the theatres. Subsequently, after the Bank (D) acquired title to the theatres, McKnight (P) continued managing the theatres until he entered the military service. However, just prior to McKnight's (P) military separation, he requested additional compensation from George Brothers for his services in developing the theatres for sale, and when they refused to pay anything additional, taking the position that full payment had been made for the services rendered, McKnight (P) instituted this action for damages to recover additional compensation from the Bank (D). In support of this claim, McKnight (P) averred that his services in managing and developing the theatres were rendered pursuant to an express contact with the Bank (D), orally made with W.D. George, a partner of George Brothers as well as director for the Bank (D), as the Bank's (D) duly authorized agent. In opposition to McKnight's (P) claim, however, the Bank (D) averred that its contract for the management and control of the theatres was made exclusively with George Brothers, through W.D. George, and that any services performed by McKnight (P) were performed as an employee of George Brothers. At the conclusion of McKnight's evidence on liability, the court below entered a directed verdict in favor of the Bank (D). McKnight (P) appealed.

ISSUE: Except where there is an express or implied promise otherwise, does a principal have an obligation to compensate his sub-agent for services the latter rendered to him pursuant to a contractual agreement between the sub-agent and the principal's immediate agent?

HOLDING AND DECISION: (Patterson, J.) No. Except where there is an express or implied promise otherwise, a principal has no obligation to compensate his sub-agent for services the latter rendered to him pursuant to a contractual agreement between the sub-agent and the principal's immediate agent. In distinguishing between an agent and a sub-agent, the inference, in looking at the agent-sub-agent contract, is that the regular employees of agents are sub-agents, although, where it is clear, an agent can perform his agency function by hiring a third party, thereby making the latter the presumptive agent of the principal. In the instant case, viewing all the evidence in the light most favorable to Mc-Knight (P) and giving him the benefit of every legitimate inference, it would justify at most a finding that McKnight (P) was a sub-agent of the Bank (D), whose agent in the management of these properties was George Brothers. Consequently, the Bank (D) is not obligated to compensate McKnight (P) for the services he rendered it pursuant to his contract with George Brothers. Affirmed.

ANALYSIS

The principal laid down in *McKnight* aims to protect the principal from undue burden and expense from compensating third parties his agent had hired to perform at least part of his duties to the principal. An obvious reason for this may be that although the principal benefits from the third party's services, since he is not in privity with the latter, then he is not obligated to make compensation. However, another not-so-obvious reason for this may be that courts want to encourage an agent to fully satisfy his obligations to his principal without delegating them to someone else, thereby defeating the purpose of his being hired in the first place.

Taylor v. Cordis Corp.

Employee (P) v. Employer (D)

634 F. Supp. 1242 (S.D. Miss. 1986).

NATURE OF CASE: Action to rescind a non-competition clause in an employment contract.

FACT SUMMARY: After Cordis Corp. (D), Taylor's (P) employer, allegedly failed to notify him of problems it was having with its pacemakers whereby he allegedly suffered harm, Taylor (P) brought this rescission action upon seeking employment elsewhere, in order to void a non-competition clause that appeared in his employment contract with Cordis (D).

RULE OF LAW

A principal has a duty to deal fairly with his agent so that the agent will not be subjected to physical or pecuniary loss in dealing with his product.

FACTS: Taylor (P) began his employment on February 13, 1981 as a salesman for Cordis Corp. (D) authorized to sell heart pacemakers. Since Cordis (D) intended to exclusively train Taylor (P) on the marketability of its products, it encouraged him to sign, on his first day of employment, an agreement not to compete for one year after termination of his employment. During his subsequent employment, Taylor (P) became increasingly concerned about the quality and marketability of Cordis (D) pacemakers, stemming from the frequency with which Cordis (D) distributed notices to its sales force regarding defects in the design and performance of its pacemakers. However, Cordis (D), although having reason to know of varied problems associated with some of its pacemakers several years beforehand, as implied in research and customer feedback, did not distribute its first notice until December 1983, where it detailed problems associated with certain defectively designed pacemakers. Subsequently, Taylor (P), after allegedly suffering humiliation and embarrassment as a result of informing his clientele of recall and liability problems associated with Cordis (D) pacemakers, voluntarily resigned from Cordis (D). Furthermore, Taylor (P), seeking employment for another similar company, filed this rescission action on the same day as his resignation in order to void the non-competition clause he had agreed to comply with by executing his signature on his employment contract for Cordis (D), contending that since Cordis (D) failed to timely provide him with material information relating to problems it had discovered in its pacemakers prior to his receipt of its December 1983 notice, then it had breached its implied duty that it owed him as its agent, thereby entitling him to the equitable remedy of rescission. In opposition to this, Cordis (D) counterclaimed for a preliminary injunction to enforce the agreement.

ISSUE: Does a principal have a duty to deal fairly with his agent so that the agent will not be subjected to physical or pecuniary loss in dealing with his product?

HOLDING AND DECISION: (Lee, J.) Yes. A principal has a duty to deal fairly with his agent so that the agent will not be subjected to physical or pecuniary loss in dealing with his product. This rule is derived from the principle as laid down in Restatement (Second) of Agency § 435 which, in effect, imposes a duty on a principal to deal fairly with his agent as determined from the circumstances. Moreover, if the circumstances call for it, the comment for Restatement of Agency § 437 demands that the principal maintain a standard of conduct that will not harm the agent's business reputation or reasonable self-respect. In this respect, in the instant case, the duty of fair dealing that Cordis (D) had to fulfill involved providing Taylor (P) with information regarding the nature of its product problems in order not to harm his business reputation as a result of his clientele being dissatisfied with the product. However, Cordis (D) fulfilled its duty by informing the sales force of its product problems in the December 1983 notification. Furthermore, although it knew of the product problems several years prior to this notification, its failure to disclose such information was reasonable under the circumstances since its research into the safety of its products had not revealed how widespread the problems were until 1983, and customer complaints relating to product performance were not so numerous as to lead them to imply that there were widespread product problems. Hence Cordis's (D) failure to inform Taylor (P) of all product problems before the issuance of the 1983 notification does not entitle him to the equitable remedy of rescission. As a result, Cordis's (D) injunction to enforce Taylor's (P) non-competition agreement, with the specific clause in question included, issued.

ANALYSIS

In *Taylor*, had there been an industry-wide study published about the defectiveness of the particular pacemakers Cordis Corp. (D) marketed prior to its first notification, then the result may have been different. In that instance, Cordis Corp. (D), even without having actual knowledge of the study, may have been held to know of the problems associated with its product since certain industry standards are generally held to be within the knowledge of those taking part in the specific industry. Generally, this ensures that companies will use means at their disposal to become informed of developments in their industry in order to minimize the risks involved with marketing their products.

Carrier v. McLlarky

Principal (P) v. Agent (D)

N.H. Sup. Ct., 693 A.2d 76 (1997).

NATURE OF CASE: Appeal of damages award for breach of agent's duties to principal.

FACT SUMMARY: When Bruce McLlarky (D) installed a replacement hot water heater in the home of Janet Carrier (P) but failed to obtain warranty recovery from its manufacturer which he said he would "try" to do, Carrier (P) sued McLlarky (D), arguing he had breached his agency duties to her as principal.

RULE OF LAW

The promise to act as an agent is ordinarily interpreted as being a promise only to make reasonable efforts to accomplish the directed result.

FACTS: Bruce McLlarky (D) installed a replacement hot water heater in the home of Janet Carrier (P). When he installed the new hot water heater, he told Carrier (P) he believed the old unit was under warranty and he would "try" to obtain a credit against the cost of the new heater from the manufacturer. McLlarky (D) subsequently returned the defective unit to the supplier, but never gave Carrier (P) the desired credit, claiming that he himself never received payment from the manufacturer. Carrier (P) sued McLlarky (D) in small claims court for the replacement value of the water heater and assorted costs. The district court found for Carrier (P), and McLlarky (D) appealed.

ISSUE: Is the promise to act as an agent ordinarily interpreted as being a promise only to make reasonable efforts to accomplish the directed result?

HOLDING AND DECISION: (Johnson, J.) Yes. The promise to act as an agent is ordinarily interpreted as being a promise only to make reasonable efforts to accomplish the directed result. Agents have a duty to conduct the affairs of the principal with a certain level of diligence, skill, and competence. As the Restatement (Second) of Agency § 377, comment b (1957) states, such promise requires only "reasonable efforts." Here, McLlarky (D) did make a reasonable attempt to obtain a refund for Carrier (P). Specifically, the evidence revealed that after agreeing to act on behalf of Carrier (P), McLlarky (D) gave the old heater to the supplier to return to the manufacturer. The record shows that McLlarky (D) was only charged with returning the defective heater for a possible credit; McLlarky (D) did not guarantee that a credit would be obtained. The record does not indicate that more was required of McLlarky (D) in his agent capacity beyond executing the actual return and seeking the credit. He merely promised "to attempt" to obtain a credit from the manufacturer. Furthermore, an agent cannot be held liable to the principal simply because the agent failed to procure something to which the principal was not entitled. In this regard, McLlarky (D) correctly argued that any finding by the lower court that there was a valid warranty in place is unsupported by the record. Notably, Carrier (P) never produced a warranty for her actual unit. Reversed.

ANALYSIS

The *Carrier* court noted there was no evidence to support the lower court's finding that McLlarky (D) breached his duty to remit funds actually received on behalf of Carrier (P). In this regard, the Restatement (Second) of Agency § 427 provides that an agent who has received money on behalf of the principal has the duty to deliver it to the principal on demand.

Olsen v. Vail Associates Real Estate, Inc.

Real property seller (P) v. Real estate agency (D)

Colo. Sup. Ct., 935 P.2d 975 (1997).

NATURE OF CASE: Appeal from defense verdict in action alleging breach of fiduciary duty, fraudulent concealment, and negligence.

FACT SUMMARY: When Vail Associates Real Estate, Inc. (D), a real estate agency, failed to disclose to its clients, the Olsens (P), the much higher price paid for adjacent property, the Olsens (P) sued.

RULE OF LAW

To discharge its fiduciary duty of good faith and loyalty, a real estate broker or agent must disclose all facts relative to the subject matter of the agency relationship that may be material to the decision the principal is about to make.

FACTS: The Olsens (P) inherited estate property which they listed with Vail Associates Real Estate, Inc. (D). After a potential buyer was found, the same buyer also purchased adjacent land for a much higher price. Vail Associates (D) did not negotiate the other sale, since the owner insisted on negotiating directly with the buyer himself. The Olsens (P) sued Vail Associates (D) for breach of fiduciary duty, fraudulent concealment, and negligence when they learned of the much higher price that had been paid for the adjacent property. The trial court found in favor of Vail Associates (D). The trial court's determination that Vail Associates (D) did not make any material omissions and did not engage in a dual agency was appealed by the Olsens (P).

ISSUE: To discharge its fiduciary duty of good faith and loyalty, must a real estate broker or agent disclose all facts relative to the subject matter of the agency relationship that may be material to the decision the principal is about to make?

HOLDING AND DECISION: (Scott, J.) Yes. To discharge its fiduciary duty of good faith and loyalty, a real estate broker or agent must disclose all facts relative to the subject matter of the agency relationship that may be material to the decision the principal is about to make. Since Vail Associates (D) did not know the price of the other property sold prior to the signing of the sale contract for the Olsens (P) estate property, it could not have disclosed it to the Olsens (P). The trial court was correct in concluding that Vail Associates (D) did not engage in a dual agency and did not breach its fiduciary duty of good faith and fair dealing. Affirmed.

ANALYSIS

A duty of disclosure is imposed on any agent if the information is "material." A matter is "material" if a reasonable person would attach importance to its existence or nonexistence in determining his choice of action in the transaction in question, according to the Restatement (Second) of Torts. In the case above, the Olsens (P) could not show how knowledge of the sale price of the adjacent property after the sale of their own property would have in any way affected their decision making. Therefore the omission by Vail Associates (D) was immaterial. Since the information known to and withheld by Vail Associates (D) as the agent was not material, there was no breach.

Gelfand v. Horizon Corp.

Employee (P) v. Employer (D)

675 F.2d 1108 (10th Cir. 1982).

NATURE OF CASE: Appeal from trial court's determination of damages.

FACT SUMMARY: In Gelfand's (P) suit for damages against Horizon Corp. (D), his former employer, the trial court determined that Horizon (D) was not entitled to offset profits which third parties made as a result of Gelfand's (P) breach of fiduciary duty with what it owed him for services rendered.

RULE OF LAW

Where a fiduciary has, by violating his obligation of loyalty, made it possible for others to make profits, he can be held accountable for these profits regardless of whether he has realized them.

FACTS: Gelfand (P), while working as a real estate salesman for Horizon Corp. (D), a real estate concern, sold, without Horizon's (D) knowledge, an option to buy on a tract of land to a dummy corporation that he had previously formed, with his wife and two associates each owning interest. Moreover, soon after paying for the option, the dummy corporation sold the option to a third corporation and made a $57,500 profit, which was split three ways among the dummy corporation's owners. The dummy corporation subsequently went out of business after this transaction. After determining what had occurred, Horizon (D) fired Gelfand (P) and refused to pay him commissions and overrides he was allegedly owed on the previously-mentioned transaction as well as on some other completed transactions. As a result, Gelfand (P) brought suit for damages against Horizon (D), alleging that he was owed for commissions made on the option sale to his dummy corporation as well as on several other completed sales. However, Horizon (D), in connection with the trial court's determination of damages for Gelfand (P), argued that Gelfand (P) breached his fiduciary duty with respect to the dummy corporation sale, and, as a result, it was entitled to an offset not only for the profits accruing directly to Gelfand (P) for this sale, but also for profits which accrued to third parties allied with him. However, the trial court, despite Horizon's (D) arguments, merely offset the profits that directly accrued to Gelfand (P) from the sale involving the dummy corporation. Horizon (D) appealed.

ISSUE: Where a fiduciary has, by violating his obligation of loyalty, made it possible for others to make profits, can he be held accountable for these profits regardless of whether he has realized them?

HOLDING AND DECISION: (Doyle, J.) Yes. Where a fiduciary has, by violating his obligation of loyalty, made it possible for others to make profits, he can be held accountable for these profits regardless of whether he has realized them. This rule is consistent with various cases which have allowed a principal to recover from an agent fiduciary who has breached his obligation of loyalty owed to his principal through making profits for third parties. These cases have generally held that the purpose for restoring profits under these circumstances is to discourage potential conflicts of interest and duty, and that complaining principal or employer need not prove that any loss was caused by a fiduciary's misconduct. Hence, restitution of profits under these circumstances serves a deterrent function. (See Bogert, Trusts and Trustees § 543). However, a court is not obligated to compel a fiduciary to reimburse the beneficiary for third-party profits. On the contrary, justice requires a case-by-case evaluation of all relevant circumstances whenever restitution of third party profits is sought. In the instant case, the weight of the evidence conclusively supports the trial court's decision. Accordingly, even if this court finds some support for Horizon's (D) position, it is not obligated to reverse the trial court's ruling merely because reasonable inferences may be drawn which counter the reasonable inferences drawn by the trial court. Affirmed.

ANALYSIS

In connection with *Gelfand*, see *Tarnowski v. Resop*, 236 Minn. 33, 51 N.W. 2d 801 (1952), in which a principal recovered not only the agent's secret commission, even though he had rescinded the contract and recovered that with which he had parted, he also recovered attorney's fees, all expenses, and loss of time devoted the operation; and *Boston Deep Sea Fishing & Ice Co. v. Ansell*, 39 Ch.D. 339 (1888), where the agent had to pay to his principal a one percent commission he had received for placing a ship building contract with the third party. The principal was also absolved from paying this agent's current salary. See also *Donemar, Inc. v. Molloy*, 252 N.Y. 360, 169 N.E. 610 (1930), where a third party was ordered to pay a $4,555 "gratuity" over to the principal, even though he had already paid it to the agent.

Town & Country House & Home Service v. Newbery

Employer (P) v. Former employee (D)

N.Y. Ct. App., 3 N.Y.2d 554, 147 N.E.2d 724 (1958).

NATURE OF CASE: Appeal from award of damages and injunctive relief for unfair competition.

FACT SUMMARY: In Town & Country House & Home Service (P) unfair competition action for damages and injunctive relief against Newbery (D), the trial court found that Newbery's (D) enticing away of Town & Country's (P) clientele to his own similar business, after his employment with the latter terminated without a negative covenant against competition ever appearing or being included in his employment contract, was not unfair competition; however, the appellate court, on appeal, found that it was.

RULE OF LAW

Absent evidence of a negative covenant against competition, an agent may not solicit his former employer's clientele where it is clear that the latter has accumulated it through considerable effort and expenditure.

FACTS: Newbery (D), while under Town & Country House & Home Service's (P) employ, conferred with two co-employees regarding starting a new, competing house cleaning business after Town & Country's (P) president refused to increase their remuneration in the business. Furthermore, while on Town & Country's payroll, but outside of business hours, they met on a number of occasions to plan the organization of their company. Subsequently, after the new company was organized under Newbery's (D) name, Newbery (D), in soliciting clientele for his new business, persuaded a number of Town & Country's (P) customers to switch to using the services he provided. After learning of Newbery's (D) solicitation tactics, Town & Country (P), although no negative covenant prohibiting competition existed in Newbery's (D) employment contract for it, brought this injunction and damages action against Newbery (D), contending that since its enterprise was unique and Newbery (D) learned trade secrets while under its employ, then he should be enjoined from heading a competing business altogether and should pay damages to it by reason of some of its customers being enticed away. Notwithstanding Town & Country's (P) grievances, the district court dismissed its complaint. However, on appeal, the appellate court found that Town & Country (P) was entitled to relief. Newbery (D) appealed.

ISSUE: Absent evidence of a negative covenant against competition, may an agent solicit his former employer's clientele where it is clear that the latter has accumulated it through considerable effort and expenditure?

HOLDING AND DECISION: (Van Voorhis, J.) No. Absent evidence of a negative covenant against competition, an agent may not solicit his former employer's clientele where it is clear that the latter has accumulated it through considerable effort and expenditure. In the instant case, Town & Country's (P) customers were not, and could not be, obtained by looking up their names in the telephone directory or by going to any advertised location, but had to be screened from a large pool of potential customers. Moreover, during the screening process, Town & Country (P) went to considerable effort and expense to determine each potential customer's receptivity and willingness to accept its service, as evidenced by its extensive telephone solicitations and subsequent appointment schedules with interested customers. Subsequently, after all these efforts, Town & Country (P) generally only netted a small percentage of the solicited customers, whose actual numbers depended on the size of the pool in which it determined to contact. Hence, since Newbery (D) merely solicited Town & Country's (P) clientele after beginning his own similar business, without engaging in the extensive solicitation process that the latter used to build it, then Town & Country (P) is entitled to enjoin Newbery (D) from soliciting its clientele, and to recover such damages or loss of profits as may be established to have resulted from those that have been solicited to date. However, aside from this, Town & Country (P) is not entitled to enjoin Newbery (D) from engaging in a similar house cleaning business altogether since, as the lower court determined, its business was not so unique as to indicate that Newbery (D) was prima facie breaching a confidential relationship he had with it by competing. On the contrary, the only unique thing involved from Newbery's (D) dealings with Town & Country (P) was the clientele list. Hence, this portion of Town & Country's (P) complaint is dismissed. Reversed in part.

ANALYSIS

The *Newbery* opinion mentions the term "trade secret" several times. A trade secret, as defined in Restatement of Torts § 757, is "any formula, pattern, device, or compilation of information which is used in one business, and which gives" an individual or company using or possessing it "an opportunity to obtain an advantage over competitors who do not know or use it." However, the standards for determining what is a protected trade secret are not as strict as those for determining what is patentable.

Robbins v. Finlay

Employer (P) v. Former employee (D)

Utah Sup. Ct., 645 P.2d 623 (1982).

NATURE OF CASE: Appeal from award of damages for unfair competition.

FACT SUMMARY: In Robbins's (P) unfair competition action for damages against Finlay (D), the trial court awarded Robbins (P) damages as a result of Finlay's (D) competing within its service area in defiance of a negative covenant in his employment contract prohibiting such competition, and which, if breached, provided that he pay Robbins (P) $3,000 in damages.

RULE OF LAW

Covenants not to compete are enforceable if carefully drawn to protect the legitimate interests of the employer.

FACTS: Finlay (D) began working for Robbins (P) (hereinafter Beltone), a distributor of hearing aids, under an employment contract which, in part, included a non-competition clause. This clause, in effect, provided that Finlay (D) was to pay $3,000 to Beltone (P) upon his breach of the covenant not to compete in Beltone's (P) service area for a period of one year following the termination of his employment. After several years of employment, Finlay (D), despite the non-competition clause, left Beltone (P) to open his own hearing aids office within Beltone's (P) service area. As a result, Beltone (P) brought this action for damages to enforce the terms of Finlay's (D) employment contract. In opposition to this action, Finlay (D) sought to have the stipulated damages award of $3,000 set aside, arguing that the non-competition clause was unenforceable because the restraint on competition was unreasonable and his employment was a common calling not subject to a covenant not to compete. Notwithstanding Finlay's (D) arguments, the trial court found that Finlay (D) had breached his covenant not to compete with Beltone (P) and awarded Beltone (P) the $3,000 amount specified in Finlay's (D) employment contract. Finlay (D) appealed.

ISSUE: Are covenants not to compete enforceable if carefully drawn to protect the legitimate interests of the employer?

HOLDING AND DECISION: (Stewart, J.) Yes. Covenants not to compete are enforceable if carefully drawn to protect the legitimate interests of the employer. In determining whether a covenant is carefully drawn, several factors need to be taken into consideration, including the covenant's geographical extent; the duration of the limitations; the nature of the employee's duties; and the nature of the interest which the employer seeks to protect such as trade secrets, goodwill of his business, or an extraordinary investment in the training or education of the employee. In a general sense, the law balances the nature of the interest of one seeking to enforce such a covenant, whether by injunction or by stipulated damages, against the hardship imposed on the employee as a result of the restraint. In the instant case, the covenant served no purpose other than restricting an employee from competing with a former employer. First, there was no indication that Finlay's (D) competition had any greater effect on Beltone's (P) customer goodwill than the competition of any other salesman employed by Beltone's (P) competitors. Second, there was no evidence to indicate that Finlay (D) was privy to any trade secrets Beltone (P) may have possessed. Third, the record showed that Finlay's (D) job required little training and was not unlike the job of many other types of salesmen. Finally, there was no showing that Finlay's (D) services were special or unique, even if their value to Beltone (P) was high due to his expertise. However, expertise acquired through employment in a common calling cannot be appropriated as a trade secret. Hence, the covenant not to compete had the effect of preventing Finlay (D) from exploiting skills and experience which he had a right to exploit and thus was unreasonable and unenforceable. Affirmed in part and reversed in part.

ANALYSIS

In some jurisdictions, there exist statutory restrictions on covenants not to compete. Colorado's statutory version, 3 Colorado Rev. Stat. § 8-2-113(2), provides, in part, that any "covenants not to compete which restrict the right of any person to receive compensation for performance of skilled or unskilled labor for any employer shall be void." However, this statute goes on to mention specific circumstances under which covenants appear in contracts for the purchase and sale of a business as well as for the protection of trade secrets, when provisions call for recovery of any expenses in connection with training an employee, and when covenants prohibit executive and management personnel from competing.

CHAPTER 3

Vicarious Tort Liability

Quick Reference Rules of Law

CHAPTER 3

26. The Effect on Vicarious Liability of a Relatonship Between Servant and Injured Party. Where a spouse, while in the course of his or her employment, causes personal injury to the other spouse, his or her employer must answer for the damage whether there is trespass by direct command or trespass incidental to the employer's business. (Schubert v. August Schubert Wagon Co.) *56*

27. The Effect on Vicarious Liability of a Relatonship Between Servant and Injured Party. Where an employee, without authority or apparent authority from his employer, invites or gives permission to a third party to enter his employer's premises or vehicle and causes the latter injury while within the scope of his employment, his employer is not liable to the third party for his tortious conduct. (Klatt v. Commonwealth Edison Co.) *57*

Jones v. Hart

Pawnbroker (P) v. Servant's master (D)

Holt, K.B. 642, 90 Eng. Rep. 1255 (1698).

NATURE OF CASE: Tort action in trover for the cost of goods sold but not delivered.

FACT SUMMARY: Hart's (D) servant offered goods of Hart's (D) to Jones (P).

RULE OF LAW

A master is vicariously liable for the acts of his servant when they are authorized by the master.

FACTS: Hart's (D) servant took some of Hart's (D) goods to a pawnbroker, Jones (P). Jones (P) later gave the servant money for the goods. The servant then failed to turn over the goods paid for by Jones (P). It was claimed by the servant that the goods had been lost. Jones (P) brought suit in trover against Hart (D). Hart (D) claimed that he had no liability to Jones (P) since all of the actions complained of were done by the servant.

ISSUE: Where a servant commits a wrong while performing acts authorized by his master, is the master liable?

HOLDING AND DECISION: (Holt, J.) Yes. The question revolves around the servant's authority. If he is acting for the master, the master will be liable for the servant's actions. If the servant is performing duties authorized by the master, e.g. driving a cart, and an injury occurs, the master also will be liable. Here, Hart (D) authorized his servant to take the goods to Jones (P). Hart (D) therefore is liable for any harm resulting from the authorization. Judgment for Jones (P).

ANALYSIS

Vicarious liability is founded on the "deep pockets" doctrine. Where a party is injured by an employee, a judgment against the employee is often worthless. The employer, on the other hand, is normally solvent. Therefore, when the employee was performing duties in the employer's behalf at the time of the injury, it was felt that the employer should bear the ultimate burden.

Heims v. Hanke

Injured pedestrian (P) v. Car washer (D)

Wis. Sup. Ct., 5 Wis. 2d 465, 93 N.W.2d 455 (1958).

NATURE OF CASE: Appeal from award of damages for personal injuries.

FACT SUMMARY: Hanke (D) appealed from a judgment entered in favor of Heims (P) in a slip and fall personal injury action, contending that he could not be held liable for the negligence of William (D), a volunteer, on a theory of respondeat superior.

RULE OF LAW

One volunteering service without any agreement for compensation or expectation of reward may be a servant of the one accepting the services, if subject to the other's control or right to control the provision of those services.

FACTS: Hanke (D) was washing his car at the street curb on a very cold day with the help of his nephew, William (D). Water was obtained by William (D) by pail from a faucet across the sidewalk. The sun was shining on the car, but not on the sidewalk. William (D) spilled some water which froze on the sidewalk. After Hanke (D) and William (D) left, Heims (P), while walking, slipped on the ice, sustaining personal injuries. Heims (P) brought a personal injury action against Hanke (D) and William (D), and from a judgment for Heims (P), Hanke (D) appealed.

ISSUE: Can one volunteering service without any agreement for compensation or expectation of reward be a servant of the one accepting the services?

HOLDING AND DECISION: (Wingert, J.) Yes. One volunteering service without any agreement for compensation or expectation of reward may be a servant of the one accepting the service, if subject to the other's control or right to control the provision of those services. From the evidence it could be inferred that one in the exercise of reasonable care would have foreseen the formation of the ice and would have done something to protect persons using the sidewalk. Further, Hanke (D) could be held liable for William's (D) negligence. Although unpaid, William (D) was obtaining the water at Hanke's (D) direction. Thus, he had control over William's (D) activities, and his negligence can be imputed to Hanke (D). Affirmed.

ANALYSIS

This case sets forth the general rule with respect to the liability of the master based upon the negligence of an unpaid volunteer/servant. These issues arise most often when one "volunteers" to drive for another. The seemingly harshness of the rule is mitigated in most jurisdictions by the fact that the master still has the right of independent indemnification against the wrongdoing servant.

Sandrock v. Taylor

Estate of decedant (P) v. Driver (D)

Neb. Sup. Ct., 185 Neb. 106, 174 N.W.2d 186 (1970).

NATURE OF CASE: Appeal from award of damages for wrongful death.

FACT SUMMARY: Meirose (D), Taylor (D), and Co-op (D) appealed a judgment in favor of Sandrock (P) in her action for wrongful death, contending that the negligence of Meirose (D) should be imputed to Sandrock, the decedent, thus barring Sandrock's (P) recovery.

RULE OF LAW

Unless some relationship exists between a driver and his passenger which gives the passenger the authority to direct or assist in the operation of the vehicle, the passenger is a guest and the driver's negligence is not imputable to the passenger.

FACTS: Sandrock was killed when a vehicle driven by Meirose (D), in which he was a passenger, collided with a milk truck driven by Taylor (D). The evidence indicated that Meirose (D), who lived on a farm which he leased to his son, agreed to take Sandrock to town to get a broken part repaired. There was no evidence that Sandrock had any right to control Meirose's (D) operation of the car, or that Meirose (D) had agreed to act subject to Sandrock's control. The plaintiff (P) successfully recovered damages in her wrongful death action against everyone, and they appealed, with Taylor (D) and Co-op (D) contending in part that the negligence of Meirose (D) should be imputed to Sandrock, barring Sandrock's (P) recovery.

ISSUE: Absent some relationship existing between a driver and his passenger which gives the passenger the authority to direct or assist in the operation of the vehicle, is the driver's negligence imputable to the passenger?

HOLDING AND DECISION: (McCown, J.) No. Unless some relationship exists between a driver and his passenger which gives the passenger the authority to direct or assist in the operation of the vehicle, the passenger is a guest, and the driver's negligence is not imputable to the passenger. There is no evidence of such a relationship in the present case. The transportation provided by Meirose (D) was gratuitous resulting from a friendly and neighborly favor. The fact that Sandrock requested the ride is not controlling. Absent such a relationship, Meirose (D) was simply a host driver, whose negligence is not imputable to the host passenger, Sandrock. Affirmed.

ANALYSIS

The court in dictum stated that the rule of nonimputation would apply where the passenger is the owner of the car. Decisions in some states hold, however, that the passenger's ownership creates a rebuttable presumption of agency. See *Edlebeck v. Hooten* (1963) 121 N.W.2d 240. There is also statutorily imposed liability on the owner of the vehicle, apart from any vicariously liability, in some states.

Kane Furniture Corp. v. Miranda

Employer (D) v. Husband of deceased (P)

Fla. Ct. App., 506 So. 2d 1061 (1987), *review denied*, 515 So. 2d 230 (1988).

NATURE OF CASE: Consolidated appeal from summary judgment and verdict in wrongful death action.

FACT SUMMARY: Kane Furniture Corp. (Kane) (D) brought a consolidated appeal from the trial court's final summary judgment in Miranda's (P) wrongful death action that Perrone (D) was Kane's (D) employee, and Kraus (D) its subemployee, and from the jury verdict, contending that Perrone (D) and Kraus (D) were independent contractors.

RULE OF LAW
One can be found to be an independent contractor as a matter of law, if an analysis of Restatement factors so dictates.

FACTS: Kane Furniture Corp. (Kane) (D) sold carpeting as part of its retail furniture business. It had sold the carpet installation portion of its business to Perrone (D) in 1975. Kane (D) utilized Perrone (D), among others, to install the carpet it sold. After a time, Perrone (D) in turn, could hire other installers, including Kraus (D), to finish jobs it could not complete. On one of these jobs, Kraus (D) and his helper completed two installations for Perrone (D) and went drinking. Four hours later, they were involved in a traffic accident in which Miranda's (P) wife was killed. Miranda (P) brought an action for wrongful death, and successfully moved for summary judgment, holding that Perrone (D) was Kane's (D) employee, and Kraus (D) was Kane's (D) subemployee. The jury returned a verdict in favor of Miranda (P), and Kane (D) brought a consolidated appeal as to both the verdict and the entry of summary judgment.

ISSUE: Can a defendant's status as an independent contractor be determined as a matter of law?

HOLDING AND DECISION: (Ryder, C.J.) Yes. One can be found to be an independent contractor as a matter of law, if an analysis of Restatement factors so dictates. In the present case, an analysis of those factors compels the conclusion that Perrone (D) and Kraus (D) were independent contractors. Although Kane's (D) salesmen diagramed the installation layout plan, Kane (D) exercised no control over the operative details of the installation. Carpet installing can be viewed as a distinct occupation. Carpet installers, such as Kraus (D) and Perrone (D), are skilled workers who perform their duties without supervision. They supplied their own transportation and installation equipment. Perrone (D) and Kraus (D) worked on an as-needed basis and were paid by the square yard per installation, not per hour. There is no evidence that the parties intended to create an employment relationship. There were no employment agreements, and neither Kraus (D) nor Perrone (D) enjoyed the usual amenities associated with an employment relationship, such as fringe benefits, etc. Measured against the Restatement criteria, the facts in total dictate that Kraus (D) and Perrone (D) were independent contractors, and as such, Kane (D) should not be held liable for their negligence. Reversed and remanded with instructions.

ANALYSIS

As noted in the present case, the critical factor is control or the right to control the operative details of the work. Mere supervision to ensure completion of the entire project is not sufficient. Further, the description of the parties in any contract pertaining to the work to be performed will not necessarily be determinative of the status of the parties.

Lazo v. Mak's Trading Co.

Assault victim (P) v. Employer (D)

N.Y. Ct. App., 644 N.E.2d 1350 (1994).

NATURE OF CASE: Appeal from order finding no vicarious liability for tort committed by a day laborer.

FACT SUMMARY: Mak's Trading Co. (D), a grocer that hired a day laborer to unload a truck shipment, was found not liable for assault committed by the laborer.

RULE OF LAW

An employer is not vicariously liable for torts committed by a worker if the employer exercised no actual or constructive control over the performance and manner in which the work was performed.

FACTS: A day laborer who was hired by Mak's Trading Co. (D) to unload a shipment assaulted Lazo (P), the operator of the tractor trailer. Lazo (P) sued Mak's (D). The trial court found that Mak's (D) could not be held vicariously liable for the laborer's tortious conduct. An appeal followed.

ISSUE: Is an employer vicariously liable for torts committed by a worker if the employer exercised no actual or constructive control over the performance and manner in which the work was performed?

HOLDING AND DECISION: [Judge not stated in casebook excerpt.] No. An employer is not vicariously liable for torts committed by a worker if the employer exercised no actual or constructive control over the performance and manner in which the work was performed. In this case, there was no evidence that would support the existence of any question of fact that could lead to the conclusion that Mak's (D) supervised the day laborer's activities. Affirmed.

CONCURRENCE: (Titone, J.) Although Mak's (D) cannot be held liable, the conclusion that, as a matter of law, the workers exercised control over the conduct of the work is incorrect. Unskilled laborers are almost always to be considered servants, according to the Comments to the Restatement (Second) of Agency. However, since an employer cannot be held liable for the tortious conduct of an employee if not undertaken within the scope of employment or authorized by the employer, it is irrelevant whether the workers were independent contractors or employees.

ANALYSIS

Various factors are considered in deciding servant rather than employee status. The master-servant relationship is an agency relationship, and vicarious liability may be imposed. Independent contractor status, however, relieves the employer from any such liability.

Soderback v. Townsend

Accident victim (P) v. Independent broker (D)

Or. Ct. App., 57 Or. App. 366, 644 P.2d 640, *review denied*, 293 Or. 394, 650 P.2d 927 (1982).

NATURE OF CASE: Appeal from defendant's summary judgment in personal injury action.

FACT SUMMARY: Soderback (P) appealed from a summary judgment in favor of the American Quasar Petroleum Company (Quasar) (D), contending that Townsend (D) was acting as an agent of Quasar (D) at the time the accident occurred.

RULE OF LAW

Where one employs another to achieve a certain result but does not exercise control or have the right to control the operative details of the work, he will not be held liable for the incidental negligence occurring in carrying out the work.

FACTS: Townsend (D) was for 26 years an independent oil and gas broker. He was retained by American Quasar Petroleum Company (Quasar) (D) to negotiate gas leases in Oregon. Quasar (D) told him generally what areas they were interested in. Townsend (D) was given maximum authority as to price and the duration of leases, but how he obtained the leases was up to him. He had no quotas and set his own work schedule. He was paid on a per diem basis, plus expenses, and accounted to Quasar (D) at two-week intervals. While driving a rental car to check some leases, he collided with Soderback (P). Soderback (P) sued Quasar (D) for his personal injuries, contending that Townsend (D) was an agent of Quasar (D) at the time of the accident. Quasar (D) successfully moved for summary judgment of this issue, and Soderback (P) appealed.

ISSUE: When one employs another to achieve a certain result but does not exercise control or have the right to control the operative details of the work, will he be held liable for the incidental negligence which occurs in carrying out the work?

HOLDING AND DECISION: (Van Hoomissen, J.) No. Where one employs another to achieve a certain result but does not exercise control or have the right to control the operative details of the work, he will not be held liable for the incidental negligence which occurs in carrying out the work. Quasar (D) knew Townsend (D) rented a car, but had no control over its operation. Since there is no evidence that Quasar (D) had control over the manner in which Townsend (D) went about his work, Quasar (D) cannot be held liable for Townsend's (D) negligence in operating the car, and summary judgment was proper. Affirmed.

ANALYSIS

It has been said in some jurisdictions that the rule of non-liability for the acts of an independent contractor has been swallowed up by expectations such that the rule is not applied if there is any reason for not doing so. Two of the main exceptions are the non-delegable duty doctrine and the peculiar risk doctrine.

Hunter v. R.G. Watkins & Son, Inc.

Accident victim (P) v. Employer (D)

N.H. Sup. Ct., 110 N.H. 243, 265 A.2d 15 (1970).

NATURE OF CASE: Appeal from ruling on reserved and transferred issue of vicarious liability in action for damages.

FACT SUMMARY: Hunter (P) and R.G. Watkins & Son, Inc. (Watkins) (D) appealed the ruling on the reserved and transferred issue that Davis (D), in operating his vehicle in picking up parts within the course and scope of his employment by Watkins (D), was a servant of Watkins (D) for the purpose of vicariously imposing liability on Watkins (D) for the negligence of Davis (D).

RULE OF LAW

If an employee negligently operates his vehicle while conducting a task within the scope of his employment, the fact that the employer did not have the right to control the operation of the vehicle will not necessarily determine whether or not the employer will be held vicariously liable for the employee's negligence.

FACTS: Davis (D), an employee of R.G. Watkins & Son, Inc. (Watkins) (D), was operating an L.V. truck on a road construction project. The truck broke down, and the replacement part needed for its repair was in another town. Davis (D) was sent to obtain the part, using his own vehicle. Watkins (D) agreed to pay him until 5:00 p.m., to compensate Davis (D) for his time and gasoline used in obtaining the part. On the way back, at about 5:00 p.m., Davis (D) became involved in an automobile accident with Hunter (P), who brought suit for the injuries he sustained in the accident. The parties reserved and transferred the issue as to whether Watkins (D) could be held vicariously liable for Davis' (D) negligence, absent the right to control the operation of the car. It was agreed for the purpose of resolving the transferred issue that Davis (D) was acting within the scope of his employment at the time of the accident. From the ruling on that issue finding Watkins (D) vicariously liable, Watkins (D) appealed.

ISSUE: Will the lack of control over the operation of an employee's vehicle at the time of an accident preclude a finding of vicarious liability on the part of an employer based upon the employee's negligent operation of the vehicle, while within the scope of his employment?

HOLDING AND DECISION: (Griffith, J.) No. If an employee negligently operates his vehicle while conducting a task within the scope of his employment, the fact that the employer did not have the right to control the operation of the vehicle will not necessarily determine whether or not the employer will be held vicariously liable for his employee's negligence. Only a dwindling minority of states hold that a lack of evidence on the control issue in such situations will preclude a finding of vicarious liability on the part of an employer. Unless control is decisive, numerous factors must be considered. The factor of control has been overemphasized, and one must determine whether, upon all the factors, Davis (D) would be considered an employee. Neither the fact that Watkins (D) did not control the operation of the vehicle nor the fact that it was Davis' (D) personal car should be controlling. Where a regular employee is sent upon a specific errand, using his own vehicle with the permission of his employer and acting within the scope of his employment, the employer can be held liable for the acts of the employee whether or not he had detailed control over the operation of the vehicle. Therefore, in the present case, Watkins (D) can be held liable for Davis' (D) negligence in the operation of his vehicle. Affirmed and remanded.

ANALYSIS

Interesting cases can arise when, as a condition of the employment relationship, the employee expressly retains operational control over the details of their employment. One of the most visible examples is the chef, who in many cases will bar his employer from the kitchen. Although the lack of control would seem to dictate that the owner of the restaurant would not be held liable, public policy considerations dictate that liability should be imposed, especially since in many instances, the chef involved will be judgment-proof, and a contrary rule would leave an injured person without an effective remedy.

Sandrock v. Taylor

Estate of decedent (P) v. Driver (D)

Neb. Sup. Ct., 185 Neb. 106, 174 N.W.2d 186 (1970).

NATURE OF CASE: Appeal from award of damages for personal injury.

FACT SUMMARY: Co-op (D) appealed from a judgment against it in Sandrock's (P) personal injury action, contending in part that it could not be held liable for Taylor's (D) negligence because pursuant to the contract between it and Taylor (D), Taylor (D) was an independent contractor.

RULE OF LAW

A party's recitation in a written contract as to its status as either an employee or independent contractor will not necessarily be controlling for vicarious liability purposes.

FACTS: Co-op (D) and Taylor (D) entered into a carrier's contract, under which Taylor (D) agreed to render daily fresh sweet milk delivery to Co-op's (D) creamery, as well as providing other services. Under the contract, Taylor (D) was required to provide all of his own equipment and was to purchase the tank truck from Co-op (D). Co-op (D) reserved the right to revise bulk routes at three month intervals, controlled the determination as to whether the transportation service was satisfactory, controlled in part the manner of Taylor's (D) payments, exercised control over the assistants whom Taylor (D) could employ, and had the right to retain any payments made on the tank truck if Taylor (D) violated the contract. Co-op (D) also retained the right to cancel the contract on 30-days' notice. The contract expressly provided that Taylor (D) had complete control over the manner and performance of his duties under the contract, and it required him to provide workers compensation and liability insurance and to pay all taxes and license fees. While operating the tank truck, Taylor (D) became involved in an accident in which Sandrock (P) sustained personal injuries. He successfully recovered in his suit against both Taylor (D) and Co-op (D), and Co-op (D) appealed, contending in part that Taylor (D) was an independent contractor under the carrier contract, and as such, it could not be held vicariously liable for Taylor's (D) negligence.

ISSUE: Can a party to a written contract establish its relationship as either an employee or an independent contractor for vicarious liability purposes?

HOLDING AND DECISION: (McCown, J.) No. A party's recitation as to its status in a written contract as either an employee or an independent contractor will not necessarily be controlling for vicarious liability purposes. In the present case, given the nature of the control that Co-op (D) still exerted over Taylor's (D) activities, the jury could have concluded from the evidence presented that Taylor (D) had no more independence than an employee in general. As such, the issue was properly submitted to a jury, and its verdict will be upheld. Affirmed.

ANALYSIS

The determination as to whether one is an independent contractor or an employee may have some other far-reaching effects. For example, workers compensation coverage depends on the determination, as do certain tax consequences. Because there are different policy considerations that underlie the doctrine of respondeat superior and the system of workers compensation, in a particular case, although a party may be able to recover against an "employer," the "employer" may retain a contractual right to indemnification under a contract designated "independent contractor."

Hixon v. Sherwin-Williams Co.

Insurer (P) v. Contractor (D)

671 F.2d 1005 (7th Cir. 1982).

NATURE OF CASE: Appeal from grant of motion for directed defense verdict in subrogation action.

FACT SUMMARY: American States (P) appealed from a decision granting Sherwin-Williams Co.'s (D) motion for a directed verdict in its subrogation action, contending in part that Sherwin-Williams (D) could be held liable for Benkovich's (D) negligence because he was engaged in an inherently dangerous activity.

RULE OF LAW

Under the peculiar risk doctrine, a principal is not liable for the torts of an independent contractor if the activity undertaken by the independent contractor is not so hazardous so as to justify the imposition of vicarious liability.

FACTS: The Chesses sustained water damage to their kitchen floor. Their insurer, American States (P), hired Hixon (D) to make the repairs. He was too busy, so he contracted with Sherwin-Williams (D), who in turn contracted with Benkovich (D) to do the job. Because of the dampness, a plywood layer was required between the concrete and the linoleum being installed. Although an experienced installer with a good reputation, Benkovich (D) had never undertaken this procedure. He used a highly flammable glue without taking heed of the express warnings and instructions on the can's label. The glue exploded, causing an additional $27,000 in damage to the home. American States (P) paid the damage and brought a subrogation action against Sherwin-Williams (D) to recover for the monies paid. Sherwin-Williams (D) successfully moved for a directed verdict on the grounds that Benkovich (D) was an independent contractor, and from that decision, American States (P) appealed, attempting to bring the case within the peculiar risk doctrine.

ISSUE: Will a principal be liable for the torts of an independent contractor under the peculiar risk doctrine for torts committed in the performance of a non-hazardous activity?

HOLDING AND DECISION: (Posner, J.) No. Under the peculiar risk doctrine, a principal is not liable for the torts of an independent contractor if the activity undertaken by the independent contractor is not so hazardous so as to justify the imposition of vicarious liability. The rationale behind the doctrine of respondeat superior in this state is accident-prevention, and therefore the independent contractor nonliability doctrine remains in full force. There is an exception to the rule for inherently dangerous activities, where case law holds that if the activity is so hazardous, the principal should take his own precautions even though he does not supervise the operative details of the work. There is nothing hazardous, however, about laying a linoleum floor. The hazard of the independent contractor misusing materials is present in almost all construction work, and to allow recovery against the principal under those circumstances would allow the exception to swallow the rule. This accident did not occur because of the inherently dangerous activity of laying a floor, but rather from Benkovich's (D) failure to read and follow the instructions and warnings on the glue can. Imposing liability on Sherwin-Williams (D) under these circumstances would not promote the rationale of accident prevention. [The court also found that Sherwin-Williams (D) was not negligent in engaging Benkovich (D) to do the job.] Affirmed on the independent contractor issue.

ANALYSIS

The rationale underlying the imposition of the doctrine of respondeat superior in many states is purely public policy, specifically that the principal, because of its "deep pocket", is better able to bear the risks and costs of such accidents. In fact, some cases have gone so far to say that the various exceptions to the independent contractor rule now loom so large in importance that they do in fact swallow the rule, holding the principal not liable for the torts of the independent contractor, only when there is a good public policy reason for doing so. See *Van Arsdale v. Hollinger*, 437 P. 2d 508 (Cal. 1968).

Kleeman v. Rheingold

Litigant (P) v. Attorney (D)

N.Y. Ct. App., 81 N.Y.2d 270, 614 N.E.2d 712 (1993).

NATURE OF CASE: Appeal from summary judgment for the defendant in an action for legal malpractice.

FACT SUMMARY: Kleeman's (P) medical malpractice suit was dismissed due to the negligence of the process server used by her attorney, Rheingold (D).

RULE OF LAW

An attorney has a nondelegable duty to his or her clients to exercise due care in the service of process and may therefore be held liable to the client for negligent service of process, even though the task is given to an independent contractor.

FACTS: Kleeman (P) originally retained Rheingold (D) to represent her in a medical malpractice action. With only five days left before expiration of the statute of limitations, Rheingold (D) promptly prepared a summons and complaint, giving them to the law firm's regular process service agency for immediate service. Although the papers were delivered on time, they were given to the doctor's secretary, not to the doctor himself. As a result, Kleeman's (P) claim was ultimately dismissed, and she filed this action against Rheingold (D) for legal malpractice. Both parties moved for summary judgment. The trial court granted Rheingold's (D) motion for summary judgment, ruling that he could not be held vicariously liable for the process server's acts. The appellate division affirmed. Kleeman (P) appealed.

ISSUE: Does an attorney have a nondelegable duty to his or her clients to exercise due care in the service of process and may he or she be held liable to the client for negligent service of process, even though the task is given to an independent contractor?

HOLDING AND DECISION: (Titone, J.) Yes. An attorney has a nondelegable duty to his or her clients to exercise due care in the service of process and may therefore be held liable to the client for negligent service of process, even though the task is given to an independent contractor. When an attorney is retained to commence an action, timely and accurate service of process is an integral part of the task. A mistake or oversight can deprive the client of her day in court. Thus, attorneys cannot be allowed to evade responsibility by farming out service of process to independent contractors. Rheingold's (D) motion for summary judgment dismissing the complaint should not have been granted. The order of the appellate division is modified and affirmed as modified.

CONCURRENCE: (Bellacosa, J.) This case would be more prudently resolved on the narrower ground that questions of fact exist as to whether Rheingold (D) was negligent in choosing his process server. The court's result is reached instead by classifying service of process, for the first time, as a nondelegable duty of the attorney. This rationale opens up an unrealistic and undue liability channel.

ANALYSIS

The general rule is that a party who retains an independent contractor, as distinguished from a mere employee or servant, is not liable for the independent contractor's negligent acts. One of the exceptions to the general rule concerns nondelegable duties. The court saw no sound reason for permitting attorneys who use outside process servers to escape liability, while those who use in-house staff to perform the same function could be held liable under ordinary principles of respondeat superior. The court also stated, however, that Kleeman (P) must demonstrate both that the process server acted negligently and that she would have prevailed in the underlying action against the doctor.

Charles v. Barrett

Father of deceased (P) v. Borrower of van (D)

N.Y. Ct. App., 233 N.Y. 127, 135 N.E. 199 (1922).

NATURE OF CASE: Appeal from dismissal of complaint in personal injury action.

FACT SUMMARY: Charles (P) appealed from an appellate division decision dismissing his personal injury action, contending in part that the chauffeur, while operating the motor van, was in the service of Adams Express Company (Adams) (D), rendering Adams (D) liable for his negligence.

RULE OF LAW

So long as an employee is furthering the business of his general employer in rendering service to another, he will not be considered an employee of the other, unless command over the activities of the employee is surrendered.

FACTS: Steinhauser supplied Adams Express Company (Adams) (D) with a motor van and chauffeur for $2 an hour. Adams (D) loaded the van and was to unload the van when it reached its destination. En route, the van struck Charles' (P) son, killing him. The negligence of the chauffeur was undisputed. Between departure and collision, the van remained, without interference or supervision, in the chauffeur's charge. On the issue as to whether Adams (D) was liable for negligence of the chauffeur, the trial court ruled it was as a matter of law, but the appellate division reversed and dismissed the complaint. From that decision, Charles (P) appealed, contending that the chauffeur was in the service of Adams (D) at the time of the accident, making Adams (D) liable.

ISSUE: Will an employee of one person who renders services to another be considered an employee of the other, if while rendering those services he also furthers the business of his general employer?

HOLDING AND DECISION: (Cardozo, J.) No. So long as an employee is furthering the business of his general employer in rendering service to another, he will not be considered an employee of the other, unless command over his activities is surrendered. Such command had not been surrendered here. Although Adams (D) determined the ultimate destination, the chauffeur, in driving carefully, was performing a duty in furtherance of Steinhauser's business. Neither the contract with Adams (D) nor the manner in which the chauffeur performed his duties demonstrated that command had been relinquished to Adams (D). Affirmed.

ANALYSIS

In nearly every "borrowed servant" case, the interests of the general employer are served, at the very least, in furthering the business relationship between the general and borrowing employers. Subsequent cases take the rationale of the present case even further. *Beatty v. H.B. Owlsley & Sons*, 280 S.E.2d 484, petition for review denied, 285 S.E.2d 95 (1981), held that an employee will not be found to be a special employee under certain circumstances, even if the special employer retained control over the details of the work and the manner in which it was performed.

Nepstad v. Lambert

Injured laborer (P) v. Company owner (D)

Minn. Sup. Ct., 235 Minn. 1, 50 N.W.2d 614 (1951).

NATURE OF CASE: Appeal from award of damages for personal injuries.

FACT SUMMARY: Lambert (D) and Crane Company (D) appealed from a decision finding them liable for the injuries of Nepstad (P) resulting from a crane accident, contending that as a matter of law, the crane operator, Pasma (D), was a loaned servant of Arnold, Nepstad's (P) employer.

RULE OF LAW

For liability purposes, an employee will be considered a loaned servant of another employer if that other employer had the right to control the particular act of that employee which gave rise to the injury.

FACTS: Nepstad (P), an employee of Arnold, rented a crane with an operator from Crane Company (D), owned by Lambert (D). Pasma (D), the crane operator, was an employee of Crane Company (D). At the time of the accident, Pasma (D) was operating the crane to move and install steel trusses, pursuant to arm and hand signals from Morris, an employee of Arnold. Nepstad (P), who was helping to guide the trusses, was injured when a truss came into contact with a powerline. He sued Pasma (D), Lambert (D), and Crane Company (D). Crane Company (D) and Lambert (D) were both found liable on respondeat superior grounds and appealed, contending that as a matter of law, Pasma (D) was a loaned servant in the employ of Arnold at the time of the accident.

ISSUE: For liability purposes, will an employee be considered a loaned servant of another employer, if that other employer had the right to control the particular act of that employee which gave rise to the injury?

HOLDING AND DECISION: (Christianson, J.) Yes. An employee will be considered a loaned servant of another employer for liability purposes if that other employer had the right to control the particular act of that employee which gave rise to the injury. (The court first found the "whole-business" test inapplicable in the present case.) Both employers frequently had some measure of control over the employee, so the focus must fall on the injury producing act. The measure of control required is the authority to exercise detailed, authoritative control over the manner in which the employee's work is to be done. More detailed control over Pasma (D) in the present case can hardly be conceived. Arnold's foreman, Morris, controlled each and every movement of the crane through hand signals. Given the danger inherent in any action by Pasma (D) that would be considered hesitant or disobedient to these signals, there can be little doubt that the hand signals were authoritative. Therefore, since Arnold had the right to control Pasma (D) when the accident occurred, Pasma (D) was a loaned servant. Reversed as to Lambert (D) and Crane Company (D) with directions to enter judgment in their favor. Affirmed as to Pasma (D).

ANALYSIS

Plaintiffs, when in the position of an injured worker, should posture their cases taking care not to attempt to invest complete control over their activities in another employer. If that employer can establish the existence of a special employment relationship, the injured worker may be barred from bringing a civil suit against the special employer, leaving only workers' compensation remedies.

Gordon v. S.M. Byers Motor Car Co.

Wife of decedent (P) v. Company (D)

Pa. Sup. Ct., 309 Pa. 453, 164 A.334 (1932).

NATURE OF CASE: Appeal from grant of defense motion for judgment notwithstanding the verdict.

FACT SUMMARY: Gordon (P) appealed from the court's granting of Hazlett's (D) motion for judgment notwithstanding the verdict granting S.M. Byers Motor Car Co. (Byers) (D) a new trial, arguing that the decision holding both vicariously liable was correct.

RULE OF LAW

When an employee, while on loan to a second employer, negligently performs an act which is for the benefit of both employers which causes injuries, both employers will be held vicariously liable for the employee's negligence.

FACTS: Hazlett (D) negotiated with S.M. Byers Motor Car Co. (Byers) (D) for a used gasoline truck. Byers (D) agreed to furnish Hazlett (D) with a truck and a driver (Lewis), to determine if the truck was suitable. During this test period, while delivering gasoline to one of Hazlett's (D) customers at Hazlett's (D) direction, he negligently caused an explosion which killed Gordon's (P) husband. She successfully sued both Hazlett (D) and Byers (D) on vicarious liability grounds. On motion, the judge entered judgment in favor of Hazlett (D) and granted Byers (D) a new trial, and from that decision, Gordon (P) appealed.

ISSUE: When an employee, while on loan to a second employer, negligently performs an act which is for the benefit of both employers which causes injuries, will both employers be held vicariously liable for the employee's negligence?

HOLDING AND DECISION: (Linn, J.) Yes. When an employee, while on loan to a second employer, negligently performs an act, which is for the benefit of both employers, which causes injuries, both employers will be held liable for the employee's negligence. In the present case, Lewis, the employee, was performing an act which benefitted both Hazlett (D) and Byers (D). He was both dispensing gasoline to a customer at Hazlett's (D) direction, but he was also demonstrating the suitability of the truck for Byers (D). As such, he was acting for the benefit of both employers, and both can be held vicariously liable. Remitted, with instructions to enter judgment for Gordon (P).

ANALYSIS

The court's concern in the present case may have been not to set a precedent which could reduce the plaintiff's remedy. Most of these cases involve an injury to a worker, where one employer is shielded from tort liability by the Workers' Compensation system. If one is found to be a special employer, the injured worker's sole remedy, absent special circumstances, is through workers compensation. Some cases now emphasize as a factor the employee's knowledge and acquiescence to the creation of such a relationship. See *Kowalski v. Shell Oil Co.*, 23 Cal.3d 168, 177, 151 Cal Rptr. 671 (1979).

DePratt v. Sergio

Injured employee (P) v. Subcontractor (D)

Wis. Sup. Ct., 102 Wis. 2d 141, 306 N.W.2d 62 (1981).

NATURE OF CASE: Appeal from decision affirming summary judgment denial of damages for personal injuries.

FACT SUMMARY: **DePratt (P) appealed from a decision affirming the trial court's decision granting Sergio Crane Service's (Sergio) (D) motion for summary judgment, arguing to the court to discard the "borrowed servant" rule in favor of a dual liability approach.**

RULE OF LAW

The borrowing master, not the loaning master, is liable for the negligent acts of a loaned servant, if the loaned servant becomes the servant of the borrowing master.

FACTS: DePratt (P) was employed by Metal Buildings, who had contracted with Sergio Crane Service's (Sergio) (D), who agreed to provide Metal Buildings with a crane and an operator. DePratt (P) was injured by the negligence of the crane operator in the operations of the crane. He received worker's compensation benefits from Metal Buildings and sued Sergio (D). Sergio (D) moved for summary judgment successfully, arguing as a matter of law that the crane operator had become the special employee of Metal Buildings. This was affirmed on appeal, and from that affirmation, DePratt (P) appealed, seeking the adoption of a dual liability approach.

ISSUE: If the loaned servant becomes the servant of a borrowing employer, will the loaning employer be liable for the negligence of the loaned servant?

HOLDING AND DECISION: (Abrahamson, J.) No. The borrowing master, not the loaning master, is liable for the negligent acts of a loaned servant, if the loaned servant becomes the servant of the borrowing master. DePratt (P) correctly noted the deficiency in the underlying premise for the "borrowed servant" rule, since both employers exerted control, and both derived some benefit from the servant's work. The borrowed servant rule is difficult to apply. While the borrowed servant rule has deficiencies both in theory and in application, the dual liability alternative presented by DePratt (P) does not offer a simple and easily applicable alternative. Courts will still have to decide when each employer retains sufficient control. Nor would that approach provide any greater certainty or precision in its application. Its application could promote unfairness, since in most situations, the loaning master's liability is limited to worker's compensation. This is not a satisfactory alternative to the borrowed servant rule. Affirmed.

ANALYSIS

Many of these cases arise in the context of contractors and subcontractors. Some courts have speculated that the loaning employer should bear the risk of the employee's negligence because he may be better able to evaluate the accident risks. The empirical studies supporting the presumption underlying this view have yet to be concisely set forth to allow the general acceptance of this theory.

Sparger v. Worley Hospital, Inc.

Surgeon (P) v. Hospital (D)

Tex. Sup. Ct., 547 S.W.2d 582 (1977).

NATURE OF CASE: Appeal from appellate decision reversing denial of damages for medical malpractice.

FACT SUMMARY: Sparger (D) appealed from an appellate decision reversing the decision acquitting him of medical malpractice, arguing that the court erred in applying the "Captain of the Ship" doctrine in holding him liable as a matter of law.

RULE OF LAW

The "Captain of the Ship" doctrine is a false special rule of agency and does not supplant the application of ordinary "borrowed servant" principles.

FACTS: Caldwell (P), who was operated on at Worley Hospital, Inc. (Worley) (D) by Sparger (D), a surgeon, was injured by a surgical sponge which was left in her abdomen. She sued Worley (D) and Sparger (D) for medical malpractice without suing the surgical nurses. The jury found that the nurses, or one of them, was negligent in failing to make a correct sponge count, and that this negligence was the proximate cause of the injuries. The jury acquitted Sparger (D) and returned a verdict against Worley (D) only. On appeal, the appellate court reversed, applying the "Captain of the Ship" doctrine and finding Sparger (D) vicariously liable as a matter of law, contrary to the jury's conclusion that the nurses were not his borrowed servants. From that decision, Sparger (D) appealed.

ISSUE: Does the "Captain of the Ship" doctrine supplant the application of ordinary "borrowed servant" principles in the medical malpractice area?

HOLDING AND DECISION: (Pope, J.) No. The "Captain of the Ship" doctrine is a false special rule of agency and does not supplant the application of ordinary "borrowed servant" principles. This doctrine, which arose in the naval context, is an obvious reference to the complete and total responsibility of the captain for what occurs on his ship. Where there are inconsistent factual inferences concerning the servant's employer which can be reasonably drawn from the evidence, however, the borrowed servant principles apply. The vitality of the "Captain of the Ship" doctrine is unsupported by precedent, and its vitality as a legal formula results from lazy repetition and application without analysis. The question of whether Sparger (D) had the right to control the nurses is a question of fact, which was resolved in Sparger's (D) favor. The facts of the present case do not allow the court to find they were his special or borrowed employees as a matter of law. Reversed.

ANALYSIS

It is important to note that the "Captain of the Ship" doctrine may have some descriptive value but has been disapproved in the present case as adding any additional measure of responsibility on the part of a surgeon. It may have some application where, as the facts may demonstrate, the surgeon's operational control is such that as a matter of law, the surgeon will bear ultimate responsibility.

Joel v. Morison

Injured pedestrian (P) v. Owner of cart (D)

Eng. Ex., 6 Car. & P. 501, 172 Eng. Rep. 1338 (1834).

NATURE OF CASE: Action for damages for negligence.

FACT SUMMARY: Joel (P) brought this action for negligence against Morison (D), contending that Morison (D), as the owner of the horse and cart and employer of the person driving the cart which injured him, was vicariously liable for his injuries.

RULE OF LAW

A master is vicariously liable for the negligence of his servant only when the servant is acting in the course of his employment.

FACTS: Joel's (P) leg was broken when he was struck by a horse and cart owned by Morison (D) and driven by Morison's (D) servant. He sued Morison (D) for his injuries, contending that he was vicariously liable for his servant's negligence. The evidence showed that there was some deviation from the route the cart ordinarily took when on Morison's (D) business; the purpose of the deviation was in question.

ISSUE: Is a master vicariously liable for the negligence of his servant only when the servant is acting in the course of his employment?

HOLDING AND DECISION: (Parke, B.) Yes. A master is vicariously liable for the negligence of his servant only when he is acting in the course of his employment. It is uncontroverted that Joel (P) was injured, and that the servant was negligent in driving the cart. If in taking the deviation the servant was still in the course of his employment with Morison (D), Morison (D) would still be liable. If the servant was going out on his own business, Morison (D) would not be liable. (The court found Morison (D) liable and awarded Joel (P) damages in the amount of £30.)

ANALYSIS

The opinion seems to imply that the extent of the deviation will not take the servant out of the course of his employment. As can be seen in the later cases in this section, the extent of the deviation does matter. The decision in the present case was rendered without any risk-spreading rationale impacting the decision, as liability insurance was not widely available.

Fiocco v. Carver

Injured child (P) v. Employer (D)

N.Y. Ct. App., 234 N.Y. 219, 137 N.E. 309 (1922).

NATURE OF CASE: Appeal from a finding of vicarious tort liability.

FACT SUMMARY: Carver's employer (D) appealed from a court of appeals decision upholding a jury verdict finding it liable for Fiocco's (P) injuries based on Carver's (D) negligence, contending that Carver (D) was outside the course of this employment at the time of the incident.

RULE OF LAW

When an employee has so substantially departed from the course of his employment so as to constitute an abandonment of his employment, the employment relationship will not be resumed until the dominant purpose of the employee's acts is the performance of his employer's business.

FACTS: Carver (D), a driver for his employer (D), was to deliver a load of merchandise to Staten Island and then to return the truck. Instead of returning to the garage, he went to visit his mother. A neighborhood carnival was in progress, and Carver (D) took children in the neighborhood for a tour of the district, stopping at a pool hall to visit a friend. Fiocco (P) was injured when his foot was drawn under the wheel. The evidence was to how Fiocco (P) came to be on the truck was disputed, but he claimed he was climbing down from the truck when Carver (D) started without warning. Carver (D) was found liable, and so was his employer (D), since Carver (D) was found to be within the course of his employment. The appellate division upheld the verdict, and the employer (D) appealed, alleging as a matter of law, Carver (D) was outside of the course of his employment when the accident occurred.

ISSUE: Will an employee be found to have resumed his employment relationship, such that his employer will be held vicariously liable for the employee's torts, if he has so substantially departed from the course of his employment so as to constitute an abandonment of his employment?

HOLDING AND DECISION: (Cardozo, J.) No. When an employee has so substantially departed from the course of his employment so as to constitute an abandonment of his employment, the employment relationship will not be resumed until the dominant purpose of the employee's acts is the performance of his employer's business. Clearly on these facts there is no presumption that Carver (D) was discharging his employer's (D) purposes. The employment relationship was broken and suspended by the tour of the neighborhood. The act of setting the truck in motion couldn't be the act which resumed the employment relationship. It cannot be determined that the dominant purpose of the act was in the furtherance of the employer's (D) business, since so many illicit incidents of the tour still remained. As such, the act of starting the truck was bound with the effects of Carver's (D) departure. This was not a question for the jury. Reversed; instructions to dismiss complaint as to employer.

ANALYSIS

A large proportions of these cases arise in the automobile accident context, and the principles enunciated in the cases will be applicable in other situations. Many factors are involved in the determination of whether an employee's act falls outside the corner of employment, including the nature of the act, the physical extent of the deviation, and whether the act is in violation of the employer's direct instructions.

Clover v. Snowbird Ski Resort

Ski accident victim (P) v. Employer of reckless skier (D)

Utah Sup. Ct., 808 P.2d 1037 (1991).

NATURE OF CASE: Appeal from summary judgment dismissing tort action.

FACT SUMMARY: Clover (P), who was severely injured by Zulliger (D) as a result of Zulliger's (D) reckless skiing, contended that Zulliger's (D) skiing was within the scope of his employment and while he was under the supervision of his employer, Snowbird Ski Resort (Snowbird) (D), and that, therefore, Snowbird (D) was vicariously liable under the doctrine of respondeat superior for Zulliger's (D) negligence.

RULE OF LAW

Where facts do not clearly indicate that an employee's actions are within or without the employee's scope of employment, a trial judge may not decide the issue of respondeat superior as a matter of law.

FACTS: Zulliger (D) was employed by Snowbird Ski Resort (Snowbird) (D) as a chef, working in a restaurant at the base of Snowbird's (D) ski resort. Snowbird (D) also had a restaurant (called Mid-Gad) midway to the top of the mountain. Zulliger (D) was periodically directed to monitor operations of Mid-Gad. Snowbird (D) provided its employees with ski passes, and expected them to be able to ski to work. On a morning that Zulliger (D) had planned to go skiing with another chef before reporting to work, he had been asked to inspect Mid-Gad's operations before reporting to his regular work. That morning, Zulliger (D) and the other chef made four ski runs. They stopped at Mid-Gad in the middle of their first run to inspect operations there. On their final run, they took a route that would take them to their restaurant at the base of the mountain. On this run, Zulliger (D) decided to jump off a crest with significant speed, despite signs asking skiers to proceed slowly since it was impossible for skiers above the crest to see skiers below the crest. Clover (P), who had just entered the same ski run from a point below the crest, either had stopped or was traveling slowly below the crest. When Zulliger (D) went over the jump, he collided with Clover (P), who was hit in the head and severely injured. Clover (P) sued Zulliger (D) and Snowbird (D), alleging that Zulliger's (D) reckless skiing was a proximate cause of her injuries; Snowbird (D) was liable for Zulliger's (D) negligence because at the time of the collision, he was acting within the scope of his employment, and Snowbird (D) breached its duty to adequately supervise its employees. Zulliger (D) settled separately with Clover (P). The trial court dismissed Clover's (P) claims against Snowbird (D) on summary judgment because it found that, as a matter of law, Zulliger (D) was not acting within the scope of his employment at the time of the collision, and that an employer does not have a duty to supervise an employee who is acting outside the scope of employment. The state's highest court granted review.

ISSUE: Where facts do not clearly indicate that an employee's actions are within or without the employee's scope of employment, may a trial judge decide the issue of respondeat superior as a matter of law?

HOLDING AND DECISION: (Hall, C.J.) No. Where facts do not clearly indicate that an employee's actions are within or without the employee's scope of employment, a trial judge may not decide the issue of respondeat superior as a matter of law. Under the doctrine of respondeat superior, employers are held vicariously liable for the torts their employees commit when the employees are acting within the scope of their employment. Ordinarily, this is a question of fact that a jury decides, provided reasonable minds may differ as to whether the employee was wholly or partly performing his employer's business or was acting within the scope of employment. Where reasonable minds could not differ, the trial judge gets to decide the issue as a matter of law. Three criteria must be met to decide if the employee's actions are, as a matter of law, within (or without) the scope of employment. First, an employee's conduct must be of the general kind the employee is employed to perform. Second, the conduct must occur during work hours and within the ordinary spatial boundaries of the employment, and, third, the employee's conduct must be motivated at least in part, by the purpose of serving the employer's interest. Here, there is ample evidence that Zulliger's (D) trip to Mid-Gad, on the first run, was predominantly for business. Therefore, the case should be analyzed as one where an employee takes a personal detour in the process of carrying out employment duties—as opposed to being analyzed under the "dual purpose" doctrine. Under this doctrine, if the primary purpose for the activity is personal, with incidental business activity, the activity is not deemed to be within the scope of employment. If the primary purpose is business-related, the activity, though incidentally personal, is considered to be within the scope of employment. Where a personal detour leads to an accident, where the detour is so substantial as to constitute an abandonment of employment, the employee is held, as a matter of law, to have acted outside the scope of employment. However, where reasonable minds can differ as to whether the detour constituted a slight deviation from the employee's duties or an abandonment of employment, the question is left for the

Continued on next page.

jury. Here, there was evidence that could lead a jury to reasonably believe that Zulliger (D) had, at the time of the accident, resumed his employment and that his deviation was not sufficiently substantial to constitute total abandonment of employment duties. Zulliger (D) was, after all, starting to head back to his chef job at the base restaurant and to report on his observations of operations at Mid-Gad. Thus, a jury could reasonably conclude that before the accident, Zulliger (D) was setting about the employer's business. Also, the accident occurred within the normal spatial boundaries of employment. A jury could also conclude that Zulliger (D) had not abandoned his employment by taking the additional ski runs, since it could conclude he was not disregarding his employer's directions because: Snowbird (D) encouraged its employees to ski as part of their work; Zulliger (D) was on Snowbird's (D) property all day; no specific time had been set for inspecting Mid-Gad; and skiing was used by employees to travel among the different job locations. For these reasons, Zulliger's (D) actions were not, as a matter of law, outside the scope of his employment. However, Clover's (P) other theories that Zulliger's (D) actions were within the scope of his employment are rejected. These theories are based on Zulliger's (D) actions being foreseeable or on the fact that Zulliger's (D) activities occurred on Snowbird's (D) premises. Reversed and remanded.

ANALYSIS

One of the alternative theories advocated by Clover (P) and rejected by the court for determining whether Zulliger's (D) conduct was within the scope of employment is known as the premises rule, which was developed in workers' compensation cases. Under this rule, employees who have fixed hours and places of work will usually be considered to be acting outside of the scope of employment when they are traveling to and from work. However, they will be considered to be in the course of employment while traveling to and from work when they are on their employer's premises. The court here noted that the policies behind workers' compensation law differ from the policies behind respondeat superior claims, and also observed that the premises rule alone would only focus on one of the factors considered in respondeat superior cases, i.e., the spatial boundaries and work hours factor. The court concluded that where the employee has other reasons aside from traveling to work to be on the employer's premises, there is a need for a more flexible and intricate analysis in the respondeat superior context.

Bremen State Bank v. Hartford Accident & Indemnity Co.

Bank (P) v. Insurer (D)

427 F.2d 425 (7th Cir. 1970).

NATURE OF CASE: Appeal from grant of summary judgment motion.

FACT SUMMARY: Bremen State Bank (Bremen) (P) appealed from the lower court's decision granting Bekins' (D) motion for summary judgment, contending that Bekins (D) was vicariously liable for the loss occasioned by the criminal act of its employee on the theory of respondeat superior.

RULE OF LAW

An employer is not liable for the criminal acts of its employee committed during the course of his employment, unless the act is in furtherance of the business of the employer.

FACTS: Bremen State Bank (Bremen) (P) moved its banking operations to a new location in Tinley Park. The employees were told to place the money in canvas bags on the floor of the vault instead of the normal procedure of placing them in metal lockers in the vault. One teller did not and put her cash draw money, totaling $10,342.03, in one of the metal lockers. The police moved the money, and Bekins (D) was hired to move the equipment, including the lockers. One of Bekins' (D) employees, Francis, absconded with the money, which was never recovered. Bremen (P) sued Bekins (D) on a theory of respondeat superior to recover for the money lost. Bekins (D) successfully moved for summary judgment, and Bremen (P) appealed, contending that Bekins (D) could be held vicariously liable for the money loss occasioned by the criminal act of Francis on the theory of respondeat superior.

ISSUE: Is an employee liable for the criminal acts of its employee committed during the course of his employment?

HOLDING AND DECISION: (Swygert, C.J.) No. An employer is not liable for the criminal acts of its employee committed during the course of his employment, unless the act is in furtherance of the business of the employer. When the act is, as in the present case, committed solely for the benefit of the employer, the employer will not be liable to the injured third party. There is no contention that Francis stole the money in the furtherance of Bekins' (D) business. Therefore, Bekins (D) was not liable for Francis' theft, and summary judgment was proper. Affirmed.

ANALYSIS

Ordinarily, a criminal act will not be found to be in the furtherance of the employer's business. A category of cases has developed, however, where an employee acts with excessive force in the furtherance of the wishes of his employer. In these cases, an employer will be vicariously liable for the acts of their employee. See *Boehmer v. Norton*, 328 Ill. App. 3d 17, 65 N.E.2d 212 (1946).

Ira S. Bushey & Sons v. United States

Contractor (P) v. Federal government (D)

398 F.2d 167 (2d Cir. 1968).

NATURE OF CASE: Appeal from award of damages for injury to property.

FACT SUMMARY: **The Government (D) appealed from a judgment in favor of Ira S. Bushey & Sons (Bushey) (P) for damage sustained to its drydock operations, contending in part that the acts of a drunken sailor in opening flood control valves resulting in damage could not be the basis for the imposition of liability under the doctrine of respondeat superior.**

RULE OF LAW

An entity will be held liable for those activities on the part of its employees, so long as the activities of the employee were reasonably foreseen to involve risk of injury to the public.

FACTS: The Tamaroa, a U.S. Naval Vessel, was in drydock for repairs, which Ira S. Bushey & Sons (Bushey) (P) had been contracted to do. The contract required that the ship's crewmen be allowed access at all times, to the vessel, which was in a closed-off area. One night, Lane (D), one of the ship's sailor, got drunk, and on his return to the ship, he open the flood control valves on the drydock, sinking part of the drydock and causing considerable damage. Bushey (P) successfully sued the Government (D) for the damages it sustained, and the Government (D) appealed, contending that it could not be held liable for Lane's (D) actions under the doctrine of respondeat superior.

ISSUE: If the activities of an employee are reasonably foreseen by the employer to involve a risk of the injury to the public, will the employer be found vicariously liable for the acts of the employee?

HOLDING AND DECISION: (Friendly, J.) Yes. An employer will be held liable for those activities on the part of its employees, so long as the activities of the employee were reasonably foreseen by the employer to involve a risk of injury to the public. The trial court rejected the traditional application of the respondeat superior test on the grounds that an expansion of liability would lead to a more efficient allocation of resources, serving the doctrine's loss-spreading function. This policy alone is not enough to justify rejection of the application of the doctrine, since the doctrine is also rooted in the policy for assigning responsibility for activity fairly characteristic of the employer. The application of the traditional doctrine reflects a wholly realistic attitude toward the risk characteristic to the operation of the ship. In the present case, Lane's (D) conduct was not so unforeseeable as to make it unfair to charge the Government (D) with responsibility. The employer should be held to expect risks which arise out and in the course of its employment of labor. Damage to the drydock by crewmen of the ship was reasonably foreseeable, regardless of whether Lane's (D) precise actions were foreseen. Under these circumstances, it is not unfair to impose liability for the drydock damage on the Government (D). Affirmed.

ANALYSIS

The pure allocation of the resources argument rejected by the court in the present case can be criticized on a number of grounds. Taking that doctrine to extremes could result in holdings where an employee would be found not liable if the victim is better able to absorb the loss. Further, a pure application of the doctrine could lead to rejection of the consideration as to whether the activity is fairly related to the employer's activity.

Lisa M. v. Henry Mayo Newhall Memorial Hospital

Molested victim (P) v. Hospital (D)

Cal. Sup. Ct., 907 P.2d 358 (1995).

NATURE OF CASE: **Review of finding on appeal that hospital was liable under theory of respondeat superior for sexual assault during medical exam.**

FACT SUMMARY: **When Lisa M. (P), a young pregnant woman, was sexually assaulted during an ultrasound exam, she sued Henry Mayo Newhall Memorial Hospital (D), where the assault occurred.**

RULE OF LAW

An intentional tort is foreseeable, for purposes of respondeat superior, only if the employment predictably creates the risk that employees will commit intentional torts of the type for which liability is sought.

FACTS: Lisa M. (P), a pregnant teenager, went to the emergency room at the Henry Mayo Newhall Memorial Hospital (D) and was sexually molested by an ultrasound technician there. Lisa M. (P) sued the Hospital (D), as well as the ultrasound technician, for professional negligence, battery, and intentional and negligent infliction of emotional harm. The superior court granted the Hospital's (D) summary judgment motion despite Lisa M's (P) claims that there were triable issues of fact as to the vicarious liability of the Hospital (D) for the battery as a tort committed within the scope of the technicians's employment, and as to the Hospital's (D) negligence. The court of appeal reversed, relying only on the theory of respondeat superior and expressly declining to reach the question of the Hospital's (D) negligence. The Hospital's (D) petition for review was granted by the California Supreme Court in order to decide the vicarious liability issue.

ISSUE: Is an intentional tort foreseeable, for purposes of respondeat superior, only if the employment predictably creates the risk employees will commit intentional torts of the type for which liability is sought?

HOLDING AND DECISION: (Werdegar, J.) Yes. An intentional tort is foreseeable, for purposes of respondeat superior, only if the employment predictably creates the risk employees will commit intentional torts of the type for which liability is sought. The intentional tort only gives rise to respondeat superior liability if it was engendered by the employment. When the facts are undisputed, determining whether an employee acted within the scope of employment becomes a matter of law. In this case, the technician's motivating emotions were not causally attributable to his employment. The assault was the independent product of the technician's aberrant decision to engage in conduct unrelated to his duties. Although the ultrasound technician's criminal acts were not engendered by his work so as to render the Hospital (D) vicariously liable, the Hospital (D) may have been negligent in failing to exercise due care to protect its patients against such injury. Reversed and remanded.

CONCURRENCE: (George, J.) The court should overrule the holding in *Mary M. v.City of Los Angeles*, 814 P. 2d 1341 (1991), where a police officer's rape of a detainee was held to be a generally foreseeable consequence of his position.

DISSENT: (Mosk, J.) The court of appeal's judgment should be enforced.

DISSENT: (Kennard, J.) Scope of employment in this case, as in most cases, is a question of fact to be resolved by the trier of fact. Where an employee's tortious acts, although personally motivated, are so integrally entwined with his employment that reasonable minds may differ on the issue of whether the sexual misconduct was outside the scope of employment, the issue should not be resolved as a matter of law.

ANALYSIS

In determining whether respondeat superior applies, two tests may be applied. One test is whether the tortious sexual behavior was impelled by motivations other than a desire to further the interests of the employer. This is the "motivation to serve" test. An alternative test is the "enterprise liability" doctrine, whereby any acts by employees "sufficiently connected" with the enterprise are considered "as deeds of the enterprise itself."

Costos v. Coconut Island Corp.

Rape victim (P) v. Inn (D)

137 F.3d 46 (1st Cir. 1998).

NATURE OF CASE: Appeal from denial of defense motion for a directed verdict in a civil rape suit based on respondeat superior.

FACT SUMMARY: When Patricia Costos (P) was raped by the manager while a guest at an inn owned by the Coconut Island Corporation (D), she sued the Corporation on the theory of respondeat superior.

RULE OF LAW

A principal is liable for the torts of the agent when the agent purports to act on behalf of the principal or was aided in accomplishing the tort by existence of the agency relation.

FACTS: In the early morning of August 14, 1993, Charles Bonney raped Patricia Costos (P) in her room at the Bernard House which was a small seasonal inn owned by the Coconut Island Corporation (D). Bonney was the inn's manager. When Costos (P) arrived for her stay, Bonney (D) escorted her to her room. That evening, after Costos (P) went to bed, Bonney entered her room and raped her. Costos (P) sued Coconut Island (D), alleging it was negligent and vicariously liable for Bonney's tort of raping her. The jury found for Costos (P) and awarded damages. Coconut Island (D) moved for a directed verdict which was denied. Coconut Island (D) appealed.

ISSUE: Is a principal liable for the torts of the agent when the agent purports to act on behalf of the principal or was aided in accomplishing the tort by existence of the agency relation?

HOLDING AND DECISION: (Lynch, J.) Yes. A principal is liable for the torts of the agent when the agent purports to act on behalf of the principal or was aided in accomplishing the tort by existence of the agency relation. It is plain that there was an agency relationship between Coconut Island (D) and Booney who was the manager of its inn and that Booney was its servant. The law does not require that Costos (P) believed that Booney was acting on behalf of Coconut Island (D) when he assaulted her or that the use of apparent authority in any way aided Booney in accomplishing the tort. The "aid" which Coconut Island (D) supplied was simply that of having employed Bonney, and providing him with the means to accomplish the assault. Here, by virtue of his agency relationship with Coconut Island (D), as manager of the inn, Bonney was entrusted with the keys to the rooms, including Costos's (P) room. Because he was the manager of the inn, he knew exactly where to find Costos (P). Bonney had responsibilities to be at the inn or to have others there late at night. In short, because he was defendant's agent, he was able to find Costos's (P) room late at night, he had the key to the room and used the key to unlock the door, slip into bed beside her as she slept, and rape her. Affirmed.

ANALYSIS

The Restatement of Agency (2nd) § 219(2)(d) provides that a master is not subject to liability for the torts of his servants acting outside the scope of their employment, unless the servant purported to act or speak on behalf of the principal and there was reliance upon apparent authority, or he was aided in accomplishing the tort by the existence of the agency relation.

Nazareth v. Herndon Ambulance Service

Sexual assault victim (P) v. Ambulance service (D)

Fla. Ct. App., 467 So. 2d 1076 (1985), *review denied*, 478 So. 2d 53 (1985).

NATURE OF CASE: Appeal from summary judgment denial of damages in employer vicarious liability action.

FACT SUMMARY: Nazareth (P) appealed from a decision granting summary judgment in favor of Herndon Ambulance Service (Herndon) (D), contending in part that as an ambulance service, Herndon (D) could be held vicariously liable for a sexual assault upon her by Barrett, the ambulance attendant.

RULE OF LAW

A common carrier can be held liable for the torts of its employees visited upon a passenger while the contract for transport is being accomplished.

FACTS: Nazareth (P) was sexually assaulted by Barrett, an ambulance attendant working for Herndon Ambulance Service (Herndon) (D), while she was being transported by ambulance from her home. Barrett had been attending her in the passenger portion of the ambulance. Barrett's employment record to that point had been exemplary and there was nothing in his record to put Herndon (D) on notice of any tendency to commit a sexual assault. Nazareth (P) sued Herndon (D), contending that it could be held liable for Barrett's sexual assault. Herndon (D) successfully moved for summary judgment, and Nazareth (P) appealed, contending in part that Herndon (D), as a common carrier, could be liable for the sexual assault.

ISSUE: Can a common carrier be held liable for the torts of its employees visited upon a passenger while the contract for transport is being accomplished?

HOLDING AND DECISION: (Sharp, J.) Yes. A common carrier can be held liable for the torts of its employees visited upon a passenger while the contract for transport is being accomplished. [The court determined that there was no basis for a negligent hiring action against Herndon (D).] An exception to the general rule of nonliability is where the employer is a common carrier for hire to the public, and the tort or attack is by an employee upon a passenger while the paying passenger is being transported. The rationale for imposing liability upon the employer in such cases is the existence of an implied contract between the victim-passenger and the carrier for safe passage, free from attack. Once transport has begun, the high duty of care imposed upon the carrier remains until the passage is complete. This high duty of care is justified because the passenger must entrust her bodily safety to the care and control of the carrier and its employees. Since there are sufficient facts to find that Herndon (D) was a common carrier, it need not be determined what its liability might be if it were not a common carrier. Summary judgment was not proper in this case. Reversed and remanded.

DISSENT: (Cobb, J.) Nazareth (P) has not alleged, and has not offered any proof, that Herndon (D) was a common carrier. The summary judgment should be affirmed.

ANALYSIS

The cases in this section have dealt with an employer's civil liability for the criminal acts of its employees. There may be instances, however, where due to the criminal act involved, or the independent authorization or ratification by the employer, the employer can be held criminally liable as well. See *People v. Travers*, 52 Cal. App. 3d 111, 124 Cal. Rptr. 728 (1975).

Adams v. New York City Transit Authority

Transit passenger (P) v. Transit authority (D)

N.Y. Ct. App., 666 N.E.2d 216 (1996).

NATURE OF CASE: Appeal from summary judgment dismissing cause of action based on breach of carrier's duty.

FACT SUMMARY: When Adams (P), a passenger, was assaulted by a token booth clerk at a subway entrance, Adams (P) sued the New York City Transit Authority (D).

RULE OF LAW

Since the special rule of "absolute liability" previously applied to common carriers is no longer viable, conduct that is outside the scope of employment does not give rise to vicarious liability on the part of the employer.

FACTS: After Adams (P) bought a subway token, she was verbally abused and physically assaulted by the token booth clerk. When Adams (P) sued the New York City Transit Authority (D), the State supreme court dismissed the claims based on negligence, but found that Adams (P) was entitled to summary judgment on her claim arising from the Transit Authority's (D) liability as a common carrier. On appeal, this cause of action was also dismissed and the court decided that the special common-carrier rule imposing a duty on carriers to provide their passengers with transportation free "from insults or assaults" by their employees. was no longer viable. Adams (P) appealed.

ISSUE: Does the special rule of "absolute liability" applied to common carriers still give rise to vicarious liability on the part of the employer?

HOLDING AND DECISION: (Titone, J.) No. Since the special rule of "absolute liability" previously applied to common carriers is no longer viable, conduct that is outside the scope of employment does not give rise to vicarious liability on the part of the employer. The scope-of-employment limitation on employers' vicarious liability for employees' torts applies to common carriers. The apparent historic underpinnings of the carrier's absolute liability for employee misconduct are of dubious validity under current social and legal conditions. Affirmed.

ANALYSIS

The court also discussed the origins in contract law of the common carrier rule. An assault on a passenger was originally considered to be a breach of a contractual duty. It is the law of torts, however, that imposes the standard of care to be applied and it is tort law that must justify the rule. Modern tort principles underlying the vicarious liability doctrine no longer offer any justification for this rule.

Hanson v. Saint Luke's United Methodist Church

Tort claimant (P) v. Unincorporated association (D)

Ind. Sup. Ct., 704 N.E.2d 1020 (1998).

NATURE OF CASE: Appeal from a defense summary judgment in a tort suit against an unincorporated association by a member.

FACT SUMMARY: When Martha Hanson (P) slipped and fell in the parking lot of Saint Luke's United Methodist Church (D), an unincorporated association, she sued the latter for her injuries even though she was one of its members.

RULE OF LAW
Members of unincorporated associations may sue their associations for tortious conduct.

FACTS: Martha Hanson (P), a member of Saint Luke's United Methodist Church (D), an unincorporated association, slipped and fell on the ice in Saint Luke's (D) parking lot, broke her arm, and sued Saint Luke's (D) and its trustee for her injuries, alleging its negligent failure to have properly inspected the lot for dangerous conditions and failure to have removed the accumulated snow and ice. The trial court granted summary judgment in favor of both defendants, applying the common law rule that a member of an unincorporated association cannot sue the association for the negligence of another member. The court of appeals affirmed the summary judgment as to the trustees, but reversed the summary judgment as to St. Luke's (D), and Hanson (P) appealed.

ISSUE: May the members of unincorporated associations sue their associations for tortious conduct?

HOLDING AND DECISION: (Shepard, C.J.) Yes. Members of unincorporated associations may sue their associations for tortious conduct. In ruling that Hanson (P) could maintain a personal injury lawsuit against the church, the court of appeals applied an exception to the common law rule. Under the common law, a member of an unincorporated association could not sue the association itself for tort injuries. The theory was that, under the doctrine of imputed liability, members of such an association are engaged in a joint enterprise, thus to permit suit would be akin to the person suing himself since each member becomes both a principal and an agent as to all other members for the actions of the group itself. Such rule, however, no longer represents the reality of certain modern associations in that frequently the member and the association are distinct; the unincorporated association has a legal existence separate from its members; and the members may not exercise control over the operations of the association. Here, clearly Hanson's (P) relation to Saint Luke's (D) warrants her being allowed to sue, taking into consideration the size of Saint Luke's (D) congregation, the hierarchy of Saint Luke's (D) government, and the existence of a set of by-laws guiding Saint Luke's (D) decisionmaking. The reasons supporting the general rule for not permitting suit, such as the prevention of collusive lawsuits and the avoidance of suits by a member against himself, do not apply. This court, however, goes further and outright abolishes the "ancient precept" that members of unincorporated associations could not sue their associations for tortious conduct. Reversed and remanded.

ANALYSIS

Beyond applying exceptions to the common law rule, several jurisdictions, in addition to Indiana, have chosen to abolish or abrogate entirely the rule preventing members of unincorporated associations from suing their associations for tortious conduct. The theory for abrogation is that, in bringing such a suit, the member is really not "suing himself" at all. Rather, the member seeks recovery from the assets of the association, just as does any third party.

Schubert v. August Schubert Wagon Co.

Injured wife (P) v. Employer of husband (D)

N.Y. Ct. App., 249 N.Y. 253, 164 N.E. 42, 64 A.L.R. 293 (1928).

NATURE OF CASE: Appeal from award of damages for personal injury.

FACT SUMMARY: **The district court awarded Schubert (P) damages for the personal injuries she suffered after being struck by a car in August Wagon Company's (D) service, and being driven by her husband while within the scope of his employment.**

RULE OF LAW

Where a spouse, while in the course of his or her employment, causes personal injury to the other spouse, his or her employer must answer for the damage whether there is trespass by direct command or trespass incidental to the employer's business.

FACTS: Schubert (P) was negligently struck by an August Wagon Company (D) car while it was in the latter's service and being driven by Schubert's (P) husband, resulting in her personal injury. Schubert (P) brought suit against August Wagon Company (D), contending that the latter was responsible for her husband's actions since he was within the scope of his employment when he caused her injuries. On the other hand, August Wagon Company (D) contended that since a spouse cannot maintain an action against another spouse for personal injury, whether intentional or negligent, then it cannot be held liable, under the rule of respondeat superior, for a lawful act. The trial court found August Wagon Company (D) liable for the injuries and noted that this principle of liability did not collide with the established principle of exemption between spouses for personal injury claims. August Wagon Company (D) appealed.

ISSUE: Where a spouse, while in the course of his or her employment, causes personal injury to the other spouse, must his or her employer answer for the damage, whether there is trespass by direct command or trespass incidental to the employer's business?

HOLDING AND DECISION: (Cardozo, C.J.) Yes. Where a spouse, while in the course of his or her employment, causes personal injury to the other spouse, his or her employer must answer for the damage, whether there is trespass by direct command or trespass incidental to the employer's business. At common law, a wife may not maintain an action against a husband, nor a husband against his wife, for personal injuries, whether negligent or willful. However, this does not mean that the intentional or negligent act committed by the offending spouse is lawful. On the contrary, the act is unlawful though the law exempts the offending spouse. As a result, since we are governed by the legal maxim that he who acts through another acts by himself, then where the offending spouse is acting in furtherance of an employer's commands, the latter must answer for the wrongs committed to the aggrieved spouse. Besides this, in the circumstance where the employer is not personally at fault, he has a remedy against the offending spouse on the basis that the latter breached his duty to render faithful service to the former. This would avoid the consequence of allowing an indirect remedy for the aggrieved spouse against the offending spouse, where the latter's employer seeks a remedy under a theory of subrogation against the offender after the aggrieved has recovered against the employer. Notwithstanding these things, however, where the principle of exemption and the principle of liability established in this case collide, the former must yield as an exception to the latter. In the instant case, because Schubert's (P) husband negligently caused her personal injuries while in August Wagon Company's (D) service (trespass incidental to the employer's business), the latter is liable to her for the harm she suffered. Affirmed.

ANALYSIS

Justice Cardozo referred to some of the procedural implications of respondeat superior liability in this case. Among other things, he noted that a judgment of no liability in a suit against a servant may be pleaded as a bar in an action against the master, and covenants not to sue generally have the same effect as those on joint tortfeasors. These statements reflect general agency law. See Seavey, Law of Agency 169-70 (1964), where he notes that a prior judgment against either a principal or an agent "is not binding upon the other," unless the first action had been controlled by the defendant in the second action, and also the damages awarded in a judgment against a principal can be no greater than those previously obtained against the agent because of the effect of the principal's right of indemnity against the agent.

Klatt v. Commonwealth Edison Co.

Injured passenger (P) v. Employer of driver (D)

Ill. Sup. Ct., 33 Ill. 2d 481, 211 N.E.2d 720 (1965).

NATURE OF CASE: Appeal from denial of damages for personal injury.

FACT SUMMARY: The district court failed to award damages to Klatt (P) for the injuries she suffered while riding in a car owned by Commonwealth Edison Co. (D) and negligently operated by her father during the course of his employment.

RULE OF LAW

Where an employee, without authority or apparent authority from his employer, invites or gives permission to a third party to enter his employer's premises or vehicle and causes the latter injury while within the scope of his employment, his employer is not liable to the third party for his tortious conduct.

FACTS: Herbert Klatt, while in the course of his employment for Commonwealth Edison Co. (D), picked up his daughter, Klatt (P), in a company car to take her home for a visit. Subsequently, he negligently caused a severe accident in which he was killed and Klatt (P) severely injured. As a result, Klatt (P) brought suit against Edison (D), seeking to recover damages on respondeat superior grounds. After deliberation, the trial court found that Edison (D) was not liable to Klatt (P) under a respondeat superior theory. Klatt (P) appealed.

ISSUE: Where an employee, without authority or apparent authority from his employer, invites or gives permission to a third party to enter his employer's premises or vehicle and causes the latter injury while within the scope of his employment, will his employer be held liable to the third party for his tortious conduct?

HOLDING AND DECISION: (Underwood, J.) No. Where an employee, without authority or apparent authority from his employer, invites or gives permission to a third party to enter his employer's premises or vehicle and causes the latter injury while within the scope of his employment, his employer is not liable to the third party for his tortious conduct. This rule is consistent with Restatement (Second) § 242, dealing with agency. The rationale for this section is that the third party's acceptance of the servant's hospitality, in this instance, so identifies him with the latter, that this forfeits any claim he may have against the servant's master. However, the issues raised by this rule have never been squarely addressed in Illinois. In fact, there is a clear line of persuasive authority contrary to the view expressed in the Restatement. This is exemplified in the "Connecticut doctrine," which rests on the broader ground that every person who manages his affairs through agents is bound to manage them so that the third persons are not injured by the tortious conduct of his agents while they are within the scope of their employment. Furthermore, public policy dictates that a master be held liable for negligent acts of the servant performed in the course of his employment, even though they are not specially authorized or contrary to his instructions. Moreover, this court, in *Hayes v. Sampsell*, 264 Ill. 258, noted in dictum that a master is liable for willful and wanton acts of his servant injuring an adult third party while in the general course of employment, even though the third party can be a trespasser. However, this situation in *Hayes* is distinguishable from the facts in the case at bar as the Restatement embodies the more sound reasoning and logic. In *Hayes*, this court found master liability where a third party trespasser was involved. However, an employee, while in the course of his employment, permitted his daughter to accompany him in a company vehicle where she subsequently suffered injuries form his negligent conduct. Furthermore, the employee had no authority nor apparent authority to permit his daughter, Klatt (P), to accompany him because company policy provided that unauthorized persons unconnected with company business were not to be transported in company vehicles, and Klatt's (P) father had knowledge of this policy. Affirmed.

ANALYSIS

The Illinois Supreme Court distinguished the *Hayes* case, where a third party minor was injured after accepting the servant's invitation to ride gratuitously on a streetcar, on the ground that there the minor was a trespasser, whereas here Klatt (P) was an invitee. However, based on the facts in the instant case, the court could be viewed as within the scope of his employment because they might have been for the purpose of obtaining the good will of passengers to insure that they continue this mode of transportation. Hence, liability is imputed to his employer because the harm that resulted to the plaintiff would be within the range of foreseeable harm that his employer must guard against to avoid liability. A clearly visible exculpatory clause, detailing the limits of the municipal transport company's liability, may have persuaded the *Hayes* court otherwise because then a third party has notice that an agent is acting for his own purposes.

CHAPTER 4

Contractual Powers of Agents

Quick Reference Rules of Law

King v. Bankerd

Conveyer of property (D) v. Owner of property (P)

Md. Ct. App., 303 Md. 98, 492 A.2d 608 (1985).

NATURE OF CASE: Appeal from summary judgment awarding damages for breach of fiduciary duty.

FACT SUMMARY: In Bankerd's (P) suit for damages against King (D), the trial court summarily awarded Bankerd (P) damages, which was affirmed on appeal, for King's (D) gratuitous conveyance of his interest in property to his wife, a co-interest holder, even though Bankerd (P) had executed to King (D) a general power of attorney to convey his property which neither authorized nor prohibited such a conveyance.

RULE OF LAW

Unless otherwise expressed or implied, a general power of attorney that authorizes an agent to sell or convey property on terms that he deems are proper implies a sale for the principal's benefit.

FACTS: Bankerd (P) executed a power of attorney to King (D), an attorney and colleague, to convey a home which he jointly owned with his wife as a tenant by the entirety. This power of attorney provided, in part, that King (D) had the power to "convey, grant, bargain, and/or sell" Bankerd's (P) property "on such terms as to him," King (D), "may seem best." Sometime later, King (D), after Bankerd (P) had separated from his wife and King (D) had tried unsuccessfully to locate him, gratuitously conveyed Bankerd's (P) interest in the home to Mrs. Bankerd, pursuant to her request. Moreover, Mrs. Bankerd, in turn, sold the property to a third party for $62,500. After determining what had occurred, Bankerd (P) filed this suit for damages against King (D), alleging breach of trust and breach of fiduciary duty in King's (D) gratuitous conveyance of Bankerd's (P) interest in the subject property, in violation of the power of attorney. In opposition to Bankerd's (P) allegations, King (D) alleged that the surrounding circumstances indicated that he did in fact have the authority to convey gratuitously Bankerd's (P) interest in the property to Mrs. Bankerd. After completion of the discovery proceedings, both parties moved for summary judgment. However, the trial court, in opposition to King's (D) allegations, granted summary judgment in favor of Bankerd (P) and awarded damages. The appellate court affirmed. King (D) appealed.

ISSUE: Unless otherwise expressed or implied, does a general power of attorney that authorizes an agent to sell or convey property on terms that he deems are proper imply a sale for the principal's benefit?

HOLDING AND DECISION: (Cole, J.) Yes. Unless otherwise expressed or implied, a general power of attorney that authorizes an agent to sell or convey property on terms that he deems are proper implies a sale for the principal's benefit. This rule naturally flows from the rule as laid down in *Adams Express Co. v. Trego*, 35 Md. 47 (1872), where the court notes, in part, that the powers of the "agent are to be exercised for the benefit of the principal only, and not of the agent or of third parties." Consequently, in keeping with this principle, if an agency relationship is founded upon a power of attorney, then the attorney, although having some discretion with respect to his duties, is bound to act for his principal's benefit and must avoid, where possible, that which is detrimental unless expressly authorized. Moreover, this agency duty most surely applies to the real estate context, where an agent has general power to convey or sell his principal's real estate, since the principal's interest is most likely substantial. In the instant case, since the express language of Bankerd's (P) and King's (D) power of attorney agreement did not authorize King (D) to convey gratuitously Bankerd's (P) property away, then the language must be construed so as to protect Bankerd's (P) interest in the property. Moreover, the surrounding circumstances do not evidence an intent by Bankerd (P) to grant King (D) the power to convey gratuitously away his property. Hence, since there is no genuine dispute as to any material fact with respect to the powers Bankerd (P) granted King (D), then the trial court did not err in granting Bankerd's (P) motion for summary judgment. Affirmed.

ANALYSIS

In connection with determining the scope of the power of attorney, see *Von Wedel v. McGrath*, 180 F. 2d 716 (3d Cir. 1950), a case with similar facts as the *King* case. There the court, in examining the power of attorney agreement involved in the case, stated as follows: "In the absence of ambiguity or incompleteness, we must deal with the intent as actually expressed in the document itself. The power of attorney before us is neither ambiguous nor incomplete. Under the settle law, the specific language governs. That language refers solely to Von Wedel's ordinary business affairs. It contains nothing that can reasonably be construed as authority for the attorney in fact to make gifts of Von Wedel's property. The principle of eiusdem generis squarely applies, and the command of the specific language must be pursued with legal strictness."

Lamb v. Scott

Holder of power of attorney/stepbrother (P) v. Will beneficiary/daughter (D)

Ala. Sup. Ct., 643 So. 2d 972 (1994).

NATURE OF CASE: Appeal from summary judgment declaring a deed void.

FACT SUMMARY: When Lamb (D), the donee of a durable power of attorney, executed a deed transferring property to herself and her sister, their stepbrother Scott (P) sued for an equal division under the terms of the will.

RULE OF LAW

One who accepts a power of attorney covenants to use the power for the sole benefit of the one conferring the power and to use it in a manner consistent with the purposes of the agency relationship created by the power of attorney.

FACTS: Lamb (D) was given a durable power of attorney by her mother. When her mother became incapacitated, Lamb (D) later executed a deed transferring her mother's farm to herself and her sister. Scott (P) was Lamb's (D) stepbrother, who claimed to be a joint owner of the property described in the deed. The trial court granted Scott's (P) request that the deed be set aside. Lamb (D) appealed the court's decision to declare the deed void.

ISSUE: Does one who accepts a power of attorney covenant to use the power for the sole benefit of the one conferring the power and to use it in a manner consistent with the purposes of the agency relationship created by the power of attorney?

HOLDING AND DECISION: (Shores, J.) Yes. One who accepts a power of attorney covenants to use the power for the sole benefit of the one conferring the power and to use it in a manner consistent with the purposes of the agency relationship created by the power of attorney. Powers of attorney will be construed strictly, restricting the powers to those expressly granted. Lamb (D) was without power to convey land to herself because Lamb's (D) power of attorney did not specifically state that she could do so. The property division is defined under the terms of the will, which was written after the power of attorney was executed. Affirmed.

ANALYSIS

The court also ruled that the Alabama statute providing that the incapacity of the donor of a durable power of attorney does not change the effect of the actions of the donee had no bearing on the facts of this case. The general common law rule that all agency powers are revoked by the principal's incapacity may be statutorily overridden. Some states have statutes spelling out the specific types of transactions for which powers of attorney may be used.

Smith v. Hansen, Hansen & Johnson, Inc.

Agent (D) v. Builder (P)

Wash. Ct. App., 818 P.2d 1127 (1991).

NATURE OF CASE: Appeal from an award of damages in an action seeking redress based on an agent's apparent authority.

FACT SUMMARY: When a new exterior glass wall, constructed by Hansen, Hansen & Johnson (HH & J) (P) with salvage glass purchased from an agent of Fentron (D), began to leak about a year after it was finished, HH & J (P) sued for damages.

RULE OF LAW

Manifestations to a third person will support a finding of apparent authority only if they caused the one claiming apparent authority to subjectively believe that the agent had authority to act for the principal and that subjective belief was reasonable.

FACTS: To build a glass wall as part of a building renovation, Hansen, Hansen & Johnson (HH & J) (P) purchased salvage glass from Fentron (D), through its agent, Foster, who was employed by Fentron (D) as a manager of manufacturing services. Foster's duties included purchasing material needed for manufacturing but not selling products to customers. However, Foster led Hansen (P), a partner in HH & J (P), to believe that Foster had authority to sell materials on behalf of Fentron (D). HH & J (P) made checks payable to Foster at his request, in part because he said the glass was at a salvage yard and was about to be destroyed. After the new wall was finished, it began to leak. After the owner of the building obtained redress from HH & J (P), HH & J (P) sued Fentron (D) for reimbursement plus other damages. The trial court ruled for HH & J (P). Fentron (D) appealed.

ISSUE: Will manifestations to a third person support a finding of apparent authority only if they caused the one claiming apparent authority to subjectively believe that the agent had authority to act for the principal and that subjective belief was reasonable?

HOLDING AND DECISION: (Morgan, J.) Yes. Manifestations to a third person will support a finding of apparent authority only if they caused the one claiming apparent authority to subjectively believe that the agent had authority to act for the principal and that subjective belief was reasonable. The evidence in this case does not support a reasonable inference that Foster had apparent authority to sell materials and designs on Fentron's (D) behalf or that HH & J's (P) subjective belief that Foster was authorized by Fentron (D) was objectively reasonable. When Foster requested that the check be made payable to him personally and stated that the glass was at a salvage yard, not in Fentron's (D) control, HH & J (P) was put on notice that further inquiry of Fentron (D) was needed. Reversed with directions to dismiss.

ANALYSIS

The rule applied by the court is found in the Restatement (Second) of Agency § 27. Both actual and apparent authority depend upon objective manifestations. With actual authority, the principal's objective manifestations are made to the agent. Apparent authority is created as to a third person by written or spoken words or any other conduct of the principal which reasonably causes the third person to believe that the principal consents to having the act done on his behalf by the person purporting to act for him.

Sauber v. Northland Insurance Co.

Automobile owner (P) v. Insurance Co. (D)

Minn. Sup. Ct., 251 Minn. 237 (1958).

NATURE OF CASE: Action against an insurance company to enforce collision policy.

FACT SUMMARY: After Sauber (P) purchased McDonald's automobile, he called Northland Insurance (D) and asked that the insurance policy be transferred to his name.

RULE OF LAW

When a party receives information over the telephone from a business, it is binding.

FACTS: Sauber (P) purchased McDonald's automobile. Sauber (P) called McDonald's insurance company, Northland Insurance (D), and asked that McDonald's policy be transferred to his name. The girl that answered the telephone said that this could be done and that she would do it. An accident occurred and Northland (D) denied that Sauber (P) was insured by it. At trial Sauber (P) established that he had talked to one of Northland's (D) employees. She testified that Sauber (P) had merely asked if a transfer were possible and she told him it was. Northland (D) offered to prove that she was not authorized to approve a transfer, but the court rejected it. The jury found for Sauber (P).

ISSUE: Is an employee answering a business telephone presumed to have authority for any duties which are assumed by such employee?

HOLDING AND DECISION: (Knutson, J.) Yes. When a party receives information over the telephone from a business, it is binding. The public has the right to rely on information given by employees over the telephone. The company impliedly approves of such actions when it authorizes employees to answer the telephone. The jury apparently found that Northland's (D) employee had agreed to make the change. Her lack of actual authority is immaterial. Where an employer has placed an employee in a position to do injury to the public, it is ultimately liable. Having clothed the employee with apparent authority, it is bound by it absent a showing of bad faith. It is not necessary to identify the employee so long as it can be shown that the call was made to the business number. Affirmed.

ANALYSIS

The third party must rely on the agent's apparent authority or the principal will not be bound. A principal will be bound by acts of those he left "in charge" of the business. Likewise, an employer will be bound where a retailer receives authorization over the telephone to extend credit to someone purporting to represent the principal. To hold otherwise in such cases would require the principal to be personally present at every business transaction.

Foley v. Allard

Investor (P) v. Apparent broker (D)

Minn. Sup. Ct., 427 N.W.2d 647 (1988).

NATURE OF CASE: **Appeal from denial of defendant's motion for summary judgment in an action to recover damages based on apparent authority.**

FACT SUMMARY: **After Allard (D) lost money given to him by Foley (P) to invest, Foley (P) brought this suit against Allard (D) and one of his customers, Steichen & Company (D), alleging that the brokerage house had negligently clothed Allard (D) with apparent authority to transact business by letting him use its telephone.**

RULE OF LAW

A presumption of apparent authority is raised by the fact that an agent answers the business phone and purports to act for the business.

FACTS: Allard (D) offered to double $10,000 Foley (P) had obtained to forestall foreclosure on residential property which she had sold. He guaranteed there was no risk and that he would return at least her principal amount before she needed it. No one told Foley (P) that Allard (D) was employed or formally affiliated with Steichen & Company (D) as a stockbroker, although she believed him to be. Allard (D) was actually Steichen's (D) customer, with phone privileges at the brokerage house. After Allard (D) told Foley (P) he had lost her money, she filed suit, alleging that Steichen (D) had negligently clothed Allard (D) with apparent authority to transact business by taking his phone messages. The court granted Steichen's (D) motion for summary judgment. The court of appeals reversed. Steichen (D) appealed.

ISSUE: Is a presumption of apparent authority raised by the fact that an agent answers the business phone and purports to act for the business?

HOLDING AND DECISION: (Wahl, J.) Yes. A presumption of apparent authority is raised by the fact that an agent answers the business phone and purports to act for the business. However, in this case, the presumption is rebutted because Foley (P) never visited Steichen's (D) offices, transacted any business during calls made and/or received on Steichen (D) phones, or investigated the company beyond checking to see if it was listed in the yellow pages. Steichen (D) did not affirmatively hold out Allard (D) as its authorized agent. Steichen's (D) customers, including Allard (D), were merely permitted to receive calls. The fact that Allard (D) gave her no records or documents, that she made her check payable directly to Allard (D), that she received assurances of no risk, and that she was charged no commission were all highly irregular activities that would have acted as signals to a person of ordinary prudence. The court of appeals is reversed, and summary judgment for Steichen (D) is reinstated.

ANALYSIS

The court first stated the rule applied here in *Sauber v. Northland Insurance Co.*, 87 N.W.2d 591 (1958). Foley (P) argued that *Sauber*, in which the court held that apparent authority existed by virtue of one telephone call, governed here. However, in *Sauber*, an insurer's agent had the authority to answer inquiries regarding insurance policies and had assured Sauber that he could drive a car with a transferred insurance policy. Moreover, *Sauber* did not extend the principal's liability to nonemployees like Allard (D).

Herbert Construction Co. v. Continental Insurance Co.

Contractor (P) v. Insurance company (D)

931 F.2d 989 (2d Cir. 1990).

NATURE OF CASE: Appeal from judgment awarding damages and granting partial summary judgment to plaintiff in an action based on apparent authority.

FACT SUMMARY: After Dixon (D) executed a performance bond on Continental Insurance Co.'s (D) behalf for a subcontractor after Continental (D) had revoked Dixon's (D) agency privileges, Continental (D) refused to remedy any possible default by the subcontractor.

RULE OF LAW

Under apparent authority, the third party must establish that the principal was responsible for the appearance of authority and that the third party reasonably relied on the agent's representations.

FACTS: Dixon (D) issued a performance bond for Michaels, a subcontractor used by Herbert Construction Co. (P), designating Continental Insurance Co. (D) as surety and signing as attorney for Continental (D). When Michaels filed for bankruptcy, Continental (D) refused to perform as surety since it had revoked Dixon's (D) agency privileges prior to issuance of the bond. Dixon (D) had doctored a valid power of attorney form signed before the revocation. Continental (D) had, however, made no effort to inform individual clients or the public at large of the revocation. Herbert (P) filed suit. The district court awarded damages and partial summary judgment to Herbert (P) while denying Continental's (D) cross-motion for summary judgment and dismissal. This appeal followed.

ISSUE: Under apparent authority, must the third party establish that the principal was responsible for the appearance of authority and that the third party reasonably relied on the agent's representations?

HOLDING AND DECISION: (Meskill, J.) Yes. Under apparent authority, the third party must establish that the principal was responsible for the appearance of authority and that the third party reasonably relied on the agent's representations. Whether or not Continental (D) could have taken further precautions to remove Dixon's (D) indicia of authority, or bears any responsibility for not preventing the subsequent doctoring of the reacquired power of attorney form, presents a substantial question of material fact for a jury to decide. A genuine issue of material fact also exists as to whether Herbert (P) reasonably relied on Dixon's (D) appearance of authority. Continental (D) may not, however, be held liable solely for failing to notify third parties that Dixon's (D) authority had been revoked. Affirmed in part, vacated in part, and remanded.

ANALYSIS

A duty to inquire only arises where a transaction is extraordinary or its novelty alerts the third party to the danger of fraud. In finding Continental's (D) unsuccessful attempt to retrieve Dixon's (D) power of attorney unimportant, the trial court relied on § 130 of the Restatement of Agency. However, the court of appeals declared that Dixon's (D) subsequent reacquisition of a once valid and previously executed power of attorney injected a different factor into the case.

Continental Insurance Co. v. Gazaway

Bond issuer (D) v. Guardian (P)

Ga. Ct. App., 453 S.E.2d 91 (1994), *reconsideration denied*, 216 Ga. App. 901 (1995).

NATURE OF CASE: Appeal from a judgment finding liability under a guardianship bond.

FACT SUMMARY: When the attorney for Continental Insurance Co. (D) issued a bond after his authority to write bonds for Continental (D) had been revoked, Continental (D) appealed from a judgment entered against it finding it liable under the bond.

RULE OF LAW

Persons dealing with a limited agent have the duty to examine the agent's authority.

FACTS: Continental Insurance Co. (D) had revoked the authority of its attorney to write bonds. Nevertheless, two months later, the attorney issued a guardianship bond to Gazaway, who was later found to have wasted the entire estate of her ward (P). The court found that the bond had been legally issued and that Continental (D) and Gazaway were jointly and severally liable for the amount covered by the bond. On appeal, Continental (D) contended that the probate court erred in holding it liable on the bond.

ISSUE: Do persons dealing with a limited agent have the duty to examine the agent's authority?

HOLDING AND DECISION: (Smith, J.) Yes. Persons dealing with a limited agent have the duty to examine the agent's authority. In this case, the attorney issued the bond as attorney-in-fact for Continental (D). One signing as attorney-in-fact does not purport to be a general agent of the corporation. He was, at best, a limited agent. Continental (D) did nothing to knowingly cause or permit the attorney to act as its agent. The lack of diligence of both the probate court and the guardian preclude a finding of justifiable reliance. Reversed.

DISSENT: (McMurray, J.) There is sufficient evidence to support the probate court's finding that the attorney was Continental's (D) ostensible agent when he issued the surety bond.

ANALYSIS

When apparent authority is terminated may be a close question. Apparent authority is also related to the theory of estoppel. In § 8 of the Restatement (Second) of Agency, estoppel as a tort principle is distinguished from apparent authority, which was derived from the law of contracts.

Gizzi v. Texaco

Purchaser of van (P) v. Corporation (D)

437 F.2d 308 (3d Cir. 1971).

NATURE OF CASE: Appeal from directed defense verdict in personal injury action.

FACT SUMMARY: The operator of a service station which carried the Texaco (D) insignia, used Texaco (D) equipment to service cars, and sold Texaco (D) products, sold a used van to Gizzi (P) after performing brake repairs, but the brakes failed on a highway, and the van collided with a tractor trailer, seriously injuring Gizzi (P).

RULE OF LAW

Questions of apparent authority and agency by estoppel, which depend on manifestations by the principal to a third person and reasonable belief and reliance by the third person that the alleged agent is authorized to bind the principal, are ones of fact for the jury to determine.

FACTS: Gizzi (P) purchased a used van for $400 from a service station operator he frequently patronized. The service station sold Texaco (D) parts, bore Texaco (D) signs and insignia, and benefited from Texaco's (D) national advertising assuring skill in automotive servicing. Gizzi (P) bought the van after the station operator promised to perform brake repairs. However, on a trip to Philadelphia in the van, the brakes failed and Gizzi (P) was seriously injured. Although Texaco (D) had been paid no portion of the van sale proceeds, the operator had used a Texaco (D) invoice as receipt. Texaco (D) also knew and acquiesced in the fact that 30% of its dealers sold used cars. Gizzi (P) sued Texaco (D) for personal injuries arising from breaches of warranty made by the station operator, who Gizzi (P) alleged was Texaco's (D) agent. The trial court granted a directed verdict for Texaco (D), and Gizzi (P) appealed.

ISSUE: Are questions of apparent authority and agency by estoppel, which depend on manifestations by the principal to a third person and reasonable belief and reliance by the third person that the alleged agent is authorized to bind the principal, ones of fact for the jury to determine?

HOLDING AND DECISION: (McLaughlin, J.) Yes. Both concepts of apparent authority and agency by estoppel depend on manifestations by the alleged principal to a third person and reasonable belief by the third person that the alleged agent is authorized to bind the principal. The third person must have relied on the indicia of authority originated by the principal, and this reliance must have been reasonable under the circumstances. Here, there was evidence to show Texaco (D) exerted control over the service station. Reasonable people could differ over Texaco's (D) liability. These are questions of fact which are for the jury to determine. Vacated and remanded.

DISSENT: (Seitz, J.) Here, a person of ordinary prudence would believe the station operator who sold the used van to Gizzi (P) was Texaco's (D) agent only for the sale of gasoline, oil, tires and other items ordinarily sold at a filling station. A reasonable man would not believe that the operator's apparent authority extended to the sale of used cars. Where the evidence permits only one reasonable conclusion on the issue of agency, the issue must be decided by the trial court, not the jury.

ANALYSIS

Although this case points out the common elements in the doctrines of apparent authority and agency by estoppel, estoppel arises from tort law rather than from the principles of mutual assent and contract law. Estoppel is designed to compensate an innocent person who relies on the words of the principal to his detriment; yet it also requires that the party change his position in response to the principal's statements. Accordingly, the principal is held to the truth of his statements because it would be unjust for him under the circumstances to deny them. See Restatement of Torts § § 872 and 894.

Hoddeson v. Koos Bros.

Furniture buyer (P) v. Furniture store (D)

N.J. Super. Ct., 47 N.J. Super. 224, 135 A.2d 702 (1957).

NATURE OF CASE: Appeal from award of damages.

FACT SUMMARY: Hoddeson (P) paid an individual who purported to be a salesman at Koos Bros. (D) for furniture.

RULE OF LAW

A principal may be liable for failing to take reasonable precautions against an imposter claiming to be the principal's agent.

FACTS: Hoddeson (P) was shopping for furniture with her aunt at Koos Bros. (D). She had come to buy specific furniture which she had already seen. A man purporting to be a salesman asked if he could help her, and she told him what she had come to buy. He guided her to the furniture she had described and calculated the price on a pad. She gave him the calculated price of $168.50, but failed to obtain a receipt. He told her the items were not in stock but would be delivered the next month. This transaction took thirty to forty minutes. When the items did not arrive the next month, Hoddeson (P) inquired at Koos Bros. (D) and learned that no record of the transaction existed. Hoddeson (P) and her aunt were unable to positively identify any of the regularly employed salesmen at Koos Bros. (D) as the man who took the money. One of the salesmen resembled the purported salesman, but they were unsure. Koos Bros.' (D) records revealed that the salesman resembling the man who took the money was on vacation the week Hoddeson (P) gave up the money. Hoddeson (P) sued and obtained a judgment against Koos Bros. (D) reimbursing her for the money. Koos Bros. (D) appealed.

ISSUE: May a principal be liable for failing to take reasonable precautions against an imposter claiming to be the principal's agent?

HOLDING AND DECISION: (Clapp, J.) Yes. A principal who fails to act reasonably to protect a third party from an imposter claiming to be his agent is liable to the third party for the harm suffered. Generally the appearance of agency must be created by the manifestations of the principal rather than the representations of the supposed agent. And the party alleging the agency must prove the requisite facts; the principal does not have the burden of disproving these facts. Assume the purported salesman was an imposter. This does not immunize the alleged principal from liability. The third party may still recover under the theory of agency by estoppel, which amounts to "a tortious dereliction of duty owed to any invited customer." When an imposter is able to represent himself as an agent of a proprietor because of the proprietor's failure to reasonably monitor his place of business, the proprietor's breach of his duty of care to the customer constitutes conduct which creates the appearance of authority. The proprietor has more than merely the duty to remove banana peels from the floor, he has a duty to exercise reasonable care to protect the customer from losses resulting from an imposter salesman's deceptions. Where a proprietor breaches this duty and allows an imposter conspicuously and ostensibly to transact the proprietor's business with a customer in the store so that a reasonable person would conclude the imposter is an authorized agent, the proprietor cannot escape liability by denying the agency. Whether Hoddeson (P) was reasonable and Koos Bros. (D) breached their duty must be determined at trial. Reversed and new trial allowed.

ANALYSIS

An omission normally does not constitute conduct unless a duty exists. The court here likens the agency by estoppel that is possible in this case to a tortious breach of duty. Note that tort analysis focusing on the "least cost avoider" is relevant in determining the appropriate duties of care of the parties. While a principal can best police against an imposter posing as his agent under his nose, it is unreasonable to expect the principal to police the world for purported agents.

AutoXchange.com, Inc. v. Dreyer and Reinbold, Inc.

Seller (P) v. Purchaser (D)

Ind. Ct. App., 816 N.E.2d 40 (2004).

NATURE OF CASE: Appeal from grant of partial summary judgment to defendant in tort action.

FACT SUMMARY: AutoXchange.com, Inc. (P) con-tended that its corporate officer and minority shareholder, Ellingwood, had neither apparent nor inherent agency authority to request that Dreyer & Reinbold, Inc. (D) pay the purchase price of vehicles Dreyer & Reinbold (D) had purchased from AutoXchange (P) directly to AutoXchange's (P) floorplan lender, Automative Finance Corporation (AFC).

RULE OF LAW

A corporate officer and minority shareholder has apparent and inherent agency authority on which a party to a transaction may reasonably rely where the corporate officer holds himself out as the company's sole negotiator and acts within the usual and ordinary scope of his authority, and where the other party is not on notice that the officer does not have such authority.

FACTS: Dreyer & Reinbold, Inc. (D) purchased several automobiles from AutoXchange.com, Inc. (P). In its negotiations with AutoXchange (P), Dreyer & Reinbold (D) dealt exclusively with Ellingwood, AutoXchange's (P) corporate officer and minority shareholder. At Ellingwood's request, Dreyer & Reinbold (D) paid the purchase price directly to Automative Finance Corporation (AFC), AutoXchange's (P) floorplan lender and secured creditor, which would ensure Dreyer & Reinbold's (D) receipt of free and clear title to the vehicles. Dreyer & Reinbold's (D) payment to AFC was credited to AutoXchange's (P) account by AFC following receipt of the purchase price. Under the terms of the financing agreement between AutoXchange (P) and AFC, AutoXchange (P) was required to hold the proceeds of the sale of any floor planned vehicles in trust for AFC, and to transfer those proceeds to AFC within forty-eight hours of the sale. AutoXchange (P) brought suit against Dreyer & Reinbold (D), asserting numerous tort claims arising from Dreyer & Reinbold's (D) compliance with Ellingwood's request, which, AutoXchange (P) claimed, was made in bad faith under the circumstances. The trial court granted partial summary judgment to Dreyer & Reinbold (D), finding that Ellingwood had apparent and inherent authority on which Dreyer & Reinbold (D) could reasonably rely. The state's intermediate appellate court granted review.

ISSUE: Does a corporate officer and minority shareholder have apparent and inherent agency authority on which a party to a transaction may reasonably rely where the corporate officer holds himself out as the company's sole negotiator and acts within the usual and ordinary scope of his authority, and where the other party is not on notice that the officer does not have such authority?

HOLDING AND DECISION: (Riley, J.) Yes. A corporate officer and minority shareholder has apparent and inherent agency authority on which a party to a transaction may reasonably rely where the corporate officer holds himself out as the company's sole negotiator and acts within the usual and ordinary scope of his authority, and where the other party is not on notice that the officer does not have such authority. Apparent authority arises where a third party reasonably believes the agent has authority based on some act by the principal. A communication of authority made solely by the agent is inadequate; instead, it is essential that there be some form of communication, direct or indirect, by the principal, which instills a reasonable belief in the mind of the third party. Although only Ellingwood communicated with Dreyer & Reinbold (D), AutoXchange (P) indirectly communicated, through its act of letting Ellingwood be the sole negotiator, that Ellingwood had authority to do so. Therefore, Ellingwood had apparent authority to instruct Dreyer & Reinbold (D) to make payment directly to AFC. He also had inherent authority, which arises where the acts done on the principal's behalf accompany or are incidental to transactions that the agent is authorized to conduct, even if in fact the agent is not authorized to engage in such acts, provided the third party reasonably believes that the agent is authorized to do them and has no notice that he is not so authorized. Here, Ellingwood, as a corporate officer, was authorized to sell automobiles, so he was acting within the usual and ordinary scope of his authority. Also, because Ellingwood was the sole negotiator of the transaction, the formulation of payment terms was a necessary accompaniment to the ordinary scope of his authority. Here, too, Dreyer & Reinbold's (D) reliance was reasonable because Ellingwood had always been the sole negotiator on its transactions with AutoXchange (P), and since AutoXchange (P) placed Ellingwood in the position of corporate officer and sole negotiator, Dreyer & Reinbold (D) should not be required to scrutinize too carefully the mandates of this agent, who did nothing more than what is usually done by a corporate officer. Finally, there was no evidence that Dreyer & Reinbold (D) was on notice of any limitations on Ellingwood's authority. Rejected, too, is AutoXchange's (P) argument that Ellingwood's reason to change the payment terms, i.e., so Dreyer & Reinbold (D) could receive clear and free title to the vehicles, should logically have put them on

Continued on next page.

notice that Ellingwood did not have inherent agency authority to direct AutoXchange's (P) funds. If AutoXchange's (P) reasoning were followed, commerce would be impeded, since a third party would always have to inquire of the principal whether the agent had authority. Affirmed.

ANALYSIS

The inherent authority concept has been criticized as superfluous to the doctrines of apparent and actual agency authority. In fact, the Restatement (Third), Agency, rejects the doctrine of inherent authority altogether.

CHAPTER 5

Fraudulent Acts of Agents

Quick Reference Rules of Law

Grease Monkey International, Inc. v. Montoya

Company (D) v. Investor (P)

Colo. Sup. Ct., 904 P.2d 468 (1995).

NATURE OF CASE: Appeal from a judgment awarding damages for fraud and misrepresentation.

FACT SUMMARY: When the chief officer and president of Grease Monkey International, Inc. (D) accepted money from Montoya (P) under the guise that the payments were investments in Grease Monkey (D) and then used the money for his own personal benefit, Montoya (P) sued for fraud and misrepresentation.

RULE OF LAW

A principal who puts a servant or other agent in a position that enables the agent, while apparently acting within his authority, to commit a fraud upon third persons is subject to liability to such third persons for the fraud.

FACTS: Sensenig, Grease Monkey International, Inc.'s (D) President, Chief Operating Officer, and Chairman of the Board, had broad authority to act as general officer and agent for Grease Monkey (D). Sensenig solicited payments from Montoya (P) by pretending that the payments would be investments in Grease Monkey (D). In return, Montoya (P) received promissory notes, interest payments, and promotional items from Sensenig. However, none of the payments was invested in Grease Monkey (D), but were instead used for Sensenig's personal benefit. Montoya (P) sued Grease Monkey (D), as Sensenig's employer, for fraud and misrepresentation. The trial court entered judgment against Grease Monkey (D) for the outstanding balance due on the promissory notes. Grease Monkey (D) appealed, contending that the application of § 261 of the Restatement (Second) of Agency amounted to strict liability for the principal.

ISSUE: Is a principal who puts a servant or other agent in a position that enables the agent, while apparently acting within his authority, to commit a fraud upon third persons subject to liability to such third persons for the fraud?

HOLDING AND DECISION: (Erickson, J.) Yes. A principal who puts a servant or other agent in a position that enables the agent, while apparently acting within his authority, to commit a fraud upon third persons is subject to liability to such third persons for the fraud. Under § 261 of the Restatement (Second) of Agency, a servant or other agent must be found to be put in a position that enabled the agent to commit fraud, the agent must have acted within his apparent authority, and the agent must have committed fraud. These conditions were met in the instant case. Also, this holding is correct under the principle that "when one of two innocent persons must suffer from the acts of a third, he must suffer who put it in the power of the wrongdoer to inflict the injury." Affirmed.

CONCURRENCE: (Mullarkey, J.) The application of apparent authority, as opposed to respondeat superior analysis, is triggered by the nature of the tort, not by the relationship of the agent to the principal.

ANALYSIS

Fraudulent acts of agents often subject the principal to vicarious liability for their misconduct. Fraud (deceit) is a tort whose elements include a knowingly false representation made by the defendant with the intent to induce to plaintiff to act in reliance upon the misrepresentation, justifiable reliance by the plaintiff upon the misrepresentation, and damage to the plaintiff resulting from such reliance. When one relies on the apparent authority of an agent making the representation, the principal is liable for the intentional misrepresentation even where the agent acts for his own purposes.

Entente Mineral Co. v. Parker

Expectant property purchaser (P) v. Attorney/purchaser (D)

956 F.2d 524 (5th Cir. 1992).

NATURE OF CASE: Appeal from a directed verdict for the defendant in an action for vicarious liability.

FACT SUMMARY: When Parker (D), a partner in the law firm (D) representing Young, appropriated the deal for Entente Mineral Co.'s (P) purchase of Young's royalty interest in certain property, Entente (P) filed suit against Parker (D) and the law firm (D) on the basis of vicarious liability for Parker's (D) actions.

RULE OF LAW

A principal or master is vicariously liable for the torts of his agent or servant that are committed within the scope of employment.

FACTS: After Young and Sneed, an employee of Entente Mineral Co. (P), agreed that Entente (P) would purchase one-half of Young's royalty interest in certain property, they asked Parker (D), a partner in the law firm (D) that represented Young, to review the terms of the deed. Parker (D) later told Young that he would purchase the one-half royalty for more than Entente (P) had offered. Young agreed. When Entente (P) discovered that Parker (D) was the purchaser, Entente (P) sued Parker (D) and the firm (D), alleging that the firm (D) was vicariously liable for Parker's (D) tortious interference with business relations and contract. At the close of Entente's (P) evidence in a jury trial, the firm (D) moved for a directed verdict on the ground that Parker's (D) purchase of the royalty was not within the scope of his employment. The trial court granted the motion. Entente (P) appealed.

ISSUE: Is a principal or master vicariously liable for the torts of his agent or servant that are committed within the scope of employment?

HOLDING AND DECISION: (Thornberry, J.) Yes. A principal or master is vicariously liable for the torts of his agent or servant that are committed within the scope of employment. In order to be within the scope of employment, the agent's conduct must be motivated by a purpose to serve the master. Alternatively, the master may be held liable if the agency relationship aids the agent in committing the tort. In this case, however, Parker (D) purchased the royalty for himself and was acting in his own interest, not in the interest of the firm (D). The firm (D) did not receive any benefit from Parker's (D) purchase. In fact, Young was never billed by Parker (D) or the firm (D). Further, the premise underlying liability, a relationship between the principal and an innocent third party, is absent in this case. Here, it is undisputed that neither Parker (D) nor the firm (D) represented Entente (P). Therefore, as a matter of law, the firm (D) may not be held vicariously liable for Parker's (D) acts. Affirmed.

ANALYSIS

In its analysis, the court referred to § § 9(1) and 13 of the UPA. Those sections state that where, by any wrongful act of any partner acting in the ordinary course of business of the partnership, loss or injury is caused to any person, the partnership is liable to the same extent as the partner so acting. However, the court instead applied the rule as to scope of employment stated in § 219(1) of the Restatement (Second) of Agency to its analysis.

Hydrolevel Corp. v. American Society of Mechanical Engineers, Inc.

Manufacturer (P) v. Professional association (D)

635 F.2d 118 (2d Cir. 1980), *aff'd*, 456 U.S. 556 (1982).

NATURE OF CASE: Appeal from a judgment awarding trebled damages for antitrust violations.

FACT SUMMARY: After competitors caused American Society of Mechanical Engineers, Inc. (ASME) (D) to issue a letter discouraging the use, on safety grounds, of a fuel cut-off made by Hydrolevel Corp. (P), Hydrolevel (P) sued ASME (D) for conspiracy to restrain trade.

RULE OF LAW

Where harm to business relations is accomplished by defamation or other methods of untruthful publicity, a servant with apparent authority to make statements binds his employer, irrespective of his motive.

FACTS: Through work done by volunteers from its membership, the American Society of Mechanical Engineers, Inc. (ASME) (D) promulgated codes and standards that influenced the profession and the marketplace. Hydrolevel Corp. (P) had manufactured a new type of automatic cutoff for water boilers and pressure vessels. After a major purchaser of the old type of cutoffs decided to switch to Hydrolevel's (P), M & M, a manufacturer of the old cutoffs, arranged to use ASME (D) code interpretation procedures to stifle Hydrolevel's (P) competition. One of the volunteers, who was closely associated with M & M, issued a letter on ASME (D) letterhead, discouraging the use of Hydrolevel's (P) cutoff on safety grounds. After the letter reached customers in the market, Hydrolevel (P) went out of business. The jury was charged that ASME (D) could be liable for fraud only if it had ratified the agent's acts or if the agents had acted to advance ASME's (D) interests. Hydrolevel (P) was awarded treble damages under the antitrust laws. This appeal followed.

ISSUE: Where harm to business relations is accomplished by defamation or other methods of untruthful publicity, does a servant with apparent authority to make statements bind his employer, irrespective of his motive?

HOLDING AND DECISION: (Lumbard, J.) Yes. Where harm to business relations is accomplished by defamation or other methods of untruthful publicity, a servant with apparent authority to make statements binds his employer, irrespective of his motive. A conspiracy to restrain trade is so similar to fraud, injurious falsehood, and tortious interference with business relations that application of the Restatement rules governing those intentional torts is appropriate. For ASME (D) to be liable, Hydrolevel (P) had to demonstrate only that ASME's (D) agents acted within their apparent authority when participating in the conspiracy. It did not have to demonstrate that they also acted in part to benefit ASME (D) or that ASME (D) later ratified their actions. The district court's charge to the jury was thus more favorable to ASME (D) than it should have been. Affirmed on liability and remanded for a new trial on damages.

ANALYSIS

Although the Supreme Court ultimately affirmed this decision, other courts have held that fraudulent acts of agents are not within the scope of their employment and have refused to hold innocent principals liable. Imposing liability on the principal, on the other hand, is supposed to induce greater care to prevent misconduct by agents occupying especially sensitive or responsible positions that invite reliance. This is a consideration of great importance where, as here, the misuse of quasi-official standards and codes can easily injure competitors.

Rothman v. Fillette

Personal injury litigant (P) v. Driver (D)

Pa. Sup. Ct., 503 Pa. 259, 469 A.2d 543 (1983).

NATURE OF CASE: Appeal from grant of prayer to reinstate a personal injury suit for damages.

FACT SUMMARY: Madnick, Rothman's (P) attorney in a personal injury suit for damages against Fillette (D), misappropriated a check which Fillette's (D) insurer presented to him purportedly to settle Rothman's (P) claim, and Rothman (P), after discovering what had occurred, prayed to have his claim reinstated, which the lower court granted and the appellate court affirmed.

RULE OF LAW

Where an agent in the settlement process, without authority from his principal, unfaithfully performs his duties and causes harm to his principal, to the other settling party, or to both, then settlement policies require that the principal bear the loss and prohibit him from pursuing a further claim of damages against the other party.

FACTS: In 1972, Rothman (P) retained Madnick to institute a suit for damages against Fillette (D) as a result of Rothman's (P) sustaining personal injuries from an auto accident with Fillette (D). Fillette (D) was insured by Liberty Mutual Insurance Co. which agreed, after negotiations in 1974, to settle the case for $7,000. Pursuant to this settlement agreement, Liberty Mutual delivered to Madnick a release containing the terms of the proposed settlement and requiring Rothman's (P) signature. This release was returned to Liberty Mutual, purportedly signed by Rothman (P). In return, Liberty Mutual presented a $7,000 check to Madnick, payable to Rothman (P) and Madnick. Subsequently, the check was purportedly endorsed by Rothman (P) and cashed. On order of Madnick, the case was marked settled, discontinued, and ended. Five years later, Rothman (P) filed a petition seeking a rule to remove the order making the case settled. He alleged that he had no knowledge of the purported settlement and he did not sign the release, nor did he endorse the check. He concluded that since he was not aware of the settlement and did not authorize it, and since his agent acted without his authority, he should not be prevented from pursuing his claim against Fillette (D) and their insurer. The court below granted the petitioner's prayer and reinstated his action against Fillette (D). This ruling was affirmed by the appellate court. Fillette (D) appealed.

ISSUE: Where an agent in the settlement process, without authority from his principal, unfaithfully performs his duties and causes him harm to his principal, to the other settling party, or to both, then do settlement policies require that the principal bear the loss and prohibit him from pursuing a further claim of damages against the other party?

HOLDING AND DECISION: (Nix, J.) Yes. Where an agent in the settlement process, without authority from his principal, unfaithfully performs his duties and causes harm to his principal, to the other settling party, or to both, then settlement policies require that the principal bear the loss and prohibit him from pursuing a further claim of damages against the other party. This rule is consistent with the long-established principle that where one or two innocent persons must suffer because of the fraud of the third, the one who has accredited him must bear the loss. In such instances, the lack of authority of the agent has been rejected as a basis for shifting the principal's losses onto the innocent third party. This view is consistent with funda-mentally sound principles of agency and equity. Furthermore, the strong judicial policy in favor of parties voluntarily settling lawsuits bars the principal's further pursuit of his claim against the third party. To ameliorate, to some extent, the losses the principal has to sustain in these instances, this court has established a client security fund to assist clients of defalcating attorneys. Here, the fact that Fillette (D) was insured will not shift the losses Rothman (P) sustained onto the former. Liberty Mutual undertook to indemnify the Fillette's (D) against the damages arising from the motor vehicle accident; it did not assume the responsibility of insulting Rothman (P) for the losses he incurred by the defalcation of his counsel. Moreover, the better financial position of Liberty Mutual does not justify creating liability where none exists. Order affirming the Court of Common Pleas reversed; and, additionally, the petition to strike the order to settle, discontinue, and end is dismissed, and Rothman (P) may not shift the burden of his losses onto Fillette's (D) shoulders.

DISSENT IN PART: (Larsen, J.) Rothman (P) should not be pursuing his claim against Fillette (D) for amounts in excess of his $7,000 settlement sum. Since Rothman (P) never authorized the settlement, there is no reason to believe that the amount settled for was reasonable to compensate him for his injuries. Moreover, preventing Rothman (P) from establishing the true value of his loss at trial will not promote the policy favoring settlement. In addition, the client security fund, which assists clients who have suffered losses due to the misconduct of their attorneys, will not reimburse Rothman (P) for any injuries he suffered due to Fillette's (D) negligence.

Continued on next page.

ANALYSIS

Limiting Rothman (P) to the assistance provided for him by the court through the client security fund is a harsh rule. Apparently the court assumes that attorney misconduct is so uncommon that limiting clients of defalcating attorneys to this remedy far outweighs the drudgery of running counter to established settlement policies. However, many questions remain as to how widespread this type of conduct really is. Furthermore, a client forced to settle for an unreasonable amount may not have the resources to bring a malpractice claim against the malfeasant attorney, when considering the amount of damages the original defendant inflicted on him.

Light v. Chandler Improvement Co.

Purchaser of land (D) v. Seller (P)

Ariz. Sup. Ct., 33 Ariz. 101, 261 P. 969, 57 A.L.R. 107 (1928).

NATURE OF CASE: Appeal from directed verdict in land foreclosure suit.

FACT SUMMARY: Light (D) purchased land, relying on the representation of a real estate broker for Chandler Improvement Co. (P), for which it was unable to make scheduled mortgage payments as a result of crop failure, and at Chandler's (P) trial to foreclose on the land, Chandler's (P) motion for a directed verdict, which ran counter to Light's (D) prayer that Chandler (P) be vicariously liable to Light (D) for the fraudulent representations of its real estate agent, was granted.

RULE OF LAW

Where a purchaser has been deceived by the unauthorized and fraudulent representations of a real estate agent, he may set up a defense of recoupment for such representations in a vendor's action for the land's purchase price if he alleges and proves that the vendor, after knowledge of such representations and an offer of rescission on that ground by the purchaser, refused to accept the rescission.

FACTS: In 1919, a real estate broker for Chandler Improvement Co. (P), a corporation, induced Light (D), represented by Light, Berry and Berry's wife, to purchase 20 acres of land by informing the latter that, among other things, the land was fertile and would produce good crops. In reliance on these representations, Light (D) closed the deal by paying $1,500 in cash, by receiving a deed to the land from Chandler (P), and by giving notes and a mortgage back for $4,500, this being the balance of the purchase price. However, during the next four years, the land failed to produce a reasonable crop. Because of this, an officer for Light (D), in 1923, suggested to Chandler (P) that the latter take the land back because the farmer was unable to produce anything off it, and, as a result, the farmer was unable to make the scheduled mortgage payments. Sometime after this, Chandler (P) brought this action against Light (D) to foreclose the mortgage on the land. The defense to the suit was fraud and deceit in inducing the purchase, with a prayer that the notes and mortgage involved be adjudged to be fully paid and satisfied, and that Light (D) recover from Chandler (P) a judgment for $945, this being the excess actually paid in cash for the land over the real value thereof. Notwithstanding Light's (D) defense, Chandler (P) contended that Light (D) was liable for the mortgage because a real estate agent cannot bind the principal by representations made in regard to land quality and value, unless he was expressly authorized to make them, or unless they are known to his principal before the sale is consummated. On the other hand, Light (D) contended that a real estate agent is impliedly authorized by his principal to make representations in regard to land quality and value, and the principal is bound by them as though he made them himself. Subsequently, Chandler (P) moved for an instructed verdict, which was granted by the lower court. Light (D) appealed.

ISSUE: Where a purchaser has been deceived by the unauthorized and fraudulent representations of a real estate broker, may he set up a defense of recoupment for such representations in a vendor's action for the land's purchase price if he alleges and proves that the vendor, after knowledge of such representations and an offer of rescission on that ground by the purchaser, refused to accept the rescission?

HOLDING AND DECISION: (Lockwood, J.) Yes. Where a purchaser has been deceived by the unauthorized and fraudulent representations of a real estate agent, he may set up a defense of recoupment for such representations in a vendor's action for the land's purchase price if he alleges and proves that the vendor, after knowledge of such representations and an offer of rescission on that ground by the purchaser, refused to accept the rescission. This rule is consistent with the line of persuasive authority that does not allow a real estate agent to bind his principal by representations the former makes in regard to land quality and value, unless he was expressly authorized to make them, or unless they are known to his principal before the sale is consummated. This is in opposition to the persuasive authority, of English origin, which declares that a real estate agent is impliedly authorized by his principal to make representations in regard to land quality and value, and that the principal is bound by them as though he had himself made them. However, since this is a matter of first impression in this jurisdiction, the court is at liberty to adopt the rule which seems best in consonance with the jurisdiction's general practice, conditions and public policy. In this regard, the former line of authority appears the soundest because it avoids the unfortunate circumstances of an owner being bound by fraudulent representations that are entirely unknown to him and he would have repudiated, had they been called to his attention. Here, there is no evidence that any false representations were communicated to Chandler (P), or, even if they were, there is no evidence that Chandler (P) authorized its real estate agent to make them. Furthermore, there is no evidence of any offer of rescission on the ground of fraud. Although it is true that an officer for Light (D) asked Chandler (P) to take

Continued on next page.

the land back, he expressly stated that his reason for asking was that the land was unproductive, and that Light (D) could not make payments thereon. As a result, to allow recoupment under such circumstances would, in effect, be compelling an innocent owner of land to sell it against his will on terms to which he never agreed. Here, Chandler (P), as a matter of law, is not vicariously liable for its real estate broker's actions. Affirmed.

ANALYSIS

The *Light* case was cited with approval in *Jerger v. Rubin*, 106 Ariz. 114 (1970), a unanimous en banc decision. However, the court added one point to the ratification analysis in the *Light* opinion, noting that a principal who insists on a contract after being informed of his agent's fraud is not deemed to have ratified it, if he had changed his position in good faith prior to being informed of the fraud, citing the Restatement § 99.

Leafgreen v. American Family Mutual Insurance Co.

Victim of burglary (P) v. Insurance agent's employer (D)

S.D. Sup. Ct., 393 N.W.2d 275 (1986).

NATURE OF CASE: Appeal from summary judgment in vicarious liability action for damages.

FACT SUMMARY: Ardnt, an American Family Mutual Insurance Co. (D) insurance agent, while purportedly performing his agent duties, aided burglars in burglarizing the Leafgreen (P) home, and at the Leafgreen (P) trial, where they contended that American Family (D) was vicariously liable for the damages they suffered, the court granted American Family's (D) motion for summary judgment.

RULE OF LAW

A principal is vicariously liable for tortious harm caused by his agent where a nexus sufficient to make the harm foreseeable exists between the agent's employment and the activity which caused the harm.

FACTS: Ardnt, an American Family Mutual Insurance Co. (D) insurance agent, went to the Leafgreen (P) residence for the apparent purpose of correcting lot descriptions and writing liability insurance for them. Five weeks later, while the Leafgreens (P) were away on a trip, this residence was burglarized by two professional burglars for whom Ardnt had actually been inspecting the place during his previous visit with the Leafgreens (P). After Ardnt was convicted of second-degree burglary, the Leafgreens (P) filed a complaint against American Family (D) for damages, alleging that since American Family (D) placed Ardnt in a position which enabled him, while apparently acting within his authority as an American Family (D) agent, to gain entry and subsequently have their home burglarized, then American Family (D) should be held vicariously liable for Ardnt's actions. On the other hand, American Family (D) filed a motion for summary judgment, contending that it was entitled to judgment as a matter of law because Ardnt was not acting within the scope of his employment when he conspired to burglarize the Leafgreens' (P) home. In agreement with American Family (D), the trial court granted summary judgment in its favor on the issue of vicarious liability, stating that Ardnt's tortious acts were not reasonably foreseeable by American Family (D), and, consequently, it would be inequitable to impute Ardnt's conduct to the company. The Leafgreens (P) appealed.

ISSUE: Is a principal vicariously liable for tortious harm caused by his agent where a nexus sufficient to make the harm foreseeable exists between the agent's employment and the activity which actually caused the harm?

HOLDING AND DECISION: (Wuest, J.) Yes. A principal is vicariously liable for tortious harm caused by his agent where a nexus sufficient to make the harm foreseeable exists between the agent's employment and the activity which caused them harm. This rule is consistent with Restatement (Second) of Agency § 261, which, in effect, provides that a principal may be held liable for fraud and deceit committed by an agent within his apparent authority, even though the agent acts solely to benefit himself. However, a principal's vicarious liability for his agent's conduct is not limitless. There are boundaries to be drawn. In connection with this, the Louisiana Court of Appeal, in *Lou-Con Inc. v. Gulf Building Services, Inc.*, 287 So.2d 192 (La. App. 1973), reasoned that under the facts of the case, § 261 must be read in connection with § 231 of the Restatement. Comment a of this latter section provides, in important part, that in determining whether an agent's act is within the scope of his employment, the principal is "not responsible for acts which are clearly inappropriate to or unforeseeable in the accomplishment of the authorized result." That is, where an agent's conduct appears so substantially different from what he was authorized to do, this conduct will not be viewed as within the scope of his employment, and his principal will not be held vicariously liable for it. Hence, § 231 imports an element of foreseeability which helped to delineate the limits of liability under the doctrine of respondeat superior for acts done within the scope of an agent's apparent authority. In the instant case, there is not a sufficient connection between Ardnt's employment as an American Family (D) insurance agent and the burglary, which caused harm to the Leafgreens (P), as to make the harm foreseeable. First, the burglary occurred five weeks after Ardnt used his employment with American Family (D) as a subterfuge to enter the Leafgreen (P) home and gather information used in the burglary. Thus, it appears the burglary was not incidental to his employment. Second, Ardnt learned that the Leafgreens (P) would be out of town the day of the burglary through his friendship with them and not because of his status as an America Family (D) insurance agent. Hence, the trial court's summary judgment in favor of American Family (D) on the issue of the foreseeability of Ardnt's actions was correct. As a result, American Family (D) is not vicariously liable for Ardnt's action. Affirmed.

DISSENT: (Henderson, J.) The Leafgreens (P) are entitled to a jury trial on the question as to whether Ardnt's actions were sufficiently foreseeable to American Family

Continued on next page.

(D) as to warrant holding the latter vicariously liable for them.

DISSENT: (Sabers, J.) American Family (D) may have been negligent in failing to obtain sufficient information about Ardnt's character and conduct before the former gave him authority to enter the dwellings of others.

ANALYSIS

In some circumstances, a defrauded person can lose his claim if he has not acted reasonably. Although the descriptive label "contributory negligence" is rejected when dealing with an intentional tort, nevertheless the defrauded person is not able to hold the principal liable if he "should know or otherwise has notice that an agent is acting for his own purposes or is otherwise violating his authority." Restatement of Agency § 262, Comment C.

Eamoe v. Big Bear Land & Water Co.

Purchaser of land (P) v. Land company (D)

Cal. Ct. App., 98 Cal. App. 2d 370, 220 P.2d 408 (1950).

NATURE OF CASE: Appeal from summary judgment denying damages for vicarious liability.

FACT SUMMARY: Two agents for Big Bear Land & Water Co. (D) negligently permitted Eamoe (P) to purchase lots not owned by Big Bear (D), and Eamoe's (P) suit for damages against Big Bear (D), charging the latter with vicarious liability for its agents' negligent conduct, was dismissed for failing to state a cause of action.

RULE OF LAW

Despite a disclaimer clause to the contrary, where an agent, who has been vested with full power by his principal to handle the latter's affairs, performs an unauthorized act when dealing with a third party, vicarious liability extends to his principal for any harm to the third party caused by his actions.

FACTS: Blacksaw and Lichtig, agents for Big Bear Land & Water Co. (D), a land and water company, negligently permitted Eamoe (P) to purchase lots not owned by Big Bear (D). During Eamoe's (P) interaction with these agents, he made a deposit on the land and received a receipt describing the lots he purchased as opposed to the ones he intended to purchase. At the same time, Eamoe (P) signed a contract of sale in blank, which Big Bear (D) was supposed to fill in and mail to him. Subsequently, this contract was executed by Big Bear (D) and mailed to Eamoe (P), but it contained no description of the lots he purchased. Sometime later, Eamoe (P) commenced building on the lots he purchased. However, after discovering that the lots he purchased were not the ones he intended to purchase, and the lot's true owners demanded that he remove his structure, Eamoe (P) brought this suit for damages against Big Bear (D), contending that the latter was vicariously liable for its agent's fraudulent and negligent representations which caused him $5,000 in damages for having to relocate his structure to the lots he intended to purchase. On the other hand, Big Bear (D) moved for summary judgment on the grounds that since it had an exculpatory provision in the contract that it mailed to Eamoe (P), which in effect, protected it against vicarious liability for its agents' fraudulent representations that might induce a purchaser to buy land, then Eamoe (P) has failed to state a cause of action against it. The lower court, agreeing with Big Bear (D), granted this motion. Eamoe (P) appealed.

ISSUE: Where an agent, who has been vested with full power by his principal to handle the latter's affairs, performs an unauthorized act when dealing with a third party, does vicariously liability extend to his principal for any harm to the third party caused by his actions, despite a disclaimer clause to the contrary?

HOLDING AND DECISION: (White, J.) Yes. Despite a disclaimer clause to the contrary, where an agent, who has been vested with full power by his principal to handle the latter's affairs, performs an unauthorized act when dealing with a third party, vicarious liability extends to his principal for any harm to the third party caused by his actions. This rule would appear to run counter to the rule laid down in *Speck v. Wylie*, 1 Cal. 2d 625, where the court declared that a principal may not protect himself from liability for damages arising from unauthorized fraudulent . . . representations of his agent, by means of an exculpatory provision. However, the purpose of such a provision is to protect an innocent principal against liability for statements of an agent beyond the scope of his actual authority by notifying a third party of the limits of the agent's authority. Here, on the other hand, the selling agents were acting within the scope of their ostensible authority when they negligently sold Eamoe (P) lots on a different block than what the latter wanted. This is so, despite the provision, because the agents appeared to be acting within their scope of authority when they exhibited and sold property of Big Bear (D) to Eamoe (P), discerned which property belonged to Big Bear (D) and which did not, and issued a receipt to Eamoe (P), after the sale, purportedly containing the correct description of the property displayed. Furthermore, it may be assumed that Big Bear (D) relied on its agents to correctly describe the property, since it executed and sent to Eamoe (P) a contract containing no description of the property its agent sold to Eamoe (P). Aside from this, the fact that Big Bear (D), in effect, vested its agent with authority which, through the negligence or mistaken confidence, it has allowed to be vested in the agents with whom Eamoe (P) was dealing. Hence, there are genuine issues as to the existence of Big Bear's (D) vicarious liability. Reversed and remanded.

ANALYSIS

Restatement (Second) of Agency § 27 stipulates that "apparent authority to do an act is created as to a third person by written or spoken words or any other conduct of the principal which, reasonably interpreted, causes the third person to believe that the principal consents to have the act done on his behalf by the person purporting to act for him." In the instant case, Eamoe's (P) belief that the "principal consents" to the acts of the agents he dealt with,

Continued on next page.

which incidentally were negligent, may rest on the autonomy with which Big Bear (D) gave them to carry out its duties. However, the reasonability of Eamoe's (P) belief may be at issue, especially considering the readily available contract of sale which included a disclaimer clause limiting Big Bear's (D) liability.

Dembowski v. Central Construction Co.

Home owner (P) v. Construction company (D)

Neb. Sup. Ct., 186 Neb. 624, 185 N.W.2d 461 (1971).

NATURE OF CASE: Appeal from reformation of a contract.

FACT SUMMARY: Dembowski (P) allowed Central Construction Co. (D) to install new aluminum doors, windows, and sidings in his home, based on the false claims of a salesperson that future commissions derived from use of Dembowski's (P) home as a showroom would fully cover the purchase price.

RULE OF LAW

A contract with a principal obtained by the agent's fraud will not be rescinded once the principal has performed or changed his position under the contract.

FACTS: Central Construction Co. (D) sold materials and furnished labor for home improvement. Dembowski (P) signed a contract with Central Construction (D) for the installation of new aluminum sidings, windows, and doors, based on the claims of a salesperson that Dembowski's (P) house would be used as a "model home" and that commissions derived from showings would be credited to fully cover the purchase price. The contract between Central Construction (D) and Dembowski (P), however, contained a clause stating that no agent of Central Construction (D) was authorized to agree to use of the purchaser's home as a "model" or to make representations concerning application of commissions for referral of future customers. Central Construction (D) had no knowledge of its agent's misrepresentations until after the materials and labor called for in the contract with Dembowski (P) had been furnished. At that time it refused to honor its agent's promise that future commissions would be applied toward Dembowski's (P) purchase price. Dembowski (P) sued in equity to reform the contract to omit the clause Central Construction (D) relied on in denying commissions, and the lower court so reformed the contract. Central Construction (D) appealed.

ISSUE: If a principal has performed or changed his position under a contract obtained by his agent's fraud, may the contract be rescinded?

HOLDING AND DECISION: (Newton, J.) No. A contract with, or a conveyance to, the principal obtained by his agent through misrepresentation can be rescinded by the other party to the conveyance or contract only prior to change of position by the principal. Here, Central Construction (D) did not know of its salesman's fraud until after the contract had been signed and fully performed. Therefore, rescission here will be denied. Further, Dembowski's (P) notice that Central Construction's (D) agent's authority was limited (the disclaimer clause) prevents subjecting Central Construction (D) to liability. Reversed and remanded with directions.

DISSENT: (Spencer. J.) This case has virtually the same facts as a previous one in which this court allowed introduction of parol evidence of fraud and reformed the contract.

ANALYSIS

Similarly, a principal who has been deceived (such as by an exaggeration of qualifications or abilities) into granting an agent authority, must revoke this authority prior to any transactions by the agent with third parties. Otherwise, the principal may be bound by contracts entered into under the grant of authority and will only have recourse to a lawsuit for damages against the fraudulent agent.

King v. Horizon Corp.

Purchaser of land (P) v. Lot developer (D)

701 F.2d 1313 (10th Cir. 1983).

NATURE OF CASE: Appeal from judgment against defendant for deceit.

FACT SUMMARY: The Kings (P) "traded up" property they had bought from Horizon Corp. (D) for new property Horizon's (D) agent stated was worth $75,700 but in fact had only an $8,300 value.

RULE OF LAW

If a principal knows of his agent's fraud yet accepts the fruits thereof, he has ratified his agent's conduct and will himself be liable for fraud.

FACTS: The Kings (P) bought single-family lots from Horizon Corp. (D), which on nine previous occasions they had "traded up" for more expensive units offered by Horizon (D). On the tenth such transaction, Horizon's (D) salesman falsely stated that the property to be acquired had a $75,700 value, when in fact it was worth only $8,300. The Kings (P), wined and dined by Horizon (D), did not read the sales contract which contained a clause disclaiming reliance on representations by Horizon (D). When the Kings (P) discovered the true value of the land, they sued Horizon (D) for fraud and won. An FTC proceeding before an administrative law judge also found Horizon (D) guilty of a pattern and course of fraudulent and deceptive conduct.

ISSUE: If a principal knows of his agent's fraud and accepts the fruits thereof, has he ratified his agent's conduct such that he himself will be liable for the fraud?

HOLDING AND DECISION: (Anderson, J.) Yes. If a principal accepts the fruits of a fraud with knowledge of the misrepresentations by which the fraud was accomplished, he has ratified the fraudulent act and will be liable for it. This is an exception to the general rule that a purchaser cannot rely on the oral representations of an agent of the seller where the seller has included a written disclaimer in the contract that the purchaser has negligently failed to read. Here Horizon (D) knew its agents were engaging in misrepresentation, yet it failed to stop the fraud and in fact accepted the sales procured thereby. Further, Horizon (D) exercised inadequate supervision over its agents, allowing them to commit fraud which could have been prevented. Affirmed.

ANALYSIS

For an act of an agent to be ratified, the agent must have intended to act on behalf of the principal, rather than on behalf of himself or a third party. Further, the agent's wrongful act must have resulted in a tangible benefit to the principal and must be accepted or retained by the principal with knowledge of all the relevant facts. Finally, failure to fire an employee or agent who commits fraud constitutes only slight, not conclusive, evidence of ratification.

CHAPTER 6

The Undisclosed Principal

Quick Reference Rules of Law

PAGE

1. **Exceptions.** Where an agent fraudulently represents to a third party that he is contracting on his own behalf and thus conceals the identity of his principal, the third party may rescind the contract. (Kelly Asphalt Block Co. v. Barber Asphalt Paving Co.) *86*

2. **Exceptions.** An informed vendee must limit himself to silence in order to escape the imputation of fraud only in cases where the misrepresentation or concealment was material. (Finley v. Dalton) *87*

3. **Unauthorized Transactions.** A principal is liable for all the acts of his agent which are usually confided in an agent of that character and necessary to carry on the business authorized. (Watteau v. Fenwick) *88*

4. **Unauthorized Transactions.** An undisclosed principal who entrusts an agent with managing his business will be liable to third parties who enter into transactions usual in such businesses with the agent on the principal's account, even if the transaction was contrary to the principal's directions. (Senor v. Bangor Mills) *89*

5. **Payment and Setoff: Setoff.** If an agent is authorized only to contract in the principal's name, the other party does not have a set-off for a claim due him from that agent unless the agent has been entrusted with possession of chattels which he disposes of as directed or unless the principal has otherwise misled the third person into extending credit to the agent. (Oil Supply Company, Inc. v. Hires Parts Service, Inc.) *90*

Kelly Asphalt Block Co. v. Barber Asphalt Paving Co.

Asphalt block maker (P) v. Competitor (D)

N.Y. Ct. App., 211 N.Y. 68, 105 N.E. 88 (1914).

NATURE OF CASE: Appeal from judgment for breach of warranty.

FACT SUMMARY: Kelly Asphalt Block Co. (P) wanted to buy asphalt blocks from its competitor Barber Asphalt Paving Co. (D) but feared rejection, so it appointed an agent to buy them for it; the blocks turned out to be defective.

RULE OF LAW

Where an agent fraudulently represents to a third party that he is contracting on his own behalf and thus conceals the identity of his principal, the third party may rescind the contract.

FACTS: Kelly Asphalt Block Co. (P) wanted to purchase asphalt blocks from its competitor Barber Asphalt Paving Co. (D) but feared rejection. It appointed an agent, Booth, who obtained a price and quotation from Barber Asphalt (D), and ordered them in his name. The order was accepted by defendant, the blocks were delivered and paid for by Booth with money from Kelly Asphalt (P). But the blocks were unmerchantable. Barber Asphalt (D) refused to return the purchase price, asserting that it would not have sold them at all if it had known Kelly Asphalt (P) was the true buyer.

ISSUE: Where an agent fraudulently represents to a third party that he is contracting on his own behalf and thus conceals the identity of his principal, may the third party rescind the contract?

HOLDING AND DECISION: (Cardozo, J.) Yes. If one who is in reality an agent denies his agency when questioned, and falsely asserts that his principal has no interest in the transaction, the contract entered into between the agent and the third party, becomes voidable. This is merely a variety of avoidance of contract due to fraud. Here, however, Booth made no affirmative misrepresentation. He was not asked anything, nor did he say anything, about Kelly Asphalt's (P) interest in the purchase. Therefore Barber Asphalt (D) has no right to rescind. Affirmed.

ANALYSIS

The comments to the Restatement of Agency 304 would also allow rescission in the event of mere nondisclosure by the agent that the principal was involved, if the undisclosed principal and the agent both knew the third party would not deal with the principal directly. The Restatement would also preclude enforcement by the undisclosed principal of a contract with a third party if the contract refers to the agent as the principal or indicates that the agent is the only contracting party. See Restatement §§ 150, 189.

Finley v. Dalton

Seller of land (P) v. Buyer of land (D)

S.C. Sup. Ct., 164 S.E.2d 763 (1968).

NATURE OF CASE: Appeal from an order of the lower court sustaining a demurrer to a complaint in equity seeking rescission of a real estate deed.

FACT SUMMARY: Finley (P) sued Dalton (D), the buyer of his land, for fraudulently misrepresenting the purpose for which he wanted the land.

RULE OF LAW

An informed vendee must limit himself to silence in order to escape the imputation of fraud only in cases where the misrepresentation or concealment was material.

FACTS: Dalton (D), who was the undisclosed real estate acquisition agent for the Duke Power Company (D), told Finley (P) that he wanted to purchase 183 acres of Finley's (P) property for his own use. However, Duke Power (D) actually wanted to build a large hydroelectric power plant on the property. Fifteen months after the sale, Finley (P) attempted to rescind the deed, but Dalton (D) refused. Three years later, Finley (P) sued Dalton (D) on the grounds that Dalton (D) had misrepresented the purposes for which he was buying the land. The trial judge found that the complaint failed to allege facts sufficient to show that the alleged misrepresentation or concealment was material, or that it had served to induce Finley (P) to sell. Finley (P) appealed from the judgment of the lower court sustaining a demurrer to his complaint.

ISSUE: Must an informed vendee always limit himself to silence in order to escape the imputation of fraud?

HOLDING AND DECISION: (Lewis, J.) No. An informed vendee must limit himself to silence in order to escape the imputation of fraud only in cases where the misrepresentation or concealment was material. In this case, Dalton's (D) false representation as to the purposes for which the land was purchased was not a representation as to the value of the land and in no way operated as an inducement to Finley (P) to sell. The misrepresentation was not material, but was made merely because Finley (P) would have demanded more money if Dalton (D) had revealed that the land was being acquired for Duke Power Company (D) for its planned hydroelectric project. Affirmed.

ANALYSIS

A third party is not bound to an agreement made with an agent who falsely states that he is not acting for a principal if the misrepresentation is material. Likewise, if an agent is expressly mentioned in the contract as the principal, the undisclosed principal cannot later enforce the contract. Nor can he enforce it if the agent is unaware of the falsity of his representations.

Watteau v. Fenwick

Seller (P) v. Owner of alehouse (D)

Queen's Bench Div., 1 Q.B. 346 (1893).

NATURE OF CASE: Appeal from award of damages for failure to pay price of goods delivered.

FACT SUMMARY: Fenwick (D) purchased a beerhouse named Victoria Hotel from Humble who, after being retained as manager but authorized only to buy bottled ales and mineral waters, bought cigars from Watteau (P).

RULE OF LAW

A principal is liable for all the acts of his agent which are usually confided in an agent of that character and necessary to carry on the business authorized.

FACTS: Fenwick (D), a brewing company, bought a beerhouse named Victoria Hotel from Humble. Fenwick (D) retained Humble as its manager for the purchase of bottled ales and mineral waters. Humble had no authority to buy anything else. The license for Victoria Hotel was taken out in Humble's name, and Humble's name appeared painted above the door. Humble went ahead and bought cigars, bovril and other articles for Victoria Hotel on credit from Watteau (P). Fenwick (D) refused to pay for these goods because they were unauthorized. The county court judge entered judgment for Watteau (P) against Fenwick (D).

ISSUE: Is a principal liable for all acts of his agent which are usually confided in an agent of that character and necessary to carry on the business authorized?

HOLDING AND DECISION: (Wills, J.) Yes. A principal is liable for all the acts of the agent which are within the authority usually confided to an agent of that character, notwithstanding limitations, as between the principal and the agent, put upon that authority. Here, Fenwick (D) was an undisclosed principal; it was not held out to Watteau (P) as responsible for the acts of Humble. Watteau (P) had never heard of Fenwick (D) and had dealt only with Humble, and the items purchased by Humble for Victoria Hotel were such as would usually be supplied to and dealt in at a beerhouse. Therefore, Humble was acting within the reasonable scope of his authority, and Fenwick (D) was liable for Watteau's (P) claim for the cigars and bovril. Appeal dismissed.

ANALYSIS

The holding of this case finds expression in the Restatement of Agency § 194 as this rule: "A general agent for an undisclosed principal authorized to conduct transactions subjects his principal to liability for acts done on his account, if usual or necessary in such transactions, although forbidden by the principal to do them." Although this rule has found widespread acceptance, it certainly runs counter to the expectations of the third party who contracted with the agent; the third party is not aware that an agency even exists, or that he was contracting with anyone other than the agent himself. Nevertheless, courts have refused to afford the undisclosed principal a complete defense on these grounds and allowed the third party to sue only the agent, perhaps because the principal, even if undisclosed, is obviously in a position to control the acts of his agents, and because he benefits from the authorized acts and therefore should be held accountable for the unauthorized ones.

Senor v. Bangor Mills

Seller of yarn (P) v. Purchaser (D)

211 F.2d 685 (3d Cir. 1954).

NATURE OF CASE: Appeal from denial of damages for breach of sales contract.

FACT SUMMARY: Bangor Mills (D) hired an agent to buy nylon yarn for it in the secondary market for $10 per pound; the agent obtained 1,250 pounds from Senor (P) at $11 per pound, which he resold to Bangor Mills (D) for $10 per pound.

RULE OF LAW

An undisclosed principal who entrusts an agent with managing his business will be liable to third parties who enter into transactions usual in such businesses with the agent on the principal's account, even if the transaction was contrary to the principal's directions.

FACTS: Bangor Mills (D) made tricot from nylon yarn, which was in short supply. It made large purchases of yarn in the secondary market but encountered price gouging due to its vulnerable market position. To avoid this artificial inflation, Bangor Mills (D) hired an intermediary, Shetzline, who would keep the identity of Bangor Mills (D) a secret while buying yarn in the secondary market. Shetzline was given a joint bank account with Bangor Mills (D) to use in paying cash for his purchases. He was to pay $10 per pound and to get prior consent to any purchases; however, he was free to buy as much as he wanted on his account for resale to other manufacturers. Shetzline bought 1,250 pounds at $11.35 per pound from Senor (P), which he passed through a dummy corporation, Park Lane, and re-invoiced to make it appear to Bangor Mills (D) that he had paid only $10 per pound. Shetzline's check to Senor (P) from Park Lane, drawn on his joint account with Bangor Mills (D), bounced. Senor (P) sued Bangor Mills (D) to recover his balance with Shetzline and Park Lane, lost in the district court, and appealed.

ISSUE: Will an undisclosed principal who entrusts an agent with managing his business be liable to third parties who enter into transactions usual in such businesses with the agent on the principal's account, even if the transaction was contrary to the principal's directions?

HOLDING AND DECISION: (Hastie, J.) Yes. An undisclosed principal who entrusts his agent with managing his business will be liable to third parties who enter into transactions usual in such businesses with the agent on the principal's account, even if the transaction was contrary to the principal's directions. However, cases in which the undisclosed principal is liable to third parties typically involve going concerns with established places of business operated by an ostensible proprietor who is actually an agent for a principal. Here, Bangor Mills (D) has not placed Shetzline in a deceptive position as the apparent proprietor of a "business" and, therefore, is not liable as an undisclosed principal. Further, Shetzline bought yarn from Senor (P) under the terms of his agency with Bangor Mills (D) which allowed him to buy from the secondary market on his own account and resell to other manufacturers if he wished. Because each purchase by Shetzline of yarn required prior consent from Bangor Mills (D), a separate agency was created each time a purchase was made with Bangor Mills' (D) knowledge and approval. Here, however, no agency arose at all because Shetzline bought Senor's (P) yarn without checking with Bangor Mills (D) first. Affirmed.

ANALYSIS

Another case involving the same defendant held that the agent authorized to deal only in cash did not have the power to bind the principal to a credit sale. See *Industrial Manufacturers, Inc. v. Bangor Mills, Inc.*, 283 App. Div. 113, 126 N.Y.S.2d 508 (1953). Cases such as these involving an undisclosed principal turn almost entirely on the intent of the agent. The fact that the existence of the agency suggested or created the opportunity for the agent's act is insufficient to bind the undisclosed principal; even if the agent's motive is improper, it is the agent's intent to act within the furtherance of the principal's business that binds the principal. As an example, the casebook author notes that an undisclosed principal would still be bound to unhappy vendees who purchased substandard goods deliberately sold by a malicious agent who merely disliked his principal and wanted to give him a bad reputation.

Oil Supply Company, Inc. v. Hires Parts Service, Inc.

Chattel owner (P) v. Chattel holder (D)

Ind. Sup. Ct., 726 N.E.2d 246 (2000).

NATURE OF CASE: Appeal from defense judgment in suit for return of property or damages for its value.

FACT SUMMARY: When Oil Supply Company, Inc. (P) sued Hires Parts Service, Inc. (D) for the value of Oil Supply's (P) antifreeze which Oil Supply's (P) agent (William Dolin) fraudulently delivered to Hires (D) as his own to relieve a personal debt to Hires (D), Hires (D) attempted to have the amount of the debt set-off against the value of the antifreeze.

RULE OF LAW

If an agent is authorized only to contract in the principal's name, the other party does not have a set-off for a claim due him from that agent unless the agent has been entrusted with possession of chattels which he disposes of as directed or unless the principal has otherwise misled the third person into extending credit to the agent.

FACTS: William Dolin (a commodities broker) was indebted to Oil Supply Company, Inc. (P). To obtain payment from him, Oil Supply (P) entered into an agreement with Dolin under which Dolin would arrange sales through Oil Supply (P). The profits would be split between Oil Supply (P) and Dolin. Dolin was also indebted to Hires Parts Service, Inc. (Hire) (D). To remedy this debt, Dolin represented to Hires (D) that he had a load of 720 cases of antifreeze that he would ship to Hires (D) in exchange for his debt to Hires (D). The cases were sent and received. Prior to this transaction, Oil Supply (P) and Hires (D) were unaware of each other's existence. Hires (D) has neither paid for nor returned the antifreeze. Oil Supply (P) sued Hires (D) for the cost of the antifreeze. The trial court awarded Oil Supply (P) the value of the antifreeze but set off the debt Dolin owed Hires (D). Oil Supply (P) appealed, and the court of appeals affirmed. Oil Supply (P) again appealed.

ISSUE: If an agent is authorized only to contract in the principal's name, does the other party have a set-off for a claim due him from that agent only if the agent has been entrusted with possession of chattels which he disposes of as directed or the principal has otherwise misled the third person into extending credit to the agent?

HOLDING AND DECISION: (Shepard, C.J.) Yes. If an agent is authorized only to contract in the principal's name, the other party does not have a set-off for a claim due him from that agent unless the agent has been entrusted with possession of chattels which he disposes of as directed or unless the principal has otherwise misled the third person into extending credit to the agent. Principals are generally in a better position to prevent potential fraud by their agents than are buyers. Here, Oil Supply (P) could have prevented this situation by making a confirmation of the sale, or by closer supervision of its agent Dolin. These failings by Oil Supply (P) were neglectful. On the other hand, Hires (D) might just as easily have prevented the defalcation by taking the time to ponder why some company it had never heard of had just deposited a truckload of antifreeze on its doorstep. The principle that between two innocent parties, the loss should be placed upon the party who put the agent out to deal, does not apply if the party seeking refuge in the principle has wittingly or otherwise aided an unscrupulous agent to defraud the principal. Here, because Hires (D) was chargeable with notice of the existence of Oil Supply (P) as Dolin's principal before it accepted the goods, and because Hires (D) had the last opportunity to prevent the loss before the transaction was complete, Hires (D) should bear the loss. Hence, Hires (D) was not entitled to set off its Dolin debt in the lawsuit brought by Oil Supply (P). Accordingly, we affirm the trial court's finding for Oil Supply (P) on the value of its antifreeze, and reverse with respect to the set-off of Dolin's debt.

ANALYSIS

The court in the *Oil Supply* case notes that the burden of an agent's fraud ought usually to be placed on the principal who hired him rather than on a third party stranger to the agency relationship and that the object of agency law should be the deterrence of absconding agents on the theory that "commerce will be facilitated where the law allocates burdens to those best able to thwart the absconders."

CHAPTER 7

Liability of the Agent to Third Persons

Quick Reference Rules of Law

PAGE

1. **Principal Is Unintentionally Undisclosed.** It is a question of fact whether an agent's use of corporate checks in paying corporate obligations provides sufficient notice to the obligee of the corporation's existence such as to absolve the agent of personal liability on the debts. (Jensen v. Alaska Valuation Service) *92*

2. **Principal Is Disclosed: Special Circumstances.** Where an attorney arranges for the services of an expert witness on behalf of a client, the primary responsibility of making it clear to the expert that the attorney acts in an agency capacity with no personal liability rests upon the attorney. (Copp v. Breskin) *93*

3. **Principal Is Partially Disclosed or Unidentified.** Where an agent negotiates a contract in his principal's behalf, and the latter's identity is unknown to the other contracting party, he must give complete information concerning his principal's identity so as to avoid personal liability on the contract. (Van D. Costas, Inc. v. Rosenberg) *94*

4. **Agent's Warranty of Authority.** An agent purporting to contract in his principal's name without or in excess of his authority to do so is personally liable for any damages the other contracting party suffers, unless the agent states that he lacks authority to bind his principal, or the other contracting party otherwise has knowledge that the agent lacks his principal's authority. (Husky Industries v. Craig Industries) *95*

5. **Harm to the Economic Interests of Others.** Where an agent causes pecuniary harm to a person other than his principal, he is not liable for this harm if it resulted from his failure to adequately perform his principal's duties. (Coker v. Dollar) *96*

Jensen v. Alaska Valuation Service

Homebuilder (D) v. Appraiser (P)

Alaska Sup. Ct., 688 P.2d 161 (1984).

NATURE OF CASE: Appeal from award of damages for breach of service contract.

FACT SUMMARY: Alaska Valuation Service (P) was paid for appraisal services provided Jensen (D) by checks drawn on Jensen's (D) newly incorporated business, but Jensen (D) did not officially notify Alaska Valuation (P) of the incorporation until after he was not able to make any further payments.

RULE OF LAW

It is a question of fact whether an agent's use of corporate checks in paying corporate obligations provides sufficient notice to the obligee of the corporation's existence such as to absolve the agent of personal liability on the debts.

FACTS: Jensen (D), a homebuilder, ordered by telephone appraisals from the president of Alaska Valuation Service (P). These appraisals were performed and invoices sent to "Art Jensen, Jensen Builders," which is how Jensen (D) was designated in Alaska Valuation's (P) corporate records. Some, but not all, of these services were paid for by Jensen (D) with checks drawn on his construction business, which had been recently incorporated. Jensen (D) did not inform Alaska Valuation (P) that he had incorporated, however, until after incurring charges he could not pay for. Alaska Valuation (P) sued to collect $823 in past due invoices from Jensen (D) personally, alleging that it had no notice of Jensen's (D) status as an agent of his corporation. Alaska Valuation (P) won in a judgment small claims court against Jensen (D) personally, which was affirmed on appeal. The Alaska Supreme Court accepted the case for review.

ISSUE: Is it a question of fact whether an agent's use of corporate checks in paying corporate obligations provides sufficient notice to the obligee of the corporation's existence such as to absolve the agent of personal liability on the debts?

HOLDING AND DECISION: (Compton, J.) Yes. Although officers of a corporation will not ordinarily be held personally liable for contracts they make as agents of the corporation, they must disclose their agency and the existence of the corporation before they will be absolved from liability. An agent who makes a contract for an undisclosed or partially disclosed principal will be liable as a party to the contract. Whether an agent's use of corporate checks provides sufficient notice of the corporation's existence to release the agent from liability is a matter of fact to be determined by considering all the circumstances in each case. Here, the small claims court's finding that Jensen (D) did not sufficiently disclose his agency was not clearly erroneous. Affirmed.

ANALYSIS

Because the general rule is that an agent for an undisclosed principal is liable as a party to the contract, in fulfillment of the expectations of the third party, the agent must bear the burden of proof that the principal was disclosed and that the parties intended not to impose personal liability on the agent. See, e.g., *Moore v. Seabaugh*, 684 S.W. 2d 492, 495 (Mo. App. 1984). Sometimes the effect of this rule can be rather drastic. For example, in *Ingram v. Lupo*, 726 S.W. 2d 791 (Mo. App. 1987), an attorney was held liable to a court reporter for the cost of preparation and delivery of a trial transcript, despite the fact that the reporter knew the identity of the specific client on whose behalf the transcript had been ordered. In fact, the court held the attorney liable not as an agent, but as a principal, and opined that the attorney could only have escaped responsibility for the ordering of the transcript.

Copp v. Breskin

Expert witness (P) v. Law firm (D)

Wash. Ct. App., 782 P.2d 1104 (1989).

NATURE OF CASE: Appeal from grant of summary judgment in favor of plaintiff in an action to recover fees for expert services.

FACT SUMMARY: When a client, for whom the law firm of Breskin & Robbins (D) had obtained Copp's (P) services as an expert witness, was unwilling to pay all of Copp's (P) fees, Breskin & Robbins (D) refused to make up the difference, contending that it had hired Copp (P) as agent of a disclosed principal, the client.

RULE OF LAW

Where an attorney arranges for the services of an expert witness on behalf of a client, the primary responsibility of making it clear to the expert that the attorney acts in an agency capacity with no personal liability rests upon the attorney.

FACTS: After the law firm of Breskin & Robbins (D) arranged to hire Copp (P) as an expert witness, it advised him that his fees were to be paid by the client. After trial, Copp (P) submitted a final bill, asking for payment within thirty days, as previously agreed. Because the client was willing to pay only 30% of the bill, Breskin & Robbins (D) offered to litigate on Copp's (P) behalf. Copp (P) filed this action against Breskin & Robbins (D), which admitted the amount owed but asserted that, in hiring Copp (P), it had acted as the agent of the client. The district court granted summary judgment to Copp (P) and awarded him the fees for his expert services. Breskin & Robbins (D) appealed.

ISSUE: Where an attorney arranges for the services of an expert witness on behalf of a client, does the primary responsibility of making it clear to the expert that the attorney acts in an agency capacity with no personal liability rest upon the attorney?

HOLDING AND DECISION: (Webster, J.) Yes. Where an attorney arranges for the services of an expert witness on behalf of a client, the primary responsibility of making it clear to the expert that the attorney acts in an agency capacity with no personal liability rests upon the attorney. When the circumstances indicate a probable intention that is contrary to the general rule, it should be modified to reflect this fact. A litigation service provider reasonably expects that the attorney will be responsible for his fees as surety or guarantor of the client's performance. Copp (P) relied upon a custom whereby experts look to attorneys for payment of their fees. Breskin & Robbins (D) was aware of an identical custom locally. Thus, under these circumstances, it was insufficient as a matter of law to apprise Copp (P) of a change from customary practice. Affirmed.

ANALYSIS

While other jurisdictions are split as to whether an attorney is responsible to an expert in the absence of a disclaimer, the clear trend is to hold the attorney liable. Putting the burden on the attorney promotes public trust and confidence in the legal profession, the supervision of which is the exclusive province and responsibility of the courts. Public trust in the profession and the courts would be greatly endangered and jeopardized by a technical defense of disclosed agency.

Van D. Costas, Inc. v. Rosenberg

Remodeler (P) v. Part owner of restaurant (D)

Fla. Dist. Ct. App., 432 So. 2d 656 (1983).

NATURE OF CASE: Appeal from denial of damages for mechanic's lien foreclosure and breach of contract.

FACT SUMMARY: In Costas' (P) mechanic's lien foreclosure and a breach of contract suit for damages against Rosenberg (D), the president of Seascape Restaurants, Inc., the trial court found that Rosenberg's (D) name and his restaurant's affiliate's name appearing on the contract was not enough to hold him individually liable for its breach.

RULE OF LAW

Where an agent negotiates a contract in his principal's behalf, and the latter's identity is unknown to the other contracting party, he must give complete information concerning his principal's identity so as to avoid personal liability on the contract.

FACTS: Rosenberg (D), president and 1/3 owner of Seascape Restaurants, Inc., of which the Magic Moment Restaurant was its affiliate and trade name, entered into a contract with Costas (P) to remodel the Magic Moment's entrance. Rosenberg (D) signed this contract on a line under which appeared "Jeff Rosenberg, The Magic Moment." After the work commenced, the parties became involved in a dispute over performance and payment, and Costas (P), as a result, filed a suit for mechanic's lien foreclosure and breach of contract against Rosenburg (D), which, in effect, sought to hold Rosenberg (D) individually liable for the contract's breach. However, the trial court denied Costas (P) his sought-after remedy, stating, in its final judgment, that under the circumstances, there was no individual responsibility because the proper party to the suit was Seascape Restaurants, Inc., the corporate owner of the Magic Moment Restaurant. Costas (P) appealed.

ISSUE: Where an agent negotiates a contract in his principal's behalf, and the latter's identity is unknown to the other contracting party, must the agent give complete information concerning his principal's identity in order to avoid personal liability on the contract?

HOLDING AND DECISION: (Grimes, J.) Yes. Where an agent negotiates a contract in his principal's behalf, and the latter's identity is unknown to the other contracting party, he must give complete information concerning his principal's identity so as to avoid personal liability on the contract. This rule is consistent with the line of persuasive authority that imposes a burden on an agent to adequately disclose his principal's identity to avoid personal liability. In this respect, Restatement (Second) of Agency § 321 (1957) states, in summary, that the law assumes an agent is a party to a contract unless his principal's identity can be readily distinguished. Moreover, in those instances when an agent uses a trade name as a means of distinguishing his principal's identity from his, the annotator at ISO A.L.R. 1303 (1944) notes that this is insufficient to eliminate the agent's liability. Hence, absent evidence that the other contracting party knows, or should know, the identity of the principal, an agent must disclose more than a mere trade name in a contract he is negotiating in his principal's behalf to avoid personal liability. In the instant case, there is no evidence that Costas (P) knew, or should have known, the identity of Rosenberg's (D) principal when the former signed the contract. Furthermore, the fact that Rosenberg (D) signed his name on a line under which appeared "The Magic Moment" (Seascape's trade name) on the contract he negotiated in Seascape's behalf is insufficient to eliminate his liability. Reversed and remanded.

ANALYSIS

Where an agent signs a contract in a manner clearly indicating his agency status, but the signature leaves the identity of his principal, which can be discovered through public registration procedures, undisclosed, courts have split on whether to hold the agent personally liable. One line of authority is reflected in *Mayer v. Buchanan*, 50 A.2d 595 (D.C. Mun. App. 1946), in which a rental agent signed a lease "A, as agent for the owner only." Although the agent argued that the owner's identity was a matter of public record under the building's address, the court held him personally liable for collecting rent in excess of rent control ceilings. The other line of authority is reflected in *Instituto Cubano v. The S.S. Theotakos*, 155 F. Supp 945 (S.D.N.Y. 1957), in which a shipping agent signed a contract "Transworld Marine Transport Corp., As Agents for Owners of the good ship Theotokos." The court did not find the agent personally liable, relying on the fact that the name of the ship's owner could be learned by checking a shipping Index.

Husky Industries v. Craig Industries

Intended buyer of manufacturing plant (P) v. Seller of plant (D)

Mo. Ct. App., 618 S.W.2d 458 (1981).

NATURE OF CASE: Appeal from award of damages for misrepresentation in a contract of sale.

FACT SUMMARY: In Husky Industries' (P) suit for damages against Craig (D), an agent for Craig Industries (D), the trial court found that Craig (D) misrepresented his authority to contractually bind Craig Industries (D) when he tried to sell the latter's manufacturing plant to Husky Industries (P), and the court awarded Husky Industries (P) $14,400 in damages as a result.

RULE OF LAW

An agent purporting to contract in his principal's name without or in excess of his authority to do so is personally liable for any damages the other contracting party suffers, unless the agent states that he lacks authority to bind his principal, or the other contracting party otherwise has knowledge that the agent lacks his principal's authority.

FACTS: Craig (D), an agent for Craig Industries (D), contracted with Gideon, an agent for Husky Industries (P), to sell one of the former corporation's charcoal manufacturing plants. During the contracting process, Craig (D) indicated that he did not personally own the property to be sold. Subsequently, "D.C. Craig, President" (D) signed the contract, in which "Craig Industries, Inc." (D) was inserted as the seller, on the corporation's behalf, and Gideon gave Craig (D) a $25,000 check as down payment on the transaction. Sometime later, the attorneys for Craig Industries (D) wrote Husky Industries' (P) attorney and stipulated that the former Corporation's board of directors decided to reject the latter's "offer" to purchase the plant, and Gideon's uncashed check was returned with the letter. As a result, Husky Industries (P) commenced this suit against Craig Industries (D) and Craig (D), seeking specific performance of the contract by the former, or damages for its breach, and seeking damages against the latter because, as contended, Craig (D) misrepresented his authority to bind contractually Craig Industries (D) to sell the plant. The trial court rendered a judgment in favor of Craig Industries (D), but found Craig (D) personally liable to Husky Industries (P) for damages in the sum of $14,400. Craig (D) appealed.

ISSUE: Is an agent purporting to contract in his principal's name without or in excess of his authority to do so personally liable for any damages the other contracting party suffers, whether or not the agent states that he lacks authority to bind his principal, or the other contracting party has knowledge that the agent lacks his principal authority?

HOLDING AND DECISION: (Titus, J.) No. An agent purporting to contract in his principal's name or in excess of his authority to do so is personally liable for any damages the other contracting party suffers, unless the agent states that he lacks his principal's authority. Liability under this rule is predicated upon the agent's breach of the express or implied covenant or warranty of authority. Moreover, the agent is personally liable for this breach even if he acts in the utmost good faith and honesty believes he has the principal's authorization. Liability results here because, as Restatement § 329, Comment a, in effect, points out, the other party to a contract, in which an agent purports to make a contract for his principal, may reasonably assume that the agent has the power to bind his principal when he lacks knowledge to the contrary. Hence, liability emerges from the mere fact that the agent in fact does not have the authority the Restatement implies he has as a result of the other contracting party's reasonable assumption. Furthermore, any damages the other contracting party suffers from the agent's breach should justly and properly be born by the latter. In the instant case, there is no evidence that Craig (D) expressly indicated that he possessed, or did not possess, authority to make an agreement to bind Craig Industries (D). Furthermore, there is no evidence that Gideon or Husky Industries' (D) attorney knew, or should heave known, of any limitation on Craig's (D) ostensible authority to contractually bind Craig Industries (D). As a result, since there is no evidence that the trial court's findings that Craig (D) had no authority, that Husky Industries (P) was unaware of this fact, and that Husky Industries (P) suffered damages as a result of Craig's (D) breach of implied warranty of authority are clearly erroneous, then Craig (D) is liable for the damages Husky Industries (P) suffered. Affirmed.

ANALYSIS

Liability stems in the above circumstances because the law entitles a third party to reasonably presume that an agent has the authority that he purports to have. However, as restatement (Second) of Agency § 125 states, this reasonable presumption acquiesces when the third party has notice of (1) termination of the agent's authority; (2) a manifestation by the principal that he no longer consents; or (3) the failure to reveal, which, were the transaction with the principal in person, would be grounds for rescission by the principal.

Coker v. Dollar

Agent (D) v. Injured party (P)

846 F.2d 1302 (11th Cir. 1988).

NATURE OF CASE: Appeal from award of damages for negligence.

FACT SUMMARY: In the Dollars' (P) negligence suit for damages against Coker (D), the trial court found Coker (D) liable for the pecuniary harm the Dollars (P) suffered as a result of his failure to set up an escrow account for them as authorized by Jackson, his principal.

RULE OF LAW

Where an agent causes pecuniary harm to a person other than his principal, he is not liable for this harm if it resulted from his failure to adequately perform his principal's duties.

FACTS: Jackson, Coker's (D) principal, contracted with the Dollars (P), promising them that 30% of all net proceeds derived from the sale of condominium units, which he had converted from apartments for the purpose of selling, would be placed in an escrow account for them. In turn, the Dollars (P) promised to assign their 30% interest in the project to Jackson. After Jackson executed this contract with the Dollars (P), he sent a copy of it to Coker (D), with instructions to set up the escrow account provided therein. However, Coker (D) misunderstood the instructions after receiving them and failed to set up the account. Moreover, the Dollars (P) were unaware that Jackson had delegated this task to Coker (D). Sometime later, after determining that Coker (D) was remiss on his responsibility to Jackson to set up the account, the Dollars (P) brought this negligence claim for damages against Coker (D), contending that he negligently failed to set up the escrow account and, as a result, caused them an injury actionable under Florida law. The district court, agreeing with the Dollars (P), found Coker (D) liable to them for the pecuniary harm they suffered as a result of his negligence. Coker (D) appealed.

ISSUE: Where an agent causes pecuniary harm to a person other than his principal, is he liable for this harm if it resulted from his failure to adequately perform his principal's duties?

HOLDING AND DECISION: (Tjoflat, J.) No. Where an agent causes pecuniary harm to a person other than his principal, he is not liable for this harm if it resulted from his failure to adequately perform his principal's duties. This rule merely restates the general principal that, in effect, absolves an agent from liability for pecuniary harm he causes to a party other than his principal due to his failure to perform his principal's duties. The law refuses to impose liability for this type of harm because it is outside the range of foreseeable harm an agent must guard against in order to avoid liability. In the instant case, although Coker (D), Jackson's agent, had an obligation to carry out Jackson's instructions and the Dollars (P) were pecuniarily injured as a result of his failure to perform that obligation, Coker (D) owed no duty of care to the Dollars (P), and therefore he is not liable for the resulting harm. Reversed in part.

ANALYSIS

In *Bescor, Inc. v. Chicago Title and Trust Co.*, 113 Ill. App. 3d 65 (1983), the court noted, "Traditionally, an agent is not liable for injuries to third persons resulting solely from a mere breach of duty which he owes to his principal, unless at the same time the agent owes a separate duty to the third party." This rule places the responsibility of a negligent agent's conduct squarely on his principal's shoulders, thereby encouraging a principal to be more selective with respect to whom he chooses to perform his duties. Furthermore, this rule increases the likelihood that an injured third party may recover for his losses, since it is more likely that a principal has more resources to handle risks incidental to his enterprise than his agent.

CHAPTER 8

The Doctrine of Ratification

Quick Reference Rules of Law

Evans v. Ruth

Subcontractor (P) v. Hiring contractor (D)

Pa. Super. Ct., 129 Pa. Super. 192, 195 A. 163 (1937).

NATURE OF CASE: Action to hold principal liable for services rendered to his agent.

FACT SUMMARY: Ruth's (D) independent subcontractor hired workers in Ruth's (D) name in excess of his authority.

RULE OF LAW

When a principal ratifies the unauthorized acts of his agent or those who purport to be his agent, the ratification relates back to, and binds, the principal for the work performed.

FACTS: Ruth (D) needed gravel to perform a contract. Ruth (D) subcontracted the work to an independent contractor. The contractor hired workers, presumably in Ruth's (D) name, to load rock for crushing. The contractor was not Ruth's (D) agent and had no authority to bind him. Weighing slips bore Ruth's (D) name and were delivered to him daily. Ruth (D) exercised no supervisory control over the operation. Evans (P) was hired by the contractor's foreman and was told that Ruth (D) would pay him. When Evans (P) went to Ruth (D) for payment, Ruth (D) assured him that he would pay Evans (P) as soon as an affidavit was submitted to show that the work had been performed. Evans (P) was never paid and he refused a 53% settlement offer. The court found that Ruth (D) had ratified the contractor's unauthorized employment of Evans (P) when he stated that Evans (P) would be paid by him. The ratification related back to the original employment and made it binding on Ruth (D). Judgment was rendered for Evans (P).

ISSUE: Is a principal bound by the acts of those without authority to act on his behalf after he has subsequently ratified the act?

HOLDING AND DECISION: (Baldrige, J.) Yes. Ratification is the subsequent approval of an unauthorized act. It relates back in time and validates and makes binding the original act. No new consideration is required since the acts performed on the basis of the agent's alleged authority are sufficient. It is immaterial that the party originally making the promise was not the principal's agent. The ratification supplies the agency relationship. By agreeing to pay Evans (P), Ruth (D) approved of the original hiring. Affirmed.

ANALYSIS

Ratification can occur in a number of ways. A principal may ratify an account by keeping the benefits of the contract. A board of directors, or shareholders, may validate an otherwise unauthorized or ultra vires act. Illegal acts cannot be ratified. However, with respect to corporate acts, those ratifying the illegal act are precluded from later maintaining a derivative suit. Normally, ratification is based on an inequitable gain theory where the principal attempts to retain the benefits without having to pay for them.

Dempsey v. Chambers

Purchaser of coal (P) v. Deliverer of coal (D)

Mass. Sup. Jud. Ct., 154 Mass. 330, 28 N.E. 279 (1891).

NATURE OF CASE: Appeal from award of damages for trespass.

FACT SUMMARY: In Dempsey's (P) vicarious liability suit for damages against Chambers (D), McCullock's principal, the superior court ruled that Chambers' (D) ratification of McCullock's unauthorized cool delivery to Dempsey (P), in Chambers' (D) name and for his benefit, which involved a trespass, made him vicariously liable for the damages McCullock caused Dempsey (P).

RULE OF LAW

Where a principal ratifies an agent's unauthorized act, which was done in his name and for his benefit, and which involved tortious conduct, then this conduct, though not specifically ratified, is imputed to the principal so as to make him liable to an injured third party.

FACTS: McCullock, without authority from his employer, Chambers (D), delivered coal to Dempsey (P), which Dempsey (P) had ordered from Chambers (D). While engaged in delivering the coal, McCullock broke a plate glass window in front of Dempsey's (P) building. Subsequently, Chambers (D), with full knowledge of the accident and the coal delivery by McCullock, presented Dempsey (P) with a bill for the coal. As a result, Dempsey (P) brought this vicarious liability action for damages against Chambers (D), contending that since Chambers (D) ratified McCullock's actions after having knowledge of what occurred, then Chambers (D) was vicariously liable for the damages Dempsey (P) suffered. On the other hand, Chambers (D) contended that since McCullock undertook to deliver the coal without his authority or knowledge, then he is not responsible for McColluck's negligence. The superior court, agreeing with Dempsey's (P) contentions, rendered a judgment in his favor. Chambers (D) appealed.

ISSUE: Where a principal ratifies an agent's unauthorized act, which was done in his name and for his benefit, and which involved tortious conduct, then is this conduct, though not specifically ratified, imputed to the principal so as to make him liable to an injured third party?

HOLDING AND DECISION: (Holmes, J.) Yes. Where a principal ratifies an agent's unauthorized act, which was done in his name and for his benefit, and which involved tortious conduct, then this conduct, though not specifically ratified, is imputed to the principal so as to make him liable to an injured third party. The ratification doctrine, detailed in this rule, is another aspect of the same tradition involving master/servant liability. Specifically, in the latter case, a servant's tortious conduct is imputed to his master if the former was acting within the scope of his authority at the time the tortious act occurred. Likewise, in the former case, when a principal ratifies an agent's unauthorized actions, which were done in the former's name and on his behalf, and which involved tortious conduct, then the law views this conduct as so connected with the agent's employment that it warrants the principal taking responsibility for this conduct as against injured third parties. Hence, both aspects function under the respondeat superior tradition. Aside from this, the ratification doctrine, as far as this court has been able to discern from authority, is broad enough to cover a case like the present when ratification is established. Here, McCullock took it upon himself to deliver Chambers' (D) coal in the latter's name and for his benefit, and afterwards, Chambers (D) contested to (ratified) this assumption by presenting a bill to Dempsey (P) for the coal. As a result, Chambers (D) is responsible for McCullock's negligence in delivering the coal to Dempsey (P). Exceptions overruled.

ANALYSIS

In *Goldstick v. ICM Realty*, 788 F.2d 456, 460 (7th Cir. 1986), Judge Posner justified the ratification concept by stating, in important part, that the best explanation for its existence may be that "the principal would not have ratified the contract unless he had seen a commercial advantage in doing so, and that advantage would be less if the ratification had no binding effect." He goes on to say that a principal normally "ratifies an agent's unauthorized transaction in order to protect" his relationship "with the other party to the transaction, ordinarily a customer or supplier; and for ratification to have this protective effect it has to be more than an idle gesture, signifying nothing because unenforceable."

Manning v. Twin Falls Clinic & Hospital, Inc.

Family of deceased (P) v. Hospital (D)

Idaho Sup. Ct., 830 P.2d 1185 (1992).

NATURE OF CASE: Appeal from a damages award in a medical malpractice action.

FACT SUMMARY: When Manning died shortly after his oxygen supply was disconnected while he was being moved to a private room in Twin Falls (D), his family (P) brought this wrongful death action.

RULE OF LAW

A principal is liable for punitive damages based upon the acts of his agents only where a clear showing indicates that the principal participated in, authorized, or ratified those acts.

FACTS: When Manning was admitted to Twin Falls (D), his pulmonary disease was in its final stages, and his family (P) was told that death was imminent. When Manning was very close to death, the hospital staff attempted to move him to a private room. The nurses did not use a portable oxygen unit during the move because of the relatively short distance. When his oxygen was disconnected, Manning suffered extreme respiratory distress and died soon after. Because the hospital committee concluded that the brief removal of oxygen probably did not cause Manning's death, it did not reprimand or fire the nurses involved. However, it implemented a policy requiring patients on oxygen to be moved with a portable oxygen supply. The Manning family (P) filed this wrongful death action. The jury awarded compensatory, emotional distress, and punitive damages. Twin Falls (D) appealed the award of punitive damages since it had not ratified the nurses' conduct.

ISSUE: Is a principal liable for punitive damages based upon the acts of his agents only where a clear showing indicates that the principal participated in, authorized, or ratified those acts?

HOLDING AND DECISION: (Per curiam) Yes. A principal is liable for punitive damages based upon the acts of his agents only where a clear showing indicates that the principal participated in, authorized, or ratified those acts. The requirement of a clear showing of ratification is particularly important when the doctrine of implied ratification is asserted. Here, Twin Falls' (D) failure to punish or reprimand the nurses does not constitute sufficient evidence of ratification, nor is it indicative of an intent to ratify. The failure to punish or reprimand does not support a finding of ratification. Similarly, Twin Falls' (D) failure to apologize and its defense at trial that the nurses did nothing wrong do not support a finding of ratification. The adoption of a policy requiring all patients on oxygen to be moved with oxygen clearly rejects any contention of ratification or failure to repudiate the nurses' conduct. Affirmed, and remanded but reversed as to punitive damages against Twin Falls (D).

ANALYSIS

Implied ratification is a means by which the principal is estopped from denying the unauthorized act of his agent because to do so would result in the unjust enrichment of the principal. An employer's reasons for continuing an employment relationship or declining to reprimand an employee may be varied. From a public policy standpoint, it would be unwise to mandate disciplinary action whenever misconduct is alleged.

Lewis v. Cable

Union representative (P) v. Employer representative (D)

107 F. Supp. 196 (W.D. Pa. 1952).

NATURE OF CASE: Motion for summary judgment specific performance in action to compel compliance with a contract.

FACT SUMMARY: Cable (D), an employer representative, stopped making payments to Lewis (P), a representative for Cable's (D) employees and their union, contrary to their wage-output agreement, even though Cable's (D) agent had previously executed (thereby finalizing) the agreement on Cable's (D) behalf.

RULE OF LAW

Where a principal shows a willingness to ratify an agreement his agent has entered into on his behalf, and thereby causes the other party to the agreement through reasonable reliance to suffer a detriment, then he is estopped from denying his agent's authority.

FACTS: Lewis (P), representing various coal mine workers and their union, contracted with Cable (D), their employer's representative, in 1948 and 1950 to receive a certain wage per ton of coal that Cable (D) was able to produce. As a way to finalize the 1948 coal wage agreement, Cable's (D) agent, the Somerset County Coal Operators Association of Pennsylvania (Association), of which Cable (D) was a member, executed the agreement on Cable's (D) behalf. Subsequently, when payments on the production of the coal, according to the 1948 agreement, ceased on April 30, 1949, and Lewis (P) tried later to compel compliance by letter, Cable (D), on October 12, 1949, replied, in effect, that he was in "no position to pay anything on this debt," but he would as soon as possible. Sometime later, the Association executed the 1950 coal wage agreement on Cable's (D) behalf. However, Cable (D) never resumed his payments on his coal production subsequent to the 1950 agreement. As a result, Lewis (P) brought this specific performance action against Cable (D) to recover the amount Cable (D) owed according to the terms of the 1948 and 1950 coal wage agreements. In support of his claim, Lewis (P) filed a motion for summary judgment, contending that the Association had apparent authority to execute the contracts on Cable's (D) behalf, or, if not, then Cable (D) ratified the contracts by making payments thereunder. In opposition to this motion, Cable (D) urged that he did not ratify the 1948 agreement because he did not have knowledge of all the material facts concerning it. Furthermore, Cable (D) filed an affidavit in which he, in effect, stated that he did not subjectively intend to ratify the 1948 agreement. On the contrary, he merely did so out of a fear of strikes and repercussions. Lewis (P) moved for summary judgment.

ISSUE: Where a principal shows a willingness to ratify an agreement his agent has entered into on his behalf, and thereby causes the other party to the agreement, through reasonable reliance, to suffer a detriment, is he estopped from denying his agent's authority?

HOLDING AND DECISION: (Marsh, J.) Yes. Where a principal shows a willingness to ratify an agreement his agent has entered into on his behalf, and thereby causes the other party to the agreement, through reasonable reliance, to suffer a detriment, then he is estopped from denying his agent's authority. This rule is consistent with Restatement of Agency § 27, which states, in summary, that a principal is held to ratify an agreement where his conduct, when reasonably interpreted, "causes a third person to believe that the principal consents to have the act done on his behalf by the person purporting to act for him." Moreover, although a principal subjectively does not intend to ratify an agreement, it is his conduct and not his undisclosed intention which controls in determining whether he has ratified the agreement. In the instant case, Cable's (D) payments on the production of coal up to April 30, 1949, and his October 12, 1949 reply to Lewis's (P) letter indicate a willingness on his part to ratify the 1948 coal wage agreement. Consequently, Cable's (D) purported subjective intention not to ratify this agreement is not controlling. Cable (D) cannot by his acts and declarations pretend to be bound by the 1948 agreement so as to prevent strikes and repercussions and, then, when full liability is asserted, seek to disaffirm it. Furthermore, although Cable (D) did not make payments under the 1950 coal wage agreement, his ratification of the 1948 agreement created apparent authority in the Association to enter into the later agreement on Cable's (D) behalf. Finally, because Cable's (D) conduct under the 1948 agreement and the apparent authority it created for the Association with respect to the 1950 agreement, the employees and their union, through the only reasonable inference to be drawn from this conduct, did not undertake to enter into a separate contract with Cable (D), although they had a right to insist that Cable (D) bargain collectively. As a result, Cable's (D) actions caused the employees and union to forego a valued right of labor—or, in other words, to suffer a detriment because they reasonably relied on Cable's (D) purported interest in coming to an agreement. Hence, Cable (D) is estopped from disaffirming the Association's authority. And as a result, Lewis' (P) motion for summary judgment is granted so that Cable (D) is liable to Lewis (P) for the amount shown to be due by the number of tons he admittedly produced. Motion granted and summary judgment entered.

Continued on next page.

ANALYSIS

The court in *Lewis* found that Lewis (P) reasonably relied on Cable's (D) actions to his detriment. However, if the facts were different, i.e., if Cable (D) honestly attempted to come to terms with Lewis (P) but could not comply with the subsequent terms of the agreement, then the result might have been different. In that instance, the reasonability of Lewis's (P) reliance would depend on various factual considerations, including whether Lewis (P) knew, or should have known, that Cable (D) would have difficulty complying with the agreement and/or whether Lewis (P) pressured Cable (D), by fear of strikes, into agreeing to unreasonable conditions.

Computel, Inc. v. Emery Air Freight Corp.

Seller of computers (P) v. Delivery company (D)

919 F.2d 678 (11th Cir. 1990).

NATURE OF CASE: Appeal from an award of damages for breach of contract.

FACT SUMMARY: Computel, Inc. (P) contended that Emery Air Freight Corp. (D), a shipper, failed to collect the correct form of payment when it delivered computer goods to a customer.

RULE OF LAW

Principals effectively ratify the acts of their agents if they purposely refrain from seeking information and are willfully ignorant of the material facts.

FACTS: Computel, Inc. (P) contracted with Emery Air Freight Corp. (D) to deliver various computer goods to a customer. The goods were to be shipped COD with a cashier's check. Emery (D) delivered the computers but collected a corporate check instead. Computel (P) received the check and attempted to deposit it. However, Computel (P) discovered that it was not a cashier's check when the check bounced. Computel (P) then brought a breach of contract action against Emery (D), who responded that Computel (P) had ratified Emery's (D) unauthorized acceptance of the corporate check by accepting and depositing it. The trial court ruled for Computel (P) and awarded $38,625 in damages.

ISSUE: Do principals effectively ratify the acts of their agents if they purposely refrain from seeking information and are willfully ignorant of the material facts?

HOLDING AND DECISION: (Fay, J.) Yes. Principals effectively ratify the acts of their agents if they purposely refrain from seeking information and are willfully ignorant of the material facts. In actions where shipping customers sue their carriers for collecting an unauthorized form of payment, most jurisdictions hold that the customer ratifies the act of the agent if it deposits the unauthorized form of payment with knowledge of its deviation. However, a principal may also assume the risk of lack of knowledge if a reasonable person should have investigated further. In the present case, the evidence might show that Computel (P) intentionally refrained from checking incoming payments. If Emery (D) could prove that Computel (P) chose to remain ignorant of the form of payment, ratification was effective upon deposit of the payment by Computel (P). Accordingly, the judgment is vacated and remanded for trial on the issue of ratification.

DISSENT: (Johnson, J.) The evidence does not allow for the inference that Computel (P) intentionally established a purposefully ignorant payment acceptance procedure to insulate itself from an affirmative defense of ratification.

ANALYSIS

This decision seems to be in accord with the Restatement (Second) of Agency. Comment e to § 91(1) is directed to the circumstances in which a principal assumes the risk of lack of knowledge. The comment states that a principal is presumed to assume the risk when he affirms without qualification and investigation.

Inn Foods, Inc. v. Equitable Cooperative Bank

Holder of judgment (P) v. Bank (D)

45 F.3d 594 (1st Cir. 1995).

NATURE OF CASE: Appeal from grant of defense summary judgment motion in an action for conversion.

FACT SUMMARY: Inn Foods, Inc. (P), seeking to collect on a default judgment against Atlantic, claimed that a U.S. Treasury check had been converted and deposited in the personal bank account of Atlantic's president.

RULE OF LAW
Ratification can be implied when a principal with knowledge makes no effort to repudiate a transaction.

FACTS: Inn Foods, Inc. (P) had secured a default judgment against Atlantic Brands. During discovery, Inn Foods (P) learned that Atlantic's president, Hodge, had indorsed and deposited a large U.S. Treasury check in his own personal account at Equitable Cooperative Bank (D). Inn Foods (P) subsequently sought to reach and apply a cause of action for conversion of the Treasury check as a judgment creditor of Atlantic's. Atlantic had never filed such a claim and had no intent to do so. The lower court granted Equitable's (D) motion for summary judgment. Inn Foods (P) appealed, claiming that since Atlantic did not have full knowledge of the facts, it could not have ratified Hodge's signature.

ISSUE: May ratification be implied when a principal with knowledge makes no effort to repudiate a transaction?

HOLDING AND DECISION: (Stahl, J.) Yes. Ratification can be implied when a principal with knowledge makes no effort to repudiate a transaction. An affirmance of an unauthorized transaction can be inferred from a failure to repudiate it. In this case, there is no indication that Atlantic ever sought to rupudiate the Treasury check transaction. Thus, Atlantic ratified Hodge's endorsement and deposit. Because Hodge's signature was authorized, Atlantic has no conversion cause of action against Equitable (D) and, thus, Inn Foods' (P) claim must fail. Affirmed.

ANALYSIS

The Restatement (Second) of Agency § 91(1) states that the purported principal must have knowledge of all the material facts before being held to an apparent affirmance. Ratification requires either knowledge of the material facts or circumstances sufficient to put a reasonable person on notice to inquire into the facts. Estoppel might be an alternative ground in some cases.

Bruton v. Automatic Welding & Supply Corp.

Owner of tractor (D) v. Repair shop (P)

Alaska Sup. Ct., 513 P.2d 1122 (1973).

NATURE OF CASE: Appeal from finding of joint and several liability in an action for damages.

FACT SUMMARY: In Automatic Welding & Supply Corp.'s (AWS) (P) action for damages against Bruton (D) and Ekvall (D), the district court found Bruton (D) jointly and severally liable with Ekvall (D) for the unauthorized repairs Ekvall (D) suggested that AWS (P) make on Bruton's (D) tractor.

RULE OF LAW

A principal's silence constitutes affirmance of his agent's unauthorized actions when a third party involved in carrying out those actions reasonably expects him to speak if he does not consent.

FACTS: Bruton (D) agreed to loan Ekvall (D) his D8 Caterpillar tractor (Cat) rent-free. By their informal oral agreement, Ekvall (D) was to provide an operator, pay for fuel consumed, and perform routine maintenance. Subsequently, after the Cat developed minor problems, Ekvall (D) called Automatic Welding & Supply Corp.'s (AWS) (P) to make field repairs, which, coincidentally, proved only temporarily effective. When these repairs failed, Ekvall (D), after conferring with Roetman, owner and manager of AWS (P), authorized AWS (P) to remove the Cat to an AWS (P) shop for major repairs. While the Cat was there, Bruton (D) entered the shop on other business, recognized his Cat and authorized some additional work. However, during his visit, the major repairs Ekvall (D) authorized were completed, or nearly so, and Burton (D), although being briefed by an AWS (P) agent on the scope of the repairs, had no knowledge of their cost. When the repairs were completed, AWS (P) billed Bruton (D) for the major and minor repairs to the Cat that Ekvall (D) authorized as well as for the additional work he authorized. Notwithstanding this, AWS (P) was unable to get any portion of the bill paid. As a result, AWS (P) brought suit for damages against Bruton (D) and Ekvall (D) to recover for the cost of all the repairs made. During the suit, Bruton (D) contended that Ekvall (D) was liable and cross-claimed against him for the cost of repairs made during the period the latter used the Cat. However, although the district court found Ekvall (D) liable for the minor repairs he authorized, it also found Bruton (D) jointly and severally liable with Ekvall (D) for the major repairs, with Ekvall (D) to have judgment against Bruton (D) for any part of the joint and several liability which Ekvall (D) would be compelled to pay. Bruton (D) appealed.

ISSUE: Where a third party involved in carrying out an agent's unauthorized actions reasonably expects a principal to speak out against these actions, does the latter's silence constitute affirmance?

HOLDING AND DECISION: (Boochever, J.) Yes. A principal's silence constitutes affirmance of his agent's unauthorized actions when a third party involved in carrying out those actions reasonably expects him to speak if he does not consent. This rule presumes that the principal has knowledge of his agent's unauthorized actions. Otherwise, the third party's expectation that a principal's silence constitutes affirmance would be unreasonable because a principal cannot be held to affirm that which he has no knowledge of. In the instant case, this court will assume that Ekvall (D) purported to be acting for Burton (D) when he authorized the Cat to be brought into the AWS (P) shop. (If not, Bruton (D) would not be held to have ratified the major repairs because it is requisite for ratification that an agent holds himself out to the third party as an agent.) However, there was no evidence that Ekvall (D) notified Bruton (D) that any major repairs were to be made. Furthermore, Bruton (D) had not discussed the cost of repairs with Roetman when he authorized additional work to be done to his Cat. Additionally, although Bruton (D) knew of the major repairs (not their cost), it was reasonable for him to assume that Ekvall (D) would pay for them because they had orally agreed that Ekvall (D) would perform routine repairs, and the major repairs were nearly complete when Bruton (D) came into the AWS (P) shop. Hence, AWS (P) could not reasonably presume that Bruton's (D) silence constituted affirmance. As a result, Bruton (D) was not jointly and severally liable with Ekvall (D) for the cost of the major repairs. Reversed in part.

ANALYSIS

In *Myers v. Cook*, 87 W. Va. 265, 104 S.E. 593 (1920), the defendant's husband, after purchasing a piece of property on credit, signed his wife's name, without her consent, to the note. Later, the wife found out about this but said nothing to the prior property owner. Soon after this, the defendant's husband sold the property. After examining these facts, the court held that no ratification took place on the ground that the wife's silence, after being informed by her husband of his use of her name, was not sufficient evidence of ratification in the absence of a pre-existing agency relationship or of receipt and retention of the benefits. In connection with this, see Restatement § 94, requiring circumstances "which reasonably justify an inference of consent" before there is ratification by silence.

Rakestraw v. Rodrigues

Forgery victim (P) v. Creditor (D)

Cal. Sup. Ct., 8 Cal. 3d 67, 500 P.2d 1401 (1972).

NATURE OF CASE: Appeal from a denial of motion for judgment notwithstanding the verdict in an action for damages.

FACT SUMMARY: In Rakestraw's (P) cross-claim for damages against Rodrigues (D), the trial court denied the latter's motion for judgment notwithstanding the verdict after ruling that he was liable for the balance owed on a loan which was secured by forging Rakestraw's (P) name.

RULE OF LAW

Where an individual, holding out as an agent, commits forgery without authority from the person he binds by his fraudulent act, the latter's subsequent ratification of the act creates an agency relationship between them and relieves the purported agent from civil liability to the principal.

FACTS: Rakestraw's (P) former husband, William (D), forged her name on both a promissory note for $75,000 in favor of Acme Financial Corporation (Acme) and a deed of trust on her woodside property securing the loan in order to obtain funds for a business venture. Shortly after this, the forged signatures were notarized by Ellinghouse, at which time Rodrigues (D), a business associate of William (D), attested that Rakestraw (P) acknowledged the instrument's execution. Rakestraw (P) learned of these forgeries a few days after she endorsed a check that Acme had made payable to her and William (D). As a result, Rakestraw (P) consulted an attorney, but she failed to follow any of the attorney's advice. Sometime later, Acme, after receiving no payments to satisfy the loan, initiated this action for damages against Rakestraw (P) to enforce payment on the loan amount. However, Rakestraw (P) cross-claimed against both Rodrigues (D) and William (D), contending that since her name was forged on the documents, Rodrigues (D) and William (D) were liable for the balance owed on the loan. On the other hand, Rodrigues (D) asserted that since Rakestraw (P) ratified the forgeries by having knowledge of them and failing to pursue remedies on her own accord, he was relieved from any liability to her. In rebuttal, Rakestraw (P) contended that she had not ratified the forgeries since, according to Civil Code § 2310, she had to ratify the deed of trust in writing, and she had not done so. The trial court, agreeing with Rakestraw (P), entered a verdict in her favor and denied Rodrigues's (D) subsequent motion for judgment notwithstanding the verdict. Rodrigues (D) appealed.

ISSUE: Where an individual, holding out as an agent, commits forgery without authority from the person he binds by his fraudulent act, does the latter's subsequent ratification of the act create an agency relationship between them and relieve the purported agent from civil liability to the principal?

HOLDING AND DECISION: (Wright, C.J.) Yes. Where an individual, holding out as an agent, commits forgery without authority from the person he binds by his fraudulent act, the latter's subsequent ratification of the act creates an agency relationship between them and relieves the purported agent from civil liability to the principal. This rule is derived from traditional principles of agency law. Specifically, ratification is defined as the voluntary election by a person to adopt in some manner as his own an act which was purportedly done on his behalf by another person, the effect of which is to treat the act as if originally authorized by him. Moreover, this act may be adopted expressly or adopted by implication based on conduct reasonably indicating the principal's consent, even though the principal did not intend to ratify it. Aside from this, it is well settled in California that a principal may ratify the forgery of his signature by his agent. Hence, it naturally follows that a principal may ratify the forgery of an individual purporting to be his agent, even though there was no previous agency relationship between them. In the instant case, Rakestraw (P) was aware of the forgeries within a few days after she had endorsed the check from Acme and thereafter consulted an attorney in connection therewith. Accordingly, the requirement of knowledge of the material facts essential to voluntary ratification is satisfied. Furthermore, Rakestraw (P) elected not to rescind at a time when she was fully informed and legally had the power to do so. In addition, Rakestraw's (P) contention that she did not ratify Rodrigues's (D) acts since, as authorized by Civil Code § 2310, ratification of the deed of trust had to be in writing must fail. On the contrary, Rakestraw's (P) liability arises from the promissory note (the deed of trust only secured it), and an agent's authority to execute a promissory note need not be in writing. Moreover, Civil Code § 2310 was not intended to apply to ratification as between a principle and an agent. Hence, Rakestraw's (P) ratification of the fraudulent transaction relieved Rodrigues (D) of liability to her as a matter of law. Reversed and remanded.

ANALYSIS

As the court observed in an omitted footnote, since a promissory note was involved in the case, article 3 of the Uniform Commercial Code (U.C.C.) should be consulted. U.C.C. § 3-404 declares that an unauthorized signature (which includes both a forgery and a signature made by

Continued on next page.

an agent in a transaction which exceeds his actual or apparent authority) may be ratified but that such ratification "does not of itself affect any rights of the person signing against the actual signer." This leaves the resolution of any dispute between such parties to conventional principles of agency law.

CHAPTER 10

Termination of the Agency Relationship

Quick Reference Rules of Law

Want v. Century Supply Co.

Employee (P) v. Employer (D)

Mo. Ct. App., 508 S.W.2d 515 (1974).

NATURE OF CASE: Appeal from dismissal of petition for accounting and imposition of constructive trust, for failure to state claim.

FACT SUMMARY: Want (P) agreed to obtain customers for Century Supply Co. (D) for as long as he wanted in return for commissions, but he was discharged after only seven months.

RULE OF LAW

An agent may state a claim for damages against his principal for termination of the agency despite the right of either party to end the relationship at will.

FACTS: Want (P) agreed to try to obtain his prior customers for Century Supply Co. (D). "No deadline was placed" on the term of the agreement, and Want (P) could have "as long as he wanted." Want (P) would advance costs and receive a 5% commission on business brought to Century Supply (D). After seven months, Want (P) had brought Century Supply (D) $10,000 in business a month and spent $3,600 in expenses; however, at that time Century Supply (D) terminated Want (P). Want (P) petitioned for an accounting for all commissions due from the date of employment to the date of filing, and for the imposition of a constructive trust on a lump sum representing future commissions. The trial court dismissed Want's (P) petition for failure to state claims on which relief could be granted.

ISSUE: May an agent state a claim against his principal for damages for termination of the agency even though both parties possessed the right to terminate the agency at will?

HOLDING AND DECISION: (Clemens, J.) Yes. Although agreements between principal and agent for an indefinite time generally can be terminated at the will of either party, an agent may sue in quantum meruit for damages arising from the termination of an agency. Here it was conceded that the principal had the right to terminate the agency. Nevertheless, limitations on the revocation of an indefinite agency do exist, as for example when an agent in good faith has incurred expense and devoted time and labor in the matter of his agency without having had a sufficient opportunity to recoup expenditures. Century Supply (D) could not retain Want's (P) investment which Want (P) was unable to recover in commissions. Reversed; remanded.

ANALYSIS

This case demonstrates the necessity of distinguishing between a principal's power to terminate an agency and an agent's right, if facts warrant, to sue the principal for damages arising from such termination. Of course, an agency may terminate for reasons other than its express revocation by the principal, such as by expiration of its term, by accomplishment of its purpose, or by an unanticipated change of circumstances which change the value of the subject matter of the agency (such as destruction or loss of property).

Hunt v. Rousmanier's Administrators

Lender (P) v. Borrower (D)

21 U.S. 379, 8 Wheat. 174 (1823).

NATURE OF CASE: Appeal from sustaining of defense demurrer to bill to compel joinder.

FACT SUMMARY: Hunt (P) loaned Rousmanier (D) monies for which he received powers of attorney to sell two vessels belonging in part to Rousmanier (D), but before the loans were repaid, Rousmanier (D) died.

RULE OF LAW

If an agent's powers are "coupled with an interest," or conferred for the benefit of the agent himself or some other third person, they become irrevocable and survive the death of the principal.

FACTS: In 1820, Hunt (P) made two loans to Rousmanier (D). The first was for $1,450. Rousmanier (D) executed a note in this amount as well as a power of attorney authorizing Hunt (P) to make and execute a bill of sale of Rousmanier's (D) three-quarters interest in the brig Nereus. This power also authorized Hunt (P) to collect monies on the policy which insured the Nereus payable in the event of its loss. The second loan was in the amount of $700. Rousmanier (D) also gave Hunt (P) a note for this sum as well as a power of attorney to dispose of his interest in the schooner Industry. Powers of attorney rather than mortgages were used to create security interests upon the advice on an attorney. However, a month and a half after this second loan, Rousmanier (D) died insolvent, having paid only $200 on both notes. Hunt (P) took possession of the Nereus and the Industry on their return from sea and offered decedent's interest in them for sale. Hunt (P) filed this bill to compel Rousmanier's estate administrators (D) to join in the decree of sale, which they refused to do voluntarily. The administrator's demurrer to the bill was sustained, and Hunt (P) appealed.

ISSUE: If an agent gives consideration for an interest in the subject matter of an agency at the time the agency power is created, does the agency become irrevocable such that it survives the death of the principal?

HOLDING AND DECISION: (Marshall, C.J.) Yes. If an agent's powers are "coupled with an interest," or conferred for the benefit of the agent himself or some other third person, they become irrevocable and survive the death of the principal. Here, Rousmanier (D) gave Hunt (P) letters of attorney which constituted the security for loans of money. Rousmanier (D) was personally bound by these powers and could not during his lifetime have revoked them. Nevertheless, there is a general rule that powers, even if irrevocable during the life of the party, are extinguished by the death of the principal. There is one exception to this rule: if the power is "coupled with an interest," then it survives the death of the principal and may be executed after his death. For this exception to be applicable, the power and the interest must be united in the same person, i.e., the agent. If the agent has an interest in the subject matter of the agency, for which he supplied consideration, then when he acts to effectuate the agency he acts in his own name, not as a substitute for the principal. Consequently, the agent's power is not extinguished by the death of the principal. Here Hunt (P) had only a naked power not coupled with an interest and this exception does not apply. Affirmed.

ANALYSIS

The confusion created by Marshall's distinction between "naked" powers and those "coupled with an interest" prompted an attempt at clarification by the drafters of the Restatement of Agency. Section 138 provides that for an agency power to be considered irrevocable, it must: (1) have been granted to secure the performance of a duty or to protect the title of the power holder or a third person; and (2) have been given when the duty or title was created or given for consideration. Section 139 provides that in such an instance, the power is not terminated by revocation by the principal, surrender of the power by the agent if he holds the power for the benefit of a third party, loss of capacity during lifetime by either the agent or the principal, or the death of the holder of the power. The basis for these rules, as implied by Justice Marshall, is that if a power is "coupled with an interest," it is not created for the benefit of the principal and thus is not really an agency at all.

In re Berry's Estate

Power of attorney revocation.

N.Y. Surrogate Ct., Queens Cty., 329 N.Y.S.2d 915 (1972).

NATURE OF CASE: Motion to file amended objections in accounting proceeding.

FACT SUMMARY: Agent, niece of principal, transferred funds under power of attorney into a Totten trust account shortly after her principal suffered a stroke and became comatose.

RULE OF LAW

An agent's authority to act under a power of attorney is suspended or revoked when the principal becomes mentally incompetent or incapacitated.

FACTS: During a hospital stay, Margaret Berry executed a power of attorney designating her niece, Irene Montanye, as her agent. Subsequent to discharge from the hospital, Berry suffered an apoplectic attack or stroke and was readmitted to the hospital, where she remained in a comatose or semi-comatose condition until her death two months later. The day after Berry's attack Montanye transferred $109,000 of Berry's funds into a Totten trust account in Berry's name for the benefit of Montanye's mother and Berry's sister, Anne R. Scully. In this probate accounting, distributees of Berry's estate at first challenged the agency created by the power of attorney as void because Berry did not understand what she was doing. Subsequently by motion they sought to amend their objections to allege that whatever agency existed was revoked prior to the transfer of funds as a result of Berry's incapacity.

ISSUE: Is an agent's authority under a power of attorney revoked by the principal's incompetency or incapacity?

HOLDING AND DECISION: (Laurino, Surrogate) Yes. A principal has the right to supervise his agency. Acts done by an agent are those which could have been accomplished by the principal herself, if present. Insanity or mental incapacity before the agent has the chance to perform her duties terminates the agency as a matter of law, whether or not the principal has been judged insane. Here, if the objectors can prove that Berry was mentally incompetent or incapacitated due to her coma at the time Montanye transferred the funds, then the agency would have been revoked or suspended. Therefore, the proposed amended objections state valid issues of fact and law. Permission granted for their filing.

ANALYSIS

Under the Model Probate Code, if Berry had provided in her power of attorney that it would not be revoked by incompetency, the objectors would not have been allowed to file their amended claims. Under the Uniform Partnership Act, § 32(1)(a), a court decree is required to formally adjudge a partner insane and thereby dissolve the partnership. Comparison of these rules with the contrasting results of the *Campbell* and *Berry* cases reveals considerable confusion in the area of termination of agency by incompetency. Less confusion exists when bankruptcy is the reason for termination of agency. Under the Restatement § 114, comment c, bankruptcy of the principal terminates the agent's authority to deal with the principal's assets, although notice to the agent is required to terminate his authority to bind the principal personally.

Campbell v. United States

Holder of power of attorney (P) v. Federal government (D)

U.S. Ct. of Claims, 231 Ct. Cl. 744, 657 F.2d 1174 (1981).

NATURE OF CASE: Suit for damages for government failure to redeem bond; government counterclaim for unpaid estate tax.

FACT SUMMARY: The Government (D) refused to redeem "flower bonds" Campbell (P) purchased to pay his father's estate taxes.

RULE OF LAW

If a principal suffers an incapacity which appears permanent from the outset, the agent is automatically deprived of authority; otherwise, an agent's actions subsequent to the onset of the incapacity are merely voidable.

FACTS: In 1965, when healthy, Campbell, Sr. granted his son Campbell, Jr. (P) a broad power of attorney. In 1976, Campbell, Sr. suffered a stroke and became incapacitated. The day after Campbell, Sr.'s stroke, Campbell, Jr. (P) purchased "flower bonds" from the U.S. Treasury with his father's funds, at a face value of $200,000, an interest rate of 3½% and maturing in 1998. These "flower bonds" were special issues which were offered at interest rates substantially below those prevailing (and which therefore sold below par) and which could be redeemed before maturity to pay federal estate taxes. Campbell, Sr. died soon after the purchase. In 1979, after the decedent's estate tax liability had been determined at $103,219, the Government's (D) Bureau of Public Debt refused to redeem the "flower" bonds. Campbell, Jr. (P) sued for the difference between the $106,000 par value of the bonds in 1979 and their market value ($81,885), for the difference in interest rates between those earned on the bond and those accrued on unpaid estate taxes, and for administrative costs. The Government (D) counterclaimed for the amount of the unpaid estate tax.

ISSUE: When an agent acts under a power of attorney subsequent to the time his principal becomes incapacitated, but it does not necessarily appear that the incapacity will be permanent, may that action be ratified by the principal's estate upon his death?

HOLDING AND DECISION: (Friedman, C.J.) Yes. If a principal suffers an incapacity which appears permanent from the outset, the agent is automatically deprived of authority; otherwise, an agent's actions subsequent to the onset of the incapacity are merely voidable. The Government (D) contends that when Campbell, Sr. suffered his stroke he became permanently incapacitated, thus immediately terminating Campbell, Jr.'s (P) authority to purchase bonds under the power of attorney granted when Campbell, Sr. was healthy. In other words, Campbell, Jr.'s (P) power "lapsed" upon Campbell, Sr.'s stroke, and thus he was not the "owner" of the bonds when they were presented for redemption. Although the Restatement of Agency (Second) § 122(1) appears to support this position, Texas courts and the Second Circuit have not followed this position. In most instances where a principal is incapacitated, the duration of the incapacity is not immediately clear. Here, when Campbell, Sr. suffered his stroke, Campbell, Jr. (P) could not have been certain his father's incapacity would be permanent. Consequently, his purchase of bonds was merely voidable at the election of the executors of Campbell, Sr.'s estate. The estate ratified the purchase by submitting the bonds for early redemption, and the purchase remained valid and enforceable. Recovery for plaintiff.

ANALYSIS

This decision seems inconsistent by holding that Campbell, Jr. (P) could not have known that his father's condition would be permanent, while in its recitation of stipulated facts stating that Campbell, Sr. was "stricken with a cerebral hemorrhage, and became permanently and irreversibly mentally incompetent . . . " Nevertheless, it represents a reasonable attempt to provide a rule for determining when incapacity is, for legal purposes, akin to death in terminating an agent's authority.

CHAPTER 11

The Creation of a Partnership

Quick Reference Rules of Law

Cox v. Hickman

Creditor (D) v. Debtor (P)

House of Lords, 8 H.L. Cas. 267, 11 Eng. Rep. 431 (1860).

NATURE OF CASE: Appeal from creditor's award in suit against debtor's partners.

FACT SUMMARY: Creditors, including Cox (D), agreed with the Smiths, debtor-parties in interest, to have trustees manage the latter's business as a means of satisfying their debt, and a trustee ordered goods from Hickman (P) to aid in the management. When Hickman (P) was not paid, he sued Cox (D) and all the trustees.

RULE OF LAW

Where a debtor contractually agrees to temporarily grant his creditors authority to continue his business as a means of discharging his debits, the law will not imply a creditor partnership, and each creditor cannot contractually bind the others by entering contracts while running the business.

FACTS: The Smiths carried on a business. When unable to pay their debts, they arranged with their creditor Cox (D) and other creditors to manage the business as trustees. The net income was to be used to pay off the outstanding debts. Together they formed the Stanton Iron Company. Subsequently, Hickman (P) supplied goods to the Stanton Iron Company, for which he was never paid. Hickman (P) sued the trustees of the company, including Cox (D) and the other creditors, under the theory that the creditors, as principals responsible for their manager's (agents) actions, are liable for payment. The Court of Common Pleas entered a verdict for Hickman (P). On appeal, the Exchequer Chamber affirmed. Cox (D), as creditor representative, appealed.

ISSUE: When a debtor contractually agrees to temporarily grant his creditors authority to continue his business as a means of discharging his debts, will a creditor partnership form such that each creditor can contractually bind the others by entering contracts while running the business?

HOLDING AND DECISION: (Lord Cranworth, J.) No. Where a debtor contractually agrees to temporarily grant his creditors authority to continue his business as a means of discharging his debits, the law will not imply a creditor partnership, and each creditor cannot contractually bind the others by entering contracts while running the business. Agency principles dictate that the liability of one partner for the acts of his co-partners is the same as the liability of a principal for the acts of his agent. However, the right to share in a business' profits does not make one liable for the business' debts. The debtor is still the person solely interested in the profits except that he has mortgaged them to his creditors. He receives the benefit of the profits as they accrue, although he has precluded himself from applying them to any purpose other than the discharge of his debts. The business is not carried on by or, on account of, the creditors even though their consent is necessary in such a case since without it all the property might be seized by them in execution. However, the business still remains the business of the debtor or his trustees; the debtor or the trustees are the persons by, or on behalf of whom, it is carried on. Reversed.

DISSENT: (Blackburn, J.) Here, the business is to be carried on by the trustees under the control of the creditors, who may give any directions they see fit as to the management of the business. The creditors have a voice in nominating new trustees, as well as the right to inspect the books. Moreover, it is the creditors alone who have these powers, no similar powers being given to the Smiths.

ANALYSIS

In the *Cox* case, the court uses agency principles to argue that a partnership relation stems from whether a business is carried on in one's behalf, as opposed to merely looking at whether profits are being shared.

Martin v. Peyton

Creditor (P) v. Lender (D)

N.Y. Ct. App., 246 N.Y. 213, 158 N.E. 77 (1927).

NATURE OF CASE: Action to hold parties as partners in an existing firm.

FACT SUMMARY: Peyton (D) and others (D) loaned a partnership money so that it could carry on its brokerage business.

RULE OF LAW

While words are not determinative, where a transaction bears all of the aspects of a loan, no partnership arrangement will be found.

FACTS: The partnership of Knauth (D), Nachod (D) and Kuhne (D) was in financial difficulty. Hall (D), one of the partners, arranged a loan from Peyton (D) and other friends (D). In exchange for the loan of $2,500,000 in liquid securities, Peyton (D) and the others were to receive a percentage of the profits until the loan was repaid. Peyton (D) was to have a veto over speculative investments; an insurance policy was to be taken out on Hall's (D) life; the securities could be pledged as a loan; Peyton (D) and the others were to receive dividends from the securities; plus many other controls and provisions existed. Peyton (D) could not bind the partnership, nor could he initiate any action on his own. The agreement specifically stated that it was a loan and not a partnership arrangement. It stated that no liability was to accrue to Peyton (D) and the others (D) for partnership debts. Martin (P), a creditor of the partnership, brought suit against it, plus Peyton (D) and the others (D). Martin (P) alleged that a partnership interest had been formed by the agreement. The court found for Peyton (D).

ISSUE: Where the only control exerted or sharing of profits occurs to protect and pay off a loan, will a partnership arrangement be found?

HOLDING AND DECISION: (Andrews, J.) No. Words alone are not determinative of a relationship. Merely declaring that no partnership is intended will not be dispositive of the issue. If the words, acts, and agreements establish the existence of a partnership arrangement, the parties will be liable as partners. Nothing in Peyton's (D) words or actions establishes a partnership. Therefore, we must look to the contract alone. Nothing in it is other than what were necessary precautions to protect the loan. Any control was negative in nature and was to prevent any misuse of the funds. Peyton (D) had no right to control, to initiate policy, or to bind the contract. This was a loan and Peyton (D) and the others are not liable. Judgment affirmed.

ANALYSIS

A partnership results from either express or implied contracts. An arrangement for the sharing of profits is often an important factor in determining the existence of a partnership. Of equal importance is the right to share in the decision-making function of the partnership and/or to bind the partnership to contractual obligations.

Serapion v. Martinez

Law firm partner (P) v. Law firm (D)

119 F.3d 982 (1st Cir. 1997).

NATURE OF CASE: Appeal from a defense summary judgment in a partner's Title VII suit against her law firm.

FACT SUMMARY: When her former partners folded the Martinez Law Firm (Firm) (D), Serapion (P) sued them and their new firm for violation of Title VII.

RULE OF LAW

A bona fide equity partner of a law firm may be ineligible to claim Title VII protection.

FACTS: Margarita Serapion (P) was a senior or proprietary partner in the Martinez Law Firm (Firm) (D). The Firm's (D) four name partners (all males) were the only other proprietary partners. When Serapion (P) requested fuller partnership status and more of a voice in operating the Firm (D), the other partners dissolved the Firm (D) and formed a new firm, which Serapion (P) sued, contending that the partners' specific intention in forming the new firm was to prevent her, because she was a woman, from attaining equal partnership status with them. The Firm (D) moved for summary judgment on the grounds that Serapion (P), as a partner in the Firm (D), was not an employee, and therefore had no recourse under Title VII. The federal district court granted the motion, and Serapion (P) appealed.

ISSUE: May a bona fide equity partner of a law firm be ineligible to claim Title VII protection?

HOLDING AND DECISION: (Selya, J.) Yes. A bona fide equity partner of a law firm may be ineligible to claim Title VII protection. The anti-discrimination provisions of Title VII apply to "any individual" which, for purposes of this legislation, is defined to mean, and only protects, employees and potential employees. Since a single individual in a single occupational setting cannot be both an employer and an employee for purposes of Title VII, equity partners usually have not been deemed to be employees. Here, the evidence is uncontradicted that Serapion (P) had an ownership interest in the Firm (D). Her compensation depended substantially on the Firm's (D) fortunes. She enjoyed significant voting rights in the Firm's (D) two principal governing bodies. It is not significant that Serapion (P) may have possessed less power than the other four partners; that her name was never added to the Firm's (D) name; that her compensation may have been less than the other partners; or that she did not head any of the Firm's (D) departments. A person, such as Serapion (P), with the requisite attributes of partnership status, is properly considered a partner, not an employee, regardless of the fact that others in the Firm (D) may wield more power. Given these facts, no reasonable factfinder could conclude that Serapion (P) was other than a bona fide equity partner, and, as such, a person ineligible to claim the protection which Title VII reserves for those who are employees. Affirmed.

ANALYSIS

As pointed out in the *Serapion* case, partnerships are mutable structures, and partners come in varying shapes and sizes. Consequently, attempting to delineate the circumstances in which a particular partner should be regarded as an employee for Title VII purposes is tricky business. The courts have been clear that merely affixing labels cannot conclusively resolve such status questions. The correct course, as was done here, is to undertake a case-by-case analysis aimed at determining whether an individual described as a partner actually bears a close enough resemblance to an employee to be afforded the protections of Title VII. After all, as said by the *Serapion* court, "Form should not be permitted to triumph over substance when important civil rights are at stake."

Lupien v. Malsbenden

Purchaser of constructed car (P) v. Manufacturer (D)

Maine Sup. Jud. Ct., 477 A.2d 746 (1984).

NATURE OF CASE: Appeal from judgment ordering specific performance of written contract.

FACT SUMMARY: Cragin, doing business as York Motor Mart, agreed to construct a Bradley automobile for Lupien (P), and the latter, not having received his completed automobile, brought a specific performance action against Malsbenden (D), the financier of the Bradley portion of York Motor Mart's business.

RULE OF LAW

UPA § 6(1) defines a partnership as "an association of two or more persons . . . to carry on as co-owners a business for profit," and this relationship is inferred by law based on established facts.

FACTS: On March 5, 1980, Lupien (P) entered into a written agreement with Stephen Cragin, doing business as York Motor Mart, for the construction of a Bradley automobile. Subsequently, Lupien (P) made visits to York Motor Mart on an average of once or twice a week to check on his car's progress. During those visits, Lupien (P) generally dealt with Malsbenden (D), the financier of the Bradley portion of York Motor Mart's business, because Cragin was seldom present. However, Lupien (P) never received the Bradley he contracted to purchase. Lupien (P) brought this action against Malsbenden (D) seeking specific performance of the contract he entered into with Cragin. He asserted that Malsbenden's (D) interest in York Motor Mart made him a co-partner with Cragin, and therefore liable for any partnership obligation Cragin had incurred. On the other hand, Malsbenden (D) contended that his interest in York Motor Mart was merely as a banker, not as a partner, and as a result he should not be required to specifically perform the contract that Cragin entered into with Lupien (P). Notwithstanding Malsbenden's (D) contentions, the district court found that his "total involvement" in the Bradley operation made him a partner in the company and thus liable to Lupien (P) for the Bradley the latter contracted to purchase. Malsbenden (D) appealed.

ISSUE: Will the partnership relationship defined in UPA § 6(1) as "an association of two or more persons . . . to carry on as co-owners a business for profit" be inferred by law based on established facts?

HOLDING AND DECISION: (McKusick, C.J.) Yes. UPA § 6(1) defines a partnership as "an association of two or more persons . . . to carry on as co-owners a business for profit," and this relationship is inferred by law based on established facts. Maine adopted the Uniform Partnership Act (UPA) as a means of determining what precisely constitutes a partnership from evidence presented to the court. This evidence may take the form of either an express or implied agreement which clearly shows that the parties placed under their money, effects, labor, and skill, or some of all of them, in a lawful business with the understanding that profits will be shared. However, no one factor alone determines a partnership's existence. Here, Malsbenden's (D) financial interest and day-to-day involvement in York Motor Mart's business enterprises conclusively showed that a partnership was formed. With respect to the former, Malsbenden's (D) $85,000 interest-free loan to York Motor Mart constituted evidence that a partnership existed. This loan was made, in substantial part, to the business in the form of day-to-day purchases of Bradley kits, other parts and equipment, and in the payment of wages. Moreover, the loan was not to be repaid in fixed amounts or at fixed times but rather upon the sale of Bradley automobiles. Hence, satisfaction of the loan hinged on company profits, evidencing Malsbenden's (D) profit interest. As to the latter, Malsbenden's (D) day-to-day involvement in the business evidenced his right to participate in its control. According to a witness, Malsbenden (D) opened the business establishment each morning, remained present through part of every day, had final say on the ordering of parts, paid for parts and equipment, and paid the witness' salary. Hence, the superior court's finding that the Bradley car operation presented a pooling of Malsbenden's (D) capital and Cragin's automotive skills, with joint control over the business and intent to share the fruits of the enterprise, was correct (there was no clear error). Affirmed.

ANALYSIS

The UPA's broad definition of what constitutes a partnership leaves a court with wide discretion in determining whether evidence before it warrants an assumption that a partnership exists. The drafters of the UPA may have left it vague because of the plethora of factual considerations to take into account in determining partnership formulation.

Mazzuchelli v. Silberberg

Injured passenger (P) v. Partner (D)

N.J. Sup. Ct., 29 N.J. 15, 148 A.2d 8 (1959).

NATURE OF CASE: Appeal from judgment limiting liability to that afforded under relevant worker's compensation law.

FACT SUMMARY: Mazzuchelli (P) was injured when Silberberg (D), a co-partner with his wife, negligently operated the company car in which the former was a passenger, and at trial, Mazzuchelli (P), in addition to the worker's compensation claim he brought, pressed a common law negligence claim against Silberberg (D).

RULE OF LAW

The entity theory, which treats a partnership as a distinct legal entity in and of itself, is not consistent with worker's compensation law where a statutory employer is liable for compensation.

FACTS: Mazzuchelli (P) was injured when Silberberg (D), a co-partner with his wife, negligently operated the company car in which the former was a passenger. At trial, Mazzuchelli (P) successfully pressed a worker's compensation claim against Silberberg (D) and his wife, where it was found that he was injured by an accident arising out of, and in the course of, his employment. Notwithstanding this, however, Mazzuchelli (P) contended, for the purposes of pressing a common law negligence claim against Silberberg (D), that a partner is a third party within the meaning of the state's worker's compensation act, preserving the common law claim of an employee against third persons. Furthermore, Mazzuchelli (P), in order to buttress his negligence claim against Silberberg (D), contended that the Silverberg partnership was a jural entity distinct from the partners and was the "employer" (as opposed to an individual partner) within the meaning of the compensation act, which, for its purposes, immunizes an employer from other claims that may arise out of the same transaction as the worker's compensation claim. Despite this, the trial judge dismissed Mazzuchelli's (P) contentions and found that his exclusive remedy was that found under the worker's compensation act. Mazzuchelli (P) appealed.

ISSUE: Is the entity theory, which treats a partnership as a distinct legal entity in and of itself, consistent with worker's compensation law where a statutory-employer is liable for compensation?

HOLDING AND DECISION: (Weintraub, C.J.) No. The entity theory, which treats a partnership as a distinct legal entity in and of itself, is not consistent with worker's compensation law where a statutory employer is liable for compensation. The Uniform Partnership Act (UPA) adopted the aggregate theory of partnership, which allows a partner to be held individually liable at law for malfeasance with respect to partnership duties, and the other partners, by virtue of mutual agency, would also be held liable for the former's transgressions. This is to be contrasted with the entity theory of partnership, where a malfeasant partner cannot be individually sued, but the partnership, as a separate legal entity, would be liable for this partner's actions. Despite the UPA's theory adoption, certain provisions in it silently embrace the entity theory. However, with respect to common law liability for performance of obligations, contractual or other, including employee obligations, the uniform law does not adopt an entity theory. On the contrary, individual partners are personally liable and immediately suable, as well as their co-partners, as co-owners of the business, for these obligations. Notwithstanding this, however, the legislature determines whether the entity approach is applicable to specific situations. To this end, as was the case with performance of contractual obligations, the legislature has refrained from applying the entity theory to worker's compensation law. Specifically, under relevant worker's compensation provisions, "employer" is there defined to include "natural persons, partnerships and corporations." However, there is no evidence that the legislature intended to exclude individual partners from liability to perform the contractual obligation of paying scheduled worker's compensation benefits. In fact, it has been held that the individual partner is an "employer" within the provision's meaning, and, as such, is liable and immediately suable for compensation benefits. Yet, worker's compensation liability was intended to substitute common law liability, particularly where an employer would be simultaneously liable at common law and under worker's compensation law. An agreement to abide by worker's compensation law constitutes "a surrender by the parties thereto of their rights to any other method, form or amount of compensation . . ." Hence, in states in which a general contractor is a "statutory-employer" who is liable for compensation, it is usually held that he is entitled to this promised quid pro quo immunity from common law liability. Here, Silberberg's (D) negligent driving which caused Mazzuchelli's (P) injuries, while the latter was in the course of his employment, may be actionable at common law under a negligence theory. However, since Silberberg (D) agreed to abide by the state's compensation act, he is merely liable to Mazzuchelli (P) for the latter's compensation benefits. Affirmed.

ANALYSIS

The court probably would have reached a different result here if the nature of the wrong was different (i.e., reckless or intentional harm). In either case, the policy to protect

Continued on next page.

employers from overburdening safety standards in order to avoid common law liability, in addition to worker's compensation liability, would be inappropriate since there is a greater possibility that resulting harm could be avoided.

Fairway Development Co. v. Title Insurance Co. of Minnesota

Partnership (P) v. Insurance company (D)

621 F. Supp. 120 (N.D. Ohio 1985).

NATURE OF CASE: Motions for summary judgment in action for breach of contract.

FACT SUMMARY: Two of the three original partners for Fairway Development Co. (P) transferred their respective partnership interests to the remaining original partner and to a third party purchaser, after the original partners acquired title insurance for Title Insurance Co. (D).

RULE OF LAW

Where membership in a general partnership changes, the law assumes that a new partnership forms unless contradicting evidence indicates that the original transferring partners intended to reserve a portion of their respective bundles of partnership rights.

FACTS: Fairway Development Co. (P), a general partnership headed by Wenger and Valentine filed this action against Title Insurance Co. (D), alleging that the latter failed to pay Fairway (P) damages for breach of contract under a title guarantee insurance policy. Title Insurance Co. (D) entered into this policy agreement with Fairway (P) while the latter was run by the partner-trio of Bernabei, Serra, And Wenger. However, some time after the title agreement was reached, two of the partners, Bernabei and Serra, sold and transferred their respective undivided one-third interests in the partnership to the remaining partner, Wenger, and to Valentine, a third-party purchaser. Both Wenger and Valentine agreed to share equally in the partnership. Nevertheless, Fairway (P) maintained that there was an intent between the original partners for the new partner-duo to continue Fairway's (P) operation following the transfer without dissolving the partnership. On the other hand, Title Insurance Co. (D) argued that a new partnership resulted from the sale of Bernabei and Serra's partnership interests to Wenger and Valentine. As a result, Title Insurance Co. (D) concluded that it could not be held liable to Fairway (P) since it was not in privity with Fairway (P) as the named party guaranteed. Both parties filed motions for summary judgment.

ISSUE: When membership in a general partnership changes, will the law assume that a new partnership forms unless contradicting evidence indicates that the original transferring partners intended to reserve their respective bundles of partnership rights?

HOLDING AND DECISION: (Dowd, J.) Yes. Where membership in a general partnership changes, the law assumes that a new partnership forms unless contradicting evidence indicates that the original transferring partners intended to reserve a portion of their respective bundles of partnership rights. Ohio law, as does UPA, adopts the common law aggregate theory of partnership, which regards a partnership as a sum of persons comprising it. This theory precipitates a recognition by both that a change in a general partnership's membership creates a new partnership. This concept is embraced in § 1777 of the Ohio code, which requires a general partnership that changes its membership to file "a new certificate (of partnership) . . . for records with the county recorder." Likewise, Official Comment to UPA § 41(1) notes that "any change in (partnership) membership dissolves" it and "creates a new one." Notwithstanding these provisions, however, partnership membership may, under the UPA, be changed without dissolving it. Specifically, UPA § 27 permits a partner to assign his interest to another but allows him to take part in partnership management affairs, thereby effectively retaining the original partnership (seen especially when a partner's interest is used as collateral for loan purposes). In fact, under UPA § 24, a partner's property rights consist of "his rights in . . . partnership property, his interest in the partnership, and his right to participate in (its) management." Hence, the UPA allows a partner to transfer some, and not all, of his partnership rights without transferring management rights and without dissolving the partnership. However, absent evidence of a partner reserving some of his rights, the law will assume that a membership change dissolves the original partnership and creates a new one. In the instant case, the evidence indicates that the change in membership of the Fairway (P) partnership created a new partnership. First Fairway (P) concedes that it failed to file a new certificate of partnership, according to Ohio law, in order to retain its original partnership status. Second, in the partnership agreement between Wenger and Valentine, they address the commencement of the partnership by stating that it "shall commence upon the execution of this agreement," thereby recognizing that they are forming a new general partnership. Finally, both partnership agreements provide that the partners are to own the partnership in equal shares, although an equal division of the partnership interests of Bernabei and Serra between Wenger and Valentine would have left Wenger owning a interest in the partnership and Valentine owning a interest. Hence, the terms of the title guaranty do not extend to the current plaintiff because the change in membership created a new partnership. As a result, the current plaintiff, Fairway (P) has no standing to sue Title Insurance Co. (D) for breach of contract (not being in privity). Title Insurance Co.'s (D) motion for summary judgment granted.

Continued on next page.

ANALYSIS

The result reached by the Ohio district court may have been different if the UPA primarily embraced the entity theory of partnership. In that case, partnership membership changes would not affect the partnership's legal status since it would be an aloof entity. This would save the red-tape involved in filing new certificates of partnership as Ohio law authorizes.

Groff v. Citizens Bank of Clovis

Partner in joint venture (D) v. Bank (P)

898 F.2d 1475 (10th Cir. 1990).

NATURE OF CASE: Appeal from judgment in a bankruptcy priority action.

FACT SUMMARY: Citizens Bank (P) contended that it had an interest in cattle that Groff (D) and Pickering owned as part of a joint venture.

RULE OF LAW

Both partnerships and joint ventures own property separate and distinct from the partners.

FACTS: To secure a debt, Citizens Bank (P) took a security interest in specified cattle owned by Groff (D) and all "after-acquired" cattle. Subsequently, Groff (D) entered into a cattle feeding venture with Pickering, and they purchased cattle from Agri-Tech. Groff (D) filed for bankruptcy, and Citizens Bank (P) contended that it had a security interest in the cattle bought by Groff (D) and Pickering for the joint venture. The trial court ruled that Citizens Bank (P) had no interest in the cattle since it was a creditor of Groff (D) only, in his individual capacity. Citizens Bank (P) appealed.

ISSUE: Do partnerships and joint ventures own property separate and distinct from the partners?

HOLDING AND DECISION: (Logan, J.) Yes. Both partnerships and joint ventures own property separate and distinct from the partners. The joint venture is a legal organization which was developed recently to extend principles of partnership law to organizations that did not meet the technical requirements of a partnership. The sole characteristic distinguishing a joint venture from a partnership is its more limited purpose or scope. Generally, the substantive law of partnerships is applicable in determining the rights and liabilities of joint venturers. Under the Uniform Partnership Act (UPA), a partnership owns property as an entity, distinct and separate from the partners individually. A partner's right in specific partnership property is not subject to attachment, except on a claim against the partnership. Creditors may only reach a partner's residual interest in the partnership. Groff (D) and Pickering purchased cattle for a joint venture. Therefore, the cattle is property of the venture only, and creditors such as Citizens Bank (P) may not attach the cattle. Affirmed.

ANALYSIS

Nearly all of the rights surrounding property are owned by the partnership as a whole when a partnership owns property. Historically, the common law treated partners as tenants in common, that is, as joint owners of real property. Consequently, an individual debtor could not insulate his partnership property from creditors. Uniform partnership legislation has attempted to define more clearly partnership property rights and obligations.

Putnam v. Shoaf

Conveyor of partnership interest (P) v. Holder of interest (D)

Tenn. Ct. App., 620 S.W.2d 510 (1981).

NATURE OF CASE: Appeal from dismissal of plaintiff's claim for reformation of deed.

FACT SUMMARY: Putnam (P) quitclaimed her interest in a partnership to Shoaf (D) before learning the partnership possessed a valuable claim against its banks for payment of forged checks.

RULE OF LAW

When a partner conveys to another her interest in a partnership, she does not convey specific interests in specific assets but rather her undivided co-tenancy interest, and thus cannot retain interests in partnership assets unknown to her at the time of the conveyance.

FACTS: Mr. and Mrs. Charlton and Mr. & Mrs. Putnam (P) were equal partners in Frog Jump Gin. Mrs. Putnam (P) succeeded to her husband's interest upon his death but wanted to be relieved of a large partnership debt to the bank. Therefore, she conveyed her one-half partnership interest by quitclaim deed to Shoaf (D) and paid $21,000 into the partnership account in return for Shoaf's (D) assumption of liability for these debts. At the time Putnam (P) made this conveyance, it was believed Frog Jump Gin owned only gin, equipment, and land. After the conveyance, the partnership learned of embezzlement by a former bookkeeper which resulted in a judgment against the bank of over $68,000. Putnam (P) sued to reform the sale contract on the grounds that this right of action was unknown at the time of sale. The trial court dismissed the claim.

ISSUE: May a partner retain an interest in a specific asset of the partnership of which she was unaware at the time she conveyed her partnership interest to another?

HOLDING AND DECISION: (Nearn, J.) No. When a partner conveys to another her interest in a partnership, she does not convey specific interests in specific assets but rather her undivided co-tenancy interest, and thus cannot retain interests in partnership assets unknown to her at the time of the conveyance. Under the Uniform Partnership Act, Putnam's (P) interest is her pro rata share of the net value or deficit of the partnership. Frog Jump Gin itself at all times owned the specific property and assets; while a partner Putnam (P) held only an undivided interest in all partnership property as co-tenant. Putnam (P) intended at the time of sale to Shoaf (D) to convey the Frog Jump Gin interest she owned; the claim against the bank was the partnership's asset, not hers personally, and therefore she could not have retained it when she sold her interest, whether unknown at the time or not. Affirmed.

ANALYSIS

The Uniform Partnership Act § 6 provides that a partner's interest is personal property, a distinction that can become very important when a will seeks to dispose of real and personal property differently. Theoretically, the partnership's real property is deemed "equitably converted" to personal property from the individual partner's perspective.

Sharfman v. State

Partnership (P) v. State (D)

Cal. Ct. App., 253 Cal. App. 2d 333, 36 A.L.R. 3d 1370 (1967).

NATURE OF CASE: Appeal from dismissal of causes of action for loss of partnership profits.

FACT SUMMARY: Sharfman (P) crashed into a roadroller negligently left by the State (D), and, as a result, claimed damages to his partnership for his inability to service existing and potential clients and accounts.

RULE OF LAW

Partnership members may recover for loss of profits caused by the negligent act of a third party where the loss of profits is certain.

FACTS: Sharfman (P), a co-partner in the Armstrong and Sharfman partnership, crashed into a five-ton roadroller negligently left by the State (D) in the dark, and, as a result, was seriously injured. At trial, Sharfman (P) brought four causes of action against the State (D), of which the first two alleged two different types of negligence and sought damages for Sharfman (P) individually. However, the latter two causes of action claimed damages to the partnership as a result of Sharfman's (P) inability to service existing clients and accounts and to obtain new clients and accounts for the partnership as a result of the injury suffered in the accident. In support of these latter two causes of action, Sharfman (P) contended that although there has been no case law that directly answered this question, the partnership's right to recover had been established under California law by analogy. However, the trial court dismissed with prejudice these latter two causes of action on the ground that the partnership as a matter of law could not state a cause of action for loss of earnings and profits of the partnership business resulting from the negligent injury of one of its partners. Sharfman (P) appealed.

ISSUE: May partnership members recover for loss of profits caused by the negligent act of a third party where the loss of profits is certain?

HOLDING AND DECISION: (Roth, J.) Yes. Partnership members may recover for loss of profits caused by the negligent act of a third party where the loss of profits is certain. In this vein, California case law has endorsed the right of plaintiffs who are in a partnership to recover for loss of profits caused by the negligent act of a third party. *Johnson v. Central Aviation*, 103 Cal. App. 2d 102. Furthermore, it has been held that a sole proprietor may recover lost profits of his business, *Hollander v. Wilson Estate*, 214 Cal. 582, and a corporation may recover damages for negligent injury to its employee, *Darmour Prod. v. H.M. Baruch*, 135 Cal. App 351. Notwithstanding this authority, however, Sharfman (P) may not recover for alleged damages to his partnership. In Johnson, a partnership recovered for loss of profits from the sale of an airplane owned by it, which had been negligently damaged in a collision. However, this partnership recovered lost profits form injury to a physical asset of the partnership as defined in UPA § 40(a). This is distinguished from the claimed loss here, the services of a member partner, in which harm is highly unascertainable. Moreover, an analysis of *Hollander* indicates that a sole proprietor recovers loss of profits to his business based on his personal loss of income, i.e., salary or earnings, as a result of being unable to work. Thus, in the instant case, Sharfman (P), in order to recover, must show what his share of partnership income had been in the past and how this share diminished by his inability to work because of his injuries. But, to allow further recovery for loss of partnership profits, as Sharfman (P) demanded here, would allow double recovery for his injuries. Furthermore, it would be difficult to distinguish between the two methods of recovery because an individual partner's earnings overlap to a considerable extent the profits earned by the partnership as an entity. Next, *Darmour* is predicated upon a codified principle of common law which allows a servant to recover for an injury that affects his ability to serve his master, Civil Code § 49(c). However, this does not authorize recovery by a partnership for determinable business profits because of loss of the services of a salaried employee. Finally, a partnership involves a contractual agreement which defines the rights and obligations of its partners. However, with one exception, courts have generally refused to recognize a cause of action based on negligent conduct which interferes with the performance of a contract between third parties or renders its performance more expensive or burdensome, assuming these damages are two remote to warrant protection. Hence, Sharfman (P) had no legally recognizable cause of action. Affirmed.

ANALYSIS

As the appellate court points out, courts have generally been reluctant to recognize a cause of action based on negligent conduct which interferes with the performance of a contract between third parties. In this respect, contracting parties must take these risks into account at the agreement stage. However, courts, not wanting third parties to extensively interfere with contracting parties' ability to contract, afford the latter protection where the former recklessly, knowingly, or intentionally interfere with contract performance.

CHAPTER 12

The Operation of a Partnership

Quick Reference Rules of Law

CHAPTER 12

28. **Suits Among Partners.** Where one partner's suit against another principally concerns breach of the partnership agreement, an action at law will not lie until there has been an accounting. (Smith v. Manchester Management Corp.) *172*

29. **Suits Among Partners.** A partner may sue another partner at law for acts relating to the partnership without an accounting if there are no complex transactions involved. (Schuler v. Birnbaum) *173*

30. **Claims by Personal Creditors of a Partner Against the Partnership Interest of the Partner.** The court has the statutory power to charge and sell an interest of a partner in a partnership to satisfy a judgment, and the partnership agreement cannot divest the court of such power. (Tupper v. Kroc) *174*

31. **Claims by Personal Creditors of a Partner Against the Partnership Interest of the Partner.** Assignees of partnership interests are not entitled to interfere in the management or administration of partnership affairs. (Bauer v. Blomfield Co./Holden Joint Venture) *175*

Elle v. Babbitt

Partner (P) v. Closely held corporation (D)

Or. Sup. Ct., 259 Or. 590, 488 P. 440 (1971).

NATURE OF CASE: **Appeal from denial of unpaid royalties in action for accounting.**

FACT SUMMARY: **Beall Pipe & Tank Corp. (D) obtained pipe for a job from The Pipe Machinery Co., a partnership, at a lower royalty than normal without the knowledge or explicit consent of most of the partners.**

RULE OF LAW

The actual authority of certain partners to bind the partnership without consulting other partners may be implied from the circumstances and prior conduct of the partnership.

FACTS: Beall Pipe & Tank Corp. (D), a closely held corporation, made pipe. Beall Pipe & Tank Corp. (D) wanted to modernize by acquiring a tube mill but did not have enough capital to do so. It therefore was decided that The Pipe Machinery Co., a partnership, would be formed to buy the tube mill and lease it to Beall Pipe & Tank Corp. (D). The partnership was initially comprised of John and Franklin Beall, who together owned 95% of Beall Pipe & Tank Corp.'s (D) stock, and five employees of the corporation. Later seven more employees and one Beall Pipe & Tank Corp. (D) customer were added as partners. Beall Pipe & Tank Corp. (D) later terminated the lease and offered to buy the mill, but the offer was rejected and Beall Pipe & Tank Corp. (D) decided to build a new mill. About two years prior to this falling out between Beall Pipe & Tank Corp. (D) and The Pipe Machinery Co., The Pipe Machinery Co. had sold pipe to Beall Pipe & Tank Corp. (D) for a certain job at a 50% reduction from the usual royalty so that Beall Pipe & Tank Corp. (D) could bid low enough to get the job. The decision to accept the reduced royalty was made at a meeting attended by John and Franklin Beall, Elle (P), a partner who then worked for Beall Pipe & Tank Corp. (D) as chief engineer and estimator, and Wilkins, a partner and Beall Pipe & Tank Corp.'s (D) sales manager. Beall Pipe & Tank Corp. (D) got the job and paid the reduced royalty. No meeting of all partners was ever called to approve this cut in royalty, and none of the other partners were notified that The Pipe Machinery Co. would be asked to accept this cut before it was so agreed. Elle (P) and two other partners later sued Beall Pipe & Tank Corp. (D) on behalf of The Pipe Machinery Co. for the difference between the discounted and the usual royalty and the terminated lease. They argued that the agreement was not authorized because all partners needed to participate in the decision as all had equal management rights according to the Uniform Partnership Act. The trial court awarded Elle (P) the difference in royalties. Beall Pipe & Tank Corp. (D) appealed.

ISSUE: Can the actual authority of certain partners to bind the partnership without consulting other partners be implied from the circumstances and prior conduct of the partnership?

HOLDING AND DECISION: (McAllister, J.) Yes. The Uniform Partnership Act gives individual partners equal management powers in dealings with third parties within the scope of partnership business, with differences resolved by a majority of the partners. UPA §§ 9(1), (4) and 18(e)(h). But the equal management rights exist only in the absence of an agreement among the partners that allocates management powers otherwise. UPA § 18. An agreement allocating management power otherwise than equally may be implied from the course of conduct of the partnership and the partners. The partners may agree to give a single managing partner authority to manage the business. Here the testimony clearly evidences the fact that most of the partners never involved themselves with the management of partnership affairs. One of the plaintiffs testified that none of the partners, other than Mr. Beall and possibly Mr. Elle (P), ever acted on behalf of the partnership, and that all the other partners did was make an initial investment and collect their profits. During the period the partnership sold pipe to Beall Pipe Manufacturing Co. (D), only partners who were management level employees of Beall Pipe Manufacturing Co. (D) under John Beall's direction managed the partnership's affairs. Because no partners ever objected to this management arrangement, John Beall became managing partner with authority to conduct the partnership's ordinary business by a tacit agreement of all the partners. Here the decision to temporarily accept reduced royalties in order to make a successful bid was clearly within the partnership's business. Thus John Beall had the authority to bind his partners to the agreement with Beall Pipe Manufacturing Co. (D) because of their long acquiescence to his management. Also of significance is that Elle (P) agreed and Wilkins, another partner, either agreed or did not object. Reversed as to the award for unpaid royalties and trial court decree affirmed as modified.

ANALYSIS

This case shows that a partner must actively participate in management to avoid losing the right to participate in

Continued on next page.

management decisions by acquiescence. The court also suggests another issue in the law of business organization, conflict of interest. A managing partner is analogous to a corporation's management and board of directors. Corporations, especially public ones, are characterized by a separation of ownership and control because shareholders normally do not participate in management decisions directly. Officers and board members are subjected to fiduciary duties that regulate self dealing and prevent transactions that are not in the best economic interests of the shareholders as a body.

Summers v. Dooley

Partner (P) v. Partner (D)

Idaho Sup. Ct., 94 Idaho 87, 481 P.2d 318 (1971).

NATURE OF CASE: Action for reimbursement for partnership expenses.

FACT SUMMARY: Summers (P) sought reimbursement from Dooley (D) for expenditures made in hiring an employee.

RULE OF LAW

In the absence of an agreement to the contrary, a partnership business decision must be made by a majority of the partners.

FACTS: Summers (P) and Dooley (D) were partners in a trash collection business. In July 1966, Summers (P) approached Dooley (D) regarding the hiring of an additional employee. Dooley (D) refused. Nonetheless, Summers (P) hired the employee and paid him out of his own pocket. Upon learning of Summers' (P) actions, Dooley (D) objected, stating that additional help was unnecessary and refused to allow partnership funds to be used to pay for the new employee. Summers (P) brought suit to force reimbursement for half of the $12,000 he had expended on the new employee. The trial court found that, as a majority agreement was lacking in the decision to hire the new employee, Summers' (P) action in hiring the employee anyway must be deemed as being for his own personal benefit. Reimbursement was not ordered. Summers (P) appealed.

ISSUE: Will a partnership be bound by a business decision made by less than a majority of the partners?

HOLDING AND DECISION: (Donaldson, J.) No. All of the relevant statutory provisions and case decisions point to the fact that in the absence of an agreement to the contrary, a partnership business decision must be made by a majority of the partners. The agreement between Summers (P) and Dooley (D) contained no such contrary provision. Dooley (D) clearly voiced his objection to the hiring of the new employee, both before and after the hiring occurred, and stated he would not allow partnership funds to be used to pay the expenses. Thus, the absence of a majority agreement is clear. As such, it would be eminently unfair to force Dooley (D) to reimburse Summers (P) for Summers'(P) unilateral decision. Affirmed.

ANALYSIS

An apparent conflict arises between the concept of majority decision-making, discussed in the principal case and detailed in Uniform Partnership Act § 18, and the notion that each partner is an agent for the entire partnership in transactions which are effected for the purpose of furthering the business of the partnership (See UPA § 9). The *Summers* case seems to rest, at least in part, on the fact that the nonconsenting party expressly vetoed the decision made by his partner and the resultant inequity of forcing him to pay for it, nonetheless.

National Biscuit Co. v. Stroud

Supplier (P) v. Partnership (D)

N.C. Sup. Ct., 249 N.C. 467, 106 S.E.2d 692 (1959).

NATURE OF CASE: Appeal from award of damages for breach of judgment in contract against partnership.

FACT SUMMARY: Stroud (D) informed National Biscuit Co. (P) that he would not be personally liable for bread shipped thereafter on credit to a store he operated with his partner, but National Biscuit Co. (P) sought to recover on unpaid accounts for deliveries of bread after this notice.

RULE OF LAW

A general partner may bind an ongoing partnership for obligations within the scope of the partnership's business, thus making all partners personally liable, even though other partners have informed the obligee they will not be personally bound to certain transactions.

FACTS: Stroud (D) operated a grocery with his partner, Freeman. Stroud (D) informed an agent of National Biscuit Co. (P), a regular supplier of bread to the grocery, that he would not be personally liable for additional bread shipped to the grocery several months before the partnership was dissolved. National Biscuit Co. (P) shipped bread to the grocery after receiving this notice, until the partnership was dissolved. Stroud (D) paid all the partnership obligations except the amount charged for bread delivered during the last 19 days before the partnership's dissolution. He paid most of these partnership obligations from his personal funds after liquidating all partnership assets, except some uncollectible accounts receivable. Stroud (D) tendered National Biscuit Co. (P) payment of half the sum billed for the 19 days prior to dissolution. National Biscuit Co. (P) sued to recover the full amount billed. The trial court rendered judgment for National Biscuit Co. (P). Stroud (D) appealed.

ISSUE: May a general partner bind an ongoing partnership for obligations to a third party within the scope of the partnership's business, thus making all partners personally liable, even though other partners have informed the third party that they will not be personally bound to certain transactions?

HOLDING AND DECISION: (Parker, J.) Yes. A general partner may bind an ongoing partnership for obligations to a third party within the scope of the partnership's business, thus making all partners personally liable, even though the others have informed the third party that they will not be personally bound to certain transactions. Stroud (D) and Freeman were partners, and nothing in the agreed facts suggests or indicates Freeman's authority was limited by the partnership agreement for matters within the ordinary and legitimate business of the partnership. The purchase and sale of bread were within the scope of the partnership's ongoing business. This court has previously held that when two partners engage in a business, each can bind the partnership in any manner legitimate to the business by operation of law. Although there is contrary authority, it does not mention the effect of the Uniform Partnership Act which is law in this jurisdiction. Each partner has equal management authority to conduct partnership affairs within the scope of its business. UPA §§ 9(1),(4) and 18(e),(h). Because the purchase of bread was within the ordinary scope of this partnership's business, Stroud (D) could not restrict Freeman's authority to buy bread under UPA § 18(h) because he was not, and could not be, a majority of the partners. Crane on Partnership, 2d ed. states that when the partners are evenly divided and a third party has knowledge, there should be no restriction placed on the partnership's activities by half, which is not a clear majority. Cases where the partnership contract imposed special restrictions on the partner acting on behalf of the partnership are distinguishable. Affirmed.

ANALYSIS

Inherent authority does not exist for this transaction because a reasonable belief of authority without notice of the lack thereof is required for inherent authority. The requirements for apparent authority and estoppel also would not be satisfied in the presence of actual notice that authority is lacking. Here the actual authority is found by applying the Uniform Partnership Act, which gives all partners equal management and control except when the actual partnership agreement overrides the Uniform Partnership Act. Presumably the result in this case would have been different if Stroud (D) could have shown that the partnership agreement, when entered into, contemplated unequal allocation of management authority whereby Freeman was not authorized to order goods. When all partners have equal management power, a situation where no majority exists among partners is possible if the number of partners is equal. This court takes a preferable position on the issue of whether half the partners can restrict other partners in transacting within the scope of the partnership's business under UPA § 18(h). Otherwise a single partner in a two person partnership could veto transactions that are necessary to preserve the ongoing concern. If a partner no longer wishes to continue to be bound as a member of a partnership, he should withdraw as a partner, thus dissolving the partnership, rather than "laming" the other partner's ability to manage an ongoing business.

Burns v. Gonzalez

Buyer of airtime (P) v. Partnership (D)

Tex. Ct. Civ. App., 439 S.W.2d 128 (1969).

NATURE OF CASE: Appeal from judgment denying recovery on promissory note.

FACT SUMMARY: Gonzalez (D), a partner with Bosquez in a business selling airtime on a radio station, executed a $40,000 note to Burns (P) to compensate him for broadcast opportunities lost during the period the station was in receivership.

RULE OF LAW

The act of a partner binds the partnership, absent an express limitation of authority known to the party dealing with such partner, if such act is for the purpose of "apparently carrying" on a partnership business.

FACTS: Gonzalez (D) and Bosquez were partners in Inter-American Advertising, which sold broadcast time over a Mexican ratio station on a commission basis. Gonzalez (D) and Bosquez also owned 50% of the stock of the company that owned the station, Radiodifusora. Radiodifusora and Inter-American together agreed to allow Roloff Evangelistic Enterprises and Burns (P) to air two 15-minute segments every day over the station, in exchange for $100,000, and Burns (P) was assigned Roloff's rights in the contract. The radio station then went into receivership for two years, during which Burns (P) received no actual broadcast time for resale to third parties. To compensate Burns (P) for this lack of airtime and to prevent him from suing, Bosquez, without the knowledge of Gonzalez (D), executed a $40,000 note payable to Burns (P). When Inter-American failed to pay, Burns (P) sued to recover against both Gonzalez (D) and Bosquez.

ISSUE: Does the act of a partner bind the partnership, absent an express limitation of authority known to the party dealing with such partner, if such act is for the purpose of "apparently carrying on" a partnership business?

HOLDING AND DECISION: (Cadena, J.) Yes. Each partner is an agent of the partnership for the purpose of its business, and the act of every partner, including the execution in the partnership name of any instrument whose purpose is to carry on in the usual way the business of the partnership, unless the partner so acting has in fact no authority to act in a particular matter and the person with whom he is dealing knows he has no such authority. Here, Bosquez had no authority to sign a note for Burns (P), but Burns (P) did not know Bosquez had no such authority. Nor was Inter-American, an advertising agency, engaged in periodic, continuous, and frequent purchasing for resale to consumers such that the issuance of commercial paper to finance such purchases was a necessary aspect of its business. Inter-American sold advertising services and its hard assets were its office supplies. Thus, Bosquez's execution of the note to Burns (P) was not of the nature of the partnership business and the manner in which it was usually conducted. The note sued on was therefore not a partnership obligation. Affirmed.

ANALYSIS

The same issue arises in the context of sales or transfers of the bulk of partnership property, including its real estate holdings. The sale of all the property is not the carrying on in the usual way of the partnership business within the meaning of the Uniform Partnership Act § 9. A mortgage of all partnership property, for example, must be executed by all members of the partnership. See, e.g., *Ditzel v. Kent*, 131 Mont. 129, 308 P.2d 628 (1957).

RNR Investments Limited Partnership v. Peoples First Community Bank

Limited partnership (D) v. Bank (P)

Fla. Ct. App., 812 So. 2d 561 (2002).

NATURE OF CASE: Appeal from summary judgment for plaintiff in foreclosure action.

FACT SUMMARY: RNR Investments Limited Partnership (RNR) (D), a limited partnership, contended that Peoples First Community Bank (Bank) (P) was negligent in lending in lending $ 990,000 to RNR (D) without consent of the limited partners when, under RNR's (D) Agreement of Limited Partnership, the authority of RNR's (D) general partner was limited to obtaining financing up to $ 650,000.

RULE OF LAW

A general partner has apparent authority to bind a partnership in the ordinary course of partnership business or in the business of the kind carried on by the partnership where a third party has no knowledge, or is not on notice that, the general partner lacks actual authority.

FACTS: RNR Investments Limited Partnership (RNR) (D), a limited partnership, was formed to buy land and build a house. Its partnership agreement provided that the budget for the project, prepared by the general partner, would need to be approved by the limited partners if it was exceeded by more than 5%, and could not be exceeded by more than 10%. It also restricted the general partner's to borrow, without the limited partners' written consent, any amount that would cause the budget to be exceeded by more than 10% or that would cause the aggregate budget to be exceeded by more than 5%. The general partner then obtained a $990,000 mortgage loan from Peoples First Community Bank (Bank) (P). Over close to two years, the Bank (P) disbursed around $952,700. RNR (D) never objected to any draw of these funds. Then, RNR (D) defaulted on the loan, and the Bank (P) brought suit seeking foreclosure. In one affirmative defense to the Bank's (P) motion for summary judgment, RNR (D) alleged that the partners had an understanding and oral agreement that the general partner would borrow no more than $650,000, and that the limited partners had not consented to a higher amount. Accordingly, RNR (D) asserted that the Bank (P) was negligent in not reviewing the partnership agreement or requesting a written consent, even if such a consent had not been memorialized. There was no record of an approved budget, and the Bank (P) was never given a copy of the partnership agreement or any budget. Nor was the Bank (P) informed of the general partner's restricted authority to borrow. The trial court entered summary judgment in favor of the Bank (P), and the state's intermediate appellate court granted review.

ISSUE: Does a general partner have apparent authority to bind a partnership in the ordinary course of partnership business or in the business of the kind carried on by the partnership where a third party has no knowledge, or is not on notice that, the general partner lacks actual authority?

HOLDING AND DECISION: (Van Nortwick, J.) Yes. A general partner has apparent authority to bind a partnership in the ordinary course of partnership business or in the business of the kind carried on by the partnership where a third party has no knowledge, or is not on notice that, the general partner lacks actual authority. The extent to which a partnership is bound by the acts of a partner acting with apparent authority is governed by statute. Statutorily, even if a general partner's actual authority is restricted by the terms of the partnership agreement, the general partner possesses the apparent authority to bind the partnership in the ordinary course of partnership business or in the business of the kind carried on by the partnership, unless a third party knows or has received notice that the partner lacks authority. Knowledge means actual knowledge, and notice means that a party "(a) knows of the fact; (b) has received notification of the fact; or (c) has reason to know the fact exists from all other facts known to the person at the time in question." Also, a partnership may file a statement of partnership authority that sets forth restrictions on a general partner's authority. These statutory provisions, when taken together, mean that a third party has no duty to inspect the partnership agreement or determine a general partner's actual authority absent actual knowledge or notice. The burden is on the partnership to inform third parties of limits on partner authority. Applying these principles here, RNR's (D) general partner was carrying on RNR's (D) business in the ordinary course when he sought the loan from the Bank (P). Therefore, the dispositive issue is whether the Bank (P) had actual knowledge or notice of restrictions on the general partner's authority; there is no evidence that it did. Because there is no dispute of any material issues of fact as to whether the Bank (P) had actual knowledge or notice or restrictions on the general partner's authority to borrow, summary judgment was proper. Affirmed.

ANALYSIS

The statute at issue in this case, the Florida Revised Uniform Partnership Act (FRUPA), based on the Revised Uniform Partnership Act (RUPA), provides greater protection than the Uniform Partnership Act (UPA) by reallocating the

Continued on next page.

risk of unauthorized agency power in favor of third parties. This is consistent with notions of the expanded liability of principals since the UPA was drafted. RUPA attempts to balance its shift toward greater protection of third parties by providing several new ways for partners to protect themselves against unauthorized actions by a rogue partner. First, the partnership may notify a third party of a partner's lack of authority. Such notification is effective upon receipt, whether or not the third party actually learns of it. More significantly, the partnership may file a statement of partnership authority restricting a partner's authority. Had RNR (D) done so here, it would have prevailed. However, chances are good that the Bank (P) would never have made the loan in the amount it did if it had notice of the restrictions on the general partner's authority, so that a foreclosure suit may have been avoided altogether.

Royal Bank v. Weintraub, Gold & Alper

Lending bank (P) v. Law firm (D)

N.Y. Ct. App., 68 N.Y.2d 124, 497 N.E.2d 289 (1986).

NATURE OF CASE: Appeal from summary judgment granting recovery of loaned funds.

FACT SUMMARY: At the request of its client, Royal Bank (P) deposited a $60,000 check in escrow with Weintraub, Gold & Alper (D), which held itself out as a law firm but whose three individual members had earlier voted to dissolve.

RULE OF LAW

A partner who makes, and consents to, continued representation that a partnership in fact exists is estopped to deny that a partnership exists to defeat the claim of a creditor.

FACTS: Allen asked Royal Bank (P) for a $60,000 loan to be deposited in escrow with his lawyers, Weintraub, Gold & Alper (D). Allen gave Royal Bank (P) a letter on Weintraub (D) firm stationery signed by the name partner Weintraub, authorizing the deposit in the firm's trust account. Once the $60,000 had been used to enable Allen to qualify for an even larger loan elsewhere, the money would be returned to Royal Bank (P). Royal Bank (P) called the firm, whose receptionist identified it over the telephone as Weintraub, Gold & Alper (D), and confirmed the loan with Weintraub himself. The loan was disbursed, deposited in the firm trust account, but never returned. Later it was discovered that the members of Weintraub, Gold & Alper (D) had orally dissolved the year before but had not filed a certificate of dissolution or publicly announced dissolution. They still shared office space, had accounts in the firm name, and had loans drawn on the firm. Nevertheless, Weintraub, Gold & Alper (D) attempted to avoid liability for the $60,000 on the basis of their dissolution. From summary judgment for Royal Bank (P), Weintraub, Gold & Alper (D) appealed.

ISSUE: Is a partner who makes and consents to continued representations that a partnership in fact exists estopped from denying a partnership exists to defeat a creditor's claim?

HOLDING AND DECISION: (Kaye, J.) Yes. A partner who continues to represent that his partnership exists will be estopped from denying its existence for the purpose of avoiding partnership obligations. Here Weintraub's (D) acts with respect to the escrow deposit were apparently for the benefit of a client and in furtherance of partnership business. If the individual Weintraub lacked authority to act for Weintraub, Gold & Alper (D) in the particular matter, Royal Bank (P) had no knowledge of this. Although the firm may have privately dissolved, public indicia of partnership—use of firm space, telephone listing, stationery, etc.—remained undisturbed, giving the impression of an ongoing entity. Therefore, Weintraub, Gold & Alper (D) is estopped from asserting dissolution as a bar to Royal Bank's (P) recovery. Affirmed.

ANALYSIS

A similar problem arises when partners incorporate their partnership but do not change the public image of their business. Partners who continue to hold themselves out as such after incorporation cannot escape responsibility for contracts entered into without adequate notice of dissolution. This is especially true when the corporation operates under the same name and circumstances as the partnership. See, e.g., *Springer v. Opsahl*, 744 P.2d 884, 889 (Mont. 1987).

Brown v. Gerstein

Real property owners (P) v. Attorney (D)

Mass. Ct. App., 17 Mass. App. 558, 460 N.E.2d 1043, *review denied*, 464 N.E.2d 73 (1984).

NATURE OF CASE: Appeal from judgment notwithstanding the verdict in malpractice action.

FACT SUMMARY: The Browns (P) retained Gerstein (D), an attorney, to represent them in a lawsuit to enjoin foreclosure on real property, but when Gerstein (D) did nothing and the Browns (P) lost the property, they tried to hold Gerstein's (D) former law partner liable.

RULE OF LAW

A person must hold himself out as a partner, or consent to being held out as a partner, to be estopped from denying liability on a claim against the partnership.

FACTS: The Browns (P), who owned real estate in danger of foreclosure due to default on the mortgage, retained Gerstein (D), an attorney, to represent them in a breach of contract claim against the foreclosing bank. Although the Browns (P) signed a complaint for injunctive relief and received assurances from Gerstein (D) that "he would handle everything" and that "there would be no foreclosure," Gerstein (D) did nothing to file the complaint and the bank foreclosed. Gerstein (D) claimed he had a "deal" with the bank and had been "double-crossed." The Browns (P) sued Gerstein (D) and Weiner, whom they claimed was his partner. Although the Browns (P) had retained the firm of Gerstein & Weiner some years previous on an unrelated claim and received letters from Gerstein (D) on Gerstein & Weiner stationery, they had never met Weiner and made out their retainer check payable to Gerstein (D) alone.

ISSUE: Must a person hold himself out as a partner or consent to being held out as a partner, to be estopped from denying liability on a claim against the partnership?

HOLDING AND DECISION: (Greaney, J.) Yes. To prevail under the doctrine of partnership by estoppel a plaintiff must prove: (1) the would-be partner held himself out as a partner; (2) such holding out was done directly by the defendant or with his consent; (3) plaintiff had knowledge of such holding out; and (4) plaintiff relied on this ostensible partnership to his prejudice. Here, the Browns (P) failed to show Weiner held himself out as, or consented to being held out as, Gerstein's (D) law partner. They never met him, and they made their payment directly to Gerstein (D). Mere use by Gerstein (D) of stationery with Weiner's name did not indicate Weiner's consent. Affirmed.

ANALYSIS

The Official Comment to Restatement of Agency § 16 notes that the weight of authority requires that to be held as a partner a person must consent to the holding out and the holding out must be a matter of fact. Another train of authority discussed in the comment but finding less approval therein holds that mere knowledge of the holding out without steps to prevent it (even if this means legal action) will subject the ostensible partner to liability.

J & J Builders Supply v. Caffin

Supplier (P) v. Co-partner (D)

Cal. Ct. App., 248 Cal. App. 2d 292 (1967).

NATURE OF CASE: Appeal from judgment awarding recovery of debt.

FACT SUMMARY: Caffin (D) said nothing when introduced to the president of J & J Builders Supply (P) as the "new partner" of its customer, a masonry company.

RULE OF LAW

Failure to deny statements made in the presence of a third party creditor that one is a partner of a debtor partnership, under circumstances which suggest that a response must be made to avoid misleading the creditor, estop the ostensible partner from denying liability for the creditor's claim.

FACTS: Jeffrey, a masonry contractor, bought building materials from J & J Builders Supply (P). One day he met with J & J's (P) president and introduced Caffin (D) to him as his "new partner" who would "throw a lot of money into the business," which would have a new account under the name Perry Masonry. Caffin (D) said nothing. After deliveries to Perry Masonry construction sites and an extended failure to pay, J & J (P) cut off Perry Masonry's credit. When one of J & J's (P) officers visited Caffin (D) to collect the unpaid balance, Caffin (D) denied liability, claiming he was not personally responsible because Perry Masonry was a corporation and that he called "anybody" he went into business with a "partner no matter what the deal is." From a judgment for J & J (P), Caffin (D) appealed.

ISSUE: Does failure to deny statements made in the presence of a third party creditor that one is a partner of a debtor partnership, under circumstances which suggest that a response must be made to avoid misleading the creditor, estop the ostensible partner from denying liability for the creditor's claim?

HOLDING AND DECISION: (Hufstedler, J.) Yes. Failure to deny statements made in the presence of a third party creditor that one is a partner of a debtor partnership, under circumstances which suggest that a response must be made to avoid misleading the creditor, estops the ostensible partner from denying liability for the creditor's claim. Here, declarations of partnership by Jeffrey in Caffin's (D) presence, under circumstances in which Caffin (D) must have known that a response negativing Jeffrey's representation should have been made to avoid misleading J & J (P), estop Caffin (D) from denying liability on J & J's (P) claim against Perry Masonry. Caffin (D) was an ostensible partner whose conduct was sufficient to lead the creditor J & J (P) to believe he was a co-partner. Affirmed.

ANALYSIS

This case's holding was based on the Uniform Partnership Act § 16, and can be read to give rise to an affirmative obligation to act. In this case, however, it was relatively easy in the face-to-face setting of the J & J (P) office for Caffin (D) to deny Jeffrey's claims of partnership. In other cases in which the ostensible partner merely received bills and letters from a creditor claiming liability, and did nothing, silence and inaction did not constitute an estoppel. See, e.g., *Huron v. Schomaker*, 132 Pa. Super. 462, 464, 1 A.2d 537, 539 (1938).

Brown & Bigelow v. Roy

Seller (P) v. Partnership (D)

Ohio Ct. App., 132 N.E.2d 755 (1955).

NATURE OF CASE: Appeal from award of damages for goods sold and delivered.

FACT SUMMARY: Brown & Bigelow (P) was not paid for merchandise it supplied to a partnership consisting of Roy (D) and Lucas, both of whom had signed, filed, and posted at their place of business a vendor's license.

RULE OF LAW

The posting and filing of a public license to do business as a partnership will estop an ostensible partner who signed the license from denying liability for partnership debts.

FACTS: Roy (D) and Lucas formed a partnership named F & M Truck Stop. They both signed, filed with the state, and posted at their place of business a vendor's license. Roy (D) also made a loan to Lucas. F & M purchased merchandise from Brown & Bigelow (P) but did not pay for it. Brown & Bigelow (P) won a judgment for goods sold and delivered against Roy (D), who had claimed that Brown & Bigelow (P) had no knowledge of the vendor's license and therefore could not have relied on his signature in extending credit.

ISSUE: Does the posting and filing of a public license to do business as a partnership estop an ostensible partner who signed the license from denying liability for partnership obligations?

HOLDING AND DECISION: (Miller, J.) Yes. The public Posting and filing with the relevant government agency of a license to do business, signed by an ostensible partner, will estop the ostensible partner from denying the partnership. Here Roy (D) represented he was a partner in F & M Truck Stop when he signed the application for the vendor's license and posted it at the truck stop, where it served as notice to the public of the nature of the business being conducted on the premises. Affirmed.

ANALYSIS

Many courts, though not all, have agreed with this holding that actual reliance by a creditor in a public holding-out scenario is not required under Uniform Partnership Act § 16. See, e.g., *Anderson Hay & Grain Co.* v. Dunn, 81 N.M. 339, 467 P.2d 5 (1970) (rebuttable presumption of reliance arises when an ostensible partner holds himself out to the public as a true partner).

Reisen Lumber & Millwork Co. v. Simonelli

Supplier of lumber (P) v. Buyer (D)

N.J. Super. Ct., 98 N.J. Super. 335, 237 A.2d 303 (1967).

NATURE OF CASE: Motion for summary judgment in action based on partnership by estoppel to recover the costs of lumber sold on credit.

FACT SUMMARY: After Simonelli (D) defaulted on payments for lumber obtained from Reisen Lumber & Millwork Co. (P), Reisen (P) obtained a default judgment against Simonelli (D), then filed this action against his former partner, Millinger (D).

RULE OF LAW

An individual is liable as a partner by estoppel when he represents himself as such or consents to another representing himself as such to a creditor, even though he is not in fact a partner, where the creditor has extended credit to the partnership in reliance upon that representation.

FACTS: In buying lumber on credit, Simonelli (D) signed his name and that of Yorke Investment Co. Simonelli (D) and Millinger (D) had previously conducted business under the name of Yorke, but they had dissolved the partnership before the lumber purchase. Simonelli (D) made no mention of Millinger (D) to Reisen Lumber & Millwork Co. (P) and never represented that Millinger (D) was a partner or was in any way connected with Yorke. Reisen (P) obtained a default judgment against Simonelli (D) when Simonelli (D) failed to pay for the lumber, and Reisen (P) then sued Millinger (D), arguing that a certificate of dissolution of the Yorke partnership had never been filed. Reisen (P) admitted that it did not rely on the filing of a partnership certificate or the absence of a certificate of dissolution.

ISSUE: Is an individual liable as a partner by estoppel when he represents himself as such or consents to another representing himself as such to a creditor, even though he is not in fact a partner, where the creditor has extended credit to the partnership in reliance upon that representation?

HOLDING AND DECISION: (Larner, J.) Yes. An individual is liable as a partner by estoppel when he represents himself as such or consents to another representing himself as such to a creditor, even though he is not in fact a partner, where the creditor has extended credit to the partnership in reliance upon that representation. In this case, the only basis for Millinger's (D) liability must rest on a theory of partnership by estoppel. The party seeking to invoke that doctrine must prove that he in good faith relied upon the conduct, act, or representation of the other party. Since Reisen (P) concedes that it did not know of the filing of the partnership certificate when it extended the credit and shipped the materials, it did not rely upon that status in any respect. Thus, it cannot utilize the doctrine of partnership by estoppel to impose liability on Millinger (D). Summary judgment denied.

ANALYSIS

Section 16 of the Uniform Partnership Act (UPA) states the rule applied here by the court. The filing of the business name certificate constitutes a representation of the partnership in a public manner within the purview of the statute. However, the representation in a public manner does not obviate the necessity of reliance on that representation by the creditor in order to impose liability through the avenue of partnership by estoppel.

Smith v. Hensley

Co-partner (D) v. Co-partner (P)

Ky. Ct. App., 354 S.W.2d 744, 98 A.L.R.2d 340 (1962).

NATURE OF CASE: Appeal from award of damages for negligence.

FACT SUMMARY: Hensley's (P) truck, while being serviced by an employee of Mary Gail Coal Company, a partnership in which Smith (D) and Hensley (P) were partners, burned when gasoline from the partnership's gas station became ignited during the employee's scope of employment for the partnership, of which Hensley (P) was a member.

RULE OF LAW

Where a partner sustains a loss to his personal property resulting from the negligence of a partnership employee while in the ordinary course of firm affairs, he may bring an action against his firm for the losses he sustained.

FACTS: Mary Gail Coal Company, a partnership in which Hensley (P) and Smith (D) were two of eight partners, operated a coal mine near Hyden and had its production transported by a fleet of trucks to Manchester. Along this transportation stretch, the company owned and operated a gas station in which the truck drivers serviced their trucks between trips. During one of these trips, while hauling a load of coal to Manchester, Hensley's (P) personally owned truck, a member of the fleet, burned when the gasoline from the company-owned gas station ignited while a company employee was servicing it. At trial, there was no evidence offered as to the contractual relationship between Hensley (P) and the partnership, but Smith (D), the partnership representative, did not question Hensley's (P) assertion that his truck and driver had been "hired" by the company. As a result, Hensley (P) asserted that since the company negligently permitted gasoline to be spilled from the pumps and to remain on the ground, which subsequently resulted in damage to his truck when the gasoline became ignited, the partnership should be liable for his loss occurring while a company employee was engaging in the firm's affairs. However, Smith (D) contended that a partner cannot maintain an action against his co-partners for the negligence of firm employees because their negligence is imputable to all partners. Notwithstanding Smith's (D) contentions, the trial court awarded Hensley (P) a judgment for $4,000 against his co-partners. Smith (D) appealed.

ISSUE: Where a partner sustains a loss to his personal property resulting from the negligence of an employee while in the ordinary course of firm affairs, may he bring an action against his firm for the losses he sustained?

HOLDING AND DECISION: (Stanley, Comm.) Yes. Where a partner sustains a loss to his personal property resulting from the negligence of a partnership employee while in the ordinary course of firm affairs, he may bring an action against his firm for the losses he sustained. At common law, an action is ordinarily not maintainable between a partner and his firm. More specifically, since the negligence of a partnership employee must be imputed to the defendant partnership to establish liability, then this negligence must also be imputed to the partner plaintiff which bars recovery because a litigant cannot sue himself (doctrine of imputable negligence). However, courts have recognized that this doctrine is of artificial creation and must in particular cases yield to reason and practical considerations (i.e, social and economic necessity). In this respect, the practical realities of the business world dictate that the partners should share the loss of damage to property resulting from the negligence of the partnership employees, regardless of who owns the property. This would require a partnership to assume the risk for damages resulting from the negligence of its employees while acting in the ordinary course of firm affairs as opposed to imposing this risk on an individual partner simply because his personal property is involved. Here, since Hensley's (P) personally-owned truck was "hired" by the partnership company to haul its production, and it was negligently damaged during the course of the firm's business by a firm employee, Hensley (P) may maintain this action. However, even if, as Smith (D) contended, the use of Hensley's (P) truck was not in the partnership business but was a collateral use in the connection with an independent contract between Hensley (P) and the partnership, then there is more reason to impose a duty on the partners to share the loss because there is no basis upon which it could be said that Hensley (P) contributed his truck to the partnership's use with an intent to assume all risk for its loss. Hence, the parties, who are jointly and severally liable for firm obligations, should bear their respective proportionate share of Hensley's (P) losses as determined by the partnership contract. Remanded, and as modified, affirmed.

ANALYSIS

As the court here noted, although an action at law is not ordinarily maintainable between a partner and his firm, changing social and economic conditions dictate that the loss a partner suffers, through a partnership employee's negligence, be viewed as an ordinary business loss.

Continued on next page.

Perhaps this rule will encourage partnerships to maintain a higher standard of care for the conduct of their employees involved in firm affairs, to avoid the increased risk of intra-partnership liability between co-members.

Rouse v. Pollard

Client (P) v. Law firm partnership (D)

New Jersey Ct. of Errors & Appeals, 130 N.J. Eq. 204, 21 A.2d 801 (1941).

NATURE OF CASE: **Appeal from dismissal of vicarious liability claim for damages against principal and limiting liability to agent.**

FACT SUMMARY: **Fitzsimmons, an attorney for the law partnership in which Pollard (D) was a member, fraudulently induced Rouse (P) to invest in mortgage bonds during the course of his duties as her attorney, and Rouse's (P) subsequent claim against the firm, charging the latter with vicarious liability for damages she suffered as a result of Fitzsimmon's actions, was dismissed by the trial court and liability limited as to Fitzsimmons.**

RULE OF LAW

Where a partnership member, while participating in conduct unrelated to his partnership duties, fraudulently appropriates the property of another, vicarious liability will not attach to the entire partnership unless it participated in or otherwise authorized the malfeasant member's conduct.

FACTS: In pursuit of a separation agreement from her husband, Rouse (P) went to the firm of Riker and Riker, a law partnership in which Pollard (D) was a member, and was referred to Fitzsimmons, another member of the firm. During the course of Rouse's (P) conferences with Fitzsimmons, the latter requested that she sell her securities and turn over the proceeds to the firm so that the firm, at its own discretion, could allegedly make future, undisclosed investments in mortgage bonds as well as discharge her legal obligations. In compliance with this request, Rouse (P) endorsed roughly a $28,000 check, representing the amount of her security proceeds, which read "Pay to the order of Thos. E. Fitzsimmons." Subsequently, Fitzsimmons deposited this check in his personal bank account. Although Rouse (P) received personal checks from Fitzsimmons representing the interest from her investment, the firm merely received the $350 Rouse (P) had incurred in legal fees by retaining Fitzsimmons. Some time later, after receiving only a portion of her principal, just prior to Fitzsimmons' arrest for embezzlement, Rouse (P) brought this action for damages against the firm and Fitzsimmons, its agent, contending that Fitzsimmons' actions were within the scope of his employment, or within his apparent authority, and therefore the firm should be held vicariously liable for the balance of her invested security proceeds. However, the lower court, in its decree, dismissed Rouse's (P) vicarious liability claim against the firm and limited liability to Fitzsimmons. Rouse (P) appealed.

ISSUE: Where a partnership member, while participating in conduct unrelated to his partnership duties, fraudulently appropriates the property of another, will vicarious liability attach the entire partnership whether or not it participated in or otherwise authorized the malfeasant member's conduct?

HOLDING AND DECISION: (Case, J.) No. Where a partnership member, while participating in conduct unrelated to his partnership duties, fraudulently appropriates the property of another, vicarious liability will not attach to the entire partnership unless it participated in or otherwise authorized the malfeasant member's conduct. In the case at bar, although the firm engaged in a "real estate practice," it did not conduct a general investment business, nor did it accept funds for future, unspecified investment at the firm's discretion, in mortgages or otherwise. Moreover, this investment practice has not occurred with enough frequency in this jurisdiction as to become a characteristic function of the practice of law. Hence, Fitzsimmons' conduct was outside the scope of his duties for the firm, e.g., the practice of law. Furthermore, there is no evidence that Fitzsimmons' conduct was participated in, or authorized by, the firm. Albeit, the firm did receive $350 from Rouse (P) as a result of Fitzsimmons' meetings with her. However, this was not received because the firm participated in a tortious transaction. On the contrary, it was legitimately received as payment for the legal services Fitzsimmons, as a member of the firm, performed for her. Therefore, the lower court's decree dismissing Rouse's (P) vicarious liability claim against the firm and limiting liability to Fitzsimmons is correct. Affirmed.

ANALYSIS

The case of *Cerniglia v. Pretty*, 674 F. Supp. 1167, 1169-70 (D. Md. 1987), addressed the issue of the appropriate remedy for an agent's fraud in the dual agency context in the following terms: "It is well established that 'one principal is not civilly liable to another for the tortious acts of an agent who acts for both parties with their consent, unless he in some manner participates in the wrong.' " The court treated this as dispositive of a claim for damages, but did observe that rescission and restitution are available to the defrauded party. "This rule is based upon the general equitable principle that a person should not benefit from the fraud of another—a principle which is fully applicable in a case involving dual agency."

Cook v. Brundidge, Fountain, Elliot & Churchill

Client (P) v. Law firm partnership (D)

Tex. Sup. Ct., 533 S.W.2d 751 (1976).

NATURE OF CASE: Appeal from summary judgment denying damages for liability.

FACTSUMMARY: Lyon, a partner in the law partnership of Brundidge, Fountain, Elliot & Churchill (D), while representing Cook (P) in a divorce proceeding, misappropriated investment funds she gave to him in order to invest in a fast-food franchise in which he was a stockholder, and Brundidge's (D) motion for summary judgment at Cook's (P) trial for damages, where the former was charged with vicarious liability for Lyon's actions, was granted by the court and affirmed on appeal.

RULE OF LAW

When non-legal actions of a partner in a law partnership occur during the existence of the attorney-client relationship in recognized legal matters and result in harm to the client, vicarious liability will extend to his firm if his actions appear to carry in on the usual way the business of his partnership.

FACTS: Lyon, a partner in the law partnership of Brundidge, Fountain, Elliot & Churchill (D), represented Cook (P) in a divorce proceeding. During a conference with Lyon concerning her divorce, Cook (P) decided to invest in a fast-food franchise in which Lyon was a stockholder, after consulting with him regarding real estate advice. Subsequently, Cook (P) invested and made payable a $60,000 check to "Warren Lyon as Attorney for" Betty Cook (P), et al. This check was mailed to and received by Lyon, but there is no evidence that it was deposited in or handled by the law firm. Shortly after this, after conferring with Lyon, Cook (P) loaned Lyon $50,000 of her investment to be used in the construction of a store in Lyon's franchise. Thereafter, Lyon persuaded Cook (P) to exchange her rights under the loan for stock in his franchise. Sometime later, Lyon's franchise was adjudged bankrupt. As a result, Cook (P) brought this suit for damages against Brundidge, et al. (D), contending that the latter was vicariously liable for Lyon's misappropriation of her funds because Lyon was acting within the scope of his apparent authority. To buttress her claim, Cook (P) filed an affidavit stating, in effect, that at no time did Lyon indicate that his actions were for his own benefit. On the other hand, Brundidge, et al. (D) filed a motion for summary judgment, on the grounds that Lyon was acting in his individual capacity when he misappropriated Cook's (P) funds. This motion was granted by the trial court and affirmed by the court of civil appeals. Cook (P) appealed.

ISSUE: When non-legal actions of a partner in a law partnership occur during the existence of the attorney-client relationship in recognized legal matters and result in harm to the client, will vicarious liability extend to his firm if his actions appeared to carry on in the usual way the business of his partnership?

HOLDING AND DECISION: (Steakley, J.) Yes. When non-legal actions of a partner in a law partnership occur during the existence of the attorney-client relationship in recognized legal matters and result in harm to the client, vicarious lability will extend to his firm if his actions appear to carry on in the usual way the business of his partnership. Liability in this context is of first impression in this jurisdiction. However, this court has said that one seeking to charge a principal through apparent authority of an agent must prove such conduct on the principal's part as would lead a reasonably prudent person to suppose that the agent had the authority he purports to exercise. Moreover, the extent of a partner's authority is determined essentially by some principles as those measuring the scope of an agent's authority. That is, according to the Texas Uniform Partnership Act, when a partner's actions appear to carry on "in the usual way the business of the partnership" (§ 9), then it follows that he was "acting within the scope of his apparent authority" and his firm is "bound to make good the loss" occasioned by his conduct (§ 14). In the instant case, there was no evidence that the firm expressly authorized Lyon's actions; nor was there evidence that his actions were outside his authority as a member of the partnership. Hence, Lyon's actions must be considered in light of whether they were impliedly authorized by the firm or, in other words, appeared to "carry on" his firm's business. This being so, then Lyon's acceptance of Cook's (P) check made payable to "Warren Lyon's as Attorney for" Betty Cook, et al., together with Cook's (P) affidavit, demonstrates the existence of fact issues with respect to whether Lyon's actions appeared to "carry on" his firm's business. As a result, the record does not definitely establish that the firm is not accountable to Cook (P) for Lyon's acts. Reversed and remanded.

DISSENT: (McGee, J.) The record clearly shows that Cook (P) had no justification for relying upon the responsibility of the partnership of any disconnected service assumed by Lyon outside one that was characteristically within the practice of law. When Lyon volunteered his services as a real estate and investment counselor for Mrs. Cook (P), he was not "apparently carrying on in the usual way the business of the partnership." On the contrary, Lyon was acting in a private, non-legal advisory capacity, and he was therefore outside the scope of his authority and

Continued on next page.

beyond the scope of the business carried on by his firm. Furthermore, such actions are not incidental to the business of a firm engaged exclusively in the practice of law. As a result, the record concisely established, as a matter of law, that there was no genuine issue of material fact as to the liability of Lyon's firm for the fraud he perpetrated on Cook (P).

ANALYSIS

In *Zimmerman v. Hogg & Allen*, 286 N.C. 24 (1974), a similar vicarious liability case as here, the court offered the following explanation for its decision to remand the case to a jury trial: "It is reasonable to infer . . . that the investment services rendered by Greene to the employees of Holly Farms might have been for the purpose of obtaining the good will of the corporation to insure the continuance of a profitable association between the corporate client and the Professional Association." For example, the "defendant Greene . . . accepted funds for investment purposes from employees of the corporate client . . . and . . . other employees of the Professional Association had knowledge of such dealings." Hence, this piece of evidence, together with others, is sufficient to justify a reasonable and prudent belief by plaintiff Sam Zimmerman that the Professional Association had conferred authority upon Greene to receive the funds from him for investment while acting as its agent.

Federal Deposit Insurance Corp. v. Braemoor Assocs.

Successor in interest (P) v. Partner in a joint venture (D)

686 F.2d 550 (7th Cir. 1982).

NATURE OF CASE: Appeal from denial of damages for breach of a fiduciary duty.

FACT SUMMARY: In Federal Deposit Insurance Corp.'s (FDIC) (P) suit for damages against Braemoor Assoc. (D), the district court found that FDIC (P) had failed to prove that Braemoor (D) had either actual knowledge or reason to know of a Braemoor (D) joint venture's breach of fiduciary duty to a bank he headed.

RULE OF LAW

A partner's knowledge, acquired while acting within the scope of his partnership duties, is imputed to his partnership unless he acquires this knowledge while committing or consenting to fraud against his partnership.

FACTS: Bere, former State Bank of Clearing president and joint venture in Braemoor Assoc. (D), funneled a total of $300,000 of his bank's money to Braemoor (D) through Ringbloom, a business associate, in order to satisfy Braemoor's (D) debts. The failure to disclose to the bank's board of directors that the actual destination of the loaned money from the bank to Ringbloom was an enterprise controlled by Bere was a violation of Illinois state law, requiring a bank officer, who made loans in excess of $10,000 to himself or to a business enterprise he controlled, to receive the approval of the bank's board of directors. After learning of these facts, Federal Deposit Insurance Corp. (FDIC) (P), as successor in interest to the defunct State Bank of Clearing, sued Braemoor (D), seeking to recover bank monies that Bere had funneled to Braemoor (D) in breach of his fiduciary obligations to the bank on the grounds that Bere's breach of duty should be imputed to Braemoor (D), as Bere's principal. Notwithstanding this, the district court found that FDIC (P) had failed to prove that Braemoor (D) had either actual knowledge or reason to know of Bere's breach of trust. FDIC (P) appealed.

ISSUE: Absent evidence of a fraud against his partnership, is a partner's knowledge, acquired while acting within the scope of his partnership duties, imputed to his partnership?

HOLDING AND DECISION: (Posner, J.) Yes. A partner's knowledge, acquired while acting within the scope of his partnership duties, is imputed to his partnership unless he acquires this knowledge while committing or consenting to fraud against his partnership. This rule merely restates the rule as laid down in UPA § 12, which, in effect, states that the knowledge a partner gains while acting in a particular matter for the partnership operates as knowledge of the partnership, except when this partner commits or consents to fraud on the partnership. Hence, absent evidence that the exception to § 12 applies, the UPA holds a partnership to constructive notice of a partner's knowledge gained while performing his partnership duties. In the instant case, Bere knew that in funneling $300,000 of his bank's money to Braemoor (D) through Ringbloom he was violating his fiduciary duty to the bank. However, Braemoor (D), despite its officers' lack of knowledge, had constructive notice of Bere's breach of duty, and, as a result, was liable for it because Bere committed fraud on behalf of as opposed to against the partnership, the latter of which would have negated this knowledge being imputed to the innocent officers. Moreover, the fact that the innocent officers benefited from Bere's fraud is more reason to hold them liable to FDIC (P) for the funneled money. Hence, the lower court clearly erred in limiting its analysis to the question whether Braemoor (D) had actual knowledge or reason to know of Bere's breach. Reversed and remanded.

ANALYSIS

Restatement § 282 states, in part, that a principal is "not affected by the knowledge of an agent in a transaction in which the agent secretly is acting adversely to the principal and entirely for his own or another's purposes." This is consistent with the court's finding in *Braemoor*, where it reasoned that Bere committed fraud on behalf as opposed to against his principal, Braemoor (D), thereby, holding the latter liable for Bere's breach. Moreover, to reach this result, the court found Bere's actions to have been within the scope of his partnership duties, thereby making the legal presumption that an agent communicates to his principal knowledge which he gains while performing his authorized duties apply. In this respect, if the court had found that Bere's actions were not within his partnership duties, then it would have concluded that Bere committed fraud against his principal, which would have exculpated Braemoor (D).

Corley v. Ott

Partner (P) v. Partner (D)

S.C. Sup. Ct., 485 S.E.2d 97 (1997).

NATURE OF CASE: Appeal of a final accounting between partners and an award of damages for breach of fiduciary duty.

FACT SUMMARY: Ott (D) failed to disclose to his partner Corley (P) that he had individually purchased some land which the partnership later bought at a higher price.

RULE OF LAW

A partner must account to the partnership for any benefit from any transaction connected with the formation of the partnership.

FACTS: Ott (D) purchased some land and then resold it to the partnership he had formed with Corley (P), but at a higher price, pocketing the difference. When Corley (P) commenced an action to dissolve the partnership, he discovered the scam, and sued Ott (D) for breach of fiduciary duty. The trial court ruled for Corley (P) and found that he had been damaged in the amount of the difference between the purchase price and the value of the land purchased. Ott (D) appealed, claiming that he had breached no fiduciary duty since, at the time of the land purchase, the partnership did not yet exist.

ISSUE: Must a partner account to the partnership for any benefit from any transaction connected with the formation of the partnership?

HOLDING AND DECISION: (Moore, J.) Yes. A partner must account to the partnership for any benefit from any transaction connected with the formation of the partnership. A partnership may be found to exist by implication from the parties' conduct. Here, Corley (P) and Ott (D) entered into the purchase agreement as "a general partnership." Thus the partnership was formed concurrently with that transaction. Since Ott's (D) prior undisclosed purchase of the property was intimately connected with the formation of the partnership, the evidence supports the trial court's finding that Ott (D) breached his fiduciary duty as a partner. Affirmed.

ANALYSIS

The Uniform Partnership Act (1914) and the Revised Uniform Partnership Act (1994) differ in some respects. The RUPA deleted the word "formation" from § 404(b)(1), signifying that the duty of loyalty need not be extended to the pre-formation period when parties are dealing at arm's length. Once the partnership is formed, however, each partner becomes a fiduciary in the "conduct" of the business, according to the Comment to § 401.

Meinhard v. Salmon

Partner (P) v. Partner (D)

N.Y. Ct. App., 249 N.Y. 458, 164 N.E. 545, 62 A.L.R. 1 (1928).

NATURE OF CASE: Appeal from award of interest in a lease.

FACT SUMMARY: In Meinhard's (P) suit for declaratory relief against Salmon (D), the trial court awarded Meinhard (P) a 25% interest in a lease, which was increased to 50% on appeal, that Salmon (D) and Gerry (D), a third party developer, had entered into without Meinhard's (P) knowledge, and which included, but was not limited to, a hotel that Meinhard (P) and Salmon (D) were jointly leasing under a lease which was to expire at the same time that the Salmon-Gerry (D) lease was to commence.

RULE OF LAW

A partner may not appropriate to his own use a renewal of a lease that his partnership holds, even though its term is to begin at the expiration of the partnership.

FACTS: Meinhard (P) and Salmon (D) were leased the premises known as the Hotel Bristol for a term of twenty years. Moreover, the two were co-adventurers in running the hotel for the lease's term, subject to fiduciary duties akin to those of partners. However, Salmon (D) had the added responsibility of managing the hotel. Subsequently, sometime near the lease's end, E. Gerry (D), who was owner of the reversion to the lease as well as owner of much of the adjacent property, agreed to lease to Salmon (D), doing business as Midpoint Realty company, his whole tract, involving a huge outlay of property, including the hotel. Furthermore, this new lease was to commence at the end of the former lease. However, Meinhard (P) had no knowledge of, and was not told about, the Gerry (D)-Salmon (D) lease until after it was an accomplished fact. After gaining this knowledge, Meinhard (P) demanded that Salmon (D) and Gerry (D) hold the lease in trust as an asset of the venture, and he, thereby, would share the personal obligations incident to the guaranty, which, in turn, allowed him to share in the profits. However, when this was refused, Meinhard (P) brought this suit for declaratory relief against Salmon (D) and Gerry (D), contending that since Salmon (D) failed to disclose the facts of the subsequent lease to him during their co-adventureship, then traditional rules of fair play demanded that the latter share in their new venture. Accordingly, the trial court awarded judgment to Meinhard (P), but limited his interest in the lease to 25% of the lease's value. However on appeal, the judgment was modified so as to enlarge Meinhard's (P) interest to 50% of the whole lease. Salmon (D) appealed.

ISSUE: May a partner appropriate to his own use a renewal of a lease that his partnership holds, even though its term is to begin at the expiration of the partnership?

HOLDING AND DECISION: (Cardozo, C.J.) No. A partner may not appropriate to his own use a renewal of a lease that his partnership holds, even though its term is to begin at the expiration of the partnership. This rule presupposes that a partner, in appropriating the above renewal, will not disclose his intentions to his partnership, thereby disallowing it to benefit from a preemptive business opportunity. However, traditional legal rules that require the utmost loyalty between a principal and his fiduciaries prohibit such secretive and ambitious schemes as this in order to discourage unethical conduct in a business setting. Moreover, these traditional rules apply, with equal weight, to joint venturers since, as is the case with partners, each member is required to act with the good of the enterprise in mind, thereby necessitating a certain level of trust in the relationship. Hence, in order not to jeopardize this trust, where disclosure of a member's intentions serves the good of his joint ventureship, then he is under a duty to disclose what they are to his other co-members. In the instant case, it will be assumed that Meinhard (P) and Salmon (D) were joint venturers, even though Salmon (D), to the eye of the observer, appeared to solely own the hotel, since both served to benefit equally from the Bristol enterprise. With this aside, since the subject matter of the lease renewal was merely an extension and enlargement of the subject matter of the Meinhard (P)-Salmon (D) lease, then Salmon's (D) undisclosed deal with Gerry (D) denied Meinhard (P) the preemptive business opportunity potentially to capitalize on a new venture. As a result, Meinhard (P) has an interest in the new enterprise. However, Salmon (D) has an option of choosing whether to allow the lease to be held in trust, with a percentage of the interest going to Meinhard (P), or to allow Meinhard's (P) interest to attach to a percentage of the shares of the stock in his company. If the latter is chosen, then Salmon (D) should receive 51% of the shares since he solely managed the Bristol enterprise under the old lease. Affirmed with modifications.

DISSENT: (Andrews, J.) As the new lease was not a renewal of the old, Meinhard (P) cannot claim any interest in it. However, even if it was a renewal, since Meinhard's (P) and Salmon's (D) venture had in view a limited object and was to end at a certain time, then any benefit resulting from the chance of renewal should solely belong to the individual to which the opportunity lent itself. Moreover,

Continued on next page.

the strict principles of loyalty applying to general partnerships do not apply to joint venturers anyway.

ANALYSIS

In connection with the above case, see *Levy & Surrick v. Surrick*, 362 Pa. Super. 510, 524 A. 2d 993, 994 (1987), where a 50% shareholder (Surrick) in a professional law corporation purchased for private investment a mini-mall which had a long-term leasehold relationship with one of the clients of the law firm. Levy, the other shareholder, brought suit in the name of the corporation alleging breach of fiduciary duty by Surrick for preempting a business opportunity. The court held in *Surrick*, stating that the purchase was not within the scope of the agency relationship. "[N]othing in the record suggests that the corporation existed for any purpose other than to practice law. It was not in the land acquisition business."

Meehan v. Shaughnessy

Law partners (P) v. Law firm (D)

Mass. Sup. Jud. Ct., 535 N.E.2d 1255 (1989).

NATURE OF CASE: Appeal of an award of damages for breach of contract.

FACT SUMMARY: Meehan (P) and Boyle (P), former partners in the law firm of Parker Coulter (D), sought to recover money under the partnership agreement, while Parker Coulter (D) claimed it was owed for cases that the former partners took when they left.

RULE OF LAW
Partners have the obligation to provide true and full information of all matters affecting the partnership to other partners.

FACTS: Meehan (P) and Boyle (P) were partners in the law firm of Parker, Coulter, Daley & White (D) but decided to leave and form their own firm. Meehan (P) and Boyle (P) made arrangements for the new firm while continuing to work at Parker Coulter (D), including drafting a letter to clients of the firm notifying them of the separation. During this period, other Parker Coulter (D) partners asked Meehan (P) and Boyle (P) if they had plans for leaving, but Meehan (P) denied it. Following the announcement that they were leaving, Meehan (P) and Boyle (P) sent out the client letters and were able to obtain nearly half of the contingent fee cases the firm had, including cases that came to Parker Coulter (D) through the efforts of other attorneys. Meehan (P) and Boyle (P) then filed suit for money they claimed was owed to them under the partnership agreement, and Parker Coulter (D) counterclaimed for damages as a result of their breach of fiduciary duty to the other partners. The trial court awarded money under the partnership agreement to Meehan (P) and Boyle (P) but allowed Parker Coulter (D) to recover for its time billed and expenses for the cases that were taken by Meehan (P) and Boyle (P).

ISSUE: Do partners have the obligation to provide true and full information of all matters affecting the partnership to other partners?

HOLDING AND DECISION: (Hennessey, C.J.) Yes. Partners have the obligation to provide true and full information of all matters affecting the partnership to other partners. Partners owe each other a fiduciary duty of the utmost good faith and loyalty. However, partners may plan to compete with the entity to which they owe allegiance provided that in the course of such arrangements they do not act in violation of their fiduciary duties. Meehan (P) and Boyle (P) violated this duty through their secret plans to take clients and the substance and method of their communications to the clients. Meehan (P) and Boyle (P) obtained an unfair advantage by denying their plans and sending a one-sided announcement, on Parker Coulter (D) stationery, to the clients. By engaging in these preemptive tactics, Meehan (P) and Boyle (P) violated their duty of good faith and loyalty. Accordingly, on remand, if the trial court determines that as a result of this breach Meehan (P) and Boyle (P) obtained certain clients, they must return the profits on those cases. Reversed and remanded.

ANALYSIS

The court's decision to impose a constructive trust on profits derived from breach of the duty of loyalty is in accord with the Uniform Partnership Act. UPA § 21 states that "every partner must account to the partnership for any benefit, and hold as a trustee for it any profits derived by him without the consent of the other partners from any transaction connected with the . . . liquidation of the partnership."

Gibbs v. Breed, Abbott & Morgan

Former law partner (P) v. Former law partnership (D)

N.Y. Sup. Ct., App. Div., 271 A.D.2d 180, 710 N.Y.S.2d 578 (2000).

NATURE OF CASE: Appeal from favorable ruling on a defense counterclaim in suit by former law partner against former partnership for monies due.

FACT SUMMARY: When Charles Gibbs (P) sued Breed Abbott & Morgan (BAM) (D), his former law firm of which he was a partner, for monies due, BAM (D) counterclaimed for damages, alleging that Gibbs (P) had violated his partnership duty of loyalty by supplying a competitor with confidential employee information from BAM's (D) personnel files.

RULE OF LAW

Members of a partnership owe each other a duty of loyalty and good faith which includes refraining from acting for purely personal gain.

FACTS: Charles Gibbs and Robert Sheehan (collectively Gibbs) (P) are former partners of Breed Abbott & Morgan (BAM) (D) who specialize in trust and estate law. They withdrew to join another firm (Chadbourne firm). While still at BAM (D), Gibbs (P) conducted employment interviews with other firms. When he left, he took case files. Also, while still working at BAM (D), Gibbs (P) supplied detailed and confidential information to the Chadbourne law firm as to possible BAM (D) employees to recruit. After leaving, Gibbs (P) brought suit for monies due him under the BAM (D) partnership agreement. BAM (D) asserted various counterclaims alleging that Gibbs (P) breached his fiduciary duties to BAM (D). The counterclaims were severed and tried without a jury. Gibbs (P) appeals from the trial court's determination that, in the course of planning and eventually implementing his withdrawal from BAM (D), he breached his fiduciary duty to the partnership, and awarded damages to the defendants in the amount of $1,861,045.

ISSUE: Do members of a partnership owe each other a duty of loyalty and good faith which includes refraining from acting for purely personal gain?

HOLDING AND DECISION: (Mazzarelli, J.) Yes. Members of a partnership owe each other a duty of loyalty and good faith which includes refraining from acting for purely personal gain. Partners are constrained by such duties throughout the life of the partnership, and the manner in which partners plan for and implement withdrawals is still subject to constraints imposed on them by virtue of their status as fiduciaries. Accordingly, Gibbs (P) breached his fiduciary duties as a partner of the firm he was about to leave by supplying confidential information to Chadbourne while still a partner at BAM (D). By sending a detailed memorandum to Chadbourne detailing personal information and confidential employee data about the individuals in BAM's (D) trusts and estates department (T/E), Gibbs (P) had the intention of at least partially crippling BAM's (D) T/E department, thus constituting a breach of his loyalty to his firm. Such action gave the Chadbourne firm, a competitor, a competitive advantage in offering employment to other members of the department. This action, coupled with taking away various chronology files from BAM's (D) T/E department, "to a large degree hobbled" his former law firm in its effort to rebuild the T/E department, and in its ability to serve clients without undue interruption. Affirmed. However, we vacate the damage award and remand for recalculation.

CONCURRENCE AND DISSENT: (Saxe, J.) The standards here employed, if applied generally, would too severely restrict attorneys' rights to change affiliations, compete with former partners, and offer clients full freedom of choice with respect to retaining counsel. Furthermore, should two partners finally agree on a move, and ultimately arrive at an arrangement with another firm acceptable to both, the orchestration of the move cannot serve as a basis for liability in the absence of sneaky or malicious conduct.

ANALYSIS

In the *Gibbs* case, the key factor in upholding the BAM (D) counterclaim was that Gibbs (P) began the recruiting of BAM's (D) employees while still a partner of the firm, and even prior to serving notice of his intent to withdraw from the firm. Furthermore, Gibbs (P) did so without informing the other partners that he was disseminating confidential firm data to competitors. The data was obtained from BAM (D) personnel files to which Gibbs (P) "had unique access" as a BAM (D) partner.

Jerman v. O'Leary

Limited partner (P) v. General partners (D)

Ariz. Ct. App., 145 Ariz. 397, 701 P.2d 1205 (1985).

NATURE OF CASE: Appeal from award of damages for breach of fiduciary duty.

FACT SUMMARY: In negotiating to purchase 25 acres of land from a limited partnership in which it held a majority interest, general partners the O'Learys (D) withheld important information concerning the fair market value of the land.

RULE OF LAW

Partners stand in fiduciary relationships to each other, requiring them to act in the utmost good faith and to disclose all knowledge affecting the value of the partnership.

FACTS: Rincon Country Mobile Home Park was a limited partnership with 38 investors. The O'Learys (D) were general partners and owned 62.1% of the limited partnership units. Although most of the mobile home park was sold in 1978, the price was payable on an installment basis, and therefore the partnership remained in existence. It retained 36 acres of property zoned SR (suburban ranch), of which 25 were developable. In late 1977, the O'Learys (D) had requested a change in zoning from SR to TH, which allowed the land to be used to construct a trailer park. The O'Learys (D) in 1978 decided to buy the 25 acres and hired an appraiser to value the property but did not tell him of the zoning change. By letter to the limited partners, the O'Learys (D) offered $110,000 as a purchase price based on the O'Learys' (D) forgiveness of limited partner debts to them and deferred receipt of other payments. In response to a claim by certain limited partners that the true land value was closer to $300,000-400,000, the O'Learys (D) claimed by another letter that the offer was in good faith, and threatened reduced distributions if the sale was not approved. The limited partners approved the sale, and a group of limited partners with a 5% overall interest sued the O'Learys (D) for breach of fiduciary duty. The O'Learys (D) appealed an adverse judgment.

ISSUE: If the general partners in a limited partnership fail to disclose facts revealing the true value of partnership property they wish to buy, have they breached their fiduciary duties?

HOLDING AND DECISION: (Howard, J.) Yes. Partners stand in fiduciary relationships to each other, requiring them to act in the utmost good faith and to disclose all knowledge affecting the value of the partnership. The O'Learys (D) had the right under the partnership agreement to purchase the 25 acres without the consent of any of the limited partners. However, as general partners they still stood in a fiduciary relationship with their limited partners, requiring them to exercise the utmost good faith in fully disclosing all knowledge which would affect the value of the property proposed to be sold. The O'Learys (D) were obliged to pay fair market value for the property and to not conceal information affecting fair market value. Here, the O'Learys (D) breached their duty by failing to advise both the limited partners and the original appraiser of the change in zoning, which resulted in a lower than market purchase price. Reversed and remanded for new trial for recomputation of damages.

ANALYSIS

This case presents a notable example of self-dealing. Any partner in a partnership owes a duty to the other members to provide a full accounting and to render complete information about personal profits from transactions connected with the conduct of the partnership. See Uniform Partnership Act § 21. Nor does a partner have the right to engage in a competitive business without the consent of the other partners or appropriate a business opportunity when offered to the venture for himself alone.

Singer v. Singer

Partner (P) v. Partner (D)

Okla. Ct. App., 634 P.2d 766 (1981).

NATURE OF CASE: Appeal from judgment imposing constructive trust.

FACT SUMMARY: Two members of a family partnership purchased for themselves land the partnership itself was considering for acquisition.

RULE OF LAW

Parties to a partnership agreement that expressly allows intra-partnership competition and who independently pursue investment opportunities presented to the partnership generally do not violate their fiduciary duties.

FACTS: In July 1979, members of the Josaline partnership, comprised of members of the Singer family organized to produce oil, discussed purchase of 95 acres of mineral-rich land. Stanley and Andrea Singer (D) were asked to consult a broker concerning the purchase. Instead, they formed Gemini Realty Co. and in September 1979, purchased the land in Gemini's name without consulting the other Josaline partners. After learning of this, Joe L. Singer (P) demanded that he be able to purchase 50% of the land, but Gemini refused. Stanley and Andrea (D) maintained that paragraph 8 of Josaline's partnership agreement, which stated that each partner could conduct business for separate individual accounts in conflict with the partnership, expressly allowed them to buy the land. Joe L. (P) won a judgment declaring the land held in constructive trust for Josaline.

ISSUE: May partners agree among themselves to allow any one of them to acquire or pursue investment opportunities presented to the partnership generally?

HOLDING AND DECISION: (Boydston, J.) Yes. Partners may agree among themselves to allow one of them to acquire or pursue investment opportunities presented to the partnership generally. Typically, partners owe fiduciary duties to each other not to engage in intra-partnership competition by pursuing areas of investment interest similar to the partnership itself. However, partners may contract away their right to this noncompetitive fiduciary relationship. Here, paragraph 8 of the Josaline agreement allowed individual members to do just as Stanley and Andrea Singer (D) did. However, Stanley and Andrea (D) would have violated their fiduciary duties if they had pirated existing Josaline assets, used Josaline funds, or financially encumbered Josaline itself. Reversed and remanded for order judgment in favor of defendants.

ANALYSIS

As fiduciaries to each other, partners generally cannot run a competitive business without the consent of all other partners. But here that consent was obtained by the partnership agreement itself. In the absence of an agreement, whether the property acquired is considered partnership property depends on whether the partnership intended that it be a partnership asset. Under the Uniform Partnership Act § 8 this is determined by: (1) in whose title the property is held; (2) whether it was purchased with partnership funds; (3) whether partnership funds improved the asset; or (4) close association of the asset with partnership business.

Bane v. Ferguson

Retired partner (P) v. Former partners (D)

890 F.2d 11 (7th Cir. 1989).

NATURE OF CASE: Appeal from dismissal of action seeking to recover unpaid pension benefits.

FACT SUMMARY: Retired attorney Bane (P), who lost pension rights due to a dissolution of his former law firm, contended that his former partners were liable to him for causing the dissolution.

RULE OF LAW

A retired partner has no action for breach of fiduciary duty against former partners whose acts led to partnership dissolution.

FACTS: Bane (P) retired from the firm of Lincoln and Beale, receiving a pension of approximately $27,000 per year. That same year, the firm merged with Reuben & Proctor. In 1988, Reuben & Proctor dissolved, thus terminating Bane's (P) pension. Bane (P) sued his former partners, alleging that the merger was negligently effected and that they had thus breached fiduciary responsibilities to him. The district court dismissed, and Bane (P) appealed.

ISSUE: Does a retired partner have an action for breach of fiduciary duty against former partners whose acts led to partnership dissolution?

HOLDING AND DECISION: (Posner, J.) No. A retired partner does not have an action for breach of fiduciary duty against former partners whose acts led to partnership dissolution. Section 9(3) of the Uniform Partnership Act prohibits a partner from undertaking acts, without consent of all partners, which makes it impossible to carry out the business of the partnership. This section does not help Bane (P). It exists to protect partners from the unauthorized acts of other partners; it does not relate to former partners like Bane (P). In terms of general fiduciary duties, partners owe such duties to other partners, not former partners. When Bane (P) terminated his partnership, his partners' duties to him also ended. Affirmed.

ANALYSIS

No scienter was alleged here. Bane's (P) allegations consisted of negligence only. Had the former partners deliberately attempted to avoid their obligations to Bane (P), he probably would have had a viable action. However, his causes of action would probably sound in fraud, not breach of fiduciary duty.

Moren v. Jax Restaurant

Injured child of partner (P) v. Partnership (D)

Minn. Ct. App., 679 N.W.2d 165 (2004).

NATURE OF CASE: Appeal from summary judgment dismissing a third-party negligence complaint.

FACT SUMMARY: Jax Restaurant (D) contended that its partner, Nicole Moren, owed it an indemnification duty in a negligence action brought against the partnership on behalf of her two-year-old son, Remington Moren (P), who had injured his hand on the partnership's premises while Nicole was making pizzas there.

RULE OF LAW

A partnership does not have an indemnity right against a partner acting in the ordinary course of partnership business.

FACTS: Nicole Moren was a partner of Jax Resturant (D). While covering for an absent employee, she brought her two-year-old son, Remington (P), to work one day. Because she did not want him running around the restaurant, she brought him into the kitchen with her, set him on top of the counter, and began rolling out pizza dough using the dough-pressing machine. As she was making pizzas, Remington (P) reached his hand into the dough press. His hand was crushed, and he sustained permanent injuries. Through his father, Remington (P) commenced a negligence action against the partnership (D). The partnership (D) served a third-party complaint on Nicole, arguing that, in the event it was obligated to compensate Remington (P), the partnership (D) was entitled to indemnity or contribution from Nicole for her negligence. The trial court granted summary judgment to Nicole, ruling that she had no obligation to indemnify Jax Restaurant (D) so long as the injury occurred while she was engaged in ordinary business conduct. The appellate court granted review.

ISSUE: Does a partnership have an indemnity right against a partner acting in the ordinary course of partnership business?

HOLDING AND DECISION: (Crippen, J.) No. A partnership does not have an indemnity right against a partner acting in the ordinary course of partnership business. Under the Uniform Partnership Act (UPA), a partner has a right to indemnity from the partnership, but the partnership's claim of indemnity from a partner is not authorized or required. The trial court was correct in concluding that Nicole's conduct was in the ordinary course of business of the partnership and, as a result, indemnity by the partner to the partnership was inappropriate. Her conduct was no less in the ordinary course of business because it also served personal purposes. It was undisputed that Nicole was acting for the benefit of the partnership by making pizzas when her son was injured, and even though she was simultaneously acting in her role as a mother, her conduct remained in the ordinary course of the partnership business. Affirmed.

ANALYSIS

A related, converse rule under the UPA is that an act of a partner that is not apparently for carrying on the ordinary course of the partnership business or business of the kind carried on by the partnership binds the partnership only if the act was authorized by the other partners. RUPA § 301 (2). Where such act was authorized by the other partners, the partner may seek indemnification from the partnership.

Walter v. Holiday Inns, Inc.

Former partners (P) v. Casino (D)

985 F.2d 1232 (3d. Cir. 1993).

NATURE OF CASE: Appeal from judgment dismissing action seeking damages for breach of fiduciary duty.

FACT SUMMARY: Walter (P) and other former partners of Holiday Inns, Inc. (D) contended that the latter breached fiduciary duties during a buyout of their interests by not disclosing all information it possessed.

RULE OF LAW

A partner does not breach fiduciary duties to another partner by mere nondisclosure of all information it possesses.

FACTS: Several individuals were collective 50-50 partners in a casino hotel in Atlantic City with Holiday Inns, Inc. (D). In separate sales in 1981 and 1983, Holiday (D) purchased the individuals' entire ownership interest. The casino proved more profitable than expected, and the various individual former partners (P) sued Holiday (D), contending that it had breached a fiduciary duty by nondisclosure of relevant information, in particular a long-term projection of profits it had prepared. The district court granted summary judgment in favor of Holiday (D), and an appeal was taken.

ISSUE: Does a partner breach fiduciary duties to another partner by nondisclosure of all information it possesses?

HOLDING AND DECISION: (Sloviter, C.J.) No. A partner does not breach fiduciary duties to another partner by mere nondisclosure of all information it possesses. The extent of one partner's duty to another in disclosing information is determined by their relative sophistication. When both sides are sophisticated, the duty only goes so far as prohibiting one side to make informed judgments. Here, both sides were sophisticated. Holiday (D) did not hide any material fact from Walter (P) or his co-investors; it merely drafted an internal study making profit projections based on facts equally available to the individual investors. Holiday (D) was under no obligation to share this report with the individual investors, so no breach of fiduciary duty occurred. [The court partially reversed on a separate issue.] Affirmed in part, reversed in part.

ANALYSIS

It is a legal rule that partners owe fiduciary duties to each other. As with most legal rules, however, this rule is more easily stated than applied. The extent and nature of the duties are determined by a multiplicity of factors such as sophistication, bargaining power, type of partnership, and length of partnership.

Holman v. Coie

Expelled partners (P) v. Law firm (D)

Wash. Ct. App., 11 Wash. App. 195, 522 P.2d 515 (1974).

NATURE OF CASE: Appeal from dismissal of a complaint alleging breach of good faith and fiduciary duty by partners in a law firm.

FACT SUMMARY: When law partners William (P) and Francis Holman (P) were expelled under the terms of their partnership agreement, they sued the firm (D) for breach of the partnership agreement and of the fiduciary duty of good faith.

RULE OF LAW

Additional requirements should not be added to unambiguous expulsion provisions in partnership agreements.

FACTS: When William (P) and Francis Holman (P), brothers and partners in a law firm, were expelled, they sued Coie (D), the firm. The Holmans (P) alleged that Coie (D) had breached the partnership agreement by failing to give proper notice of meetings, expelling them without cause, failing to state the reason for the expulsions, and failing to allow the Holmans (P) an opportunity to be heard. The terms of the partnership agreement, however, did not require any advance notice or opportunity for a hearing. Holman (P) also alleged that a requirement of good faith should be inferred. The trial court dismissed the complaint. The Holmans (P) appealed.

ISSUE: Should additional requirements be added to unambiguous expulsion provisions in partnership agreements?

HOLDING AND DECISION: (Munson, J.) No. Additional requirements should not be added to unambiguous expulsion provisions in partnership agreements. Since the executive committee in this case had the right to expel the Holmans (P) without stating the reason or cause pursuant to the partnership agreement, there was no breach of any fiduciary duty. These parties had contractually agreed to the very method of expulsion exercised by the Holmans (P), i.e., a clean, quick, and expeditious severance, with a clear method of accounting. Affirmed.

ANALYSIS

The court noted that implying terms not expressed in the partnership agreement would frustrate the unambiguous language of the agreement and the result contemplated. This "guillotine" approach does not include any due process guarantees. Some commentators have argued for the application of the rules of "natural justice" in such situations.

Winston & Strawn v. Nosal

Law partnership (P) v. Expelled partner (D)

Ill. App. Ct., 279 Ill. App. 3d 231, 664 N.E.2d 239 (1996).

NATURE OF CASE: Appeal from summary judgment granted to defendant, validating expulsion of law partner.

FACT SUMMARY: When Nosal (D) was expelled from the partnership of Winston & Strawn (P), Winston (P) filed suit seeking a declaration that Nosal's (D) expulsion was effectuated validly under the partnership agreement.

RULE OF LAW

The discretion conferred upon partners under a partnership agreement does not abrogate their high duty to exercise good faith and fair dealing in the execution of such discretion.

FACTS: Winston & Strawn (P) expelled Nosal (D) from their law partnership pursuant to the terms of their agreement. Nosal (D) claimed that his expulsion was void because it was in violation of the implicit duty of good faith that exists between partners and was a result of his frequent requests to view Winston's (P) financial statements. Winston (P) was granted summary judgment by the court below, and Nosal (D) appealed, contending that there were triable issues on the question of his bad faith expulsion from the firm.

ISSUE: Does the discretion conferred upon partners under a partnership agreement abrogate their high duty to exercise good faith and fair dealing in the execution of such discretion?

HOLDING AND DECISION: (Hoffman, J.) No. The discretion conferred upon partners under a partnership agreement does not abrogate their high duty to exercise good faith and fair dealing in the execution of such discretion. In this case, the fact that the out placement occurred just after Nosal's (D) threatened lawsuit to enforce his right to examine books and records raises an inference that Nosal (D) was expelled solely because he insisted on invoking rights belonging to him under the partnership agreement, and that the reasons advanced by Winston (P) were pretextual. Reversed and remanded.

ANALYSIS

Even though there was no "for cause" requirement in Winston & Strawn's (P) partnership agreement, a good faith and fair dealing requirement was read into the terms of the agreement in this case. For policy reasons, a clean break may be preferable to a long lawsuit. Many law firms will now come under the terms of the Revised Uniform Partnership Act.

Bohatch v. Butler & Binion

Former law firm partner (P) v. Law firm (D)

Tex. Sup. Ct., 977 S.W.2d 543 (1998).

NATURE OF CASE: Appeal from a defense summary judgment in a suit by a former partner against her law firm for wrongful expulsion.

FACT SUMMARY: When Colette Bohatch (P) was expelled as a partner from her law firm, Butler & Binion (Butler) (D), for making a good faith but incorrect accusation of overbilling by one of the partners, she sued the firm for violating its duty not to expel a partner under such circumstances.

RULE OF LAW

The fiduciary relationship between partners does not create an exception to the at-will nature of partnerships to give rise to a duty not to expel a partner who reports suspected overbilling by another partner.

FACTS: Colette Bohatch (P), a partner in the law firm Butler & Binion (Butler) (D), accused another partner of the firm of overbilling clients. Although her accusation was made in good faith, the accusation was mistaken. Because of the accusation which she made, Bohatch (P) was discharged from the firm. She sued Butler (D), contending, among other things, that Butler (D) breached a fiduciary duty to her as a partner by discharging her for the whistleblowing, notwithstanding that she had been mistaken in making the accusation. The trial court found in Bohatch's (P) favor, however, the court of appeals reversed. Bohatch (P) appealed.

ISSUE: Does the fiduciary relationship between partners create an exception to the at-will nature of partnerships so that there is a duty not to expel a partner who reports suspected overbilling by another partner?

HOLDING AND DECISION: (Enoch, J.) No. The fiduciary relationship between partners does not create an exception to the at-will nature of partnerships to give rise to a duty not to expel a partner who reports suspected overbilling by another partner. A partnership exists solely because the parties choose to place personal confidence and trust in one another. Partners have no obligation to remain partners. At the heart of the partnership concept is the principle that partners may choose with whom they wish to be associated. Just as a partner can be expelled, without a breach of any common law duty, over disagreements about firm policy or to resolve some other "fundamental schism," a partner can be expelled for accusing another partner of overbilling without subjecting the partnership to tort damages. Such charges, whether true or not, may have a profound effect on the personal confidence and trust essential to the partner relationship. Once such charges are made, partners may find it impossible to continue to work together to their mutual benefit and the benefit of their clients. Here, the partnership agreement contemplated expulsion of a partner and prescribed procedures to be followed. The agreement did not, however, specify or limit the grounds for expulsion. Thus, while Bohatch's (P) claim that she was expelled in an improper way is governed by the partnership agreement, her claim that she was expelled for an improper reason is not. Butler (D) did, however, breach the partnership agreement by reducing Bohatch's (P) tentative distribution share to zero without the requisite notice, and Butler (D) is liable for such breach. Affirmed.

CONCURRENCE: (Hecht, J.) The majority's holding that part-ners in a law firm have no common law liability for expelling one of their number for accusing another of unethical conduct is directly contrary to that of some of the leading scholars on the subject. Here, however, the report of unethical conduct, though made in good faith, was incorrect. That fact alone does justify expulsion of the accusing partner for bad judgment.

DISSENT: (Spector, J.) In light of the court's role in setting standards to govern attorneys' conduct, it is particularly inappropriate for the court to deny recourse to attorneys wronged for adhering to the Disciplinary Rules. The majority sends an inappropriate signal to lawyers and to the public that the rules of professional responsibility are subordinate to a law firm's other interests.

ANALYSIS

Courts in some states have held that a partnership may expel a partner for purely business reasons. Further, courts recognize that a law firm can expel a partner to protect relationships both within the firm and with clients. Finally, many courts have held that a partnership can expel a partner without breaching any duty in order to resolve fundamental disagreements within the firm. Some legal scholars, however, have suggested that public policy requires a "limited duty" to remain partners, i.e., that a partnership should be liable for failure to retain a whistleblower partner.

Cadwalader, Wickersham & Taft v. Beasley

Law firm (D) v. Former partner of law firm (P)

Fla. Ct. App., 728 So. 2d 253 (1998).

NATURE OF CASE: Appeal from a damages award to a former partner against his law firm for wrongful expulsion.

FACT SUMMARY: When James Beasley (P) was expelled as a partner from his law firm Cadwalader, Wickersham & Taft (D), he sued the firm, contending that the partnership agreement contained no provision for partner expulsion except under strictly limited circumstances.

RULE OF LAW

Under the Uniform Partnership Act, partners have no common law or statutory right to expel or dismiss another partner from the partnership, although they may provide in the partnership agreement for expulsion under strictly prescribed conditions.

FACTS: In 1989, James Beasley (P) laterally transferred to become a partner in the Palm Beach Office of the law firm Cadwalader, Wickersham & Taft (D). After his arrival, the office suffered from internal discord and, by 1994, the office was operating at a loss. In mid-1994, Cadwalader (D) informed several partners, including Beasley (P), that they would be transferred. Beasley (P) rejected this offer as impractical since he had been practicing in Southern Florida for 22 years and deemed such a transfer as tantamount to an expulsion. Beasley (P) sued Cadwalader (D), arguing wrongful expulsion, and the trial judge agreed, awarding him damages. Cadwalader (D) appealed.

ISSUE: Under the Uniform Partnership Act, do partners have no common law or statutory right to expel or dismiss another partner from the partnership, although they may provide in the partnership agreement for expulsion under strictly prescribed conditions?

HOLDING AND DECISION: (Polen, J.) Yes. Under the Uniform Partnership Act, partners have no common law or statutory right to expel or dismiss another partner from the partnership, although they may provide in the partnership agreement for expulsion under strictly prescribed conditions. Cadwalader (D) intended to remove Beasley (P) as a partner in the firm when it announced it was closing its Palm Beach office by year-end 1994. Here, Cadwalader (D) anticipatorily expelled Beasley (P) from the firm. Although Cadwalader (D) was authorized to close the Palm Beach office pursuant to the partnership agreement, and Beasley (P) would have left Cadwalader (D) by year-end 1994 in any event, nevertheless, since the partnership agreement lacked provisions for the expulsion of a partner except in one limited situation, Cadwalader (D) breached the partnership agreement when it announced its plans to close the Palm Beach office in August, and then actually breached the agreement when it sent Beasley (P) a subsequent letter of termination. Any partner has the right to a formal accounting as to partnership affairs if, as here, he is wrongfully excluded from the partnership business or possession of its property by his copartners or whatever circumstances render it just and reasonable. Affirmed in part, reversed in part, and remanded.

ANALYSIS

In reaching its conclusion that Beasley (P) had been wrongfully expelled as a partner from Cadwalader (D), the court rejected Cadwalader's (D) argument that Beasley (P) voluntarily withdrew from the firm, rather than having been expelled, since Beasley (P) had been practicing exclusively in South Florida for 22 years, where he had built a substantial client base. To suddenly uproot to New York or Washington and leave his clients and contracts behind, said the court, would have severely diminished his rainmaking abilities. Under these circumstances, his rejecting the offer as impractical was not equivalent to a voluntary withdrawal.

Smith v. Manchester Management Corp.

Partner (P) v. Partnership (D)

N.H. Sup. Ct., 117 N.H. 361, 373 A.2d 361 (1977).

NATURE OF CASE: Interlocutory appeal from denial of motion for jury trial in suit for mismanagement of funds.

FACT SUMMARY: Manchester Management Corp. (D) did not maintain its capital account and engaged in self-dealing in its partnership with Smith (P) for the development of an "antique fair."

RULE OF LAW

Where one partner's suit against another principally concerns breach of the partnership agreement, an action at law will not lie until there has been an accounting.

FACTS: Smith (P) entered into a partnership with Manchester Management Corp. (D) for the development of an "antique fair." The fair was a financial failure. Smith (P) alleged that Manchester (D): (1) undercontributed to its capital account; (2) mismanaged its partnership duties by awarding contracts without competitive bidding and hiring bad supervisors; and (3) engaged in self-dealing by optioning land on which the partnership had an easement. Smith (P) petitioned for constructive trust and moved for jury trial; his motion was denied.

ISSUE: Must a partner who wishes to recover damages from another partner for breach of the partnership agreement first bring an equitable suit for a final accounting?

HOLDING AND DECISION: (Per curiam) Yes. Actions at law cannot be maintained by one partner against another for breach of the general provisions of the partnership agreement unless there has been an accounting or final settlement of partnership matters. Only when there is an allegation of breach of an agreement by one partner individually will an action at law be allowed without an investigation of partnership accounts. Smith's (P) claims that Manchester (D) undercapitalized and mismanaged the partnership go to the heart of the conduct of the partnership and do not involve any express agreement by Manchester (D) running individually to Smith (P). Thus, Smith (P) may not maintain a legal action until after an equitable suit for an accounting, which does not allow for a jury trial. Exceptions overruled.

ANALYSIS

Although at common law the right to an accounting existed only when the partnership was dissolved or if a partner was wrongfully excluded from the business, the Uniform Partnership Act, § 22 also allows accountings when partners are withholding benefits or profits belonging to the partnership or there are other "just and reasonable" circumstances. Typically, two hearings are held, i.e., to determine that an accounting is required and to determine the sum certain due plaintiff.

Schuler v. Birnbaum

Partner (P) v. Partner (D)

N.Y. Sup. Ct., App. Div., 62 A.D.2d 461, 405 N.Y.S.2d 351 (1978).

NATURE OF CASE: Appeal from denial of defendant's motion to dismiss and granting of plaintiff's cross-motion for summary judgment.

FACT SUMMARY: Schuler (P), who formed a partnership with Birnbaum's decedent to build a nursing home, sued Birnbaum (D) at law after the decedent failed to pay his pro-rata share of a settlement with the proposed home's architects.

RULE OF LAW

A partner may sue another partner at law for acts relating to the partnership without an accounting if there are no complex transactions involved.

FACTS: Schuler (P) and Hurlbut formed a partnership with Birnbaum's testator to construct and run a nursing home. An architectural firm prepared plans, and an application was filed with the state agency. The license was not granted, and the partnership was abandoned. The architectural firm sued Schuler (P) for unpaid services, a claim Schuler (P) settled 10 years later. Decedent did not approve the settlement or reimburse Schuler (P) for his one-third liability, so Schuler (P) sued Birnbaum (D) at law.

ISSUE: May an action at law by one partner against another be maintained without a final accounting when few or simple transactions are involved?

HOLDING AND DECISION: (Simons, J.) Yes. The general rule is that parties cannot sue each other at law for acts relating to the partnership unless there is an accounting. However, an exception exists which allows a partner to maintain an action at law against his co-partner when no complex accounting is required or when only one transaction is involved which is fully closed but unadjusted. Here, the retention of the architects and the filing of the license application was the sole business conducted by the partnership, so the exception applies and this action at law may be maintained. Affirmed.

ANALYSIS

Another exception to the requirement that a partner's sole initial remedy against a co-partner is an equitable suit for an accounting exists when the co-partner commits fraud or wrongfully converts partnership assets. See, e.g., *Eichberger v. Reid*, 728 S.W. 2d 533 (Ky. 1987).

Tupper v. Kroc

Partner (D) v. Partner (P)

Nev. Sup. Ct., 88 Nev. 146, 494 P.2d 1275 (1972).

NATURE OF CASE: Appeal from orders in a dissolution.

FACT SUMMARY: Kroc (P) got the court to order the sale of Tupper's (D) interest in the limited partnerships they had formed, to satisfy a judgment he obtained on notes signed by Tupper (D), then Kroc (P) purchased the partnership interests of Tupper (D) at the sheriff's sale for a minimal sum.

RULE OF LAW

The court has the statutory power to charge and sell an interest of a partner in a partnership to satisfy a judgment, and the partnership agreement cannot divest the court of such power.

FACTS: Tupper (D) and Kroc (P) entered into three limited partnerships for the purpose of holding title to, and leasing parcels of, real estate. When Tupper (D) could not pay his share of partnership debts, Kroc (P) paid them and took notes from Tupper (D) for his share. Eventually, Kroc (P) sued on the notes and obtained a judgment. He then sought a charging order from the court in which he had filed a petition to dissolve the partnerships, and the court appointed a receiver. The court entered a charging order directing the sheriff to sell Tupper's (D) interests in the partnerships, and Kroc (P) purchased the interests at the sale for only $2,500. More than a year later, Tupper (D) moved to have the sale set aside, a motion which the court denied, at the same time it granted Kroc's (P) motion to terminate the receivership.

ISSUE: Does the court have the power to charge one's partnership interest and have it sold to satisfy a money judgment?

HOLDING AND DECISION: (Batjer, J.) Yes. The court has the statutory power to charge and sell an interest of a partner in a partnership to satisfy a judgment, and the partnership agreement cannot divest the court of such power. However, once that was accomplished, Tupper (D) became entitled to once again participate in the management, even though he no longer had any interest in the profits or surplus of the partnerships. The purchase by another of Tupper's (D) interest in the partnerships did not divest him of his other rights. Orders affirmed.

ANALYSIS

There was another option which would have had a less financially devastating impact on Tupper (D). The receiver could have been ordered to collect Tupper's (D) share of the profits or, upon dissolution, his share of the surplus. Thereafter, when Kroc (P) satisfied his judgment, Tupper (D) would have had his rights restored to receive part of the profits or surplus. Kroc's (P) action foreclosed that possibility.

Bauer v. Blomfield Co./Holden Joint Venture

Assignee of partnership (P) v. Partnership (D)

Alaska Sup. Ct., 849 P.2d 1365 (1993).

NATURE OF CASE: Appeal from dismissal of a declaratory relief action.

FACT SUMMARY: Bauer (P) sought income payments from a partnership that he was assigned an interest in to secure a loan.

RULE OF LAW

Assignees of partnership interests are not entitled to interfere in the management or administration of partnership affairs.

FACTS: In 1986, Bauer (P) loaned Holden $800,000. To secure the loan, Holden assigned his interest in the Blomfield Joint Venture (D). The other members of the partnership consented to the assignment. Holden defaulted on the loan, and Bauer (P) gave notice to Blomfield (D) that he should receive all distributions of income from the partnership. Subsequently, the partners stopped making income payments and agreed to use the income to pay a substantial commission to one of the partners. Bauer (P) was not consulted and was not paid the $207,000 he would have received if there had been no commission. Bauer (P) filed suit for declaratory relief, asserting that his rights had been violated. The trial court dismissed the action, ruling that Bauer's (P) assignment did not make him a member of the partnership.

ISSUE: Are assignees of partnership interests entitled to participate in the management or administration of partnership affairs?

HOLDING AND DECISION: (Burke, J.) No. Assignees of partnership interests are not entitled to interfere in the management or administration of partnership affairs. Assignments of interests in a partnership or joint venture entitle the assignee to receive any resulting profits. Assignees are not members of the partnership. Accordingly, they are not entitled to interfere or participate in the management or administration of the business affairs of the partnership. Bauer (P) was an assignee of Holden's interest in the Blomfield (D) partnership. Thus, Bauer (P) was not entitled to interfere with the other partners' decision to give a commission in lieu of making income payments. Affirmed.

DISSENT: (Matthews, J.) While assignees have no management rights, partners must make decisions regarding income distributions in good faith. There is no basis in the law for allowing partners to deny profits to an assignee for wrongful reasons.

ANALYSIS

The dissent also noted that the Uniform Partnership Act considers the rights of assignees. Under the UPA, assignees may petition a court for dissolution of the partnership. However, the Alaska version of the UPA mistakenly did not include that provision.

CHAPTER 13

Dissociation of a Partner and Dissolution of a Partnership

Quick Reference Rules of Law

Dreifuerst v. Dreifuerst

Brothers/partners (P) v. Brother/partner (D)

Wis. Ct. App., 280 N.W.2d 335 (1979).

NATURE OF CASE: Appeal from decision dissolving a partnership.

FACT SUMMARY: In the Dreifuersts' (P) case against their brother, Dreifuerst (D), to dissolve a partnership in which they were all partners, Dreifuerst (D) contended that under Wisconsin law, he had a right to force a sale of partnership assets in order to obtain his fair share of the assets in cash upon dissolution.

RULE OF LAW

A partnership at will is a partnership which has no definite term or particular undertaking and can rightfully be dissolved by the express will of any partner.

FACTS: The Dreifuersts (P) and their brother, Dreifuerst (D), formed a partnership operating two feed mills. There were no written articles of partnership governing the partnership. The Dreifuersts (P) served Dreifuerst (D) with a notice of dissolution and windup of the partnership. The dissolution complaint alleged that the Dreifuersts (P) elected to dissolve the partnership, and there were not allegations of fault, expulsion, or contravention of an alleged agreement as grounds for dissolution. The partners were not, however, able to agree to a winding up of the partnership. Hearings on dissolution were held, and Dreifuerst (D) requested that the partnership be sold and that the court allow a sale, at which time the partners would bid on the entire property. By such sale, Dreifuerst (D) argued that he could obtain his fair share of the assets in cash upon dissolution, while the Dreifuersts (P) could continue to run the business under a new partnership. The trial court denied Dreifuerst's (D) request and divided the partnership assets in kind according to the valuation presented by the Dreifuersts (P). Dreifuerst (D) appealed.

ISSUE: Is a partnership at will a partnership which has no definite term or particular undertaking and can be rightfully dissolved by the express will of any partner?

HOLDING AND DECISION: (Brown, J.) Yes. A partnership at will is a partnership which has no definite term or particular undertaking and can be rightfully dissolved by the express will of any partner. In the present case, the Dreifuersts (P) wanted to dissolve the partnership. This being a partnership at will, they could rightfully dissolve it with or without the consent of Dreifuerst (D). Here, the Dreifuersts (P) never claimed that Dreifuerst (D) violated any partnership agreement, and, therefore, there has been no wrongful dissolution of the partnership. Partners who have not wrongfully dissolved a partnership have a right to wind up the partnership. Lawful dissolution gives each partner the right to have the business liquidated and his share of the surplus paid in cash. Thus, the trial court erred in ordering an in-kind distribution of the assets of the partnership. A sale is the best means of determining the true fair market value of the assets. Reversed and remanded.

ANALYSIS

"Dissolution" sometimes designates the completion of the winding up of partnership affairs. This, the end of the association, should be called termination of the partnership. Again, the term is sometimes used in referring to the process of liquidation or winding up. Lastly, the term may be used to designate a change in the relation of partners caused by any partner's ceasing to be associated in carrying on the business.

Girard Bank v. Haley

Partner's decedent (P) v. Partners (D)

Pa. Sup. Ct., 332 A.2d 443 (1975).

NATURE OF CASE: Appeal from order dissolving partnership.

FACT SUMMARY: The executors (P) of Mrs. Reid's estate (Reid) appealed from the decision of the trial court, in their suit in equity to dissolve the partnership and distribute its assets, that the partnership was dissolved at Mrs. Reid death, and not at the time of Mrs. Reid's written request to dissolve the partnership.

RULE OF LAW

A partnership can be dissolved upon the express will of any partner, unless the partnership articles provide otherwise.

FACTS: Mrs. Reid entered into a written partnership agreement with three others, Haley, et al. (D), to lease certain real property for profit. The agreement provided that upon Mrs. Reid's death, the other partners had the option to purchase her interest. After 13 years, Mrs. Reid notified Haley (D) by letter that she was dissolving the partnership and requesting a liquidation and distribution of the partnership assets. This could not be accomplished amicably among the partners, so Mrs. Reid brought suit praying for a winding up of the affairs of the partnership and a liquidation of its assets. Mrs. Reid died during the course of the proceedings and was replaced by Mrs. Reid's decedent, Reid (P). The trial court found there was no evidence to justify the termination, and thus the partnership was not terminated at Mrs. Reid's request but by her death, allowing Haley and the others (D) to exercise their option to purchase her interest. Reid (P) appealed, contending no justification was present and the partnership had been dissolved at the time of Mrs. Reid's request.

ISSUE: Can a partnership be dissolved upon the express will of any partner?

HOLDING AND DECISION: (Pomeroy, J.) Yes. A partnership can be dissolved upon the express will of any partner, unless the partnership articles provide otherwise. The articles in the present case were silent as to winding up and liquidation; thus, the provisions of the Uniform Partnership Act apply. Reid's (P) assertion that there is no "justification" requirement was correct. Since the partnership was dissolved when Mrs. Reid gave notice of her desire to do so, the provisions allowing Haley (D) and the others to purchase her interest are not germane. [The court also concluded that Mrs. Reid's unilateral dissolution of the partnership was not in violation of the partnership agreement.] Decree reversed and remanded.

ANALYSIS

It is important to note that dissolution of a partnership is not the equivalent to termination of the partnership. The partnership continues until the winding up of partnership affairs is completed. Court action is often required to compel a more rapid winding up, where a partner wishes to limit his liability for obligations incurred by the partnership during the winding up.

Page v. Page

Partner (P) v. Partner (D)

Cal. Sup. Ct., 55 Cal. 2d 192, 359 P.2d 41 (1961).

NATURE OF CASE: Action for a declaratory judgment.

FACT SUMMARY: Page (P) sought a declaratory judgment that the partnership he had with Page (D) was a partnership at will which he could dissolve.

RULE OF LAW

A partnership may be dissolved by the express will of any partner when no definite term or particular undertaking is specified.

FACTS: Page (P) and Page (D) were partners in a linen supply business they had entered into in 1949, pursuant to an oral agreement. Each had contributed about $43,000 to purchase linen, equipment, and land. It was not until 1958 that business began to show a profit. Page (P) was the sole owner of the corporation which was the partnership's major creditor, holding a $47,000 demand note, and in 1959, he sought a declaratory judgment that it was a partnership at will which he could terminate. The trial court found the partnership to be for a term, namely such reasonable time as was necessary to repay from profits the original outlays of Page (P) and Page (D) for equipment, etc.

ISSUE: Can a partnership be dissolved by the express will of any partner when no definite term or particular undertaking is specified?

HOLDING AND DECISION: (Traynor, J.) Yes. When no definite term of particular undertaking is specified, a partnership may be dissolved by the express will of any partner. Partners may impliedly agree to continue in business until certain debts are paid, until one or more partners recoups his investment, etc., but there is no evidence in this case to suppose any implied agreement of that nature. All partnerships are ordinarily entered into with the hope they will be profitable, but that alone does not make them all partnerships for a term and obligate the partners to continue in the partnerships until all of the losses over a period of many years have been recovered or original investments recouped. In holding that this is a partnership terminable at will, it is noted that the power to dissolve it must be exercised in good faith and not to "freeze out" a co-partner. Reversed.

ANALYSIS

An important aspect of this leading case is the introduction of the concept that a partner holds his dissolution power as a fiduciary. That means he owes his partners fraternal duties of good faith and fair dealing in exercising his dissolution rights.

Potter v. Brown

Partners (P) v. Senior partner (D)

Pa. Sup. Ct., 328 Pa. 554, 195 A. 901, 118 A.L.R. 1415 (1938).

NATURE OF CASE: Appeal from order granting decree for dissolution of partnership.

FACT SUMMARY: Brown (D) appealed from the trial court's order granting Potter's (P) bill for dissolution of the partnership, contending that his actions did not disrupt the harmonious operation of the partnership sufficiently to justify entering an order of dissolution.

RULE OF LAW

The remedy of dissolution is not available for trivial misconduct, but only for such conduct by a partner of such a nature that it becomes no longer reasonably practical to carry on the business of the partnership.

FACTS: The firm of Henry W. Brown & Co. was a partnership composed of ten partners. The written partnership agreement provided that Brown (D) "shall own a majority of the shares," which gave him control over nearly every decision pertaining to the partnership business, except as to the admission of new partners or the termination of the interest of any partner other than Brown (D). The partnership was very profitable. The record indicated that Brown (D) proposed admission to the partnership for Moore, who was rejected by seven of the partners (Potter) (P). Since he had control over the salaries of the various partners by virtue of the partnership agreement, Brown (D) sought to compel Moore's admission by reducing the dissenting partners' (P) salaries. He was unsuccessful and shortly thereafter abandoned his attempts to coerce Potter (P) in this matter. Even though Brown (D) restored the original salary levels, Potter (P) refused to attend any further partnership meetings on the grounds that Brown (D) had breached the agreement. Potter (P) then brought this action for dissolution, requesting the right to continue the business under the same name until the partnership term expired. They were successful, and Brown (D) appealed, contending that his actions were not of such a character as to wholly disrupt the harmonious operation of the partnership sufficient to justify dissolution.

ISSUE: Is the remedy of dissolution available only for such conduct by a partner of such a nature that it becomes no longer practical to carry on the business of the partnership?

HOLDING AND DECISION: (Barnes, J.) Yes. The remedy of dissolution is not available for trivial misconduct, but only for such conduct by a partner of such a nature that it becomes no longer practical to carry on the business of the partnership. Even though Brown's (D) tactics in attempting to coerce the other partners to accept Moore were not commendable, there is no evidence on the record to show that he had caused any serious or permanent injury to the partnership business. The partnership remained as profitable as ever during the turmoil. There is no evidence that Potter, et al. (P) were denied participation in the management of the partnership, and any complaints they might have in that regard are probably due to the degree of control maintained in the partnership agreement itself by Brown (D). Bills in equity for dissolution are not available to resolved partnership squabbles. It appeared that Potter (D) sought dissolution merely as a way to acquire the business to the exclusion of Brown (D). The evidence does not sustain the conclusions reached by the court below. Reversed and bill dismissed.

ANALYSIS

The present case expresses a widely held sentiment of the courts, that partners resolve their own difficulties either through mechanisms provided for in the partnership agreement itself or by civilized discussion among themselves. There is a limit to how many trifling interferences a partner may be able to bear, however. When there exists a pattern of trivial acts so pervasive so as to destroy all confidence and cooperation in the business, dissolution may be appropriate. See *Owen v. Cohen*, 119 P. 2d 713 (1941).

Horizon/CMS Healthcare Corp. v. Southern Oaks Health Care, Inc.

Dissolved partnership (D) v. Former partner (P)

Fla. Ct. App., 732 So. 2d 1156 (1999).

NATURE OF CASE: Appeal from a ruling denying future profit damages to a partner against a dissolved partnership.

FACT SUMMARY: When Southern Oaks Health Care, Inc. (P) sued Horizon/CMS Healthcare Corporation (D) for damages for the wrongful dissolution of its partnership, Horizon (D) argued that the partnership agreement permitted dissolution for irreconcilable differences.

RULE OF LAW

The incapability of partners to continue to operate a business together constitutes "irreconcilable differences" which is a permissible reason for dissolving a partnership under express terms of partnership agreements.

FACTS: Horizon/CMS Healthcare Corporation (D) entered into several 20-year partnership and management agreements with Southern Oaks Health Care, Inc. (P) under which Horizon (D) would manage both a Southern Oaks (P) nursing facility and a new facility of its own. Three years later, when both health care partners encountered serious differences of opinion as to how the profits from their nursing facilities were to be determined and divided, Southern Oaks (P) sued Horizon (D) for default and breach of agreement. The trial court ordered that the partnership be dissolved, finding that a dissolution was proper where partners developed irreconcilable differences making it impracticable to carry on the partnership business. Southern Oaks (P) appealed, seeking damages for loss of future profits.

ISSUE: Does the incapability of partners to continue to operate a business together constitute "irreconcilable differences" which is a permissible reason for dissolving a partnership under express terms of partnership agreements?

HOLDING AND DECISION: (Goshorn, J.) Yes. The incapability of partners to continue to operate a business together constitutes "irreconcilable differences" which is a permissible reason for dissolving a partnership under express terms of partnership agreements. The partnership agreement at issue provided, inter alia, that the partnership between Southern Oaks (P) and Horizon (D) could be dissolved if, upon due notice, either partner elected to dissolve the partnership on account of an irreconcilable difference which arises and cannot, after good faith efforts, be resolved. Here, irreconcilable differences were shown by evidence of a good faith difference of opinion as to how the profits of the partnership were to be determined and provided. Evidence further revealed that these differences of opinion had a material and adverse impact on the conduct of the partnership business. Furthermore, Southern Oaks' (P) argument that Horizon's (D) dissolution of the partnership was wrongful under the Revised Uniform Partnership Act (RUPA) is misplaced. The RUPA permits a partnership to be dissolved and its business to be wound up upon a determination that it is not otherwise reasonably practicable to carry on the partnership business in conformity with the partnership agreement, as was the case here. While "reasonably practicable" is not defined in the RUPA, the term is broad enough to encompass the inability of partners to continue working together, which is what the trial court found. Only when a partner dissociates *and* the dissociation is wrongful can the remaining partners sue for damages. And here, the dissociation was not wrongful. Affirmed.

ANALYSIS

The *Horizon* court made clear that, in the instant case, because the partnership dissolution either came within the partnership agreements or the Revised Uniform Partnership Act [RUPA § 801(5)(c)(judicial dissolution where it is not reasonably practical to carry on the partnership business)], Southern Oak's (P) claim for lost future profits was without merit.

Warner v. Modano

Creditor (P) v. Partner (D)

Mass. Sup. Jud. Ct., 340 Mass. 439, 164 N.E.2d 904 (1960).

NATURE OF CASE: Appeal from equitable decree ordering payment of trade accounts.

FACT SUMMARY: Beale (D), Modano's (D) physician, entered into a secret partnership with Modano (D) to operate Modano's (D) supermarket, but after written dissolution of the partnership, a creditor sued for overdue trade accounts.

RULE OF LAW

If a member of a partnership is unknown as a partner to the partnership's creditors, and is so inactive in partnership affairs that the partnership's business reputation does not depend on him, then he will not be personally liable for partnership debts incurred after dissolution to creditors who had no notice of the dissolution.

FACTS: Modano (D) owned and operated a supermarket. Beale (D), Modano's (D) physician, lent Modano (D) $3,500. In return, Modano (D) gave Beale (D) a $4,000 note and agreed to make him a partner in the market if he discharged the debt. After Modano (D) bought out his existing partner, Beale (D) and Modano (D) entered into a secret agreement to operate the market. Beale (D) began to engage employees and examine company books. He also warned one salesman not to deal with the manager or else Beale (D) would not be responsible for the bill. Beale (D) also identified himself in a letter firing the manager as a "co-partner." However, Beale's (D) partnership was not recorded with the city clerk, nor did he order merchandise, work at the market, direct its operations, keep the books, or sign anything. Shortly thereafter, Beale (D) and Modano (D) terminated their partnership by written agreement; however, the market's creditors generally were unaware of the secret partnership between Beale (D) and Modano (D), and no notice of dissolution was published in a local newspaper. Certain suppliers continued to deliver goods on account to the market after the dissolution, but some were not paid. One assignee of four of these accounts sued in equity to reach assets of the market given by Modano (D) to Beale (D), and the trial judge ruled that Beale (D) was known enough to creditors to hold him personally liable for debts incurred by the market after the partnership's dissolution.

ISSUE: If a member of a partnership is unknown as a partner to the partnership's creditors, and is so far unknown and inactive in partnership affairs that the partnership's business reputation does not depend on him, will he still be held personally liable for partnership debts incurred after dissolution to creditors who had no notice of the dissolution?

HOLDING AND DECISION: (Whittemore, J.) No. The Uniform Partnership Act, § 35 does state that a partnership will remain liable to creditors who extended credit to the partnership prior to dissolution and who had no knowledge or notice of the dissolution. But it also states that the liability of a former partner must be satisfied from partnership assets alone if he was so unknown and inactive in partnership affairs such that the business reputation of the partnership was not in any degree connected with it. Here, there was no evidence that any creditors knew of the partnership and there was no evidence of the business reputation of the partnership. Although one salesman and some others in the business community may have heard of Beale's (D) connection with the market, reputation depends on general knowledge and standing in the business community. Thus, Beale (D) was not sufficiently known for him to be held personally liable for debts incurred by the partnership after the dissolution. [The trial court's decree was modified to reduce Beale's (D) obligation to Warren (P) to the two debts incurred prior to dissolution.] Affirmed as modified.

ANALYSIS

This case demonstrates the importance of notifying creditors of dissolution of partnership or the withdrawal of a partner, whether by advertisement or otherwise. An interesting variant on this problem arises when a partnership decides to incorporate. Some courts hold that the use and repeated acceptance of corporate checks is sufficient to constitute notice of dissolution of the partnership. See, e.g., *Jensen Sound Lab v. Long*, 113 Ill. App. 331, 69. Ill. Dec. 247, 447 N.E. 464, 465-66 (1983).

Seattle-First National Bank v. Marshall

Executor bank (P) v. Partner (D)

Wash. Ct. App., 31 Wash. App., 641 P.2d 1194 (1982).

NATURE OF CASE: Appeal from judgment enforcing partnership agreement.

FACT SUMMARY: The Marshalls (D) appealed from a judgment in favor of Seattle-First National Bank (Bank) (P) compelling them to purchase Olsen's interest in the partnership, contending that Bank (P) incorrectly valued that interest in failing to take into account costs which would be incurred when the purchase was made.

RULE OF LAW

The courts will enforce the parties' agreement with respect to buy-sell provisions and the valuation of a partner's interest.

FACTS: Burt Marshall (Marshall) (D), Roy Marshall, and Blanche Olsen entered into a partnership. Roy died, and the partnership agreement was amended to show Burt Marshall's (D) 80% interest in the property and Olsen's 20% interest. The agreement provided that upon the death of one partner, the surviving partners would purchase the interest of the deceased partner (the buy-sell provision). The agreement provided that the purchase price was the reasonable market value of the interest and further provided a method for determining that value. The valuation procedure was silent as to sales costs, minority interest, or capital gains taxes, all costs which would be paid at the time of the sale of the partnership interest. Olsen died, with the Seattle-First National Bank (Bank) (P) named as the executor of her will. After unsuccessfully attempting to have Marshall (D) purchase Olsen's interest pursuant to the buy-sell provision, Bank (P) brought suit to compel enforcement of that provision. Marshall (D) objected, contending the interest was overvalued because it was not discounted by the costs which would be incurred upon the purchase. Bank (P) was successful in compelling Marshall (D) to purchase the interest in conformity with the partnership agreement, and Marshall (D) appealed.

ISSUE: Will the reasonable fair market value of a partner's interest to be purchased pursuant to a buy-sell provision necessarily be discounted for costs to be incurred by the purchaser at the time of the sale?

HOLDING AND DECISION: (Durham, J.) No. The courts will enforce the parties' agreement with respect to buy-sell provisions and the valuation of a partner's interest. A buy-sell provision in a partnership agreement represents an effort to resolve conflicts likely to arise upon the death of a partner and represents a compromise rather than a precise formula for valuation. The evidence supports the decision of the trial court not to allow the discounts sought by Marshall (D). The agreement requires the purchase and provides a method for valuation which is silent as to costs incurred upon purchase. Furthermore, the interest is valued as a percentage of the partnership's entire inventory, not merely Olsen's interest. Although discounts might be appropriate in other circumstances, in this case, the law of this partnership is the agreement. Affirmed.

ANALYSIS

As the present case aptly points out, the Uniform Partnership Act provisions take a back seat to the express provisions of the agreement. Buy-sell provisions can be drafted to favor the buyer or seller, as the partners should desire, but because the partner usually does not know ahead of time that the provision will be applicable to him as a buyer, as opposed to a seller, or vice versa, most provisions will be drafted as in the present case in an attempt to strike a fair compromise between the two positions.

Hunter v. Straube

Partner (P) v. Partner (D)

Or. Sup. Ct., 273 Or. 720, 543 P.2d 278 (1975).

NATURE OF CASE: Appeal from denial of judicial dissolution and dismissal of counterclaim for breach of partnership agreement.

FACT SUMMARY: Hunter (P) and Straube (D) were doctors who formed a partnership for the provision of radiology services; Hunter (P) and another doctor later sued to dissolve it but refused Straube's (D) right—expressly set forth in the partnership agreement—as a non-withdrawing partner to continue the partnership business.

RULE OF LAW

Although a partner under Uniform Partnership Act § 31 may dissolve the partnership at any time, the exercise of such power, if in violation of the terms of the partnership agreement, may give rise to a claim for damages for breach of the agreement.

FACTS: Doctors Hunter (P) and Straube (D) were radiologists who formed a partnership named Lloyd Center X-Ray by written agreement in 1969. In 1971, by addendum, they added a third doctor, Haugen. In 1974, Hunter (P) and Haugen filed suit to dissolve the partnership and to wind up its affairs. Straube (D) counterclaimed, alleging that he was entitled to continue the partnership business under an express provision to that effect in the partnership agreement and to recover damages for breach of the partnership agreement. The trial court found that the filing of the suit did not cause dissolution of Lloyd Center X-Ray, and denied jurisdiction to wind up the partnership and dismissed Straube's (D) counterclaim because the partnership had not been dissolved. Both parties appealed.

ISSUE: Although a partner under Uniform Partnership Act § 31 may dissolve the partnership at any time, does the exercise of such power, if in violation of the terms of the partnership agreement, give rise to a claim for damages for breach of the agreement?

HOLDING AND DECISION: (McAllister, J.) Yes. Although a partner under Uniform Partnership Act § 31 may dissolve the partnership at any time, the exercise of such power, if in violation of the terms of the partnership agreement, may give rise to a claim for damages for breach of the agreement. Here Hunter (P) expressed his will to dissolve Lloyd Center X-Ray by filing the lawsuit. He had this power under general partnership law, as represented by Uniform Partnership Act § 31, which gives partners the power to dissolve whether or not such dissolution violates the partnership agreement. However, the "power" to dissolve is not equivalent with the "right" to dissolve; if dissolution involves noncompliance with the terms of the partnership agreement, the partner causing the dissolution may be subject to damages for breach of the partnership agreement. Here the agreement required Hunter (P) to give Straube (D) six months' notice of his desire to withdraw from Lloyd Center X-Ray; it also expressly allowed non-withdrawing partners such as Straube (D) to continue to carry on the partnership business. Hunter (P) filed this suit to avoid giving the proper notice and to escape from the liabilities he assumed when he signed the agreement. Thus, his election to dissolve, while fully within his power, breached the partnership agreement. Straube (D) is entitled to continue work as Lloyd Center X-Ray, and his counterclaim for damages for breach of the agreement will stand. Reversed and remanded.

ANALYSIS

The clause in the partnership agreement at issue in this case, sometimes called a "continuation clause" or "denial of dissolution" clause, presents risks of litigation because typically when one or more partners wish to dissolve a partnership, there are one or more who wish to continue on with the partnership business. Partners sometimes agree to such clauses despite the risks because they clarify the tax status of the partnership upon the death or withdrawal of a partner. Internal Revenue Code § 708(b)(1) requires that for a partnership to be terminated for tax purposes, within the meaning of the tax code, "no part of any business, financial operation, or venture . . . continues to be carried on by any of its partners."

Redman v. Walters

Client (P) v. Attorney (D)

Cal. Ct. App., 88 Cal. App. 3d 448 (1979).

NATURE OF CASE: Appeal from order dismissing action for damages for negligent legal representation.

FACT SUMMARY: When Walters (D), a former partner in a law firm, was sued for negligence, he claimed that he was not liable since the partnership had been dissolved.

RULE OF LAW

The dissolution of a partnership does not in and of itself discharge the existing liability of any partner.

FACTS: Redman (P) employed a law firm to represent him in 1969. In 1970, Walters (D) severed his relationship with that law firm and began practicing law elsewhere. When Redman's (P) lawsuit was dismissed for failure to bring it to trial within five years, Redman (P) commenced an action for damages against the firm and against Walters (D) for negligence. The lower court held that because of partnership's "dissolution" in 1970, Walters (D) was not the attorney of record for Redman (P) on the date of the alleged negligent act in 1974 and that the other attorneys in the firm had become Redman's (P) attorneys and therefore his agents. Their knowledge of the dissolution was therefore imputed to Redman (P) as their principal, under agency law principles. When his case against Walters (D) was dismissed, Redman (P) appealed.

ISSUE: Does the dissolution of a partnership in and of itself discharge the existing liability of any partner?

HOLDING AND DECISION: (Elkington, J.) No. The dissolution of a partnership does not in and of itself discharge the existing liability of any partner. An individual partner's liability in such a case will not be terminated except by performance of an agreement creating the liability, or by express or implied consent of the other contracting party that he need not so perform. It follows that unless Redman (P) had in some manner consented to nonrepresentation by Walters (D), Walters (D) continued as a partner and would be liable for the negligent act of the partnership. Reversed.

ANALYSIS

The unilateral decision to dissolve the partnership was not within the scope of authority granted to it by Redman (P). Therefore, the court found that knowledge of the dissolution could not be imputed to Redman (P) under agency principles. The Uniform Partnership Act § 36 states the correct rule.

Munn v. Scalera

Homebuilders (P) v. Construction partnership (D)

Conn. Sup. Ct., 181 Conn. 527, 436 A.2d 18 (1980).

NATURE OF CASE: Appeal from judgment discharging partner liabilities in breach of contract action.

FACT SUMMARY: The Munns (P) appealed from a judgment in favor of Peter Scalera (D), discharging him from liability for breach of contract, contending in part he was not relieved of liability for the Munn (P) construction project because there had not been a material alteration in the nature or payment of the obligation owed to the Munns (P).

RULE OF LAW

When a person agrees to assume the existing obligations of a dissolved partnership, the partner whose obligations have been assumed shall be discharged from any liability to any creditor of the partnership, who, aware of such agreement, consents to a material alteration in the nature or time of payment of such obligation.

FACTS: Peter Scalera (D) and Robert Scalera (D) were partners in Constructors I. They agreed to construct a home for the Munns (P). The project fell into default almost immediately. The Scaleras (D) decided to dissolve the partnership and informed the Munns (P), who elected to have Robert Scalera (D) complete construction individually. Construction was substantially completed, but the Munns (P) incurred substantial financial liability to a materialman, as well as other costs, to have the home completed. They brought suit for breach of contract, recovering against Robert (D). The trial court ruled in favor of Peter Scalera (D), finding that he had been discharged from liability for the construction of the Munns' (P) home under the Uniform Partnership Act (UPA). The Munns (P) appealed from this judgment, contending in part that there was no discharge from liability because there had not been a material alteration in the nature or payment of the obligation owed them.

ISSUE: When a person agrees to assume the existing obligations of a dissolved partnership, shall the partner whose obligations have been assumed be discharged from any liability to any creditor of the partnership, who, aware of such agreement, consents to a material alteration in the nature or time of payment of such obligation?

HOLDING AND DECISION: (Peters, J.) Yes. When a person agrees to assume the existing obligations of a dissolved partnership, the partner whose obligations have been assumed shall be discharged from any liability to any creditor of the partnership, who, aware of such agreement, consents to a material alteration in the nature or time of payment of the obligation. [The court first concluded the trial court had correctly determined that the partnership had been dissolved and Robert Scalera (D) had assumed the partnership obligation to complete the construction project. The court also determined that there was no reason to distinguish the situation where all of a partner's partnership obligations are assumed, from the present situation, where only one obligation, the one to complete the construction project, was assumed.] Although in the present case, the changes agreed to by the Munns (P) were in the nature and time of the payment to Robert Scalera (D), as opposed to changed in the nature and time of payment by Robert Scalera (D), since the Munns (P) essentially underwrote the procurement of materials, there is no doubt the contract was materially altered with respect to its payment terms. As such, Peter Scalera (D) was properly discharged from liability.

ANALYSIS

In a practical sense, a withdrawing partner must be concerned not only with existing obligations of the partnership, but also obligations incurred after withdrawal. The withdrawing partner must provide notice of dissolution, or could be held liable for such obligations, especially with respect to those he had previously dealt with as a partner. In some jurisdictions, when a creditor sues, the burden of proving notice of dissolution will be placed upon the defendant.

Ellebracht v. Siebring

Injured farm worker (P) v. Partnership (D)

525 F. Supp. 113 (W.D. Mo. 1981), *aff'd without opinion*, 676 F.2d 706 (8th Cir. 1982)

NATURE OF CASE: Motion to dismiss and to quash service in products liability action.

FACT SUMMARY: The partners of Siebring Manufacturing Company (D) moved to quash service of process and to dismiss Ellebracht's (P) product liability action, contending in part that they were not members of the partnership which manufactured the farm implement which injured Ellebracht (P).

RULE OF LAW

The doctrine of successor corporate liability is inapplicable to partnerships.

FACTS: Several different partnerships had been formed under the name Siebring Manufacturing Company (D). The first one, Partnership A, was formed in 1941 by Claude Siebring, Owen Siebring, and Grace Siebring. This partnership was terminated in 1967, when Claude died, and Owen purchased his interest. Through several changes, none of the partners in Siebring Manufacturing Company (D) now sued was a partner in Partnership A, a manufacturer of farming tools. Partnership A manufactured the farm implement which injured Ellebracht (P) sometime between 1958 and 1964. He brought his products liability action against the partners in the Siebring Manufacturing Company (D), contending in part that the partnership now operating as Siebring Manufacturing Company (D) was a "successor in interest" to Partnership A, such that the personnel jurisdictions could be asserted over the partners (D). They in turn moved to quash service of process and to dismiss, contending in part that they were not members of the partnership which manufactured the farm implement which injured Ellebracht (P).

ISSUE: Is the doctrine of "successor corporation liability" applicable to partnerships?

HOLDING AND DECISION: (Wright, J.) No. The doctrine of successor corporation liability is inapplicable to partnerships. The burden of proving a continuing partnership is on Ellebracht (P). He did not meet his burden, since the undisputed facts make clear that original partnership which manufactured the farm implement was terminated when Owen purchased Claude's interest from one Burton in 1967. Nor did Gary Siebring's (D) purchase in 1968 of Grace Siebring's interest in the partnership, and his assumption of one-third of its liabilities, make him responsible for the torts of the prior partnership; he did not expressly assume responsibility for these torts and therefore cannot be bound by them. The doctrine of successor corporation liability renders a successor corporation liable for the torts of its predecessor. This doctrine has not been recognized in this jurisdiction, and no collective inclination exists to apply it to partnerships. Ellebracht (P) has been unable to establish personal jurisdiction over any of the current partners of Siebring Manufacturing Company (D). Motions granted.

ANALYSIS

As the present case suggests, a change in the constitution of a partnership business can have some long-term effects on a particular partner's individual liability status. The successor corporation doctrine has found widespread acceptance and is based in part on the policy that the successor corporation is in a better position to absorb losses. Since partnerships, like corporations, benefit economically from their business activities, the doctrine would appear to be equally applicable to partnerships.

Case v. Paul Troester Maschinenfabrik

Accident victim (P) v. Partnership (D)

129 F. Supp. 2d 428 (W.D.N.Y. 2001).

NATURE OF CASE: Motion for summary judgment in tort action.

FACT SUMMARY: Case (P) claimed that Paul Troester Maschinenfabrik (PTM) (D), a German partnership, and Troester Machinery, Ltd. (TML) (D), an American corporation, were successors-in-interest to Troester Maschinenbau GmbH & Co. (TMG), which had manufactured a machine that had injured him, and, therefore, were liable to him under various tort theories.

RULE OF LAW

(1) A motion for summary judgment to dismiss an action on the basis of successor liability is defeated where evidence is presented that a partnership has been carrying on the business of a former partnership.

(2) A motion for summary judgment to dismiss an action on the basis of successor liability is not defeated where no evidence is presented that a purported successor entity is any way connected to the predecessor entity.

FACTS: Case (P) suffered injuries when his arm got caught in a machine manufactured by Troester Maschinenbau GmbH & Co. (TMG), a German partnership which was no longer in business. Case (P) claimed that Paul Troester Maschinenfabrik (PTM) (D), a German partnership, and Troester Machinery, Ltd. (TML) (D), an American corporation, were successors-in-interest to TMG, and, therefore, were liable to him under various tort theories. When TMG dissolved, certain raw materials, two or three used machines and certain furniture were purchased by PTM (D). Also, some, but not all, of TMG's former partners, management and/or shareholders served as partners and/or in management of PTM. After TMG dissolved, PTM (D) made machines similar to the machine that injured Case (P). PTM (D) never assumed TMG's tort liabilities or any of its debts. TML (D) was established to sell certain types of machines in the U.S. It never produced anything, and its management, personnel, assets and partners are all different from those of TMG. Case (P) claimed that PTM (D) and TMG were closely related prior to TMG's dissolution. He maintained that their products shared the trade name "Troester;" the machine at issue was assembled pursuant to a cooperation agreement between the two partnerships; the type of machine at issue was among the machines the partnerships manufactured together and under supervision of the same technical director; and all partners of TMG were partners of PTM (D). Also, all TMG intellectual property transferred to PTM (D) and PTM (D) continued to service TMG's former customers.

ISSUE:

(1) Is a motion for summary judgment to dismiss an action on the basis of successor liability defeated where evidence is presented that a partnership has been carrying on the business of a former partnership?

(2) Is a motion for summary judgment to dismiss an action on the basis of successor liability defeated where no evidence is presented that a purported successor entity is any way connected to the predecessor entity?

HOLDING AND DECISION: (Larimer, C.J.)

(1) Yes. A motion for summary judgment to dismiss an action on the basis of successor liability is defeated where evidence is presented that a partnership has been carrying on the business of a former partnership. The general rule is that a business entity, such as a partnership, that acquires the assets of another similar business entity is not liable for the torts of its predecessor. One of several exceptions to this rule occurs when the purchaser is a mere continuation of the seller, and carries on the same business. Here, Case (P) contends that PTM (D) and TML (D) are carrying on the same business previously operated by TMG. Several factors are applied to determine if the successor is a mere continuation of the predecessor. These include whether the successor (1) retained the same employees, supervisory personnel, the same production facilities in the same location and the same business name, (2) continued production of the same products, (3) maintained the same assets and general business operations and (4) held itself out to the public as the continuation of the previous enterprise. Here, some of these factors are clearly satisfied: TMG partners were also PTM (D) partners; TMG was created to extend PTM's (D) capacity; PTM (D) retained most of TMG's management; some of TMG's assets and customers were transferred to PTM (D) partners; and PTM (D) had exclusive access to TMG's designs. Also, there was a question of fact as to whether the machines that PTM (D) manufactured after TMG's dissolution were very similar to the machines produced by TMG. There was also evidence that PTM (D) and TMG were held out to the public as being affiliated. For these reasons, sufficient fact issues are raised to defeat summary judgment, and the court does not need to decide other successor liability issues raised by Case (P) as between PTM (D) and TMG, such as whether successor

Continued on next page.

liability might exist on the so-called product line exception to the general rule.

(2) No. A motion for summary judgment to dismiss an action on the basis of successor liability is not defeated where no evidence is presented that a purported successor entity is any way connected to the predecessor entity. Here, Case's (P) attempt to impose successor liability on TML (D) must fail. TML (D) is a separate corporation with separate management based in a separate country. It does not manufacture any products; it merely sells them in the United States. Indeed, TML (D) was not even incorporated many years after the machine at issue was manufactured, and a year after TMG was dissolved. Moreover, TML (D) has neither expressly nor impliedly agreed to assume TMG's debts, and TML (D) was not a party to the cooperation agreement between PTM (D) and TMG. Therefore, the motion for summary judgment is granted with respect to TML.

ANALYSIS

The product line exception to the general rule of successor liability, which the court here avoided reaching, provides that when a business entity purchases substantially all of the assets of a manufacturer and thereafter continues essentially the same manufacturing operation it may be strictly liable for defects in products in the same line even though they were in fact made by the predecessor. To prove this exception, a plaintiff bears the burden of proving: (1) the plaintiff's remedy against the original manufacturer was virtually destroyed by the successor's acquisition of substantially all of predecessor's assets; (2) the successor entity continued to manufacture essentially the same product line as its predecessor; (3) the succeeding entity had the ability to assume the original manufacturer's risk-spreading role; and (4) the successor benefited from the original manufacturer's goodwill.

Seattle-First National Bank v. Marshall

Executor bank (P) v. Partner (D)

Wash. Ct. App., 641 P.2d 1194 (1982).

NATURE OF CASE: Appeal of award of prejudgment interest.

FACT SUMMARY: Marshall (D) challenged the award of prejudgment interest as part of the judgment entered in favor of Seattle-First National Bank (Bank) (P) in its action, brought in its capacity as executor for Olsen's estate, to compel compliance with the partnership agreement's buy-sell provision, contending the court erred in awarding prejudgment interest on an unliquidated sum.

RULE OF LAW

The rule barring the award of prejudgment interest on a judgment for an unliquidated sum is inapplicable when valuing a deceased partner's interest in the assets of a dissolved partnership.

FACTS: Seattle-First National Bank (Bank) (P), in its capacity as executor for Olsen's estate, successfully brought suit against Marshall (D) to compel compliance with the buy-sell provision of a partnership agreement, which required Marshall (D) to purchase the partnership interest of a deceased partner. As part of the award, prejudgment interest, in the amount of $78,071.04, was awarded to the estate. Marshall (D) appealed, contending that the court was barred from awarding prejudgment interest on a judgment for an unliquidated sum.

ISSUE: Is the rule barring judgment interest on a judgment for an unliquidated sum applicable when valuing a deceased partner's interest in the assets of a dissolved partnership?

HOLDING AND DECISION: (Durham, J.) No. The rule barring the award of prejudgment interest on a judgment for an unliquidated sum is inapplicable when valuing a deceased partner's interest in the assets of a dissolved partnership. The Uniform Partnership Act (UPA) controls, where, as here, the partnership agreement is silent on the issue of interest. The UPA provided that a deceased partner's estate is entitled to either interest or profits on the value of the deceased partner's interest. To enforce the rule in this situation would thwart the purpose of UPA § 42. The effect of that section can be avoided by properly drafting the partnership agreement to preclude an award of prejudgment interest. That was not done here. Affirmed.

ANALYSIS

The holding in this case does not preclude the parties to a partnership agreement from expressly agreeing that prejudgment interest shall not be payable, under any circumstance, to the estate of a deceased partner on the value of that partner's interest in the partnership. Nevertheless, the rule in this case is sound for two reasons: (1) it is a means of compelling those continuing the partnership affairs after the death of a partner; (2) it also serves to compensate the estate of the decedent partner for the use of decedent's assets or capital in the continuing conduct of the business until final winding up.

Blut v. Katz

Wife of deceased partner (P) v. Partners (D)

N.J. Sup. Ct., 99 A.2d 785 (1953).

NATURE OF CASE: Appeal in action for dissolution and accounting of partnership share.

FACT SUMMARY: **Blut (P) appealed the Chancery Division's determination of the value of her late husband's partnership share, contending she should be entitled to the profits of the partnership attributable to the use of her dead husband's capital since his death.**

RULE OF LAW

Unless the representative of a deceased partner consents to the continuation of the partnership business, the deceased partner's estate is not entitled to profits attributable to the use of the deceased partner's share of the partnership assets.

FACTS: Blut's (P) husband and four others entered into a partnership in 1925. The partnership agreement had a term of one year, provided weekly allowances, an even distribution of the profits, and provided for paying off any partner who voluntarily withdrew. In 1940, two partners withdrew. From that point until Blut's (P) husband's death, the partners operated the business as equal one-third partners. In 1946, Blut's (P) husband became ill. He continued to receive his salary and share of profits, although because of his illness, he rendered no services to the business. At his death in 1949, Blut (P), as the executrix of his estate, instituted this action, seeking a dissolution of the partnership and an accounting. The remaining partners, Katz et al. (D), continued to operate the business. Blut (P) never consented to the continued operation of the business. On appeal, a judgment representing Blut's (P) husband's share of the business was remanded to the Chancery Division to determine the value of that interest, including goodwill. From that valuation, both sides appealed with Blut (P) contending in part that she was entitled to a share of the profit of the partnership attributable to the use of her late husband's capital since his death.

ISSUE: Is the deceased partner's estate entitled to the profits attributable to the use of his share of the partnership assets, absent consent from a representative of the estate to the continuation of the partnership business?

HOLDING AND DECISION: (Wachenfeld, J.) No. Unless the representative of a deceased partner's estate consents to the continuation of the partnership business, the estate is not entitled to profits attributable to the use of the deceased partner's share of the partnership assets. The Uniform Partnership Act (UPA) § 41, upon which Blut (P) relied, was designed to protect the estate of the deceased partner from creditor's demands should the executor liquidate. The consent serves as the quid pro quo because by granting consent, the estate would be liable to new claims of creditors to the extent of the estate's interest in the partnership. This is how the provision is construed and applied in this jurisdiction. Blut (P) never gave consent to the continuation of the partnership business. As such, her husband's estate was not entitled to profits, which were due to the skill, time, and diligence of the remaining partners in the furtherance of the partnership business. Blut (P) is only entitled to interest on the value of her late husband's share of the partnership assets. Affirmed and remanded.

DISSENT: (Heher, J.) The principle of unjust enrichment is applicable here and should require Kutz (D) to turn over profits resulting from the unauthorized use of partnership assets.

ANALYSIS

From the foregoing case, it is clear that where business is going well, consent should be given, since profits will ordinarily be greater than interest and could receive a more favorable tax status. Where business is not so good, by withholding consent, the remaining partners bear the risk of continuing business. Where the execution's judgment is recklessly or negligently exercised, an action may lie against him by the deceased's beneficiaries for lost profits, for failure to consent to a continuation of the business.

In re Brown

Partnership determination of good will.

N.Y. Ct. App., 242 N.Y. 1, 150 N.E. 581, 44 A.L.R. 510 (1926).

NATURE OF CASE: Appeal from decision surcharging executors' accounts for failing to account for good will.

FACT SUMMARY: The executors (D) of the estate of Steven H. Brown appealed from the affirmation of a decision surcharging their accounts for acquiescing in the determination of Brown's surviving partners that there was no good will to be accounted for, arguing that there was no good will in the partnership which they were required to account for.

RULE OF LAW

Good will, when it exists as incidental to the business of a partnership, is presumptively an asset to be accounted for like any other by those who liquidate the business.

FACTS: Stephen H. Brown was a partner in Vernon C. Brown & Company, a stockbroker business which was quite profitable. New members were admitted from time to time, but the firm name remained the same. One partner, Schoonmaker, retired, and nothing was paid him for the "good will" of the business. The business consisted of four departments. The first was the general commission business. The second was the "odd-lot" business, the orders for which did not come through the office but from the trading floor. The third department was the "two-dollar" business, similar in operation to the odd-lot business. The fourth department handled speculative business for the firm itself. When Steven H. Brown died in 1917, his share of the profits was 15½%. The surviving partners denied that there was any good will in the business to be accounted for, continuing the business under the old name and at the same location. The executors (D) acquiesced in that determination. However, the decision not to include in Brown's estate a portion of Brown & Company was challenged, and a referee decided to calculate a value for the decedent's share of the goodwill. This value was based on an estimation of the partnership's profits over the previous two years attributable to the non-speculative aspects of the business (i.e., the first three branches or departments of the venture). The executor's accounts were surcharged Brown's 15½% of this profit by the referee; the surcharge was confirmed by the surrogate and affirmed on appeal.

ISSUE: Is good will, when it exists as incidental to the business of a partnership, presumptively an asset to be accounted for like any other by those who liquidate the business?

HOLDING AND DECISION: (Cardozo, J.) Yes. Good will, when it exists as incidental to the business of the partnership, is presumptively an asset to be accounted for like any other by those who liquidate the business. However, the partners themselves may nonetheless expressly or impliedly agree that even though good will exists it shall not be considered property or an asset of the partnership. Evidence of such an agreement is present in this case. Assuming for disposition of this case, however, that the presumption remains intact, there was good will to be accounted for. The two chief elements of value upon any sale of good will are continuity of place and continuity of name. Both are present in this case, although the continuity of name would have been at most the continuity of name associated to a successor. (The court went on to determine that although there was good will associated with the "commission" department, there was no good will to be accounted for with respect to the odd-lot and two-dollar business, since those departments' business arose for the most part through individual broker effort on the trading floor, and not due to the name or location of the business.) Reversed; rehearing ordered.

ANALYSIS

Good will is not presumptively recognized as an asset of the partnership when the relationship between the partners is personal or preferential. The theory appears to be that the good will consists of personal skills or professional qualifications, which are incapable of transfer. Even if the presumption against recognition can be overcome, or is provided for by the agreement, problems still remain with valuation of the interest.

Dawson v. White & Case

Former partner (P) v. law firm (D)

N.Y. Ct. App., 88 N.Y.2d 666, 672 N.E.2d 589 (1996).

NATURE OF CASE: Appeal from judgment in favor of plaintiff ordering an accounting in suit for wrongful termination.

FACT SUMMARY: When an accounting was ordered pursuant to the dissolution of White & Case (D), a law firm, good will was valued, despite a provision in the partnership agreement excluding it.

RULE OF LAW

Partners are free to exclude particular items from the class of distributable partnership property, and such an agreement will be enforced in an accounting proceeding.

FACTS: Dawson (P) was a partner at White & Case (D), a law firm, who refused to withdraw from the firm when asked to do so. White & Case (D) voted to dissolve the partnership and reform it without Dawson (P). Dawson (P) sued, alleging wrongful termination, breach of fiduciary duty, breach of contract, and various other tort claims. The lower court granted Dawson (P) an injunction prohibiting White & Case (D) from interfering with Dawson's (P) access to his client files and also ordered an accounting pursuant to § 43 of the Uniform Partnership Act. A Special Referee valued the assets of White & Case (D), including the firm's good will. White & Case (D) appealed, claiming that the terms of the partnership agreement deemed good will to be "of no value."

ISSUE: Are partners free to exclude particular items from the classification of distributable partnership property?

HOLDING AND DECISION: (Ciparick, J.) Yes. Partners are free to exclude particular items from the classification of distributable partnership property, and such an agreement will be enforced in an accounting proceeding. Therefore, a partnership agreement deeming good will to be "of no value" is binding. Since new White & Case (D) partners never paid anything for good will and departing partners never received any payment for good will, the terms of the agreement should be enforced. The judgment should be modified and the case is remitted for further proceedings in accordance with this opinion. Affirmed as modified.

ANALYSIS

There is no longer any blanket prohibition against valuing law firm good will. The Code of Professional Responsibility authorizes the sale of a law practice, including its good will. Ethical constraints against the sale of good will may still apply, however.

Resnick v. Kaplan

Former partner (D) v. law firm (P)

Md. Ct. Spec. App., 49 Md. App. 499, 434 A.2d 582 (1981).

NATURE OF CASE: Appeal from allocation of fees in suit for partnership accounting.

FACT SUMMARY: Resnick (D) left his old law firm, Kaplan (P), to open his own office; however, both Resnick (D) and Kaplan (P) continued to work on matters begun prior to Resnick's (D) departure, and to receive fees for such continuing matters.

RULE OF LAW

A partnership is not terminated on dissolution but continues until the winding up of partnership affairs is completed.

FACTS: Resnick (D) left his old law firm, Kaplan (P), and opened his own law office. He continued to represent clients of the old firm in about 150 cases; most were personal injury claims taken by the firm on a contingency fee basis, and quickly settled. Resnick (D) collected about $385,000 in fees from these matters. He had obtained authorizations from the clients to continue to represent them in his new capacity as an independent lawyer. Kaplan (P) also continued to represent clients of the firm in about 600 cases which had been commenced prior to Resnick's (D) departure; Kaplan (P) collected fees of about $843,000 from these cases. Neither Resnick (D) nor Kaplan (P) paid each other any part of the fees they separately collected. Kaplan (P) sued Resnick (D) for an accounting, and the trial court held that the collective fees received by both Resnick (D) and Kaplan (P) should be distributed between them in accordance with their respective distributive shares under the partnership agreement. Resnick (D) appealed.

ISSUE: Does a partnership which is dissolved continue until the winding up of partnership affairs is completed?

HOLDING AND DECISION: (Moore, J.) Yes. A partnership is not terminated on dissolution but continues until winding up of partnership affairs is completed. Dissolution occurs when there is a change in the relations of the partners caused by any partner ceasing to be associated in the carrying on—as distinguished from the winding up—of the business. Here the law partnership between Kaplan (P) and Resnick (D) was dissolved on Resnick's (D) departure; however, until the firm was "wound up," both Kaplan (P) and Resnick (D) had continuing obligations, both professionally and contractually, to represent clients who retained the firm prior to Resnick's (D) departure. The trial court properly held that the aggregate of the fees collected should be allocated according to the percentages specified in the agreement for the distribution of profits and losses. Affirmed.

ANALYSIS

The proposition is universally accepted that a law partner in dissolution owes a duty to his old firm to wind up the old firm's pending business, and that he is not entitled to any extra compensation therefor. See, e.g., *Frates v. Nichols*, 167 So.2d 77 (Fla.3d D.C.A. 1964) (fees of over $200,000 attributable to settlement of ten negligence cases by former partner of law firm held to be firm assets as to which the former partner could only receive partnership interest therein). Further, a former partner is not entitled to receive payments in quantum meruit based on the value of services rendered on behalf of the old firm, even after dissolution.

Marr v. Langhoff

Law partnership (P) v. Former partner (D)

Md. Ct. App., 589 A.2d 470 (1991).

NATURE OF CASE: Appeal of an award of damages for breach of fiduciary duty.

FACT SUMMARY: **Marr (P), a partner in a law firm, sought to recover the fee that Langhoff (D), a former partner, had earned while representing a client in a lawsuit since Langhoff (D) had taken the case from the firm.**

RULE OF LAW

Partners' mutual fiduciary duties cease when the winding up after dissolution is completed.

FACTS: Langhoff (D), Marr (P), and Bennett established a law firm. In 1981, serious differences arose between Langhoff (D) and Marr (P), and it was agreed that Langhoff (D) would officially leave the firm on January 1, 1982. On his last day, Langhoff (D) discussed pending cases with Bennett, and they agreed that Langhoff (D) would take those cases that were his. When Langhoff (D) left the firm, he took a file that was not one of the agreed-upon cases. Langhoff (D) earned a substantial fee on the case, and Marr (P) filed suit for breach of fiduciary duty. The trial court ruled for Marr (P), and Langhoff (D) appealed.

ISSUE: Do partners' mutual fiduciary duties cease when the winding up after dissolution is completed?

HOLDING AND DECISION: (Rodowsky, J.) Yes. Partners' mutual fiduciary duties cease when the winding up after dissolution is completed. Work in progress at the time of dissolution is an asset of the dissolved firm. During the winding up of partnership business following dissolution, partners continue to owe one another fiduciary duties with respect to the business of the dissolved partnership. However, the mutual fiduciary duties cease when the winding up is completed. When Langhoff (D) and Bennett agreed to a method of splitting the work in progress at the law firm, it had the immediate effect of winding up the firm. Thus, the firm was immediately terminated, and the mutual fiduciary duties were ended. While Langhoff's (D) action in taking the file may have breached that agreement with Bennett, it was not a breach of any fiduciary duty. Reversed and remanded.

ANALYSIS

This decision is in accord with the Uniform Partnership Act. UPA § 30 states that upon dissolution, "the partnership is not terminated, but continues until the winding up of partnership affairs is completed." Section 43 discusses the rights of partners at dissolution, "in the absence of any agreement to the contrary."

Ohlendorf v. Feinstein

Partner (P) v. Partner (D)

Mo. Ct. App., 636 S.W.2d 687 (1982).

NATURE OF CASE: Appeal from judgment ordering winding up of partnership and awarding damages.

FACT SUMMARY: Ohlendorf (P) appealed from a judgment against him on cross-claims by Feinstein (D) and Whaley (D) for a winding up of the partnership and for damages, contending that the damages for lost profits were not proximately caused by his wrongful conduct.

RULE OF LAW
Partners who have not wrongfully dissolved a partnership have the option but not the duty to continue the partnership business.

FACTS: Feinstein (D) submitted the highest bid for seven tracts of state land, delivering a check for 10% of the purchase price and signing a sales agreement. The balance was due when the purchase closed. Feinstein (D) formed a partnership with Whaley (D) and Ohlendorf (P) to obtain individual purchasers for the seven tracts for profit. They were partially successful in lining up buyers, with Ohlendorf (P) indicating that he considered the partnership dead. He notified the state that the partnership would not complete the purchase and sued Feinstein (D) and Whaley (D) to recover his third of the down payment. They cross-claimed for a winding up of the agreement. From a judgment in favor of Whaley (D) and Feinstein (D) on the cross-claim, Ohlendorf (P) appealed, contending that Feinstein (D) and Whaley (D) failed to prove that the lost profits were due to his wrongful conduct.

ISSUE: Do partners who have not wrongfully dissolved a partnership have the duty to continue the partnership business?

HOLDING AND DECISION: (Pudlowski, J.) No. Partners who have not wrongfully dissolved a partnership have the option, but not the duty, to continue the partnership business. (The court concluded that there was no doubt that Ohlendorf (P) had breached the partnership agreement.) Since they did not wrongfully dissolve the partnership, Feinstein (D) and Whaley (D) have an election of remedies. To uphold Ohlendorf's (P) position that their damages were not due to his wrongful conduct is a backhanded attempt to limit the options available to Feinstein (D) and Whaley (D), and would impose upon them a duty to continue the business if there was a reasonable certainty that it would be profitable. Imposing such a duty would erroneously make Ohlendorf's (P) wrongful conduct the proximate cause of the lost profits. Reversed and remanded for a determination of lost profits on Tracts 1, 2, and 6; otherwise affirmed.

ANALYSIS

This case addresses the rights of "innocent" partners when a partnership dissolution occurs as the result of an act in violation of the partnership agreement. If the partners decide to retain the business as a going concern, they must pay the partner causing dissolution the value of his interest in the partnership. The greatest difficulty in valuing the wrongdoer's share is ascertaining the partnership's business goodwill; if the partners have had foresight, a formula based on capitalization of expected income stream or discounting the value of the enterprise will have been included in the partnership agreement itself. However, more likely than not the partners will not have planned ahead for the value of the going concern at dissolution, and debates will occur on whether goodwill should account for human talent, managerial expertise, customer or brand loyalty, etc.

Prentiss v. Sheffel

Majority partners (P) v. Partner (D)

Ariz. Ct. App., 20 Ariz. App. 411, 513 P.2d 949 (1973).

NATURE OF CASE: Appeal from order allowing partners to bid on dissolved partnership's assets at judicial sale.

FACT SUMMARY: Sheffel (D) was a minority partner in a three-man partnership-at-will, in which Prentiss (P) was one of two majority partners; when the partnership was dissolved and its assets, principally a shopping center, sold at a judicial sale, Prentiss (P) was allowed to bid despite Sheffel's (D) objection that he had been wrongfully excluded from management of the partnership.

RULE OF LAW

Absent any showing of bad faith, a partner may bid upon partnership assets at a judicial sale of those assets.

FACTS: Prentiss (P) and another individual were majority partners in a three-man partnership-at-will, in which Sheffel (D) was the minority partner. The partnership was formed to acquire and operate a shopping center. When the center suffered losses, Sheffel (D) did not contribute all of his share of the deficit incurred by the center. Consequently, the majority partners, including Prentiss (P), who collectively owned 85% of the partnership, excluded Sheffel (D) from management of the business. Eventually Prentiss (P) sued for dissolution of the partnership, on the ground that Sheffel (D) had been derelict in his duties. Sheffel (D) counterclaimed, seeking a winding-up of the partnership and appointment of a receiver. A receiver was appointed and ordered a judicial sale of the shopping center owned by the partnership; the receiver, however, denied Sheffel's (D) request for an order prohibiting Prentiss (P) from bidding on the assets on the grounds that Sheffel (D) had been wrongfully excluded from the partnership business. Prentiss (P) was high bidder at the sale, and the court confirmed the sale of the center to Prentiss (P) and the other majority partner. Sheffel (D) appealed from the order of confirmation.

ISSUE: Absent any showing of bad faith, may a partner bid upon partnership assets at a judicial sale of those assets?

HOLDING AND DECISION: (Haire, J.) Yes. Absent any showing of bad faith, a partner may bid upon partnership assets at a judicial sale of those assets. Sheffel (D) contended that he was wrongfully excluded from the management of the shopping center, but there is no evidence that Prentiss (P) did so in bad faith or with the intent to wrongfully obtain Sheffel's (D) interest in the Center. Further, it appeared that Sheffel (D) was not disadvantaged at all by the bidding; Prentiss' (P) bid may have even enhanced the value of Sheffel's (D) interest. There was no evidence that Prentiss (P) acted fraudulently, in bad faith, or with the intent to pay less than adequate consideration for Sheffel's (D) interest. Nor is there case law which prohibits a partner from bidding at a judicial sale of the partnership assets. Finally, this sale was properly conducted. Affirmed.

ANALYSIS

In many instances, a dissolution, liquidation, and subsequent purchase of partnership assets at a judicial sale is an attempt by the majority partners to buy out a minority partner's interest for less than fair value. In the present case, it is unclear whether dissolution was absolutely necessary. Prentiss (P) already had management control of the business, and it may have been merely a move to forestall Sheffel (D) from bringing a dissolution of the partnership on his own terms.

Kovacik v. Reed

Partner (P) v. Partner (D)

Cal. Sup. Ct., 315 P.2d 314 (1957).

NATURE OF CASE: Judgment for plaintiff in suit for dissolution of joint venture and accounting.

FACT SUMMARY: Kovacik (P) and Reed (D) entered into a joint venture to remodel kitchens; Kovacik (P) agreed to supply money and credit and job opportunities, and Reed (D) agreed to provide his own labor as job superintendent and estimator.

RULE OF LAW

In a partnership where one partner has agreed to contribute only money and the other has agreed to contribute only services or labor, neither partner is liable to the other for losses sustained by the partnership.

FACTS: Kovacik (P) informed Reed (D) that he had opportunities to do kitchen remodeling in San Francisco. Kovacik (P) agreed to invest $10,000, if Reed (D) would act as job superintendent and estimator. Kovacik (P) and Reed (D) agreed that they would share profits equally, but Kovacik (P) did not ask Reed (D) to share any loss—indeed, the subject of loss was not even discussed. Thereafter, Reed (D) commenced work, supplying only his own services in addition to purchasing materials on his own account, for which he was reimbursed. Kovacik (P) supplied credit which provided the venture's financing. Although a number of bids were won and completed by the venture, it lost money. Kovacik (P) demanded contribution from Reed (D) of his purported share of expenditures in excess of income. Reed (D) refused, and as a result of a subsequent dissolution and accounting action by Kovacik (P) faced a judgment for half of the venture's monetary losses.

ISSUE: In a partnership where one partner has agreed to contribute only money and the other has agreed to contribute only services or labor, is either partner liable to the other for losses sustained by the partnership?

HOLDING AND DECISION: (Schauer, J.) No. Where, as here, one partner or joint venturer contributes the money capital as against the other's skill and labor, neither party is liable to the other for contribution for any loss sustained. There is an implied agreement in such ventures that the value of each partner's contribution is equal, and therefore in the event of loss each loses his own capital—the one his money and the other his labor. Thus, although Kovacik (P) lost $8,680 in actual money advanced and invested in the venture, and Reed (D) lost nothing out-of-pocket but his labor time, Kovacik (P) is not entitled to a judgment against Reed (D). Reversed.

ANALYSIS

This case demonstrates an exception to the general rule that in the absence of an agreement to the contrary the law presumes that partners and joint venturers intended to participate equally in the losses and profits of the common enterprise. However, as this court notes, in the cases in which this general rule has been applied, each of the parties had contributed capital consisting either of money or land or other tangible property or else was to receive compensation for services rendered to the common undertaking. Here, Reed (D) did not receive payment for his labor, so his "losses" were in effect his donation of time to the venture.

CHAPTER 14

The Limited Partnership

Quick Reference Rules of Law

Direct Mail Specialist, Inc. v. Brown

Company (P) v. Limited partnership (D)

673 F. Supp. 1540 (D. Mont. 1987).

NATURE OF CASE: Motions for summary judgment in debt collection action.

FACT SUMMARY: Direct Mail Specialist (P) provided services to Peaceful Bay Resort and Club, of which Brown (D) was the general partner; when it was not paid for these services, it sued Brown (D) and Peaceful Bay's limited partners on the grounds that its certificates of limited partnership and registration of assumed business name were defective.

RULE OF LAW

Where there is a failure substantially to comply with the statutory formalities for formation of a limited partnership, and the limited partners fail to renounce their interests as soon as they learn of defects in formation, the limited partners will be liable as general partners to third persons with no knowledge of the limited nature of the partnership.

FACTS: Direct Mail Specialist (P) provided services to Peaceful Bay Resort and Club, of which Brown (D) was the general partner. When it was not paid for these services, it sued Brown (D) and Peaceful Bay's limited partners on the grounds that its certificates of limited partnership and registration of assumed business name were defective. Further, Direct Mail (P) had no knowledge at the time it provided services that Peaceful Bay was a limited partnership. The certificate of limited partnership was not recorded with the Secretary of State as required by Uniform Limited Partnership Act (UPLA) § 2(1)(b), nor did it attach a schedule as required by UPLA § 1(a) showing the respective capital contributions and profit participations of each partner. The application for certificate of assumed business name did not indicate that Peaceful Bay had any limited partners. Both Direct Mail (P) and Brown (D) filed motions for summary judgment.

ISSUE: Where there is a failure substantially to comply with the statutory formalities for formation of a limited partnership, and the limited partners fail to renounce their interests as soon as they learn of defects in formation, will the limited partners be liable as general partners to third persons with no knowledge of the limited nature of the partnership?

HOLDING AND DECISION: (Smith, J.) Yes. Where there is a failure substantially to comply with the statutory formalities for formation of a limited partnership, and the limited partners fail to renounce their interests as soon as they learn of defects in formation, the limited partners will be liable as general partners to third persons with no knowledge of the limited nature of the partnership. Here, Direct Mail (P) had no independent knowledge of, and due to the defects in formation could not have known of, the limited nature of the Peaceful Bay partnership. Nor did any of the limited partners attempt to renounce, until at least three years after this lawsuit was filed, their interest in Peaceful Bay. This belated attempt did not satisfy the requirements of UPLA § 11 that a person must renounce any interest in the profits of the business or other compensation by way of income as soon as he learns there is something wrong with the organizational set-up. Because no effort was made to comply with the spirit of the law, either in formation of Peaceful Bay, or in renunciation of limited partner interests upon discovery of the formation defect, Direct Man's (P) motion for summary judgment is granted and Brown's (D) denied.

ANALYSIS

Unlike a general partnership, formalities are required for the formation of a limited partnership. This makes absolute sense given that limited partnerships are creatures of statute. Under UPLA (1976) § 203, these formalities are: (1) execution of a limited partnership certificate stating the partnership name, character of business and location of principal office, setting forth the name and address of each partner, the capital contributions of each partner and whether each partner is general or limited, and the respective rights and priorities of each partner; (2) filing of the limited partnership certificate with the County Clerk, recordation with the county of principal place of business, and central filing with the Secretary of State.

Briargate Condominium Ass'n v. Carpenter

General partnership (P) v. Investor/partner (D)

976 F.2d 868 (4th Cir. 1992).

NATURE OF CASE: Appeal from an award of damages for breach of contract.

FACT SUMMARY: Carpenter (D) claimed that she should not have to pay the debts of a partnership because she believed that she was only a limited partner.

RULE OF LAW

A person is not a general partner if he had a good-faith belief that he was a limited partner and corrects the mistake upon discovery.

FACTS: Briargate Homes was a partnership that purchased several units in the Briargate Condominium (P) complex in South Carolina. Carpenter's (D) accountant convinced her to invest in the partnership for tax reasons. Carpenter (D) believed that she was to be a limited partner. However, Briargate Homes was operated as a general partnership from the beginning. After the partnership failed to pay assessed fees by the Briargate Condominium Association (P) in the amount of $85,106, the Association (P) filed a collection action against the partners (D). When Carpenter (D) discovered that she was a general partner, she immediately notified all parties that she was withdrawing from any equity participation and renouncing all profits. The trial court ruled for the Association (P), and Carpenter (D) appealed.

ISSUE: Is a person a general partner if he had a good faith belief that he was a limited partner and acts to correct the mistake upon discovery?

HOLDING AND DECISION: (Hamilton, J.) No. A person is not a general partner if he had a good-faith belief that he was a limited partner and corrects the mistake upon discovery. According to the law, a person contributing to a business enterprise is not a general partner in an enterprise if two requirements are met. First, the person must have a good-faith belief that he was a limited, rather than general, partner at the time of contribution. Second, the person must take an appropriate course of action upon discovering the mistake. Giving notice and withdrawing from future equity participation in the business qualifies as appropriate action to establish status as a limited partner. If these two elements are satisfied, personal liability as a general partner is cut off. The trial court did not apply this standard to Carpenter's (D) actions. Accordingly, the judgment is vacated, and the case is remanded.

ANALYSIS

The decision also discussed whether the good-faith belief requirement was an objective or subjective test. The court determined that an objective standard was more appropriate. In other words, a person claiming no liability as a general partner must have a reasonable belief that he held limited partner status.

Holzman v. De Escamilla

Trustee (P) v. Limited partners (D)

Cal. Ct. App., 86 Cal. App. 2d 858, 195 P.2d 833 (1948).

NATURE OF CASE: Appeal from a finding that the defendants were general partners and were personally liable to creditors.

FACT SUMMARY: Hacienda Farms was formed as a limited partnership with Russell (D) and Andrews (D) acting as limited partners.

RULE OF LAW

If a limited partner exercises control over the partnership business, he becomes a general partner.

FACTS: De Escamilla (D) was the only general partner of Hacienda Farms. Russell (D) and Andrews (D) were limited partners. However, Russell (D) and Andrews (D) exerted control over business operations and decisions. Hacienda Farms went bankrupt and Holzman (P), the trustee, sought to hold Russell (D) and Andrews (D) personally liable for partnership debts. The court found that, by taking an active interest in the business, Russell (D) and Andrews (D) had lost their limited partnership protection. The court found them liable.

ISSUE: May a party participate in a partnership business while retaining his status as a limited partner?

HOLDING AND DECISION: (Marks, J.) No. Limited partnership protection is lost if there is participation in, or control over, the business. These are the actions of general partners. Where a limited partner assumes such duties, his protection ceases. He becomes personally liable for partnership debts just as though he were a general partner. Judgment affirmed.

ANALYSIS

A limited partner is considered similar to the shareholder of a corporation. To encourage and facilitate investments in partnerships, most states have accorded limited partners personal immunity from partnership debts. Their potential loss is limited to the capital contributed to the partnership. To preserve this immunity, the limited partner must not assume any active interest in partnership affairs.

Gateway Potato Sales v. G.B. Investment Co.

Supplier (P) v. Limited partnership (D)

Ariz. Ct. App., 822 P.2d 490 (1991).

NATURE OF CASE: Appeal from summary judgment in an action to recover payment for goods.

FACT SUMMARY: Gateway Potato Sales (P) sought to recover money it was owed by Sunworth (D) from G.B. Investment Co. (D) since Sunworth (D) had claimed that G.B. (D) was a general partner.

RULE OF LAW

A limited partner is liable as a general partner if he takes part in the control of the business.

FACTS: In 1985, Ellsworth, the president of Sunworth (D), contacted Gateway Potato Sales (P) to buy seed potatoes. Although Gateway (P) was hesitant, they proceeded with the deal when Ellsworth informed them that G.B. Investment Co. (D) was in partnership with Sunworth (D) and was providing the financing. In fact, only a limited partnership existed between the two operations. G.B. (D) did not exert any control over the daily management of Sunworth (D). Gateway (P) did not attempt to verify what Ellsworth told them about the partnership and shipped substantial quantities of goods. When Sunworth (D) failed to pay, Gateway (P) filed suit against Sunworth (D) and G.B. (D). The trial court granted summary judgment to G.B. (D), and Gateway (P) appealed.

ISSUE: Is a limited partner liable as a general partner if he takes part in the control of the business?

HOLDING AND DECISION: (Taylor, J.) Yes. A limited partner is liable as a general partner if he takes part in the control of the business. If a limited partner's participation in the control of the business is not substantially the same as the exercise of powers of a general partner, he is liable only to persons who transact business with the limited partnership with actual knowledge of the control. However, a creditor of a partnership is not required to have direct contact with the limited partner in order to discover control or operation. The creditor's reasonable belief is not required to be based upon the limited partner's conduct; it must only arise from some actual knowledge. Accordingly, it would be possible for Gateway (P) to establish that it had a reasonable belief that G.B. (D) acted in control of the limited partnership even though it never had contact with G.B. (D). Therefore, it was improper for the trial court to grant summary judgment to G.B. (D). Reversed and remanded.

ANALYSIS

The court did note that Revised Uniform Limited Partnership Act (RULPA) included amendments which reflected a reluctance to hold a limited partner liable if there was no direct contact with the creditor. However, Arizona had not revised the RULPA to correspond to these amendments at the time of the case.

Pitman v. Flanagan Lumber Co.

Limited partner (D) v. Lumber company (P)

Ala. Sup. Ct., 567 So. 2d 1335 (1990).

NATURE OF CASE: Appeal from an award of damages in a debt recovery action.

FACT SUMMARY: Flanagan (P) sought to recover a debt owed by Ramsey Homebuilders, a partnership, from Pitman (D), a limited partner, because he had secured credit in the partnership's name.

RULE OF LAW

Securing credit for a partnership is considered exercising control for purposes of liability of a limited partner.

FACTS: Pitman (D) was one of two limited partners in Ramsey Homebuilders, a business that engaged in residential construction. Ramsey, the sole general partner, had poor credit. Pitman (D) had a personal relationship with Flanagan Lumber's (P) credit manager and was able to secure an account in the partnership's name. Ramsey was unable to pay the account, and Flanagan (P) sued Pitman (D), alleging that Pitman (D) was liable because he had exercised control of the partnership. The trial court ruled for Flanagan (P), and Pitman (D) appealed.

ISSUE: Is securing credit for a partnership considered exercising control for purposes of liability of a limited partner?

HOLDING AND DECISION: (Houston, J.) Yes. Securing credit for a partnership is considered exercising control for purposes of liability of a limited partner. Limited partners are not responsible for the debts of the partnership unless they have participated in the control of the operation. Control is defined as the "power or authority to manage, direct, superintend, restrict, regulate, govern, administer or oversee." A limited partner who intercedes to secure credit for the partnership can be considered to have participated in the control of the operation. At the time Pitman (D) directly contacted Flanagan (P) to secure credit, and Flanagan (P) reasonably relied on this participation, Pitman (D) lost his limited partner status. Accordingly, Pitman (D) is liable for the debt. Affirmed.

ANALYSIS

Limited partnerships enjoy partnership tax status under the Internal Revenue Code. However, where the general partner is a corporation, the partnership agreement must be drafted with precision to take advantage of the tax benefits. The corporate general partner is required to have a net worth that relates to the partnership contributions.

Zeiger v. Wilf

Creditor (P) v. Limited partnership partner (D)

Superior Ct. of N.J., Appellate Div., 339 N.J. Super 258, 755 A.2d 608 (2000).

NATURE OF CASE: **Appeal from the granting of a defense motion for summary judgment in a creditor's suit for personal liability against a limited partner.**

FACT SUMMARY: **When Zeiger (P) brought a suit for personal liability against Wilf (D) for the breach of a contract by a limited partnership of which Wilf (D) was a member, Wilf (D) argued that personal liability may not be imposed on a limited partner unless such partner actually participates in the control of the business.**

RULE OF LAW

The Revised Uniform Limited Partnership Act does not impose a general partner's liability on an individual who simply takes part in the control of the partnership business.

FACTS: Zeiger (P), a seller of property to be renovated, entered into an agreement from a redevelopment company (a limited partnership), to receive a consultant fee of $23,000 per year for sixteen years. The payments ceased after two years, and Zeiger (P) sued the redevelopment company. A jury found the redevelopment company liable for those payments. Zeiger (P) also sued Wilf (D), the individual who led the various redevelopment entities (including the redevelopment company which was a limited partnership), contending that Wilf (D) should be held personally liable for the consultant payments and that such liability should also be imposed on a general partnership owned by Wilf (D) and members of his family. There was no claim that Wilf (D) personally, or his general partnership, ever guaranteed the consultant payments or that Zeiger (P) ever believed Wilf (D) had made such guarantees. The trial court granted Wilf's (D) motion for summary judgment, and Zeiger (P) appealed.

ISSUE: Does the Revised Uniform Limited Partnership Act impose a general partner's liability on an individual who simply takes part in the control of the partnership business?

HOLDING AND DECISION: (Lesemann, J.) No. The Revised Uniform Limited Partnership Act does not impose a general partner's liability on an individual who simply takes part in the control of the partnership business. Were this court to find individual liability against Wilf (D) because of his "control" here, the court would be encouraging precisely the instability and uncertainty which are anathema to widespread use of the limited partnership as a business entity. The modern, sound view, epitomized by the Revised Uniform Limited Partnership Act (RULPA), New Jersey legislation, and judicial decisions from most jurisdictions, is in the other direction: to curtail the threat of personal liability unless there is some reliance on the part of the outsider dealing with the limited partnership. Here, since there was no such reliance, there is no basis for imposing personal liability on Wilf (D). Zeiger (P), an insider in the project, does not claim he was ever misled as to the entities with whom he was dealing. Zeiger (P), furthermore, was a sophisticated, experienced developer and businessman. He does not claim that he ever sought or obtained any individual guarantee or promise from Wilf (D). Nor does Zeiger (P) deny that he understood completely that he was dealing with a limited partnership. The RULPA sharply limits the circumstances under which the exercise of "control" could lead to imposition of general partner liability. To impose liability on a limited partner, the limited partner's control activities need to be so extensive as to be "substantially the same as" a general partner. However, but for that extreme case, mere participation in control, as here, does not impose liability on a general partner. Affirmed.

ANALYSIS

As made clear in the *Zeiger* decision, there is no inherent fraud or injustice in an individual having two roles in a business transaction: one as a limited partner, and one as an officer or director of a corporation functioning as a general partner. The "Safe Harbor" provision of the Revised Uniform Limited Partnership Act [RULPA § 303(b)(1)] provides that a limited partner does not participate in the control of the business solely by serving as an officer, director, or shareholder of a corporate general partner.

Obert v. Environmental Research & Development Corp.

Limited partners (P) v. General partner (D)

Wash. Sup. Ct., 771 P.2d 340 (1989).

NATURE OF CASE: Appeal from an award of damages for breach of a partnership agreement.

FACT SUMMARY: Obert (P), one of a group of limited partners in Campus Park, sought to remove and replace ERADCO (D) as general partner.

RULE OF LAW

Limited partnership agreements may provide for the removal of a general partner upon a vote of the limited partners without dissolving the partnership.

FACTS: ERADCO (D) sold limited partnership units in the Campus Park Limited Partnership, which owned a parcel of land in Washington, to Obert (P) and fifty other entities and individuals. Each of the limited partners entered into a limited partnership agreement with ERADCO (D), which acted as the general partner. The agreement provided that the general partner could be removed for cause by vote of two-thirds of the ownership. Subsequently, 74% of the ownership of Campus Park amended the agreement and voted by proxy to remove ERADCO (D) as general partner and elected Pace as successor. Obert (P) and the limited partners also alleged that ERADCO (D) had violated fiduciary duties owed to the partners. The trial court ruled for Obert (P), denying ERADCO (D) its profits for breaching the fiduciary duties. However, the court of appeals reversed, ruling that under the Revised Uniform Limited Partnership Act (RULPA), the failure to unanimously elect a successor general partner resulted in dissolution of the partnership. Obert (P) appealed.

ISSUE: May limited partnerships remove their general partners without dissolving the partnership?

HOLDING AND DECISION: (Pearson, J.) Yes. Limited partnership agreements may provide for the removal of a general partner upon a vote of the limited partners without dissolving the partnership. Under § 801 (4) of the RULPA, a limited partnership is dissolved when the general partner is removed unless all partners agree to continue the business and appoint another general partner. However, § 801(4) is inapplicable to any valid, conflicting contractual provision entered into prior to the adoption of the Act. The Campus Park limited partnership agreement was filed prior to the enactment of RULPA and contained a provision that allowed for removal and replacement of the general partner with a 66% vote. Accordingly, the partnership was not dissolved when ERADCO (D) was removed by the limited partners' vote. Thus, the denial of profits to ERADCO (D) was not inappropriate given the trial court's determination of a fiduciary breach. The court of appeals is reversed.

ANALYSIS

Washington adopted RULPA in 1981. This case seems to suggest that partnerships formed after this date will not be able to remove general partners except as provided for in § 801(4). This decision was the first to thoroughly address and interpret the rules that § 801(4) establishes.

Obert v. Environmental Research & Development Corp.

Limited partners (P) v. General partner (D)

Wash. Ct. App., 752 P.2d 924 (1988).

NATURE OF CASE: Appeal from an award of damages for breach of a partnership agreement.

FACT SUMMARY: Obert (P), one of a group of limited partners in Campus Park, sought to remove and replace ERADCO (D) as general partner.

RULE OF LAW

Under RULPA § 801(4), dissolution of a limited partnership occurs by operation of law where a general partner is removed and there is no unanimous approval of a substitute within ninety days.

FACTS: ERADCO (D) sold limited partnership units in the Campus Park Limited Partnership, which owned a parcel of land in Washington, to Obert (P) and fifty other entities and individuals. Each of the limited partners entered into a limited partnership agreement with ERADCO (D), which acted as the general partner. The agreement provided that the general partner could be removed for cause by vote of two-thirds of the ownership. Subsequently, 74% of the ownership of Campus Park amended the agreement and voted by proxy to remove ERADCO (D) as general partner and elected Pace as successor. Obert (P) and the limited partners also alleged that ERADCO (D) had violated fiduciary duties owed to the partners. The trial court ruled for Obert (P), denying ERADCO (D) its profits for breaching the fiduciary duties.

ISSUE: Does dissolution of a limited partnership occur by operation of law where a general partner is removed and there is no unanimous approval of a substitute within ninety days?

HOLDING AND DECISION: (Pekelis, J.) Yes. Under RULPA § 801(4), dissolution of a limited partnership occurs by operation of law where a general partner is removed and there is no unanimous approval of a substitute within ninety days. According to RULPA § 401, additional general partners may be admitted only with the specific written consent of each partner unless otherwise provided in the partnership agreement. The "unless" clause was added to Washington's version of the RULPA. The Washington version of § 801(4), which governs substitutions of general partners, does not contain a similar clause. This evinces a legislative intent that all limited partners must consent to the substitution of a general partner, whether there is a contrary agreement or not. Thus, dissolution of the limited partnership occurs by operation of the law if there is not unanimous approval of a substitute general partner within ninety days of the removal of the prior general partner. Campus Park was dissolved since there was not unanimous approval for Pace. Reversed.

DISSENT: (Ringold, J.) The limited partners in this action have resisted dissolution. It would be illogical to interpret the RULPA in a way that forces dissolution on the partnership. Furthermore, since general partners may also be limited partners, the majority opinion would allow the general partner to prevent removal and replacement by dissenting.

ANALYSIS

The dissent argued that § 801 should be read as applying to situations in which there was more than one general partner or where the general partner sought to add another partner. Thus, § 801 could be read to preclude adding other general partners without approval from all of the limited partners. Actions by limited partners resemble shareholder derivative suits.

Anglo American Security Fund v. S.R. Global International Fund

Limited partners (P) v. Limited partnership (D)

Del. Ch. Ct., 829 A.2d 143 (2003).

NATURE OF CASE: Motion to dismiss action for breach of fiduciary duty, fraud, aiding and abetting, and breach of limited partnership agreement.

FACT SUMMARY: Limited partners (P) of S.R. Global International Fund, L.P. (Fund) (D), a limited partnership, brought various claims based on the withdrawal by the general partner, Sloane Robinson Investment (Cayman), Ltd. (Sloane) (D) from its capital account, allegedly in violation of the partnership agreement. Sloane (D) contended that these claims were derivative and that, therefore, the limited partners (P) did not have standing to bring them and that they should be dismissed on these grounds.

RULE OF LAW

1. In a limited partnership that is structured in such a way that whenever the value of the partnership is reduced the injury accrues irrevocably to current partners but not to later partners, a claim based on the diminution of value to the partnership is a direct claim.
2. In a limited partnership hedge fund where the general partner is contractually obligated to provide the limited partners with certain financial statements, a claim that those statements are incomplete or materially false or misleading is a direct claim.

FACTS: S.R. Global International Fund, L.P. (Fund) (D) was a limited partnership hedge fund through which its limited partners (P) could make various financial investments. The general partner was Sloane Robinson Investment (Cayman), Ltd. (Sloane) (D). Each partner had a capital account that accounted for the partner's original capital contribution, plus any additional capital contributions, minus any capital withdrawals, and adjusted at the end of each fiscal period for the partner's proportional share of net profits and losses. The Fund (D) was obligated to provide the partners with unaudited quarterly reports and an audited annual financial statement as well as information necessary for federal income tax purposes. As of December 31, 1999, Sloane's (D) capital account in the Fund (D) was credited with $22,350,704 or 15% of the net profits to the limited partners (P) in 1999. On February 18, 2000, Sloane (D) withdrew $22,350,704 from its capital account. The credit to Sloane's (D) capital account was recorded in the Fund's (D) audited 1999 financial statement. This statement was provided to the limited partners (P) in March 2000. Although it did report other post-year-end capital contributions and withdrawals as "Subsequent Events," the 1999 statement did not report Sloane's (D) February 18 withdrawal. This withdrawal was reported in the Fund's (D) quarterly statement for the first quarter of 2000, which statement was received by the limited partners (P) on May 9, 2000. Based on these events, the limited partners (P) brought suit, alleging, inter alia, breach of fiduciary duty, fraud, aiding and abetting, and breach of limited partnership agreement. They claimed that the withdrawal was material since it overdrew Sloane's (D) capital account because substantial losses sustained by the Fund (D) during January and February 2000 had reduced the available balance in Sloane's (D) capital account below $22,350,704—i.e., that Sloane (D) had "bailed" from the Fund (D); the partnership agreement permitted the general partner to withdraw funds only on the last day of the month; and the withdrawal should have been disclosed as a Subsequent Event in the 1999 statement. Sloane (D) and the Fund (D) moved to dismiss all claims on the basis that they were derivative, as opposed to direct, and that the limited partners (P) did not have standing to bring derivative claims. Sloane (D) and the Fund (D) argued that the claims either alleged a diminution in the value of the fund, or misdisclosures of the withdrawal, which they asserted are both derivative claims.

ISSUE: 1. In a limited partnership that is structured in such a way that whenever the value of the partnership is reduced the injury accrues irrevocably to current partners but not to later partners, is a claim based on the diminution of value to the partnership a direct claim? 2. In a limited partnership hedge fund where the general partner is contractually obligated to provide the limited partners with certain financial statements, is a claim that those statements are incomplete or materially false or misleading a direct claim?

HOLDING AND DECISION: (Chandler, J.) 1. Yes. In a limited partnership that is structured in such a way that whenever the value of the partnership is reduced the injury accrues irrevocably to current partners but not to later partners, a claim based on the diminution of value to the partnership is a direct claim. In the partnership context, a claim is direct if a partner alleges either an injury that is different from what is suffered by other partners or one that involves a contractual right of partners that is independent of the partnership's rights. If the injury is one that affects all partners proportionally to their pro rata interests in the partnership, the claim is derivative. A key factor in deciding whether a claim is direct or derivative where a limited partnership is involved (as distinguished from a corporation) is the limited partnership agreement, which

Continued on next page.

specifies or modifies the entity's function and structure and the rights and responsibilities of the general and limited partners. There are two purposes for classifying claims as derivative: (1) to ensure that any remedy accrues to the entity that sustained the injury but does not confer benefits on wrongdoers nor provide windfalls to the uninjured and (2) to provide a gatekeeping function that will both promote entity resolution of internal problems and deter strike suits. Here, these purposes are not served. Whenever the value of the Fund (D) is reduced, the injury accrues irrevocably and almost immediately to the current partners but will not harm those who later become partners, since the value of the current partners' capital accounts is reduced immediately. If a current partner withdraws, and if the claim is characterized as derivative, the partner has no remedy for recovery, since any recovery by the Fund (D) is not passed on to the withdrawn partner nor to any successor-in-interest. If additional partners are later admitted, they suffer no injury from previous reductions in value, and if the Fund (D) obtains a recovery, such later partners get a windfall. Therefore, the claims here relating to Sloane's (D) withdrawals are direct, and the limited partners (P) have standing to bring them. 2. Yes. In a limited partnership hedge fund where the general partner is contractually obligated to provide the limited partners with certain financial statements, a claim that those statements are incomplete or materially false or misleading is a direct claim. The claimed misdisclosures here raise concerns that are different if they were raised in the corporate context. In a corporation, the misdisclosures would be an injury shared by all stockholders in proportion to their pro rata ownership. Here, the structure of the Fund (D) is not at all similar to a corporate structure, and the limited partners' (P) claims implicate a contractual right that is not similarly a right of the Fund (D) itself. The Fund (D) was a hedge fund vehicle used for investment purposes, with minimal going concern value. The limited partners (P) had no capacity to replace Sloane (D) for failing properly to represent their interests. Instead, the only alternative available to a dissatisfied limited partner (P) was to withdraw from the Fund (D). A delay in withdrawal could severely impact the value of a limited partner's (P) account. Therefore, claims of misdisclosures are highly material in this context. The only protection the limited partners (P) have is in the partnership agreement, which requires Sloane (D) to provide accurate financial statements. Thus, any claim that these statements in general, and that the 1999 statement in particular, were incomplete, materially false or misleading states a direct claim. The motion to dismiss for failure to state a claim is denied.

ANALYSIS

As this case demonstrates, courts typically look to precedent set in the corporate context to start their analysis of whether a claim is derivative or direct, but then adapt such precedent, and the policies supporting it, to the particular facts of the particular entity involved. As happened here, the parties' contractual agreement(s) usually plays a key role in the decision.

Temple v. White Lakes Plaza Assocs., Ltd.

Substitute limited partner (P) v. Limited partnership (D)

Kan. Ct. App., 15 Kan. App. 2d 771, 816 P.2d 399 (1991).

NATURE OF CASE: Appeal from judgment ordering plaintiff be made limited partner.

FACT SUMMARY: When the general partner of White Lakes Plaza Assocs., Ltd. (D), a limited partnership, refused to admit Temple (P), the assignee of an interest in the partnership as a substituted limited partner, Temple (P) sued.

RULE OF LAW

An assignee may not become a limited partner merely by virtue of the assignment of a limited partnership interest.

FACTS: Temple's (P) husband was a limited partner in White Lakes Plaza Assocs., Ltd. (D), a Kansas limited partnership formed for the purpose of operating an apartment complex. The partnership agreement provided that all limited partners and the general partner must consent to termination of the partnership, amendment of the agreement, and sale of the partnership's assets. The certificate of limited partnership stated that any purchaser shall only be admitted as a Substituted Limited Partner if the Assignor so designates and the General Partner consents thereto. As part of the property settlement following divorce proceedings in Florida, Temple (P) was awarded the interest in White Lakes (D). However, the general partner would not allow the partnership interest transfer, and Temple (P) filed suit, claiming she wanted to become a limited partner in White Lakes (D) for advantageous tax law treatment. When the district court ordered that Temple (P) be made a substituted limited partner, White Lakes (D) appealed, claiming that the district court had improperly substituted its discretion for that of the general partner.

ISSUE: May an assignee become a limited partner merely by virtue of the assignment of a limited partnership interest?

HOLDING AND DECISION: (Rulon, J.) No. An assignee may not become a limited partner merely by virtue of the assignment of a limited partnership interest. Temple (P) is an assignee of her ex-husband's interest, but she cannot be made a substituted limited partner outside of the agreement or in contravention of the Revised Uniform Limited Partnership Act. That portion of the district court judgment that awarded Temple (P) the earnings from the assigned partnership interest being held in escrow is affirmed, but the portion of the judgment making Temple (P) a substituted partner in the partnership is reversed.

ANALYSIS

Since this was a small group of limited partners who were experienced in the management of real estate, the court considered the nature of the limited partner's role. In general, a limited partner's role in the management of the partnership's business differs from that of a general partner in either a general or a limited partnership. Most limited partners play a passive role, unlike the limited partners in White Lakes (D).

KE Property Management, Inc. v. 275 Madison Management Corp.

General partner (P) v. Limited partnership (D)

Del. Ch. Ct., 1993 Del. Ch. LEXIS 147 (July 21, 1993).

NATURE OF CASE: Request for declaratory judgment enjoining management firm from acting as a managing general partner.

FACT SUMMARY: When the President of the original managing general partner of a limited partnership misappropriated Partnership funds, a limited partner acted to remove the managing general partner, 275 Madison Corp. (D).

RULE OF LAW

Under the Delaware Uniform Partnership Law, all partners owe each other fiduciary obligations.

FACTS: KE Property Management, Inc. (P), one of the general partners of 275 Madison Associates L.P., a Delaware limited partnership (the Partnership), sought a declaratory judgment that the purported removal of 275 Madison Corp. (D), the managing general partner, by the Kawaski Partners, was effective. 275 Madison Corp. (D) was removed purportedly because its President had misappropriated $2 million of Partnership funds. KE Property (P) thus sought to enjoin 275 Madison Corp. (D) from purporting to act as the managing general partner. 275 Madison Corp. (D) alleged that the Kawasaki Partners, the limited partner, acted in bad faith in that their real motivation in removing 275 Madison Corp. (D) was to prevent 275 Madison Corp. (D) from filing for bankruptcy on behalf of the Partnership.

ISSUE: Under the Delaware Uniform Partnership Law, do all partners owe each other fiduciary obligations?

HOLDING AND DECISION: (Hartnett, V. Chan.) Yes. Under the Delaware Uniform Partnership Law, all partners owe each other fiduciary obligations. An allegation of bad faith raises essentially a question of fact, but must be supported by competent evidence to defeat a motion to dismiss or a motion for summary judgment. The presumption of the good faith of the Kawasaki Partnership in removing 275 Madison Corp. (D) has not been overcome by any competent evidence in this case. Summary judgment must therefore be granted to KE Property (P) on its claim against 275 Madison Corp. (D).

ANALYSIS

Since the limited partner in this case was controlled by the same entity that controlled the general partner, the fiduciary duty could have been imputed. However, since Delaware law imposes fiduciary duties on all partners, this issue never came up. Since no real evidence was offered to prove 275 Madison Corp's (D) allegation of bad faith, the presumption of good faith prevailed in this case.

Baybank v. Catamount Construction, Inc.

Creditor (P) v. Limited partnership (D)

N.H. Sup. Ct. 693 A.2d 1163 (1997).

NATURE OF CASE: Appeal from a judgment dissolving a limited partnership.

FACT SUMMARY: When Baybank (P), a creditor of the Connors, obtained a charging order against the Connors' interest in the limited partnerships East Street and Catamount Construction, Inc. (D), and dissolution of Catamount Construction (D), the Connors contended that additional remedies against the limited partnerships were improper.

RULE OF LAW

A creditor with a charging order on a limited partnership interest may enforce that interest if necessary.

FACTS: Baybank (P) obtained a judgment against the Connors as guarantors on a promissory note made by Catamount Construction, Inc. (D). To satisfy its judgment, Baybank (P) sought to reach the Connors' interest in East Street Associates Limited Partnership and Catamount (D), in which the Connors were limited partners. Baybank (P) requested a charging order against the Connors' interest in East Street, the appointment of a receiver for any monies due to the Connors as limited partners in East Street, and, if the judgment was not satisfied, dissolution of East Street and Catamount (D). The Connors responded by conceding Baybank's (P) entitlement to a charging order under the Revised Uniform Limited Partnership Act, but objecting to the additional relief sought. The trial court did, however, grant all the relief sought. The Connors (D) appealed, challenging the trial court's authority to order the additional relief, particularly the dissolution of East Street.

ISSUE: May a creditor with a charging order on a limited partnership interest enforce that interest if necessary?

HOLDING AND DECISION: (Johnson, J.) Yes. A creditor with a charging order on a limited partnership interest may enforce that interest if necessary. A trial court has broad equitable powers to grant to creditors of a limited partnership relief which is additional to the relief set forth in the Revised Uniform Limited Partnership Act (RULPA). As here, the trial court may properly import a variety of creditors' rights and remedies found in the Uniform Partnership Act (UPA) into RULPA cases. In fact, the UPA § 6(2) specifically provides that the UPA applies to limited partnerships except insofar as the statutes relating to such partnerships are inconsistent with the UPA. The trial court properly found that here there was no conflict between the UPA and anything in the RULPA. In addition, the trial court based its order of dissolution on UPA § 32(2) which provides that a court may decree a dissolution on the application of the purchaser of a partner's interests. Again, the trial court properly found that this section did not conflict with anything in RULPA and was, therefore, applicable. In sum, a court may properly look to the UPA's remedies for the *means* to enforce a charging order under RULPA when the latter remedy alone would be insufficient. In the instant case, however, the trial court did not actually grant the type of relief contemplated by the UPA since, although the trial court purported to order the appointment of a receiver to dispose of various interests in the limited partnership to satisfy the judgment debt, such relief would have been unnecessary in light of the trial court's order that the partnership be dissolved. Affirmed in part; reversed in part; vacated in part; remanded.

ANALYSIS

The statutory remedy of a charging order was designed to prevent the personal creditors of a limited partner from disrupting the partnership by seizing partnership assets on execution. The statutory remedy forces a judgment creditor to look solely to the debtor's partnership interest, which the RULPA § 101(10) defines as a partner's share of the profits and losses of a limited partnership and the right to receive distribution of partnership assets.

Appletree Square I Limited Partnership v. Investmark, Inc.

Limited partners (P) v. General partners (D)

Minn. Ct. App., 494 N.W.2d 889 (1993).

NATURE OF CASE: Appeal from dismissal of an action for fraud.

FACT SUMMARY: Appletree Limited Partnership (P) bought an office building which was contaminated with asbestos and sought recovery from the partners who were part of Investmark, Inc. (D), the sellers.

RULE OF LAW

General partners have a broad obligation to disclose material facts to limited partners.

FACTS: Appletree Limited Partnership (P) was formed in 1981 to purchase and operate an office building. The general partners of Investmark, Inc. (D) owned the property, and Appletree (P) was made up of limited partners in Investmark (D). CRI, an affiliate of Appletree (P), represented them in the transaction. CRI requested that Investmark (D) provide all information regarding the building to the investors. In response, CRI was told to inspect the building. In 1986, Appletree (P) learned that the building was contaminated with asbestos and filed suit against the Investmark general partners (D) for failure to disclose the asbestos information. The trial court ruled that the general partners' (D) only fiduciary duty in the purchase was to render true information when it was demanded and dismissed the suit. Appletree (P) appealed.

ISSUE: Do general partners have a broad obligation to disclose material facts to limited partners?

HOLDING AND DECISION: (Crippen, J.) Yes. General partners have a broad obligation to disclose material facts to limited partners. Absent a fiduciary duty, one party to a transaction has no duty to disclose material facts to the other party. The relationship of partners, however, is fiduciary, and partners are therefore held to high standards of integrity in their dealings with each other. Parties in a fiduciary relationship must disclose material facts to each other; silence as to material facts may constitute fraud. Under the RULPA, limited partners have the right, upon reasonable demand, to obtain information from general partners. This right under the RULPA addresses the narrow duty of partners to respond to requests for information. It does not negate the general partners' broad fiduciary duty to disclose all material facts. Additionally, partners may destroy this duty through contract provisions. Here, the general partners of Investmark (D) were partners with the investors in Appletree (P). Accordingly, they had a fiduciary duty to disclose information about the asbestos even though there was no direct demand for information. Therefore, the trial court should not have dismissed the fraud action. Reversed and remanded.

ANALYSIS

General partners also owe the limited partners a duty of good faith and fair dealing. In *Brooke v. Mt. Hood Meadows Oregon Ltd.*, 725 P.2d 925 (1986), the limited partners sued the general partners for not distributing all profits. The general partners successfully defended the suit on the basis that reinvesting a portion of the profits did not violate their duty of good faith.

Gotham Partners, L.P. v. Hallwood Realty Partners, L.P.

Limited partnership (P) v. General partnership (D)

Del. Ch. Ct., 795 A.2d 1 (2001).

NATURE OF CASE: Suit for judicial rescission of a general partner's acquisition of partnership units under a reverse stock split.

FACT SUMMARY: When Gotham Partners L.P. (P) sought to hold Hallwood Realty Partners, L.P. (D) liable for breach of fiduciary duties to the partnership, Hallwood (D) contended that its good faith misreading of an ambiguous provision in the partnership agreement shielded it from liability.

RULE OF LAW

A general partner is not necessarily shielded from liability for breach of the partnership agreement for a good faith misreading of an ambiguous provision.

FACTS: Gotham Partners L.P. (P) was a limited partnership controlled by Hallwood Realty Partners, L.P. (D), a corporate general partner. Hallwood (D) engaged in a series of transactions that resulted in a reduction of the number of partnership units held by the limited partners and an increase in the number of units held by Hallwood (D). This was accomplished by a reverse split and an odd-lot offer. The effect was to increase the control of the general partner and virtually eliminate the possibility that the general partner could be ousted by a vote of the limited partners. One of the limited partners, Gotham (P), challenged these transactions in a derivative action, claiming that the process employed by the general partner to approve the transactions was in violation of the partnership agreement. Hallwood (D) argued that the challenged transaction involved the simple sale of partnership units which, according to its reading of the partnership agreement, was expressly permitted.

ISSUE: Is a general partner necessarily shielded from liability for breach of the partnership agreement for a good faith misreading of an ambiguous provision?

HOLDING AND DECISION: [Judge not stated in casebook excerpt.] No. A general partner is not necessarily shielded from liability for breach of the partnership agreement for a good faith misreading of an ambiguous provision. Here, it was only because the partnership agreement imposed specific standards of conduct that default fiduciary duties were held not to apply to the general partner's actions in effecting the challenged transactions. The safe harbor for the general partner from fiduciary liability is thus compliance with the agreement. If the Revised Uniform Limited Partnership Act (RULPA) were interpreted otherwise, the general partner would be free to escape fiduciary liability in a self-interest context that would not fall within the exculpatory clause of the instant contract if it mistakenly read the agreement in its own conflicted favor. This approach is less favorable to general partners, more protective of investors, and in keeping with the traditional approach of construing exculpatory provisions narrowly. The approach holds a general partner and other fiduciaries responsible under traditional fiduciary principles when they do not comply with the contractual provisions that supplant their duties. That is, to the extent that the general partner and other interested fiduciaries do not properly avail themselves of a contractual safe harbor in implementing a conflict transaction, they will suffer liability unless they can prove fairness. In other words, RULPA will only shield a partner when the partner accurately read, applied, and relied on an agreement provision in taking action. Under this analysis, the general partner is protected from a fiduciary duty or other non-contractual claim only where its actions are contractually authorized. Damages are awarded to Gotham (P). Rescission, however, is not granted because of Gotham's (P) unjustifiable delay in challenging the transactions, and the action undertaken by the defendants was not a deliberate effort to control or enrich the corporation.

ANALYSIS

The *Gotham* case reflects the general policy of courts to read exculpatory clauses narrowly and construe them as not conferring immunity if that is reasonably possible.

Brickell Partners v. Wise

Limited partner (P) v. General partner's directors (D)

Del. Ch. Ct., 794 A.2d 1 (2001).

NATURE OF CASE: Motion to dismiss derivative action brought by limited partner on behalf of partnership asserting breach of fiduciary duties in connection with a conflict transaction.

FACT SUMMARY: Brickell Partners (P), a limited partner in El Paso Energy Partners, L.P. (El Paso) (D), brought a derivative action challenging the purchase by El Paso (D) of Crystal Gas Storage, Inc. as a conflict transaction that involved breaches of fiduciary duty by directors (D) of El Paso's (D) corporate general partner, DeepTech International, Inc. (DeepTech) (D). DeepTech's directors (D) claimed that the acquisition was insulated by El Paso's (D) partnership agreement, which provided that conflict transactions were deemed approved by the partnership if "Special Approval" was obtained from a majority of the members of the partnership's Conflicts and Audit Committee—which had been obtained in this instance.

RULE OF LAW

Where a limited partnership agreement unambiguously provides a procedure for approving conflict-of-interest transactions, and such a procedure is followed and the transaction is approved, a derivative action challenging the transaction must be dismissed.

FACTS: El Paso Energy Partners, L.P. (El Paso) (D), a limited partnership, acquired Crystal Gas Storage, Inc. (Crystal Gas). Crystal Gas was owned by El Paso Energy Corp. (Energy), which also owned and controlled El Paso's (D) general partner, DeepTech International, Inc. (DeepTech) (D). Energy also held 34.5% of El Paso's (D) units, which were publicly traded. El Paso (D) purchased Crystal Gas for $ 170 million in newly issued El Paso preference units. Brickell Partners (P), one of El Paso's (D) limited partners, brought a derivative action challenging the acquisition of Crystal Gas as substantively unfair to El Paso (D), claiming that the transaction consideration exceeded the value of Crystal Gas. Brickell Partners (P) also claimed the procedure used to effect this conflict transaction was "impaired" because the only procedural protection used by El Paso (D) to ensure the interests of unitholders other than Energy was to subject the transaction to "Special Approval" by DeepTech's (D) "Conflicts and Audit Committee." This committee was made up of two DeepTech directors (D). Brickell Partners (P) claimed that since the directors (D) owed fiduciary duties to DeepTech (D), they could not fairly opine on a transaction in which DeepTech (D) and El Paso (D) had conflicting interests. However, El Paso's (D) partnership agreement provided for just such a procedure in case of conflict transactions, and provided that if "Special Approval" was obtained, the transaction was deemed approved by all the partners. Accordingly, the various defendants (D) moved to dismiss on the grounds that the partnership agreement displaced traditional default fiduciary duties.

ISSUE: Where a limited partnership agreement unambiguously provides a procedure for approving conflict-of-interest transactions, and such a procedure is followed and the transaction is approved, must a derivative action challenging the transaction be dismissed?

HOLDING AND DECISION: (Strine, V.Chan.) Yes. Where a limited partnership agreement unambiguously provides a procedure for approving conflict-of-interest transactions, and such a procedure is followed and the transaction is approved, a derivative action challenging the transaction must be dismissed. Here, the partnership agreement supplants the traditional default fiduciary duties that would otherwise apply to the Crystal Gas deal in the absence of contractual modification. The fiduciary duty of loyalty would, if unmodified, have required the defendants (D) to demonstrate that the Crystal Gas acquisition was entirely fair. Limited partnerships are permitted by statute to restrict traditional fiduciary duties owed by the general partner, and, as precedent indicates, principles of contract preempt fiduciary principles where the parties' intentions are unambiguously indicated in their partnership agreement. The language of the partnership agreement is unambiguous, providing that "Special Approval" of the Conflicts and Audit Committee is conclusive evidence of the fairness and reasonableness of a conflict transaction. Since the agreement's process was followed, Brickell Partners (P) should not be allowed to challenge the transaction. Rejected is Brickell Partners' (P) argument that the agreement is ambiguous insofar as it does not specify who will serve on the Conflicts and Audit Committee. Brickell Partners (P) maintains that no reasonable limited partner would expect that anyone with ties to DeepTech (D) would be allowed to serve. However, the very term "committee" implies that the group will be made up of DeepTech directors (D). Thus, while a reasonable investor might conclude that the committee would not be comprised of management directors, it would be unreasonable for such an investor to conclude that the committee would be comprised of members with no relationship to DeepTech (D) whatsoever. Here, neither member of the committee was in management. Moreover, Brickell Partners (P) has failed to adduce additional evi-

Continued on next page.

dence that would show that either director was beholden to Energy. The complaint is dismissed with prejudice.

ANALYSIS

As the court points out, directors of corporate general partners occupy a position that is significantly different from the position occupied by independent outside directors of a non-partner corporation. By definition, the directors of the corporate general partner find themselves in a position of on-going conflict because they owe fiduciary duties to the corporate general partner (on whose board they serve) and fiduciary duties to the limited partnership governed by the corporate general partner. Even when such directors have no material self-interest in the success of the corporate general partner as an entity or the partnership itself, they owe duties to two entities with potentially conflicting interests. Thus, their situation is subtly but critically different from the position of an outside, "independent" director of a corporation, since a corporate independent director owes his fidelity only to the corporation and its stockholders, to the exclusion of any potentially conflicting constituency. That can never be the case with the director of a corporate general partner forced to opine on a transaction between an affiliate of the corporate general partner and the partnership.

CHAPTER 15

The Limited Liability Company

Quick Reference Rules of Law

		PAGE
1.	**Creation of an LLC.** A limited liability company may assume, by operation of law, the interests and obligations of a sole proprietorship. (C & J Builders and Remodelers, LLC v. Geisenheimer)	223
2.	**Creation of an LLC.** A limited liability corporation is bound by a contractual provision directing all disputes to be resolved exclusively by arbitration or court proceedings in another jurisdiction. (Elf Atochem North America, Inc. v. Jaffari)	224
3.	**Creation of an LLC.** The limitation of liability of all LLC members is a substantial difference especially relevant to the provisions of state liquor laws. (Meyer v. Oklahoma Alcoholic Beverage Laws Enforcement Commission)	225
4.	**The Entity Theory and the LLC.** A creditor may reach the assets of a limited liability company when the partners so dominate and control it that justice requires piercing the corporate veil. (Litchfield Asset Management Corporation v. Howell)	226
5.	**The Entity Theory and the LLC.** A limited liability company is "another person" within the meaning of business practices legislation. (Abrahim & Sons Enterprises v. Equilon Enterprises, LLC)	227
6.	**The Entity Theory and the LLC.** A transfer of property by its owner to a limited liability company (LLC) does not constitute a sale or exchange supported by consideration that triggers the payment of a brokerage fee. (Premier Van Schaack Realty, Inc. v. Sieg)	228
7.	**Management of an LLC.** Where a limited liability company's regulations and articles conflict, but the regulations expressly provide that in case of such conflict the articles control, the articles control. (Pinnacle Data Services, Inc. v. Gillen)	229
8.	**Management of an LLC.** A limited liability company may provide for dissolution upon a member's bankruptcy filing, with the remaining members having the right to continue the business and elect a new manager. (Broyhill v. DeLuca)	230
9.	**Authority and Apparent Authority of Members.** A limited liability company is liable for instruments and documents relating to property disposition if they were executed by a manager, even if the other members did not authorize the manager's actions because they were unaware of them. (Taghipour v. Jerez)	231
10.	**Fiduciary Duties of Members.** The operating agreement of a limited liability company may limit or define the scope of the fiduciary duties imposed upon its members. (McConnell v. Hunt Sports Enterprises)	232
11.	**Fiduciary Duties of Members.** Members of a limited liability company owe a fiduciary duty of loyalty to one another. (VGS, Inc. v. Castiel)	233
12.	**Fiduciary Duties of Members.** A non-manager member of a manager-managed limited liability company (LLC) does not owe fiduciary duties to the LLC or its manager where the member does not exercise any managerial authority pursuant to the operating agreement, and, therefore, cannot breach any fiduciary duties to the LLC's manager or the LLC that could support a collusion claim. (Katris v. Carroll)	234

C & J Builders and Remodelers, LLC v. Geisenheimer

Contractor (P) v. Customer (D)

Conn. Sup. Ct. 733 A.2d 193 (1999).

NATURE OF CASE: Appeal from a court-ordered arbitration in contractor's suit against a customer.

FACT SUMMARY: When C & J Builders (P) sought contractual arbitration to recover against Geisenheimer (D) for a residential renovation project, Geisenheimer (D) contended that because C & J (P) statutorily changed its business form from a sole proprietorship into a limited liability company, the new C & J (P) was not a successor in interest and had no standing to enforce the original contract.

RULE OF LAW

A limited liability company may assume, by operation of law, the interests and obligations of a sole proprietorship.

FACTS: C & J Builders (P) contracted to renovate Geisenheimer's (D) summer residence. The contract contained an arbitration clause. At the time the contract was formed, C & J (P) was a sole proprietorship. Subsequently, C & J (P) accomplished a conversion, under Connecticut legislation, from a sole proprietorship to a limited liability company. C & J (P) assumed the same name as before, operated at the same business address, and carried on the same business operations as the prior sole proprietorship. In its new business form, C & J (P) continued the renovation. When a fee dispute arose, C & J (P) brought suit against Geisenheimer (D) and requested the trial court to order contractual arbitration. Geisenheimer (D) argued that the present C & J (P) was not a party to its contract with the original sole proprietorship and therefore was not entitled to compel arbitration of the dispute. The trial court, however, concluded that C & J (P) was entitled to enforce the contract and ordered arbitration. Geisenheimer (D) appealed.

ISSUE: May a limited liability company assume, by operation of law, the interests and obligations of a sole proprietorship?

HOLDING AND DECISION: (Callahan, C.J.) Yes. A limited liability company may assume, by operation of law, the interests and obligations of a sole proprietorship. Connecticut legislation governs the conversion of a general or limited partnership to a limited liability company. Specifically, statutory provision provides that a general or limited partnership that has been converted to a limited liability company is deemed "for all purposes the same entity that existed before the conversion," except that the converted entity is governed by other legislation. Moreover, legislation provides that, upon the conversion, all property owned by the converting partnership remains vested in the converted entity and "all obligations" of the converting partnership "continue as obligations of the converted entity." Thus, the legislation expressly provides that the actual business operations of the converting partnership are not affected by the conversion, and that all of the converting partnership's property and obligations are transferred to the newly converted limited liability company by operation of law. In effect, the statute treats the converted limited liability company as the "successor in interest" to the converting partnership. The legislation, furthermore, mandates that the conversion has no effect on claims pending against the converting partnership or its partners, and that the members of the newly converted company retain personal liability for the preexisiting debts and obligations incurred by the converting partnership. Hence, it is readily apparent that the statute evidences an intent to facilitate "seamless transition" between the converting partnership and the converted company. Accordingly, there is no reason to distinguish between the conversion of a sole proprietorship to a limited liability company and the conversion of a general partnership to a limited liability partnership. Affirmed.

ANALYSIS

In the *C & J Builders* case, the court stressed that the legislative mandate recognized the importance of protecting the interests and expectations of third parties who, prior to the conversion, had contracted with, or had maintained claims against, the converting partnership. As such, the Connecticut legislation embodies the general policy of treating the limited liability company as the successor in interest to the earlier entity, while ensuring that its preconversion creditors and claimants are not precluded by the business' change in organizational form.

Elf Atochem North America, Inc. v. Jaffari

LLC partner (P) v. LLC partner (D)

Del. Sup. Ct., 727 A.2d 286 (1999).

NATURE OF CASE: Appeal from grant of a defense motion to dismiss a complaint for lack of subject matter jurisdiction.

FACT SUMMARY: When Elf Atochem North America, Inc. (Elf) (P), a member of an LLC, sued, in Delaware, another member, Cyrus Jaffari (D), for breach of fiduciary duties, Jaffari (D) moved to dismiss on the grounds that the LLC Agreement expressly made arbitration in California the exclusive forum for disputes under the Agreement.

RULE OF LAW

A limited liability corporation is bound by a contractual provision directing all disputes to be resolved exclusively by arbitration or court proceedings in another jurisdiction.

FACTS: Elf Atochem North America, Inc. (Elf) (P), a Pennsylvania manufacturing corporation, and Cyrus Jaffari (D), president of a California corporation, undertook a joint venture to manufacture solvent-based materials for the aerospace and aviation industries. The joint venture was carried out using a limited liability company as the vehicle. Accordingly, their LLC was duly formed in Delaware. The certificate of incorporation did not contain a comprehensive agreement among the parties. Rather, the Delaware LLC statute contemplated that the certificate of formation was to be complemented by the terms of the Agreement. Elf (P) and Jaffari (D) created their LLC Agreement, a clause of which provided that arbitration was to cover all disputes and that California was to be the exclusive forum for all disputes. Subsequently, Elf (P) sued Jaffari (D) in the Delaware Court of Chancery for breach of fiduciary duties under the LLC, seeking equitable remedies. Jaffari (D) moved to dismiss for lack of subject matter jurisdiction, arguing that the LLC Agreement mandated that California was to be the exclusive forum for all disputes under the LLC. The court agreed and dismissed the action. Elf (P) appealed the dismissal of his complaint.

ISSUE: Is a limited liability corporation bound by a contractual provision directing all disputes to be resolved exclusively by arbitration or court proceedings in another jurisdiction?

HOLDING AND DECISION: (Veasey, C.J.) Yes. A limited liability corporation is bound by a contractual provision directing all disputes to be resolved exclusively by arbitration or court proceedings in another jurisdiction. While statutory provision does vest jurisdiction with the Court of Chancery in actions involving removal of managers and interpreting, applying, or enforcing LLC agreements, such a grant of jurisdiction may have been constitutionally necessary if the claims do not fall within the traditional equity jurisdiction. Nevertheless, for the purpose of designating a more convenient forum, there is no reason why the LLC members cannot alter the default jurisdictional provisions of the statute and contract away their right to file a suit in Delaware. Because the policy of the LLC legislation is to give the maximum effect to the principle of freedom of contract and to the enforceability of LLC agreements, LLC parties may contract to avoid the applicability of the Delaware forum provisions. Here, the parties contracted as clearly as practicable when, in their Agreement, they relegated to California "any" dispute "arising out of, under or in connection with [the] Agreement or the transactions contemplated by [the] Agreement." Furthermore, another section of the Agreement provides that no action at law or in equity based upon any claim arising out of or related to the agreement may be brought, except in California, and then only to enforce arbitration in California. The court's conclusion is bolstered by the fact that Delaware recognizes a strong public policy in favor of arbitration, and all doubts on arbitrability are resolved in favor of arbitration. Here, there is no doubt of the parties' intention to agree to arbitrate all disputes in California. To hold otherwise would mean that arbitration clauses in existing LLC agreements could be rendered meaningless. By resorting to the alleged "special" jurisdiction of the Court of Chancery, future plaintiffs could avoid their own arbitration agreements simply by couching their claims as derivative. Such a result could adversely affect many arbitration agreements already in existence in Delaware. Affirmed.

ANALYSIS

In *Elf Atochem*, the court noted that although the LLC statute fails to mention that the parties may agree to the exclusive jurisdiction of a foreign jurisdiction, the legislation clearly does not state that the parties must agree to either one of the delineated options for subject matter jurisdiction. Had the legislature intended to prohibit the parties from vesting exclusive jurisdiction or court proceedings in another state, it could have proscribed such an option.

Meyer v. Oklahoma Alcoholic Beverage Laws Enforcement Commission

Liquor store licensee (P) v. State commission (D)

Okla. Ct. App., 890 P.2d 1361 (1995).

NATURE OF CASE: Appeal from the district court's reversal of an administrative agency's declaratory ruling that a limited liability company is not entitled to receive and hold a retail package store license.

FACT SUMMARY: When a package liquor store became an LLC, its liquor license was revoked.

RULE OF LAW

The limitation of liability of all LLC members is a substantial difference especially relevant to the provisions of state liquor laws.

FACTS: Meyer (P) was the holder of a retail package store license. She petitioned the Oklahoma Alcoholic Beverage Laws Enforcement Commission (ABLE) (D), requesting that she be permitted to hold the license as an LLC. ABLE (D) denied the petition, and Meyer (P) appealed the decision to the district court. The trial court reversed the ABLE (D) ruling and ordered it to issue a license to Meyer (P) as an LLC. ABLE (D) appealed, claiming the order of the lower court was contrary to law.

ISSUE: Is the limitation of liability of all LLC members a substantial difference especially relevant to the provisions of state liquor laws?

HOLDING AND DECISION: (Stubblefield, J.) Yes. The limitation of liability of all LLC members is a substantial difference especially relevant to the provisions of state liquor laws. Personal responsibility for compliance with liquor laws is mandated by the Oklahoma Constitution. The Constitution prohibits the holding of a license by any LLC and thus, the lower court did err in its decision. Reversed.

ANALYSIS

Although there was testimony that an LLC was really the same as a partnership, the trial court correctly focused on the limitation on the personal liability in an LLC. However, owners of an LLC may still be held liable for personal wrongdoing. But, like shareholders in a corporation, LLC owners are immune from liability for the business' tort or contract obligations.

Litchfield Asset Management Corporation v. Howell

Creditor (P) v. Debtor (D)

Conn. Appellate Ct., 70 Conn. App. 133, 799 A.2d 298 (2002).

NATURE OF CASE: Appeal from an award of damages and injunctive relief.

FACT SUMMARY: Litchfield Asset Management Corporation (P) brought a suit to reach the assets of a limited liability company to satisfy a judgment previously obtained against Mary Ann Howell (D), a partner of the LLC. Litchfield (P) argued that the LLC was simply a shell created by Howell (D) to fraudulently shield her from the debt.

RULE OF LAW

A creditor may reach the assets of a limited liability company when the partners so dominate and control it that justice requires piercing the corporate veil.

FACTS: Litchfield Asset Management Corporation (P) obtained a damages award against Mary Ann Howell (D) and her company. Litchfield (P) subsequently brought a suit to enforce the judgment, which was granted. Howell (D) meanwhile formed a new limited liability company into which she transferred the assets of her former company. When the judgment remained unsatisfied, Litchfield (P) commenced the present suit against Howell's (D) new LLC, alleging that Howell (D) had formed the new LLC as a "mere shell" and used it to perpetrate a fraud or promote injustice by preventing him from collecting his debt on his judgment against her. The trial court agreed, holding that the new LLC was a mere alter ego of the first company and awarded damages against the new LLC. Howell (D) appealed.

ISSUE: May a creditor reach the assets of a limited liability company when the partners so dominate and control it that justice requires piercing the corporate veil?

HOLDING AND DECISION: (Lavery, C.J.) Yes. A creditor may reach the assets of a limited liability company when the partners so dominate and control it that justice requires piercing the corporate veil. In the usual veil piercing case, a court is asked to disregard a corporate entity so as to make available the personal assets of the owners to satisfy a liability of the entity. The instant case constitutes an instance of what is known as "reverse piercing" in which a creditor argues the opposite: that the assets of the corporate entity should be made available to pay the personal debts of the owner. The guiding concept behind both standard and reverse veil piercing cases is the need to avoid an over-rigid preoccupation with questions of structure and to apply the preexisting and overreaching principle that liability is imposed to reach an equitable result. Here, the element of domination and control is present. Howell (D) dominated and controlled the LLC. She used company funds to pay in excess of $30,000 in personal expenses, to purchase gifts for and make interest free loans to family members, and to pay the $8,247 balance of a loan for a vehicle titled to her husband. There was also a nearly complete overlap between Howell's (D) interest in another company she owned and the instant LLC. Furthermore, she was the general manager of both companies, each of which had no employees, but retained the same independent contractors. Both companies operated out of the same office space. Furthermore, the instant LLC's retention of revenue obtained from Howell's (D) sale of her other business evidenced a lack of arm's length dealing between the two companies. Howell (D), accordingly, deprived Litchfield (P) of any means of collecting its judgment against her and her previous company by unjustly creating the new corporate structure of a limited liability company in order to avoid her personal debt to Litchfield (P). Additionally, with knowledge that Litchfield (P) was pursuing a claim against her that she chose not to defend, Howell (D) transferred the cash value of her life insurance policies from herself to the new LLC. This prevented Litchfield (P) from securing collection of the judgment it eventually obtained against her. Affirmed.

ANALYSIS

As the *Litchfield* case demonstrates, if a creditor can show that there was such a unity of interest and ownership that the independence of the corporations or limited liability companies had in effect ceased or had never begun, an adherence to the fiction of separate identity would serve only to defeat justice and equity by permitting the economic entity to escape liability arising out of an operation conducted by one person or corporation for the benefit of the whole enterprise. What must be shown to pierce the veil is control and domination by the other person or entity, not mere majority or complete stock control, but complete domination, not only of finances but of policy and business practice with respect to the transaction attacked.

Abrahim & Sons Enterprises v. Equilon Enterprises, LLC

Gas station franchisees (P) v. Oil companies (D)

292 F.3d 958 (9th Cir. 2002).

NATURE OF CASE: Appeal of a grant of summary judgment for the defense in a suit by franchisees against franchisor for violation of business practices legislation.

FACT SUMMARY: When Shell and Texaco assigned their gas station leases and dealer agreements to Equilon Enterprises (D), an LLC, without first offering to sell such interest to Abrahim & Sons Enterprises (P) and other existing franchisees, Abrahim (P) contended that Shell and Texaco thereby violated legislation requiring a franchisor to first offer interests in a franchise to the existing franchisee before assigning an interest in the premises "to another person."

RULE OF LAW

A limited liability company is "another person" within the meaning of business practices legislation.

FACTS: Abrahim & Sons Enterprises (P) and forty-two other independent dealers who operated Shell or Texaco gasoline stations in Southern California leased their stations from Shell or Texaco with whom they had lease and retail marketing agreements in the form of franchises. Shell and Texaco subsequently combined all of their retail marketing and refining activities into a limited liability company, called Equilon Enterprises (D), assigning all the gas station leases and dealer agreements to Equilon (D) as well. In exchange, Shell and Texaco received full ownership interest in Equilon (D). Abrahim (P) sued Shell, Texaco, and Equilon (D), claiming that by transferring the gas stations to Equilon (D) without first offering the stations for sale to Abrahim (P) and the other independent gas dealers, Shell and Texaco violated California legislation prohibiting a franchisor from selling, transferring, or assigning an interest in a premises "to another person" unless first making a bona fide offer to sell that interest to the franchisee. The trial court granted Equilon's (D) motion for summary judgment on the grounds that Shell and Texaco's "contribution" of the gas stations to Equilon (D) was not a sale or assignment of the stations "to another person." Abrahim (P) appealed.

ISSUE: Is a limited liability company "another person" within the meaning of business practices legislation?

HOLDING AND DECISION: (Nelson, J.) Yes. A limited liability company is "another person" within the meaning of business practices legislation. Corporations and LLCs are distinct legal entities, separate from their stockholders or members. The acts of a corporation or LLC are deemed independent of the acts of its members. For this reason, both corporations and LLCs are included within the definition of "person" in the California Corporation Code. Shell and Texaco are incorrect in arguing that Equilon (D) is not a distinct legal entity because they own and control it. In essence, they are asking the court to disregard the corporate form they themselves created because the form does not benefit them in the instant case. While members do own and control most LLCs, yet the LLCs remain separate and distinct from their members. Indeed, the separate and distinct nature of LLCs is their reason for existence. Based on the common understanding of how an LLC works, Equilon (D) fits within the meaning of "another person." Reversed and remanded.

ANALYSIS

As the court makes clear in the *Abrahim* decision, common sense dictated that Equilon (D) was not the same entity as Shell or Texaco individually. Equilon (D) was owned jointly by Shell and Texaco. The gas stations, which previously were owned by only one oil company, now will be controlled and influenced by both companies. Therefore, the current owner of the gas station is not identical to the previous owners.

Premier Van Schaack Realty, Inc. v. Sieg

Real estate broker (P) v. Real estate owner (D)

Utah Ct. App., 51 P.3d 24 (2002).

NATURE OF CASE: Appeal from summary judgment for defendant in action to recover a real estate brokerage fee.

FACT SUMMARY: Premier Van Schaack Realty, Inc. (Premier) (P) contended that Sieg's (D) transfer of real property to a limited liability company (LLC) constituted a sale or exchange that required payment by Sieg (D) of a brokerage fee to Premier (P) under their listing agreement.

RULE OF LAW

A transfer of property by its owner to a limited liability company (LLC) does not constitute a sale or exchange supported by consideration that triggers the payment of a brokerage fee.

FACTS: Premier Van Schaack Realty, Inc. (Premier) (P) and Sieg (D) entered into a listing agreement for the sale of Sieg's (D) property that provided that Sieg (D) would pay to Premier (P) a 7% brokerage fee if during the listing period (one year) Premier (P) found a ready and willing buyer for the property. During the listing period, Premier (P) located an investor group (DVJ) who offered to purchase the property for $1.3 million. However, the sale fell through. Then, again during the listing period, DVJ and Sieg (D) formed a limited liability company (LLC), MJTM, whereby Sieg (D) conveyed the property to MJTM for a 40% interest and a preferential return of 9% on future profits. MJTM's operating agreement further provided that Sieg (D) had a beginning balance of $ 670,000 in his initial capital contribution account and that MJTM assumed $ 580,000 of Sieg's (D) debt. The other members of MJTM agreed not to encumber the property without Sieg's (D) approval. The operating agreement stated that the agreed value of the property was $ 1.3 million. Furthermore, the operating agreement provided, "No Member shall be personally liable to any other Member for the return of any part of the Members' Capital Contributions." Subsequently, MJTM borrowed $1.413 million, and each member personally guaranteed the loan. MJTM then paid off a $300,000 loan to Sieg (D) secured by the property. When Premier (P) found out about this arrangement it demanded a commission of 7% of $1.3 million. Seig (D) refused to pay, saying his contribution of property to MJTM was an investment, not a sale or exchange as defined by the listing agreement. Premier (P) brought suit, and the trial court granted summary judgment for Sieg (D). The state's highest court granted review.

ISSUE: Does a transfer of property by its owner to a limited liability company (LLC) constitute a sale or exchange supported by consideration that triggers the payment of a brokerage fee?

HOLDING AND DECISION: (Greenwood, J.) No. A transfer of property by its owner to a limited liability company (LLC) does not constitute a sale or exchange supported by consideration that triggers the payment of a brokerage fee. The core issue here is whether a sale or exchange occurred between Sieg (D) and MJTM. To have either of these, there must be consideration. Premier (P) argued that Sieg's (D) 40% interest, a capital account credited with a beginning balance of $670,000, assumption of $580,000 of Sieg's (D) debt, and a 9% preferential return on future profits all constituted consideration. Sieg (D) countered that these factors cannot be considered consideration because he continued to maintain an ownership interest in the property, and was personally liable on the $1.413 million loan. Sieg (D) is correct. He retained a substantial ownership interest in the property, and assumed the risks of an investor, so that there was only a change in the form of ownership, not a transfer of the property to another entity. Seig (D) retained the right to sell the property—and took the risk that the property's value would decrease. Thus, there was no sale or exchange. Also, any debt relief Seig (D) obtained was not consideration because he was personally liable on the loan that provided the funds for such relief. Thus, MJTM did not actually relieve Seig (D) of debt, but instead caused him to personally incur nearly three times the debt he owed on the property before joining the LLC. Thus, any debt relief was illusory. Also, the focus here is correctly on whether there was valuable consideration, not, as Premier (P) urges, on whether an LLC is an entity distinct from its owners. Whether a sale or exchange for valuable consideration has occurred is a fact-intensive inquiry that requires more than a mere showing that an owner transferred his property to a separate legal entity. Here, the evidence shows that the transaction was an investment transaction, with Seig (D) continuing to have substantially the same ownership interest in the property after the transfer to MJTM, so there was no consideration, and, thus, no sale or exchange. Affirmed.

ANALYSIS

Unlike the court in this case, other courts have found that the separate legal identity of the LLC is pivotal as to whether there has been an exchange or sale, finding that the transferor has received the benefits of limited liability. Also, § 501(a) of the Uniform Limited Liability Company Act provides that the property of an LLC is owned by the LLC, not its members.

Pinnacle Data Services, Inc. v. Gillen

50% LLC member (P) v. Combined 50% LLC members (D)

Tex. Ct. App., 104 S.W.3d 188 (2003).

NATURE OF CASE: Appeal from summary judgment for defendant in declaratory action.

FACT SUMMARY: Pinnacle Data Services, Inc. (PDS) (P), a 50% member in MJCM, LLC, a limited liability company, contended that MJCM's Regulations controlled over its articles of organization (Articles), and that, therefore, as provided in the Regulations, a vote of 66.66% of the ownership interest was required to amend the Articles, rather than a vote of two-thirds of the members as provided in the Articles.

RULE OF LAW

Where a limited liability company's regulations and articles conflict, but the regulations expressly provide that in case of such conflict the articles control, the articles control.

FACTS: Gillen (D) and Baldridge (D) each owned 25% of MJCM, L.L.C., a limited liability company, and Pinnacle Data Services, Inc. (PDS) (P), owned 50%. MJCM's articles of organization (Articles) and its Regulations (the equivalent of an operating agreement) provided that MJCM would be member-managed and that members would be paid through profit distributions. As MJCM became more profitable, the members began to disagree over how the company should be managed. At a company meeting, Gillen (D) proposed amendments to the Articles that would convert MJCM from member managed to manager managed, with Gillen (D) as manager. The Regulations provide that the Articles can only be amended by an affirmative vote of at least 66.66% of the ownership interest, whereas the Articles allow for their amendment by an affirmative vote of two-thirds of the members. The Regulations also provide that, to the extent the Regulations conflict with the Articles, the Articles control. Gillen (D) and Baldridge (D) voted to institute the proposed changes, and Gillen (D) assumed the managerial role. He also increased the number of employees and began paying himself and Baldridge (D) salaries and bonuses. PDS (P) brought suit challenging the amendments to the Articles and Regulations and the election of Gillen (D) as manager. The trial court granted summary judgment in favor of Gillen (D), Baldridge (D), and MJCM, and the state's intermediate court granted review.

ISSUE: Where a limited liability company's regulations and articles conflict, but the regulations expressly provide that in case of such conflict the articles control, do the articles control?

HOLDING AND DECISION: (Morriss, C.J.) Yes. Where a limited liability company's regulations and articles conflict, but the regulations expressly provide that in case of such conflict the articles control, the articles control. Determining whether the Regulations or Articles controls will be dispositive of all issues. If the Articles control, Gillen (D) and Baldridge (D) had the authority to amend the Articles and change the management structure of MJCM despite not having PDS's (P) consent. The state's LLC Act provides that the regulations of any LLC may contain provisions that are not inconsistent with law or the articles. Here, PDS's (P) president signed the Regulations, and the Articles were available to the public, so PDS (P) had notice of them. Rejected, as unsupported by precedent, is PDS's (P) claim that the Regulations are a contract because they were signed by all the parties, and that by virtue of rules of contract interpretation, the Regulations control over the Articles. Such a result would, instead, be contrary to the LLC Act and the Regulations' express language. Even if, as PDS (P) claims, it did not receive a copy of the Articles until two years after they were filed, this does not mean that PDS (P) tried to obtain them, and, in any event, the terms set forth in the Regulations, Articles, and the LLC Act are not rendered inoperative because PDS (P) failed to exercise diligence in obtaining a copy of the Articles before agreeing to their terms. Affirmed.

ANALYSIS

This case demonstrates the need for attorneys representing parties to an LLC operating agreement to understand, to the extent possible, all ramifications of the agreement's terms, and accordingly advise their clients of all significant potential outcomes under the agreement and state law. It also demonstrates the importance for parties entering into such agreements to be represented by an attorney.

Broyhill v. DeLuca

Successor LLC manager (P) v. Prior LLC manager (D)

U.S. Bankr. Ct., E.D.Va., 194 B.R. 65 (1996).

NATURE OF CASE: Petition to bankruptcy court for a declaration that a new LLC manager was properly appointed.

FACT SUMMARY: When the managing member of an LLC filed for bankruptcy, the LLC choose to continue the business and elect a new manager.

RULE OF LAW

A limited liability company may provide for dissolution upon a member's bankruptcy filing, with the remaining members having the right to continue the business and elect a new manager.

FACTS: D&B Countryside, a limited liability company, contained an operating agreement expressly specifying that the bankruptcy of a member would result in dissolution of the LLC and permit the remaining members to elect to continue the business and, if the bankrupt member were also the only manager, to elect a new manager. The DeLucas (D), the manager-members of D&B Countryside, filed a voluntary Chapter 11 petition, subsequent to which the LLC members executed a document in which they elected to continue the business and confirmed the election of Broyhill (P) as the new manager. Broyhill (P) sought a declaration in the bankruptcy court that the DeLucas (D) were properly removed as the managers of D&B Countryside and that Broyhill (P) was properly appointed as the successor manager.

ISSUE: May a limited liability company provide for dissolution upon a member's bankruptcy filing, with the remaining members having the right to continue the business and elect a new manager?

HOLDING AND DECISION: (Mitchell, J.) Yes. A limited liability company may provide for dissolution upon a member's bankruptcy filing, with the remaining members having the right to continue the business and elect a new manager. Here, the LLC's operating agreement explicitly provided that the bankruptcy of a member would trigger the dissolution of the company, but that within 90 days of the bankruptcy event, the remaining members could elect in writing to continue the business of the company and, if the bankrupt member were also the only manager, could elect a new manager. Broyhill (P) and the other members of the LLC have done precisely that. There is nothing in the Bankruptcy Act to prohibit their actions in this regard. Since the DeLucas (D) were properly removed as the managers of the company, the issue of their assuming the management functions specified in the operating agreement is not implicated, but upon their removal they would have had the right and duty to participate in the decision of a successor manager, acceptable to all the members, to carry on the management function. However, in view of the highly questionable conduct of the DeLucas (D) in having allowed a trust deed to be recorded against the company's property to secure a personal loan and in light of other violations of duty, the election of a new manager appeared highly appropriate. Such action does not, however, deprive the DeLucas' (D) bankruptcy estate of the right to share in the profits, losses, and distributions which resulted from their membership interest in the LLC. The court finds that the DeLucas (D) were properly removed as managers of D&B Countryside prior to the filing of the Chapter 11 petition and that Broyhill (P) was, subsequent to DeLucas' (D) Chapter 11 filing, properly elected as the successor manager.

ANALYSIS

The requirement in an LLC operating agreement for a unanimous vote in order to elect a manager presents an obvious practical difficulty. Since the manager may be removed by a majority, but less than unanimous vote, the LLC could well find itself in the difficult and untenable position of having removed a manager but being unable to elect a new one, thereby leaving the LLC essentially paralyzed. If that were to occur, the only apparent remedy would be a statutory judicial winding up. That was the potentiality which existed in the *Broyhill* case.

Taghipour v. Jerez

LLC (P) v. Manager of LLC (D)

Utah Sup. Ct., 52 P.3d 1252 (2002).

NATURE OF CASE: Appeal of the dismissal of a claim.

FACT SUMMARY: When Edgar Jerez (D), an LLC manager, acquired a loan from Mount Olympus Financial (D) by mortgaging LLC property to it, then absconded with the proceeds, Namvar Taghipour (P) and Danesh Rahemi (P), the two other LLC members (who knew nothing of the loan), brought suit against Mount Olympus Financial (D) to set aside its foreclosure on the property.

RULE OF LAW

A limited liability company is liable for instruments and documents relating to property disposition if they were executed by a manager, even if the other members did not authorize the manager's actions because they were unaware of them.

FACTS: Namvar Taghipour (P), Danesh Rahemi (P), and Edgar Jerez (D) formed a limited liability company to purchase and develop a real estate parcel pursuant to a joint venture agreement. The LLC's operating agreement designated Jerez (D) as the LLC's general manager, and specified that no loans could be contracted on behalf of the LLC unless authorized by the members. The LLC acquired the intended real estate. Subsequently, Jerez (D), unbeknownst to the LLC's other members or managers, entered into a loan agreement on behalf of the LLC with Mt. Olympus Financial (D) under which Mt. Olympus (D) loaned the LLC $25,000 and, as security for the loan, executed and delivered a trust deed that conveyed the LLC's real estate to a trustee with power to sell the property in the event of default. Mt. Olympus (D) did not investigate Jerez's (D) authority to effectuate the loan. Jerez (D) absconded with the funds, causing the LLC to default on the loan (of which they were unaware). Foreclosure was taken on the property. Taghipour (P) and Rahemi (P) filed suit against Mt. Olympus (D) and Jerez (D), arguing the loan agreement and foreclosure were invalid because Jerez (D) lacked authority to bind the LLC. Mt. Olympus (D) moved to dismiss the suit on the grounds that a statute provided that real property instruments and documents of an LLC were valid and binding on the LLC if executed by the manager. The trial court agreed and dismissed, and the court of appeals affirmed. Taghipour (P) appealed.

ISSUE: Is a limited liability company liable for instruments and documents relating to property disposition if they are executed by a manager, even if the other members did not authorize the manager's actions because they were unaware of them?

HOLDING AND DECISION: (Russon, J.) Yes. A limited liability company is liable for instruments and documents relating to property disposition if they were executed by a manager, even if the other members did not authorize the manager's actions because they were unaware of them. In support of its argument to set aside the mortgage of the LLC property, Taghipour (P) points to a statutory provision which precludes a manager from executing a loan without a resolution of the members if the operating agreement does not afford the manager authority to do so. However, another statute provides that real property instruments and documents of an LLC are valid and binding on the LLC if executed by the manager. The question of which statute the legislature intended to apply is determined by looking to the plain language of the statutes that purport to cover the same subject. Here, the statute providing that real property instruments and documents of an LLC are valid and binding on the LLC if executed by the manager is the more specific because it applies only to documents explicitly enumerated in the statute, namely, "instruments and documents" that provide "for the acquisition, mortgage, or disposition of property" of the LLC. Thus, this section is tailored precisely to address the documents and interests which Jerez (D) executed, i.e., the trust deed and trust deed note. Conversely, the other statute is more general because it addresses every situation in which a manager can bind an LLC. Affirmed.

ANALYSIS

As the *Taghipour* case points out, a statute is more specific according to the content of the statute, not according to how restrictive the statute is in operation. Indeed, a specific statute may be either more or less restrictive than the statute more general in application, depending upon the intent of the legislature in enacting a more specific statute.

McConnell v. Hunt Sports Enterprises

Member of LLC (P) v. LLC (D)

Ohio Ct. App., 725 N.E.2d 1193 (1999).

NATURE OF CASE: Appeal from a declaratory judgment.

FACT SUMMARY: **When McConnell (P), a member of an LLC, entered into a competing franchise with another LLC, he argued that the terms of the first LLC expressly did not forbid him from doing so.**

RULE OF LAW

The operating agreement of a limited liability company may limit or define the scope of the fiduciary duties imposed upon its members.

FACTS: Hunt, McConnell (P) and others formed a limited liability company entitled Columbus Hockey Limited, LLC (CHL) to seek a National Hockey League (NHL) franchise. The CHL members created an operating agreement for their LLC, a provision of which was entitled "Members May Compete." The provision stated that members were not in any way prohibited from or restricted "in engaging or owning an interest in any other business venture of any nature, including any venture which might be competitive with the business of the Company." Subsequently, and while still a member of CHL, McConnell (P) entered into a competing LLC. The new competing LLC was awarded the NHL franchise. McConnell (P) and his new franchise sought a declaratory judgment that the ownership of the franchise by his group was proper. The trial court rendered a judgment in favor of McConnell (P). Hunt Sports, an original member of the CHL limited liability company, appealed.

ISSUE: May the operating agreement of a limited liability company limit or define the scope of the fiduciary duties imposed upon its members?

HOLDING AND DECISION: (Tyack, J.) Yes. The operating agreement of a limited liability company may limit or define the scope of the fiduciary duties imposed upon its members. Fiduciary duty is a relationship in which special confidence and trust is reposed in the integrity and fidelity of another, and there is a resulting position of superiority or influence acquired by virtue of this special trust. Here, a limited liability company is involved which, like a partnership, involves a fiduciary relationship. Normally the presence of such a relationship would preclude direct competition between members of the company. However, here an operating agreement by its very terms allows members to compete with the business of the company. Since a fiduciary is a person having a duty, created by his own undertaking, to act primarily for the benefit of another in matters connected with such undertaking, the contract (or, in this case, operating agreement) may define the scope of fiduciary duties between the parties to the contract. The same principle has been applied in situations involving corporations and partnerships. In becoming members of CHL, all members agreed to abide by the terms of the operating agreement, and the agreement specifically allowed competition with the company by its members. As such, the duties created pursuant to the undertaking did not include a duty not to compete. Therefore, there was no duty on the part of McConnell (P) to refrain from subjecting CHL to the injury here complained of. Affirmed in part and reversed in part.

ANALYSIS

"Operating agreement" is usually statutorily defined as all the valid written or oral agreements of the members as to the affairs of a limited liability company and the conduct of its business. Indeed, many statutory provisions governing LLCs indicate they are, in various ways, subject to and/or dependent upon related provisions in an operating agreement. In the *McConnell* case, the operating agreement stated in its opening paragraph that it evidences the mutual agreement of the members in consideration of their contributions and promises to each other. The agreement specifically allowed its members to compete with the company.

VGS, Inc. v. Castiel

LLC (D) v. LLC member (P)

Del. Ch. Ct., 2000 Del. Ch. LEXIS 122 (Aug. 31, 2000).

NATURE OF CASE: Petition in equity to declare a merger invalid.

FACT SUMMARY: Sahagan and Quinn (two members of the Board of Managers of an LLC), without providing notice to David Castiel (P) (the third member), merged the LLC into another company, thereby depriving Castiel (P) of his majority interest. Castiel (P) sought rescission of the merger on the grounds that by failing to give him notice, Sahagan and Quinn had violated their fiduciary duty to him to act in good faith.

RULE OF LAW
Members of a limited liability company owe a fiduciary duty of loyalty to one another.

FACTS: David Castiel (P) formed a limited liability company entitled Virtual Geosatellite LLC. Subsequently Sahagan became a member and Castiel (P) appointed Quinn to the Board of managers. When dissension arose among the three members of the Board, Sahagan and Quinn fashioned a plan to oust Castiel (P). To this end, and without notice to Castiel (P), Sahagan and Quinn acted by written consent to merge the LLC into VGS, Inc. (VGS) (D). Accordingly, Virtual Geosatellite LLC ceased to exist, its assets and liabilities passed to VGS (D) which became Virtual Geosatellite's successor in interest. Castiel (P), therefore, then found himself relegated to a minority position in the surviving corporation. These "clandestine machinations" were essential to the success of Sahagan and Quinn's plan. Castiel (P) filed a petition to have the merger of Virtual Geosatellite LLC and VGS (D) declared invalid on the grounds that Sahagan and Quinn failed to discharge their fiduciary duty of loyalty to the LLC by providing Castiel (P) with notice of the proposed merger, which he surely would have attempted to prevent.

ISSUE: Do members of a limited liability company owe a fiduciary duty of loyalty to one another?

HOLDING AND DECISION: (Steele, V.Chan.) Yes. Members of a limited liability company owe a fiduciary duty of loyalty to one another. Here, while a majority of the board of Virtual Geosatellite LLC acted by written consent, had the original member's manager received notice beforehand that his appointed manager contemplated actions against his interests he would have promptly attempted to remove him. Because the two managers acted without notice to the third manager under circumstances where they knew that with notice he could have acted to protect his majority interest, they breached their duty of loyalty to the original member and their fellow manager by failing to act in good faith. It is clear that the purpose of the statute permitting action by written consent of LLC managers without notice is to enable LLC managers to take quick, efficient action in situations where a minority of managers could not block or adversely affect the course set by the majority even if they were notified of the proposed action and objected to it. The legislature, however, never intended to enable two managers, as here, to deprive, clandestinely and surreptitiously, a third manager representing the majority interest in the LLC of an opportunity to protect that interest by taking an action that the third manager's member would surely have opposed if he had knowledge of it. Equity looks to the intent rather than to the form. Here, the "majority" existed only so long as it could act in secrecy. Accordingly, the acts taken to merge Virtual Geosatellite LLC into VGS (D) are invalid, and the merger is ordered rescinded.

ANALYSIS

In the *VGS, Inc.* case, the court applied a traditional maxim of equity that equity regards and treats as done that which in good conscience ought to be done, to arrive at the conclusion that, under the particular and unique circumstances of this case, Sahagan and Quinn should have given Castiel (P) prior notice of the proposed merger.

Katris v. Carroll

LLC manager (P) v. Alleged colluder (D)

Ill. Ct. App., 842 N.E.2d 221 (2005).

NATURE OF CASE: Appeal from grant of summary judgment to defendant in action for collusion to breach fiduciary duties.

FACT SUMMARY: Katris (P), the manager for Viper Execution Systems, L.L.C. (the LLC), a manager-managed limited liability company, alleged that Carroll (D) and Ernst & Co. (Ernst) colluded with Doherty, a non-manager member, to breach fiduciary duties to Katris (P) and the LLC.

RULE OF LAW

A non-manager member of a manager-managed limited liability company (LLC) does not owe fiduciary duties to the LLC or its manager where the member does not exercise any managerial authority pursuant to the operating agreement, and, therefore, cannot breach any fiduciary duties to the LLC's manager or the LLC that could support a collusion claim.

FACTS: Viper Execution Systems, L.L.C. (the LLC), a manager-managed limited liability company, was managed by Katris (P) and Hamburg. Its articles of organization specified that management was not retained by its non-manager members, which included Doherty. A written consent in lieu of an initial meeting confirmed that only Katris (P) and Hamburg had managerial authority, but named Doherty as "Director of Technology." Prior to and at the time of the LLC's formation, Doherty worked as an independent contractor for Carroll (D), an employee of Ernst & Co. (Ernst) (D). Subsequently, Ernst (D) hired Doherty to work for Carroll (D) creating a software product that allegedly was very similar to, and that competed with, the LLC's software product. Katris (P) brought suit asserting that Doherty had breached fiduciary duties and that Carroll (D) and Ernst (D) had colluded with Doherty in doing so. Doherty settled, and only the collusion claims remained. Carroll (D) and Ernst (D) moved for summary judgment, asserting that Doherty owed neither Katris (P) nor the LLC any fiduciary duties because the state's LLC Act provided that non-manager members of a manager-managed LLC do not owe fiduciary duties unless they exercise some or all managerial authority under the LLC's operating agreement. Katris (P) countered that the written consent had operated as an amendment to the operating agreement insofar as it made Doherty the Director of Technology, a position that Katris (P) claimed entailed managerial authority. The trial court granted summary judgment for Carroll (D) and Ernst (D) and the state's intermediate appellate court granted review.

ISSUE: Does a non-manager member of a manager-managed limited liability company (LLC) owe fiduciary duties to the LLC or its manager where the member does not exercise any managerial authority pursuant to the operating agreement, and, therefore, can breach fiduciary duties to the LLC's manager or the LLC that could support a collusion claim?

HOLDING AND DECISION: (McNulty, J.) No. A non-manager member of a manager-managed limited liability company (LLC) does not owe fiduciary duties to the LLC or its manager where the member does not exercise any managerial authority pursuant to the operating agreement, and, therefore, cannot breach any fiduciary duties to the LLC's manager or the LLC that could support a collusion claim. The dispositive issue here is whether Doherty owed Katris (P) or the LLC any fiduciary duties. The state's LLC Act controls here, and Katris (P) concedes that Doherty did not owe any fiduciary duties solely by reason of being an LLC member. Instead, Katris (P) maintains that Doherty exercised some of the authority of a manager in his capacity as director of technology for the LLC, and so comes within the scope of the statute. However, the statute's plain language provides that the exercise of such authority must be exercised pursuant to the operating agreement. The LLC Act provides for the creation of an operating agreement, and here such an agreement was entered into. The language of the operating agreement clearly provides that only Katris (P) and Hamburg are the LLC's managers. The agreement's other provisions, which set forth the members' rights and obligations, do not provide for any managerial authority. Thus, Doherty did not exercise any managerial authority pursuant to the LLC's operating agreement. Rejected is Katris's (P) assertion that the written consent amended the operating agreement. First, there is no precedent for such an assertion. Second, the operating agreement itself provided for an affirmative vote of a majority of the percentage ownership to amend it; the consent was only participated in by Katris (P) and Hamburg—representing only 50% of the ownership interest. Thus, the consent was not an amendment to the operating agreement. Finally, even if the consent could be construed as an amendment, it acts to reaffirm the operating agreement by indicating that the operating agreement was adopted by all the members, and by specifying that only Katris (P) and Hamburg were the managers. Based on the plain language of the LLC Act, it would be inappropriate to look beyond the operating agreement to determine if Doherty exercised any

Continued on next page.

managerial responsibilities, so Katris's (P) arguments in this regard are unavailing. Because Doherty owed no fiduciary duties, he could not have breached them, and, therefore, neither Carroll (D) nor Ernst (D) could have colluded with him in effecting such a breach. Affirmed.

ANALYSIS

The Uniform Limited Liability Company Act (ULLCA), § 409 (h)(1) similarly provides that "[A] member who is not also a manger owes no duties to the company or to the other members solely by reason of being a member." It also provides in § 409(h)(3) that "a member who pursuant to the operating agreement exercises some or all of the rights of a manager in the management and conduct of the company's business is held to the standards of conduct [that a manager is held to] to the extent that the member exercises the managerial authority vested in a manager." Under the ULLCA, the only fiduciary duties are those of loyalty and care. In addition, managers have the fiduciary duties of an agent.

Taurus Advisory Group, Inc. v. Sector Management, Inc.

Limited liability company (P) v. Management group (D)

Conn. Super. Ct., 1996 Conn. Super LEXIS 2272 (Aug. 29, 1996).

NATURE OF CASE: Action for breach of contract and breach of fiduciary duty arising from an agreement to form the LLC.

FACT SUMMARY: Members (P) of Sector Management (D), an LLC, sought to bring a derivative action for breach of fiduciary duty, negligent misrepresentation, breach of covenant of good faith, and breach of contract.

RULE OF LAW

Members of limited liability companies may bring suit if the members or managers having authority to do so have refused to commence the action or an effort to cause those members or managers to commence the action is not likely to succeed.

FACTS: Taurus Advisory Group (TAG) (P) and Taurus, LLC (P) sued Sector (D) for breach of contract, breach of fiduciary duty and negligent misrepresentation arising from an agreement to form a limited liability company (LLC). Sector (D) moved to dismiss on the grounds that the court lacked subject matter jurisdiction because TAG (P) lacked authority to assert derivative claims individually or in the name of Taurus, LLC (D). TAG (P) argued that it was bringing the claims in its own right, as was Taurus, LLC (D), and even if the claims were derivative in nature, TAG (P) had the right to assert those claims because it was the only remaining member having authority to authorize a suit, and a member may bring a derivative action where an effort to obtain authority is not likely to succeed.

ISSUE: May the members of limited liability companies bring suit if the members or managers having authority to do so have refused to commence the action or an effort to cause those members or managers to commence the action is not likely to succeed?

HOLDING AND DECISION: (Lewis, J.) Yes. Members of limited liability companies may bring suit if the members or managers having authority to do so have refused to commence the action or an effort to cause those members or managers to commence the action is not likely to succeed. The complaint must state with particularity the effort of the plaintiff to secure initiation of the action by a member or manager or the reasons for not making the effort. The complaint in the case at bar does not state an effort or the reasons why the action is not likely to succeed. The motion to dismiss is granted as to the counts relating to breach of fiduciary relationship, and is otherwise denied.

ANALYSIS

Both parties in this case had agreed that there was no case law to guide them on derivative suits against LLC's. They accepted the analogy to a corporation whereby members are similar to shareholders. Other courts have used similar construction with limited liability partnerships, and therefore the court accepted this analogy in this case also.

Walker v. Resource Development Company Limited, L.L.C.

LLC Member (P) v. LLC (D)

Del. Ch. Ct., 791 A.2d 799 (2000).

NATURE OF CASE: Petition by LLC member to declare that other members had no authority to expel him and for recovery of interests withheld from him.

FACT SUMMARY: When Walker (P) was expelled as a member of Resource Development Company, LLC (REDECO) (D), he argued that neither the operating agreement nor the law provided for his expulsion.

RULE OF LAW

A member of a limited liability company may not be expelled where neither the operating agreement nor the law provides for an expulsion.

FACTS: Resource Development Company, LLC (REDECO) (D) was a limited liability company founded by Cox (D), Baron (D), Liedtke (D), and Walker (P). Frustrated by Walker's (P) drinking problems, financial irresponsibility, and inability to secure financing that he had promised would be forthcoming, the other members attempted to expel Walker (P) from REDECO (D) by a removal letter which stated, "We hereby terminate your member-ship interest in the Firm." Walker (P) never acknowledged nor returned the removal letter, but brought a petition in equity to declare that the three other members had no authority to expel him, and for recovery from them of the LLC interests which they withheld from him.

ISSUE: May a member of a limited liability company be expelled where neither the operating agreement nor the law provides for an expulsion?

HOLDING AND DECISION: [Judge not stated in casebook excerpt.] No. A member of a limited liability company may not be expelled where neither the operating agreement nor the law provides for an expulsion. The basic approach of the limited liability company statute is to permit members to have the broadest possible discretion in drafting their operating agreements and to furnish answers only in situations where the members have not expressly made provisions in their agreement. Thus, LLC members' rights begin with, and typically end with, the operating agreement. Here, the operating agreement includes no provision that can be read to allow the partners to deprive Walker (P) of his ownership interest under the circumstances of this case. One article deals with removal of the manager, but makes clear that removal shall be without prejudice to the manager's contract rights, implicitly including his ownership rights. Another article does address the voluntary and involuntary withdrawal from membership, but identifies no instance even arguably applicable to the instant case. The absence of such a provision is surprising, considering what the other members knew about Walker (P) at the time they entered into the agreement. These members could easily have protected themselves in the operating agreement by simply making Walker's (P) REDECO (D) interest contingent on successfully closing the deal he said he would. They failed, however, to do so. Furthermore, there is no basis in law for unilateral removal of Walker (P). There may indeed be other mechanisms available to LLC members to recast their business relations to eliminate persons from the enterprise, such as the merger provisions of the various business entity laws, but these provisions do not provide for the forfeiture of economic rights, requiring instead that the persons whose interests are eliminated are entitled to receive fair value therefor. The provision shielding members of an LLC from good faith business decisions was never intended by the legislature to allow the members of an LLC to misappropriate property from another member and to avoid returning that property or otherwise compensating the wronged member. Judgment for Walker (P).

ANALYSIS

As stressed in the *Walker* case, the operating agreement is the cornerstone of a limited liability company and effectively constitutes the entire agreement among the members with respect to the admission of members to or the expulsion from, and the creation, operation, and termination of the LLC.

Haley v. Talcott

50% LLC owner (P) v. 50% LLC owner (D)

Del. Ch. Ct., 864 A.2d 86 (2004).

NATURE OF CASE: Action to dissolve limited liability company (LLC).

FACT SUMMARY: Haley (P) and Talcott (D), each 50% owners of an LLC, were at an impasse. Haley (P) argued that dissolution was necessary, whereas Talcott (D) argued that Haley (P) was limited to an exit mechanism provided in the LLC's operating agreement, even if such exit mechanism was not equitable regarding Haley's (P) interests.

RULE OF LAW

Where co-equal members of a limited liability company are at an impasse, can no longer carry on the LLC's business, and are in disagreement about whether to discontinue the business and how to dispose of its assets, and where an exit mechanism in the LLC's operating agreement is inequitable, dissolution is necessary.

FACTS: Haley (P) and Talcott (D) each owned 50% of Matt and Greg Real Estate, LLC (the LLC). A restaurant (the Redfin Grill) owned by Talcott (D) and operated by Haley (P) leased from the LLC the land on which the restaurant operated. Contractually, Haley (P) was supposed to receive 50% of the profits from the restaurant business, which the two men operated as a joint venture. Although pursuant to an employment contract Haley (P) was technically Talcott's (D) employee at the restaurant, the other terms of the contract established a relationship more similar to a partnership. Both men contributed equally and personally guaranteed the mortgage for the property owned by the LLC. Eventually, a rift developed between them, and the rift turned into deadlock and an impasse where the LLC could no longer carry on its business. In addition, the LLC property appreciated substantially in value (from the purchase price of $720,000 to an appraised value of $1.8 million). Absent court intervention, Haley (P) would be stuck with the status quo unless he chose to avail himself of the operating agreement's exit mechanism. This mechanism provided that upon notice of election to quit the LLC, the remaining member could elect to purchase the departing member's interest at fair market value. If the remaining member fails to elect to purchase the departing member's interest, the company is to be liquidated. However, the exit mechanism did not provide expressly for a release from the personal guarantees that the two men had given for the mortgage of the LLC's real property. Nor did the exit provision state that any member dissatisfied with the status quo had to break an impasse by exit rather than a suit for dissolution. Haley (P) brought suit for dissolution; Talcott (D) maintained that Haley's (P) remedy was limited to the contractual exit mechanism. Although both were willing to buy out the other, neither was willing to sell.

ISSUE: Where co-equal members of a limited liability company are at an impasse, can no longer carry on the LLC's business, and are in disagreement about whether to discontinue the business and how to dispose of its assets, and where an exit mechanism in the LLC's operating agreement is inequitable, is dissolution necessary?

HOLDING AND DECISION: (Strine, V.Chan.) Yes. Where co-equal members of a limited liability company are at an impasse, can no longer carry on the LLC's business, and are in disagreement about whether to discontinue the business and how to dispose of its assets, and where an exit mechanism in the LLC's operating agreement is inequitable, dissolution is necessary. The applicable statute provides that on application by or for a member or manager, the court may decree dissolution of a limited liability company whenever it is not reasonably practicable to carry on the business in conformity with a limited liability company agreement. The elements of this statute are met here: the members are equal owners; they are engaged in a joint venture; and they are unable to agree upon whether to discontinue the business or how to dispose of its assets. Most importantly in this regard, Haley (P) never agreed to be a passive investor in the LLC who would be subject to Talcott's (D) unilateral dominion. Instead, the LLC agreement provided that: "no member/managers may, without the agreement of a majority vote of the managers' interest, act on behalf of the company." Because the manifest weight of the evidence is that the parties are deadlocked, if the entity were a corporation, there would be no question that Haley's (P) request to dissolve the entity would be granted. However, here, the operating agreement's exit mechanism must also be considered. First, the state's LLC statute is grounded on principles of freedom of contract. For that reason, the presence of a reasonable exit mechanism bears on the propriety of ordering dissolution. When the agreement itself provides a fair opportunity for the dissenting member who disfavors the inertial status quo to exit and receive the fair market value of her interest, it is at least arguable that the limited liability company may still proceed to operate practicably under its contractual charter because the charter itself provides an equitable way to break the impasse. Thus, so long as Haley (P) can actually extract himself fairly, it arguably makes sense for the court to stay its hand in an LLC case and allow the contract itself to solve the problem. However, forcing Haley (P) to exercise the contractual exit mechanism would not permit the LLC to proceed in a practicable way that accords with the LLC

Continued on next page.

agreement, but would instead permit Talcott (D) to penalize Haley (P) without express contractual authorization. This is so because the exit mechanism would not relieve Haley (P) of his obligation under the personal guaranty that he signed to secure the mortgage on the LLC's property. If Haley (P) is forced to use the exit mechanism, Talcott (D) and he both believe that Haley (P) would still be left holding the bag on the guaranty. It is therefore not equitable to force Haley (P) to use the exit mechanism in this circumstance. Thus, the exit mechanism fails as an adequate remedy for Haley (P) because it does not equitably effect the separation of the parties. Rather, it would leave him with no upside potential, and no protection over the considerable downside risk that he would have to make good on any future default by the LLC (over whose operations he would have no control) to its mortgage lender. For this reason, it is necessary for the court to intervene and order dissolution.

ANALYSIS

It is an interesting question whether the 50% member of an LLC that operates an on-going business, and who does not favor inertial policy, must exit rather than force dissolution, particularly when the cost of the exit procedure would, as here, be borne solely by him. Arguably, it is economically more efficient—absent an explicit requirement that the party disfavoring inertia exit if he is dissatisfied—to order dissolution, and allow both parties to bid as purchasers, with the assets going to the highest bidder (inside or outside) who presumably will deploy the asset to its most valuable use. It is also concomitantly arguable that if parties wish to force the co-equal member disfavoring inertia to exit rather than seek dissolution, then they should explicitly contract upfront in the LLC agreement that exit (or the triggering of a buy-sell procedure, giving incentives for the business to be retained by the member willing to pay the highest value) is the required method of breaking any later-arising stalemate.

Hurwitz v. Padden

LLC member (P) v. LLC member (D)

Minn. Ct. App., 581 N.W.2d 359 (1998).

NATURE OF CASE: **Appeal from a declaratory judgment for the defense in a member's suit upon dissolution of an LLC.**

FACT SUMMARY: **When the law firm of Hurwitz & Padden, LLC dissolved, Padden (D) sought recovery quantum meruit recovery of legal fees from lawsuits acquired prior to dissolution of the firm.**

RULE OF LAW

Partnership principles may properly be applied to the dissolution of a limited liability company.

FACTS: Hurwitz (P) and Padden (D) formed a two-person law firm, but failed to enter into a written partnership agreement. The partners shared all firm proceeds on a 50-50 basis, and reported all income as partnership income. Afterward, the firm filed articles of incorporation which established it as a limited liability company. Hurwitz (P) and Padden (D) subsequently dissolved their LLC and successfully resolved all business issues except for the division of attorney fees from several of the firm's contingency fee cases. Hurwitz (P) filed a declaratory judgment suit against Padden (D) seeking a formal dissolution, a post-dissolution distribution of attorney fees on the traditional 50-50 basis, and injunctive relief. Padden (D) counterclaimed, requesting a full accounting as well as attorney fees from several of the firm's contingency fee cases. The court found in favor of Hurwitz (P), and Padden (D) appealed.

ISSUE: May partnership principles properly be applied to the dissolution of a limited liability company?

HOLDING AND DECISION: (Short, J.) Yes. Partnership principles may properly be applied to the dissolution of a limited liability company. The limited liability company act specifically incorporates the definition and use of the term "dissolution" from the Uniform Partnership Act (UPA). Under both statutes, the entity is not terminated upon dissolution, but continues until all business issues are resolved. Thus, the UPA provides guidance when examining the end stages of either entity's life. Moreover, the mere fact that the parties filed an LLC document with the state does not foreclose an examination of partnership law. Here, it is undisputed that the law firm had no oral or written agreement regarding the division of contingency fees upon dissolution; such fees were acquired before the firm's dissolution; and prior to dissolution, the firm divided fees equally. Under these circumstances, partnership principles, including the "no-compensation rule," govern the division of fees obtained from pre-dissolution contingency fee files. Furthermore, Padden (D) is incorrect in his assertion that the state's rules of professional conduct prohibit an equal division of the contingency fees because the parties failed to strictly comply with the fee-splitting requirements. In fact, the model rules of professional conduct only regulate the manner in which lawyers from different firms may split a fee. Until the firm's affairs are wound-up, the entity remains intact for the purposes of completing its affairs, and lawyers remain in the same firm until that process is completed. Affirmed.

ANALYSIS

As a partnership moves toward termination, it conducts a "winding up" of its affairs. When a partnership is in this "winding up" stage, the UPA confers no right of compensation for services rendered by the partners in furtherance of the partnership business. During the period between dissolution and termination, partnership distributions continue to be made according to pre-dissolution rules. Pending contingency files are uncompleted transactions of the partnership, and the fees obtained from such cases are assets of the firm subject to distribution under the UPA.

Glossary

Common Latin Words and Phrases Encountered in the Law

A FORTIORI: Because one fact exists or has been proven, therefore a second fact that is related to the first fact must also exist.

A PRIORI: From the cause to the effect. A term of logic used to denote that when one generally accepted truth is shown to be a cause, another particular effect must necessarily follow.

AB INITIO: From the beginning; a condition which has existed throughout, as in a marriage which was void ab initio.

ACTUS REUS: The wrongful act; in criminal law, such action sufficient to trigger criminal liability.

AD VALOREM: According to value; an ad valorem tax is imposed upon an item located within the taxing jurisdiction calculated by the value of such item.

AMICUS CURIAE: Friend of the court. Its most common usage takes the form of an amicus curiae brief, filed by a person who is not a party to an action but is nonetheless allowed to offer an argument supporting his legal interests.

ARGUENDO: In arguing. A statement, possibly hypothetical, made for the purpose of argument, is one made arguendo.

BILL QUIA TIMET: A bill to quiet title (establish ownership) to real property.

BONA FIDE: True, honest, or genuine. May refer to a person's legal position based on good faith or lacking notice of fraud (such as a bona fide purchaser for value) or to the authenticity of a particular document (such as a bona fide last will and testament).

CAUSA MORTIS: With approaching death in mind. A gift causa mortis is a gift given by a party who feels certain that death is imminent.

CAVEAT EMPTOR: Let the buyer beware. This maxim is reflected in the rule of law that a buyer purchases at his own risk because it is his responsibility to examine, judge, test, and otherwise inspect what he is buying.

CERTIORARI: A writ of review. Petitions for review of a case by the United States Supreme Court are most often done by means of a writ of certiorari.

CONTRA: On the other hand. Opposite. Contrary to.

CORAM NOBIS: Before us; writs of error directed to the court that originally rendered the judgment.

CORAM VOBIS: Before you; writs of error directed by an appellate court to a lower court to correct a factual error.

CORPUS DELICTI: The body of the crime; the requisite elements of a crime amounting to objective proof that a crime has been committed.

CUM TESTAMENTO ANNEXO, ADMINISTRATOR (ADMINISTRATOR C.T.A.): With will annexed; an administrator c.t.a. settles an estate pursuant to a will in which he is not appointed.

DE BONIS NON, ADMINISTRATOR (ADMINISTRATOR D.B.N.): Of goods not administered; an administrator d.b.n. settles a partially settled estate.

DE FACTO: In fact; in reality; actually. Existing in fact but not officially approved or engendered.

DE JURE: By right; lawful. Describes a condition that is legitimate "as a matter of law," in contrast to the term "de facto," which connotes something existing in fact but not legally sanctioned or authorized. For example, de facto segregation refers to segregation brought about by housing patterns, etc., whereas de jure segregation refers to segregation created by law.

DE MINIMIS: Of minimal importance; insignificant; a trifle; not worth bothering about.

DE NOVO: Anew; a second time; afresh. A trial de novo is a new trial held at the appellate level as if the case originated there and the trial at a lower level had not taken place.

DICTA: Generally used as an abbreviated form of obiter dicta, a term describing those portions of a judicial opinion incidental or not necessary to resolution of the specific question before the court. Such nonessential statements and remarks are not considered to be binding precedent.

DUCES TECUM: Refers to a particular type of writ or subpoena requesting a party or organization to produce certain documents in their possession.

EN BANC: Full bench. Where a court sits with all justices present rather than the usual quorum.

EX PARTE: For one side or one party only. An ex parte proceeding is one undertaken for the benefit of only one party, without notice to, or an appearance by, an adverse party.

EX POST FACTO: After the fact. An ex post facto law is a law that retroactively changes the consequences of a prior act.

EX REL.: Abbreviated form of the term ex relatione, meaning upon relation or information. When the state brings an action in which it has no interest against an individual at the instigation of one who has a private interest in the matter.

FORUM NON CONVENIENS: Inconvenient forum. Although a court may have jurisdiction over the case, the action should be tried in a more conveniently located court, one to which parties and witnesses may more easily travel, for example.

GUARDIAN AD LITEM: A guardian of an infant as to litigation, appointed to represent the infant and pursue his/her rights.

HABEAS CORPUS: You have the body. The modern writ of habeas corpus is a writ directing that a person (body) being detained (such as a prisoner) be brought before the court so that the legality of his detention can be judicially ascertained.

IN CAMERA: In private, in chambers. When a hearing is held before a judge in his chambers or when all spectators are excluded from the courtroom.

IN FORMA PAUPERIS: In the manner of a pauper. A party who proceeds in forma pauperis because of his poverty is one who is allowed to bring suit without liability for costs.

INFRA: Below, under. A word referring the reader to a later part of a book. (The opposite of supra.)

IN LOCO PARENTIS: In the place of a parent.

IN PARI DELICTO: Equally wrong; a court of equity will not grant requested relief to an applicant who is in pari delicto, or as much at fault in the transactions giving rise to the controversy as is the opponent of the applicant.

IN PARI MATERIA: On like subject matter or upon the same matter. Statutes relating to the same person or things are said to be in pari materia. It is a general rule of statutory construction that such statutes should be construed together, i.e., looked at as if they together constituted one law.

IN PERSONAM: Against the person. Jurisdiction over the person of an individual.

IN RE: In the matter of. Used to designate a proceeding involving an estate or other property.

IN REM: A term that signifies an action against the res, or thing. An action in rem is basically one that is taken directly against property, as distinguished from an action in personam, i.e., against the person.

INTER ALIA: Among other things. Used to show that the whole of a statement, pleading, list, statute, etc., has not been set forth in its entirety.

INTER PARTES: Between the parties. May refer to contracts, conveyances or other transactions having legal significance.

INTER VIVOS: Between the living. An inter vivos gift is a gift made by a living grantor, as distinguished from bequests contained in a will, which pass upon the death of the testator.

IPSO FACTO: By the mere fact itself.

JUS: Law or the entire body of law.

LEX LOCI: The law of the place; the notion that the rights of parties to a legal proceeding are governed by the law of the place where those rights arose.

MALUM IN SE: Evil or wrong in and of itself; inherently wrong. This term describes an act that is wrong by its very nature, as opposed to one which would not be wrong but for the fact that there is a specific legal prohibition against it (malum prohibitum).

MALUM PROHIBITUM: Wrong because prohibited, but not inherently evil. Used to describe something that is wrong because it is expressly forbidden by law but that is not in and of itself evil, e.g., speeding.

MANDAMUS: We command. A writ directing an official to take a certain action.

MENS REA: A guilty mind; a criminal intent. A term used to signify the mental state that accompanies a crime or other prohibited act. Some crimes require only a general mens rea (general intent to do the prohibited act), but others, like assault with intent to murder, require the existence of a specific mens rea.

MODUS OPERANDI: Method of operating; generally refers to the manner or style of a criminal in committing crimes, admissible in appropriate cases as evidence of the identity of a defendant.

NEXUS: A connection to.

NISI PRIUS: A court of first impression. A nisi prius court is one where issues of fact are tried before a judge or jury.

N.O.V. (NON OBSTANTE VEREDICTO): Notwithstanding the verdict. A judgment n.o.v. is a judgment given in favor of one party despite the fact that a verdict was returned in favor of the other party, the justification being that the verdict either had no reasonable support in fact or was contrary to law.

NUNC PRO TUNC: Now for then. This phrase refers to actions that may be taken and will then have full retroactive effect.

PENDENTE LITE: Pending the suit; pending litigation underway.

PER CAPITA: By head; beneficiaries of an estate, if they take in equal shares, take per capita.

PER CURIAM: By the court; signifies an opinion ostensibly written "by the whole court" and with no identified author.

PER SE: By itself, in itself; inherently.

PER STIRPES: By representation. Used primarily in the law of wills to describe the method of distribution where a person, generally because of death, is unable to take that which is left to him by the will of another, and therefore his heirs divide such property between them rather than take under the will individually.

PRIMA FACIE: On its face, at first sight. A prima facie case is one that is sufficient on its face, meaning that the evidence supporting it is adequate to establish the case until contradicted or overcome by other evidence.

PRO TANTO: For so much; as far as it goes. Often used in eminent domain cases when a property owner receives partial payment for his land without prejudice to his right to bring suit for the full amount he claims his land to be worth.

QUANTUM MERUIT: As much as he deserves. Refers to recovery based on the doctrine of unjust enrichment in those cases in which a party has rendered valuable services or furnished materials that were accepted and enjoyed by another under circumstances that would reasonably notify the recipient that the rendering party expected to be paid. In essence, the law implies a contract to pay the reasonable value of the services or materials furnished.

QUASI: Almost like; as if; nearly. This term is essentially used to signify that one subject or thing is almost analogous to another but that material differences between them do exist. For example, a quasi-criminal proceeding is one that is not strictly criminal but shares enough of the same characteristics to require some of the same safeguards (e.g., procedural due process must be followed in a parole hearing).

QUID PRO QUO: Something for something. In contract law, the consideration, something of value, passed between the parties to render the contract binding.

RES GESTAE: Things done; in evidence law, this principle justifies the admission of a statement that would otherwise be hearsay when it is made so closely to the event in question as to be said to be a part of it, or with such spontaneity as not to have the possibility of falsehood.

RES IPSA LOQUITUR: The thing speaks for itself. This doctrine gives rise to a rebuttable presumption of negligence when the instrumentality causing the injury was within the exclusive control of the defendant, and the injury was one that does not normally occur unless a person has been negligent.

RES JUDICATA: A matter adjudged. Doctrine which provides that once a court of competent jurisdiction has rendered a final judgment or decree on the merits, that judgment or decree is conclusive upon the parties to the case and prevents them from engaging in any other litigation on the points and issues determined therein.

RESPONDEAT SUPERIOR: Let the master reply. This doctrine holds the master liable for the wrongful acts of his servant (or the principal for his agent) in those cases in which the servant (or agent) was acting within the scope of his authority at the time of the injury.

STARE DECISIS: To stand by or adhere to that which has been decided. The common law doctrine of stare decisis attempts to give security and certainty to the law by following the policy that once a principle of law as applicable to a certain set of facts has been set forth in a decision, it forms a precedent which will subsequently be followed, even though a different decision might be made were it the first time the question had arisen. Of course, stare decisis is not an inviolable principle and is departed from in instances where there is good cause (e.g., considerations of public policy led the Supreme Court to disregard prior decisions sanctioning segregation).

SUPRA: Above. A word referring a reader to an earlier part of a book.

ULTRA VIRES: Beyond the power. This phrase is most commonly used to refer to actions taken by a corporation that are beyond the power or legal authority of the corporation.

Addendum of French Derivatives

IN PAIS: Not pursuant to legal proceedings.

CHATTEL: Tangible personal property.

CY PRES: Doctrine permitting courts to apply trust funds to purposes not expressed in the trust but necessary to carry out the settlor's intent.

PER AUTRE VIE: For another's life; during another's life. In property law, an estate may be granted that will terminate upon the death of someone other than the grantee.

PROFIT A PRENDRE: A license to remove minerals or other produce from land.

VOIR DIRE: Process of questioning jurors as to their predispositions about the case or parties to a proceeding in order to identify those jurors displaying bias or prejudice.

Casenote Legal Briefs

Administrative Law	Breyer, Stewart, Sunstein & Vermeule
Administrative Law	Cass, Diver & Beermann
Administrative Law	Funk, Shapiro & Weaver
Administrative Law	Mashaw, Merrill & Shane
Administrative Law	Strauss, Rakoff, & Farina (Gellhorn & Byse)
Agency & Partnership	Hynes & Loewenstein
Antitrust	Pitofsky, Goldschmid & Wood
Antitrust	Sullivan & Hovenkamp
Banking Law	Macey, Miller & Carnell
Bankruptcy	Warren & Bussel
Bankruptcy	Warren & Westbrook
Business Organizations	Allen, Kraakman & Subramanian
Business Organizations	Bauman, Weiss & Palmiter
Business Organizations	Choper, Coffee & Gilson
Business Organizations	Hamilton & Macey
Business Organizations	Klein, Ramseyer & Bainbridge
Business Organizations	O'Kelley & Thompson
Business Organizations	Soderquist, Smiddy & Cunningham
Civil Procedure	Field, Kaplan & Clermont
Civil Procedure	Freer & Perdue
Civil Procedure	Friedenthal, Miller, Sexton & Hershkoff
Civil Procedure	Hazard, Tait, Fletcher & Bundy
Civil Procedure	Marcus, Redish & Sherman
Civil Procedure	Subrin, Minow, Brodin & Main
Civil Procedure	Yeazell
Commercial Law	LoPucki, Warren, Keating & Mann
Commercial Law	Warren & Walt
Commercial Law	Whaley
Community Property	Bird
Community Property	Blumberg
Conflicts	Brilmayer & Goldsmith
Conflicts	Currie, Kay, Kramer & Roosevelt
Constitutional Law	Brest, Levinson, Balkin & Amar
Constitutional Law	Chemerinsky
Constitutional Law	Choper, Fallon, Kamisar & Shiffrin (Lockhart)
Constitutional Law	Cohen, Varat & Amar
Constitutional Law	Farber, Eskridge & Frickey
Constitutional Law	Rotunda
Constitutional Law	Sullivan & Gunther
Constitutional Law	Stone, Seidman, Sunstein, Tushnet & Karlan
Contracts	Barnett
Contracts	Burton
Contracts	Calamari, Perillo & Bender
Contracts	Crandall & Whaley
Contracts	Dawson, Harvey & Henderson
Contracts	Farnsworth, Young & Sanger
Contracts	Fuller & Eisenberg
Contracts	Knapp, Crystal & Prince
Contracts	Murphy, Speidel & Ayres
Copyright	Cohen, Loren, Okediji & O'Rourke
Copyright	Goldstein
Copyright	Gorman & Ginsburg
Criminal Law	Bonnie, Coughlin, Jeffries & Low
Criminal Law	Boyce, Dripps & Perkins
Criminal Law	Dressler
Criminal Law	Johnson & Cloud
Criminal Law	Kadish & Schulhofer
Criminal Law	Kaplan, Weisberg & Binder
Criminal Procedure	Allen, Hoffmann, Livingston & Stuntz
Criminal Procedure	Dressler & Thomas
Criminal Procedure	Haddad, Marsh, Zagel, Meyer, Starkman & Bauer
Criminal Procedure	Kamisar, LaFave, Israel & King
Criminal Procedure	Saltzburg & Capra
Employment Discrimination	Friedman
Employment Discrimination	Zimmer, Sullivan, Richards & Calloway
Employment Law	Rothstein & Liebman
Environmental Law	Menell & Stewart
Environmental Law	Percival, Schroder, Miller & Leape
Environmental Law	Plater, Abrams, Goldfarb, Graham, Heinzerling & Wirth
Evidence	Broun, Mosteller & Giannelli
Evidence	Fisher
Evidence	Mueller & Kirkpatrick
Evidence	Sklansky
Evidence	Waltz & Park
Evidence	Weinstein, Mansfield, Abrams & Berger
Family Law	Areen & Regan
Family Law	Ellman, Kurtz & Scott
Family Law	Harris, Teitelbaum & Carbone
Family Law	Krause, Elrod, Garrison & Oldham
Family Law	Wadlington & O'Brien
Family Law	Weisberg & Appleton
Federal Courts	Fallon, Meltzer & Shapiro (Hart & Wechsler)
Federal Courts	Low & Jeffries
Health Care Law	Hall, Bobinski & Orentlicher
Health Law	Furrow, Greaney, Johnson, Jost & Schwartz
Immigration Law	Aleinikoff, Martin & Motomura
Immigration Law	Legomsky
Insurance Law	Abraham
Intellectual Property	Merges, Menell & Lemley
International Business Transactions	Folsom, Gordon, Spanogle & Fitzgerald
International Law	Blakesley, Firmage, Scott & Williams
International Law	Carter, Trimble & Weiner
International Law	Damrosch, Henkin, Pugh, Schachter & Smit
International Law	Dunoff, Ratner & Wippman
Labor Law	Cox, Bok, Gorman & Finkin
Land Use	Callies, Freilich & Roberts
Legislation	Eskridge, Frickey & Garrett
Oil & Gas	Lowe, Anderson, Smith & Pierce
Patent Law	Adelman, Radner, Thomas & Wegner
Products Liability	Owen, Montgomery & Davis
Professional Responsibility	Gillers
Professional Responsibility	Hazard, Koniak, Cramton & Cohen
Professional Responsibility	Schwartz, Wydick, Perschbacher & Bassett
Property	Casner, Leach, French, Korngold & VanderVelde
Property	Cribbet, Johnson, Findley & Smith
Property	Donahue, Kauper & Martin
Property	Dukeminier, Krier, Alexander & Schill
Property	Haar & Liebman
Property	Kurtz & Hovenkamp
Property	Nelson, Stoebuck & Whitman
Property	Rabin, Kwall & Kwall
Property	Singer
Real Estate	Korngold & Goldstein
Real Estate Transactions	Nelson & Whitman
Remedies	Laycock
Remedies	Shoben, Tabb & Janutis
Securities Regulation	Coffee, Seligman & Sale
Securities Regulation	Cox, Hillman & Langevoort
Software and Internet Law	Lemley, Menell, Merges & Samuelson
Sports Law	Weiler & Roberts
Taxation (Corporate)	Lind, Schwartz, Lathrope & Rosenberg
Taxation (Individual)	Burke & Friel
Taxation (Individual)	Freeland, Lathrope, Lind & Stephens
Taxation (Individual)	Klein, Bankman & Shaviro
Torts	Dobbs & Hayden
Torts	Epstein
Torts	Franklin & Rabin
Torts	Henderson, Pearson, Kysar & Siliciano
Torts	Schwartz, Kelly & Partlett (Prosser)
Wills, Trusts & Estates	Dukeminier, Johanson, Lindgren & Sitkoff
Wills, Trusts & Estates	Dobris, Sterk & Leslie
Wills, Trusts & Estates	Scoles, Halbach, Roberts & Begleiter